Welcome to the Theatre

Welcome to the Theatre

Sandra N. Boyce

Nelson-Hall nh Chicago

With love to Rob,
Farah, Kate, and Jim

Photographs not otherwise credited courtesy of
the Graphics Communications Department, Chowan College.

Library of Congress Cataloging-in-Publication Data

Boyce, Sandra N., 1948–
   Welcome to the theatre.

   Bibliography: p.
   Includes index.
   1. Theater.   2. Drama.   I. Title.
PN2037.B59   1987   792   87-12188
ISBN 0-8304-1187-9
ISBN 0-8304-1083-X(pbk.)

Manufactured in the United States of America

10 9 8 7 6 5 4 3 2

Contents

Preface

An introductory theatre course offers information in three primary areas: history and development; acting and play production; and the study of genres and representative plays. In searching through available texts, I found many that contained one or two of these elements, but no one textbook contained an academic study of all three. This book was written to fill that void. It offers valuable information and insights into ancient Greek Dionysian theatre, methods of acting, and play production responsibilities, as well as five full-length plays with discussion notes. My hope is that, after reading *Welcome to the Theatre*, the student will indeed *feel* welcome in the theatre.

"Thank you" to the many students of the past five years who have heard and reacted to the information contained in this book and who thereby have helped to determine its content and shape its purpose. Several individuals have made significant contributions; special thanks to Doug Gleason and Herman Gatewood for the printing of photographs; to Jackie Copeland for her artwork; to Frank Stephenson for acting as mentor; and to Farah Boyce who assisted with proofreading. To each of you I owe a debt of gratitude. Another thank you to Jane Durkott for her excellent help in editing. And a warm thank you to my husband and parents for their support and encouragement on this project.

Part One

Theatre:
Place and Mode
for Creative Expression

1

Definitions: Theatre Terminology

Communication in the theatre is a unique interpersonal experience. Each time a curtain rises to begin a performance, the audience, a heterogeneous group of people with varied backgrounds, goals, personality traits, and preferences, witnesses and reacts to a first-time experience with a group of trained, rehearsed performers. This union of performer and audience is a potentially thrilling experience, yet perilously unpredictable. So many variables affect this situation that its outcome cannot be foretold. Even if the play runs for hundreds of performances, no two will ever be quite the same. Each audience member brings a collection of memories, prejudices, and bits of information. The extent to which each member understands and appreciates the performance will be based on and modified by these personal differences.

The basic communication goal of the director is to portray, as honestly as possible, the intent of the playwright. Whether or not that intended communication reaches and involves the audience will depend largely on each member's intelligence, theatrical experience and personality. The ingredients of each actor's performance include script interpretation, historical research, pantomime, verbal skills, and many other factors too numerous to mention. All of these variables are integrated by the actor into his or her character portrayal. The actor adapts to the role and molds the character by integrating his or her ''self'' and the role into a new interpretation of a part that may have been played countless times, but never before in quite this way. Each member of the audience becomes involved in watching the performance by assimi-

Figure 1.1 A communication, or SCR, diagram.

lating the actor's characterization into his or her own preexisting set of ideas, ideals, and emotional nature.

Thus, each theatrical performance is an artistic venture in which the communication sent by the performer and the message received by the audience is colored by the inner resources of the two. This interpersonal nature of the theatre experience makes it a rare and nonrepeatable one.

In order to lay some groundwork for appreciation of a theatrical experience, it seems appropriate to begin by identifying and defining terms. In order for audience members and actors to share moments of quality, some bases defining their relationship to each other need to be established. This chapter will look at how each contributes to and participates in: communication, creativity, imagination, role playing, pantomime, improvisation, and oral interpretation. With an understanding of each of these terms, the reader will be better prepared to understand and appreciate the ideas that follow.

Communication

Communication is the all-encompassing term we use when we mean "to send and receive a message." The diagram for communication shown in figure 1.1 generally shows a *sender*, a *channel* and a *receiver*.

This widely accepted diagram shows that communication is an ongoing phenomenon that continually changes as feedback messages dictate. The message originates with a sender, travels by means of a channel, and is received. The receiver then becomes a sender in "feeding back" to the original sender (now a receiver) a response or reaction to the original communication. This feedback is acknowledged as an important part of the process in altering subsequent messages; and in most communication, we are both a sender and a receiver.

In a dramatic production, the sender is, of course, the actor. The channels available to the actor include those that can be seen as well as those that are heard and felt. The actor's total body, including his or her mental and emotional faculties, are utilized for effective and total communication to take place. The viewing audience in a particular scene, for example, should be able to *hear* the suffering of the protagonist as he wails and laments the loss of a family member. It may *see* the distress in the hands uplifted in sorrow and helplessness and in the distorted and pained facial expression. It may *feel* the agony suffered by this character. If the actor's portrayal is genuine and believable, audience involvement is achieved.

The total communication of a play is transmitted to the audience through many mediums, or channels. For example, in a performance of the all-time favorite *Dracula,* the audience members understand the desired mood by viewing the somber colors of the set and the dim lighting effects. They can hear the eerie music, wolf howls, distant church bells, and so on. They see the pale, fragile face of Lucy and hear her weak voice. All the facets of the production send this communication. Any one or two of them taken separately would not effectively transmit the mood.

When we look at the audience as "receiver" in the diagram, we must first acknowledge the many differences in each audience member. Most have brought some experience with this particular play to the performance. While some may never have seen or heard of it, others may have heard of it briefly in legend form. Others may be Dracula buffs and very interested in folklore of the occult. Still others may have seen several stage productions of this particular play and may be present to compare some facets of this production with others they have seen. Realizing that differences among members are inherent in an audience, we expect that the reactions, or "feedback," to this particular performance will reflect those differences. How, then, does this relate to the performer?

The performer must always be cognizant of the audience. If it provides feedback cues, then the performer must be mindful of those cues. Audiences are aware when watching a stand-up comic perform that the timing of jokes, punchlines, and pauses are directly related to how the audience is receiving the material. Performers of this type edit their material during a performance based on how well or how poorly it is being received by the audience. In much the same fashion, the audience viewing a full length play sends feedback to the stage performer. If half of the viewing audience is unable to hear, feedback will make it quite clear. Shuffling of programs will audibly increase, coughing and clearing of throats will become noticeable, children will exit to the restrooms, and adults will go out for a smoke. Sir Ralph Richardson, the English actor, once said, "The art of acting consists in keeping people from coughing."[1] A performer must be able to "read" these messages and appropriately alter the performance. In this case, he or she must increase projection in order to regain the audience's full attention.

Occasionally, a particular scene or pantomime within a play may be shortened, lengthened, or altered depending on how a particular audience receives it. For example, a scene may be cheered and applauded by a juvenile audience, thus encouraging the actor to push that scene to its full potential; an adult audience may find the same scene not funny at all, perhaps even embarrassing, thus encouraging the actor to get it done quickly.

Communication is the essence of the theatrical art. The director strives to communicate, through actors and the play medium, the intent of a playwright. Contributions to this communication are made by the costumer through style and color selection; the technical designer through color, shape, and form within the set; the lighting designer through intensity and hue; the property master through the collection and fabrication of stage props; and many others involved in a production. But whether or not the message received by the audience is the intended one remains to be judged by the audience.

Creativity

On the first page of her book, *Creative Communication*, Fran Tanner placed this quote: "Creativity is not just for the artist or the gifted. It is for people. It is a way of working, a way of thinking, a way of living."[2] It has been said by many a director that it is better to have an aspiring actor who is willing to work long and hard to learn and develop than to have five talented, even "gifted," persons who are lazy. And it was Constantin Stanislavski, the famous Russian producer and teacher, who said, "Always and forever, . . . we must play ourselves."[3] So how does creativity come into play? When the two ideas offered by Tanner and Stanislavski are taken together.

Often the question is asked and haphazardly answered, "Can creativity be taught?" Perhaps the question should be, "Can creativity be developed?'' The word *creativity* has often been used to describe some special talent with which a gifted few are blessed at birth. Most of us can agree with the idea that ''to create'' is to make new—either something that has not been done before or at least has not been done in this or that particular fashion. If drama is a creative art, how does this definition apply?

A beginning performer must overcome the notion that he or she is to ''pretend'' roles. When the actor comes to the realization that voice, gesture, movement, and manner must come into play, then he or she can ''create'' a role from within, based on a study of the script. Many a novice actor has appeared stilted on stage. He doesn't know how to stand still or what to do with his hands. Painfully, he anticipates a movement and then jerkily executes it. Although stagefright may be the villain, the actor's awkwardness may be related to the fact that he is *pretending* to be the character. He is not actually *creating* a character from within his own framework of ideas and movements. When an actor realizes that he must adapt an honest impression of himself to the role, then movement becomes easier and smoother. At the very least, creativity in the dramatic sense is to be willing and able to use one's inner resources, memory, intelligence, experiences, and senses to give a unique interpretation to a performance.

Why is it that a playgoer will anxiously wait in line to attend a fifth or twelfth different production of *Macbeth*? It can't be that the person doesn't understand the story or is unfamiliar with the characters. It must be because of the original creative interpretation that each new actor brings to a role. Because each person has a different set of memories and experiences, the way each views a play or a particular role is different. Each of us was born into a particular family in a specific neighborhood in a clearly defined income bracket. Each attended a certain school, had a personal group of friends, suffered heartache, and rejoiced at triumph. Taken individually, no one event was particularly grand. But the sum total of these life experiences has made each person a one-of-a-kind, multifaceted personality capable of *creating* role interpretations, sets, and costumes never seen or experienced before. Similarly, one's personality colors one's appreciation of a play. The performer who is willing to work hard at searching within the self, studying the role, and listening to direction will be able to create.

Creativity, then, in the theatrical sense, is a willingness to honestly look within oneself for newness and freshness that can be applied to an already existing character role in order to make that role new and interesting and to work diligently to develop a full and "round" character.

I believe creativity can be developed. Look at some examples from the daily life of children at play. Creative play is evident in the human at an early age; probably, it is most fertile during this time. In young children, it is unlimited and without restraint. Children arrange blocks into skyscrapers, make vehicles from shoeboxes, and build all manner of inventions from raw materials they find at hand. Their imagination seems limitless, and they do not tire of play. A child is not afraid to try something new, to experiment, or to scrap a disappointing project altogether when it is near completion.

As children grow up in our society, they seem, through the well-meaning guidance of adults, to grow out of this *joie de vivre* in creative play. Commercial television urges them to buy dolls that wet, eat, cry, and grow hair. Toy trucks come equipped with hydraulic lifts, cranes, and engine sounds. These toys demand little creative play from their users. To engender creativity, perhaps parents should favor unlined paper to coloring books and ragdolls to Barbie. In these ways, more creativity might develop.

The challenge for those who have outgrown this fertile period of creativity is to rediscover it and make it productive once more. First and foremost, one must be willing to lose or loosen some of the restraints on mind and body that have been so carefully adopted, and then to practice, to invent from existing materials, and to scrap disappointing projects—all the while striving for better performance.

Imagination

Imagination is the primary resource from which creativity is drawn. To imagine is to reorganize or to create new associations for already existing ideas or resources. The imagination of the actor is where the unique performance is born. In *The Total Actor*, Raymond Rizzo states, "A fertile imagination, which releases emotion, is the most precious asset you have as an actor. You do, of course, need an excellent voice and an expressive body, but your imagination is that unknown factor, all other talents being equal, that will make you either mediocre or outstanding."[4]

Suppose an actor is preparing to play Macbeth. In his memory bank exists information on his relationships with manipulative women such as Lady Macbeth, knowledge of and experience with desire for power and majesty, and knowledge of the historical background of the play and of sorcerers and witches. It is his active imagination that allows him to assimilate and use this information already in his memory together with the new information of the role to be played. The resulting character interpretation is a creation of the actor and provides the basis of a new and interesting performance. The actor must be able to project himself into the character to be played in order for a marriage of actor and role to take place. Exploration and experimentation with the role and the many opportunities for subtle movements and overt gestures can be discovered and played out only through the active imagination of the actor.

Imagination must also be actively used by the audience. In many plays, both historical and modern, lack of or limited use of a set challenges the audience to create its own set through imagination. We see a great deal of this in the modern theatre. In *Death of a Salesman*, for example, rooms of the house are often suggested by platforms and timbers arranged so that the imagination of the audience comes into play. Plot lines are often open-ended so that the viewer can imagine the conclusion. At the end of *Countess Julie*, for example, we wonder if she goes offstage to kill herself. It is especially true in pantomime that imagination is needed for the audience to "see" objects and people that do not actually appear on stage.

The imagination is stimulated by music, colors, sound effects, lights—all the trappings of the stage. Just as the past experiences and psychological framework of the actor come to bear on his interpretation in performance, so the past experiences and frame of reference of audience members influence their interpretation in viewing. As the discussion on communication pointed out, the message sent and the message received may or may not be the same. This imagination variable allows the viewers to discover meanings that may or may not have been intended.

Role Playing

Audiences sometimes feel a great distance between themselves and the actors on stage. They wonder how the actors can make their roles seem so believable. They are in awe of the transformation from a real-life role into a make-believe one on stage. They don't stop to think of the role playing that takes place in everyday life.

When both actor and viewer understand that role playing is basic not only to dramatic performance but also to everyday living, then the actor and viewer have a common base of understanding. Role playing is the one aspect of theatrical play in which we all have engaged. Whether or not we like to admit it, we all play roles. It was Shakespeare who said, "All the world's a stage, and all the men and women merely players." As psychologists and behaviorists continue to probe the human psyche, they find Shakespeare's statement to be more and more true. To admit we are role players immediately makes us feel more comfortable with the actor. After all, the actor is role playing too; but the actor's role playing is predetermined, rehearsed, and controlled.

But, to a large extent, aren't all of our everyday roles predetermined and to some degree rehearsed and controlled? Take, for example, the student speaking after class with a professor about why a paper was not turned in on time. The student knows the behavior and language appropriate to this situation, and so does the professor. They each begin to play out their roles. Each has a fairly accurate idea of what the other is going to say and how he or she, in turn, will react. This kind of situation plays itself out many times each day in our normal routines and activities with our employers, friends, and family. This type of role playing is not so different from that performed on the stage.

In the case of the actor, a role is clearly defined. Not only are the character type and action situation given in the script, but blocking instructions and lines or dialogue are also provided. The actor's challenge is to give the character spontaneity, believable manner, and synchronization with the other characters and the action of the play. The improvisational aspect of the actor's role playing is a part of the "role." The actor must be ready to improvise a line of conversation, or ad-lib, in the event that some line or action does not happen as rehearsed. This is one of the most exciting elements of dramatic performance.

Just as the actor plays a predetermined role in the play, so the audience at a given performance plays out a somewhat predetermined role. Its role definition includes arriving at a particular time, sitting in a seat, focusing attention on the action, and responding appropriately to the situations on stage. As intermission arrives, the role playing continues as people read their programs, discuss interesting aspects of the production, stand, stretch, and so forth.

Just as in everyday life, the unexpected can, and often does, happen in the theatre. Playing a role on the stage requires the training to control any situation whether rehearsed or spontaneous and move forward with the scene. When actors and audience fully understand this, they find that there is not much distance separating them after all.

Pantomime

Pantomime is acting without words. It is often a vital part of a dramatic performance and, as in the case of performers like Marcel Marceau and Shields and Yarnell, can become a performance in and of itself.

Pantomime requires a tremendous amount of concentration on the part of both the actor and the audience. The absence of words removes the easiest and quickest method of communication. Since speech is eliminated, physical movement, especially the use of hands and face, becomes of paramount importance. Movement in pantomime must be heightened, since it is the primary channel of the communication. The audience must see the action in order for communication to take place. The actor must define, through physical movement, the location, attitude, and size and shape of "objects" that do not actually appear. To see Marcel Marceau define an imaginary box in which he has become entrapped is to appreciate the muscular control required in pantomime.

Doing the simple pantomime exercise of pretending to make a peanut butter and jelly sandwich points out some of the problems faced by the mime. Pretend that a loaf of bread sealed in a bag, a jar of peanut butter, a jar of jelly, and a knife are before you on the table. Proceed to make a sandwich. Upon completion, ask yourself these questions: How large was the jar of jelly? How difficult was it to remove the lid? Was one hand or two required to open the bag containing the bread? Was each item closed at completion? At what angle was the knife held in order to enter the jar? How smoothly did the peanut butter spread? Did it tear the bread? Was there follow through on each of the movements? In considering such questions, one becomes acutely aware of how important every movement, every use of the hands, face, and body can be in pantomime.

Often in dramatic performance, the addition of pantomime can be the most effective kind of communication. A raised eyebrow, a slight shrug of the shoulders, a sneer, or a glare may be worth far more in characterization than words of dialogue. To carry an empty suitcase on stage as if it were full of books requires the concentrated use of vital muscles. Timing, training, and body

Figure 1.2 A pantomimist in classical whiteface.

rhythm acquired in pantomime can make this task fairly simple.

Just as the actor must carefully rehearse movements and timing for the pantomime to be sure it communicates, so too must the audience pay careful attention to be sure it "sees" what is intended in the communication.

Improvisation

Improvisational skills are imperative for the dramatic performer. Because of the unpredictable nature of performance, the actor, speaker, mime, vocalist, and other performers must always be ready for the unexpected. He or she must be ready to improvise as any situation might require. To improvise in the sense of dramatic performance is to be able to come up with suitable actions and words for a given situation on the spur of the moment. If an actor is late for an entrance or the lights do not dim at the predetermined moment, then it is up to the actors to improvise some believable words and action within the framework of the play and the characters being portrayed. Such improvisational skills demand quick thought and execution. The goal of the performers in this situation is to continue the action already in progress in a believable fashion. This is done by adapting available props, pieces of furniture, other actors, and the ideas of the dialogue or pantomime already in progress.

Improvisational skills are desirable for the total performance, not just for the emergency situation, however. An actor adept at his craft is skilled at using the resources he has within himself in conjunction with those available in the set. Sonia Moore, author of *The Stanislavski System*, observes, "There are moments of subconscious creativity when an actor improvises although his text and the pattern of his role are firmly fixed. Such creativity or inspirational improvisation is the goal and essence of . . . acting." [5] We can compare the improvisational actor with the energetic beaver. The beaver will select a suitable dwelling place on a river bank. Desiring still rather than moving water, it will improvise a dam. It finds, adapts, and uses resources close at hand. The building of the dam is no simple task. With its strong teeth the beaver gnaws around the trunk of a tree until it falls. Then it drags the tree into the water, places it properly, and secures it with mud and rocks brought up from the river bottom. No two dams are quite the same. Yet, the same intuition is used in every new construction.

Just as the "eager beaver" by instinct uses physical and intuitive abilities and available supplies to create something, so too must the performer. The actor must train through improvisation to use his or her physical, mental, and emotional resources to create whatever is needed for the fleeting scene. The intuition and instinct of the actor are not to be minimized or taken lightly. The skilled actor can handle any situation through knowledgeable use of improvisation.

The experienced director makes wise use of the actors by letting them improvise much of their own blocking. If an actor does not feel comfortable with certain lines, he or she may alter them or improvise new ones so long as the new lines are in keeping with the author's intent. Improvisation games or scenes are often used by directors at auditions, because an actor's abilities are demon-

Figure 1.3 Improvisations are often used at auditions. Here actors are "using" imaginary props.

strated by improvisation. It may well be that an actor's ability to improvise is the best measurement of his or her potential as an actor.

Oral Interpretation

Oral interpretation is one of the fundamentals of training for the actor. Although it is a form of performance in and of itself (referred to as Readers Theater), oral interpretation is used in dramatic performance primarily to train and develop an expressive voice and interpretive skills. To interpret literature is to attempt to study, to understand, and to expressively and honestly communicate the author's intent in a literary work. To do so requires much work and preparation on the part of the interpreter.

The uses of oral interpretation are as varied as are the kinds of reading matter available to us. We use interpretive skills when we read a news article aloud at breakfast, when we share a report at a business meeting, and when we read a story to a child. If we color our reading by emphasizing certain phrases or words and pause at some point to create interest or suspense, we are employing interpretation methods. Most of us know someone who is especially adept at storytelling. His words hold interest; his face is alive with expression; his delivery of a punch line is always timed perfectly for effect. He is an oral interpreter.

Historically, oral interpretation began with folk tales and legends that were handed down from generation to generation by word of mouth. The tribal storyteller passed on the anthology of tales to a younger person who would later move into the position as storyteller. In this way, history before the advent of the written word was passed along through oral interpreters.

Modern oral interpretation, however, whether for the purpose of reading a story to a child or portraying a role for an audience, must begin with and rely on the *written* word. It is from the author's words that the message must be deciphered. Charlotte Lee, in her popular book *Oral Interpretation,* says in the preface, "Interpretation . . . goes several steps beyond a mere vocalization of silent reading. It requires an appreciation of one's material as a work of literary art and the ability to communicate that work of art through voice and body. It demands both intellectual and emotional response from the interpreter and a control and channeling of the understanding and emotion to elicit the appropriate response from the audience."[6] The interpreter is an intermediary between author and audience and acts as an artist channeling the writer's art to the audience. It is the responsibility of the interpreter, therefore, to study and research the written words in order to find the purpose and intent of the author's writing.

The diligent interpreter wants to know not only what the piece says but also what it means. Why was it written? What inspired the author? What were the particular circumstances surrounding the author at the time of the writing? What was the author's frame of mind and emotional state? To what particular audience was he or she addressing this piece? (Whether it was intended for one individual or for an entire government or city will certainly have bearing on the interpreter's presentation.) The earnest interpreter needs all the information available concerning the mood and events surrounding the writing of a particular piece. The more information the interpreter can gather, the more honest and informative the interpretation will be.

Punctuation is of utmost importance in oral interpretation. Correct punctuation aids in communicating proper phrasing through pauses and expression. Without proper phrasing, the audience will not understand the material it is hearing. Take, for example, the phrase, "Woman without her man would be a savage." It can be punctuated in different ways to give it completely different meanings. Two samples are: "Woman! Without her, man would be a savage" and "Woman, without her man, would be a savage." The audience will not see the written material, so it is the interpreter's responsibility to *honestly* communicate the meaning through appropriate phrasing of words by use of pauses and emphasis. The experienced oral interpreter will have no difficulty in transmitting such phrases to an audience successfully and effectively.

The actor, then, must be an effective oral interpreter. In the final analysis, it is the dramatist's play that is to be communicated; the primary channel for that communication is the actor and his or her ability and willingness to interpret. The degree of accuracy achieved in following the intent of the playwright depends in large degree on the quality of the oral interpretation.

Readers Theatre

Oral interpretation is frequently used as a type of performance produced without the trappings of a theatre. Called Readers Theatre, it focuses primarily on the oral interpretation of the literature. Often, the materials of Readers Theatre are works that were not originally written to be performed. Short stories, novels, poetry, essays, and letters can provide the scripts, though play scripts may also be used.

Focusing primarily on the interpretation of the literature, the performer emphasizes vocal, physical, and facial techniques. Less emphasis is given to sets, costumes, and props. Performances of Readers Theatre can be as versatile as a director desires. Some incorporate movement before a painted backdrop; in others, actors sit on stools before a black curtain. Some performers use props and speak from memory. Others may hold a script, referring to it often. A Readers Theatre performance can create intimacy between performer and audience if the performers ignore the fourth wall and address the audience directly. Readers Theatre provides valuable training for the actor, emphasizing vocal variety and inflection, proper phrasing based on punctuation and meaning, use of the pause, and the interpretive value of speech tempo. Student theatre groups may find Readers Theatre to be a good "starting point" when attempting to establish a performance program.

The theatrical experience is an interpersonal communication that must be shared and participated in by both the audience and

Figure 1.4 A Readers Theatre production of *Love Is Better Than the Next Best Thing*.

the performers. The information and definitions in this chapter provide a basis for understanding how the creativity and imagination of viewer and performer must come into play if the theatrical communication is to be successful. Each of us participates in role playing, pantomime, and improvisation in everyday life. The act of oral interpretation is an aspect of performance in which we all share. Acknowledging this common ground gives us kinship with the performer; we no longer feel so far removed from the actor and his or her craft. Understanding dramatic terms lays the groundwork for the discussions of theatre craft in subsequent chapters.

Suggested Reading

Altenbernd, Lynn, and Leslie L. Lewis. *A Handbook for the Study of Drama.* New York: Macmillan, 1966.

Bowman, Walter P., and Robert H. Ball. *Theatre Language.* New York: Theatre Arts Books, 1961.

Coger, Leslie I. and Melvin R. White. *Readers Theatre Handbook.* Glenview, Ill.: Scott Foresman, 1967.

Lee, Charlotte I. *Oral Interpretation*, 3d ed. Boston, Mass.: Houghton Mifflin, 1955.

2

Theatre Conventions

In order to fully enjoy participating in an activity, one needs to understand the "rules of the game" and be willing to abide by those rules. In the game of Monopoly, for example, players must understand that the game is about economics and that buying and developing land is the goal of each player. Players receive an allotment of "money" and then compete for real estate. So long as all players abide by the rules, the game is enjoyable for all. But if one player inappropriately withdraws money from the bank, the game loses its appeal for the other players.

Just as in game playing, the theatrical experience is one in which all the participants—actors and audience members—must understand and abide by the rules of the game, or conventions, as they are often called. These are commonly accepted criteria or procedures. For example, as people assemble in a theater for a play performance, they follow a theatrical convention by finding their seats in the area of the theatre known as the house. There, rows of seats are arranged so that the audience can see and hear the action on the stage. The house is separated in some way from the acting area or stage. The differentiation may be made by changes in floor elevation, by curtains or walls, by lighting effects, or by other methods. This separation of areas and space is mutually accepted by both artist and playgoer.

While the audience assembles for the performance, the house lights are on and viewers chat amiably with each other. But at curtain time, the house lights dim, a hush falls over the audience, and the curtain, if there is one, opens to reveal a stage prepared in a manner appropriate for this particular play. Thus the transfer is made from a dark stage and lit house to a lit stage and dark house, and all attention is focused on the stage. Other conventions are opening and closing the curtain at the beginning and end of acts and changing scenes within an act by means of lighting changes. Such conventions or game rules result in enjoyment and appreciation of theatrical production. Many other generally agreed upon conventions have come to be commonly associated with playmaking.

Unities of Time, Place, and Action

Since Aristotle and, later, the Renaissance, dramatists have been cognizant of the importance of the elements of time, place, and action in the theatrical experience. Playwrights have come to acknowledge Aristotle's advice, that the elapsed time of the action in the play (that is, the length of time spanned in the lives of the characters of the play) should be the least amount necessary to present the play's theme. Aristotle advised that twenty-four hours was the maximum length of time that should elapse in any one play. Admittedly, this advice has rarely been heeded by playwrights through the years. Some plays span less time; many may cover several days, weeks, months, or years. *Antigone* and *Countess Julie* each take place in one afternoon. *The Importance of Being Earnest* spans a few days, while *Othello* is played out over several weeks. The important element is that the relevance of time as a theatrical convention is accepted by the audience. This willingness to believe will be encouraged and aided by a printed program made available to each playgoer, by the dialogue of the play, by the changing seasons reflected in costume and lighting, and by the actors themselves in their handling of the passage of time and events.

Unity of place, in the view of Greek writers, was nearly as limited as time. Although this idea was not set down specifically by Aristotle, in general, one or two locations for the action were thought to be adequate. This is reflected in Sophocles' *Antigone*. Perhaps this "place" restriction was to facilitate staging. As plays moved into the Elizabethan era, more liberty was taken with unity of place. Whereas the Greek actor only described the events that had taken place off stage (for example, the guard comes to the palace to tell Creon that Antigone has buried her brother's body), the Shakespearean actor could perform the action on stage (Othello, for example, goes to his bedroom to suffocate the sleeping Desdemona). The location moved freely and easily as the needs of the play dictated. The stage became a free-flowing space where time, place, and action could change perceptibly. In *Othello*, the location moves from the dock, to Othello's courtyard, and then to the street where Iago awaits his prey.

In the modern theatre, the unity of place varies with the play type. Tennessee Williams's plays generally occupy one setting. The Wingfield apartment in *The Glass Menagerie* and Big Daddy's plantation house in *Cat on a Hot Tin Roof* supply us with limited space for the intense, compact drama. Many other plays of this type occupy only one setting: *A Raisin in the Sun* takes place in the cramped Younger apartment, and *Countess Julie* is played out in the kitchen. However, in musical comedy and outdoor drama, which are American theatrical types, the location of the action may change dozens of times. In the popular musical *Annie*, for example, the setting moves from an orphanage to "Hooverville" to a stately mansion. The technical accomplishments involved in making these fantastic changes take place before one's eyes is part of the enjoyment.

Unity of action is more difficult to define. Aristotle insisted that the plot should be simple and easy to follow. But we have only to read a Shakespearean comedy or a Eugene O'Neill drama to realize that not all playwrights have followed that advice. Once a playwright begins to develop a plot, subplots emerge and characters become complex and interrelated. Soon, the simple plot has become anything but simple. It would be a more accurate appraisal of the unity of action in the acknowledged "good" plays to say that each has a unifying thread that helps to simplify the plot and to move the story forward. In *Death of a Salesman*, by Arthur Miller, the action is centered around Willy Loman and his slow but sure demise. In *Othello*, we see how jealousy can so blind a man that he is unable to see the truth and destroys the woman he loves. In Noel Coward's *Still Life*, a love affair begins, develops, and ends over several scenes, all in a railway station. In some plays, characters tie the action together; in some, tragic weakness in a central character provides unity of action; and in still others, it is the location. So long as the playwright has found a means of telling his story that can be clearly understood and followed by the audience, then his unity of action has been achieved. Again, the final judge is the audience. Was the action and the plot organized and propelled in such a fashion that the audience was able to follow it with relative ease?

Suspension of Disbelief

When a person enters the theatre with the intent of understanding and enjoying a play, he or she must acknowledge and participate in another commonly held theatrical convention. "Willing suspension of disbelief" is the term given to the convention dealing with the audience's belief in the action of the play. Obviously, by its very nature, we know that the play is only a play—an imitation of something in life and nothing more. This convention asks that, for the duration of the play and within the limits defined by the play, we be willing to believe it, if only for this brief span. The Kernoldles call this "the deception that deceives no one."[1] In order for the play to achieve any success, the audience must accept the deception and believe in the story, characters, and setting.

Consider the play *The Crucible,* by Arthur Miller. The viewers are asked to believe that they are being taken back in time more than two hundred years and to acknowledge that the rumor and practice of witchcraft is widespread and threatening. In actuality, an audience member may have no belief in witchcraft at all. Indeed, he or she may hold it to be foolish nonsense. Yet the convention of the theatre holds that the spectator be willing to suspend that disbelief for a while, at least until the end of the performance. If the viewer is unable to do this, then he or she is not going to understand and appreciate the performance and may even be insulted or angered by it.

Suspension of disbelief is a mental exercise that becomes easier with practice and experience. In observing audiences as they view a play, one sees that inexperienced audiences seem to have marked difficulty in believing situations and events that do not mesh with their own particular life style and customs. For example, when students view performances in which fellow students are taking part, the viewers often find it hard to forget (or to disbelieve) even for a few moments that the actors on stage are friends or roommates.

Willing suspension of disbelief is probably the most important convention of the theatre for the audience. In order for a theatrical experience of any worth or value to take place, an audience member must be free from real-world concerns for a period of time and become immersed in a world of make-believe.

The Fourth Wall

A convention that makes the suspension of disbelief easier and contributes to the make-believe world of the play is the concept of the fourth wall. This idea originated with the early proscenium stage; the audience sits on only one side of the stage and is generally separated from it by a curtain and often a change in elevation. Action is viewed through the proscenium arch, which acts as a frame surrounding the stage ''picture.'' The stage is enclosed on three sides, which often constitute the walls of the set, in which there are doors and windows. The fourth wall is an invisible barrier through which the audience views the play. Originally, in plays performed on a proscenium stage, the performers did not acknowledge the presence of the audience. The play progressed while the audience eavesdropped on the performance via the invisible fourth wall. This provided a separation of audience and actor that was thought to be desirable. This fourth wall concept provided a psychological barrier helpful to both the actor and the audience.

Although this is still a widely held convention of the theatre, it has altered somewhat so that a more open relationship generally exists now between actor and audience.

In the nineteenth century, it was widely held that actors should never turn their backs on the audience and always gesture with the upstage hand in order to remain completely open to the audience. This resulted in stiff acting and stilted characters. With the popularity of thrust and arena stages today and increased interest in realistic acting, very rarely are plays performed that totally ignore the opportunity for the actor not only to acknowledge, but also to play to the audience. Stilted movement has been replaced with more believable and realistic movement, and sometimes it is appropriate, even advisable, for an actor to turn away from the audience or to make a broad gesture with either hand. Many modern plays bridge this separation by having action progress in and through the audience. Still, the boundaries between actors and audience are generally well understood. The clear delineation, albeit invisible, encourages the audience to participate in the make-believe and to believe the play.

The Illusion of Reality

The fourth wall convention, which separates the audience from the action, and the spectator's willingness to suspend disbelief,

Figure 2.1 The fourth-wall idea originated with the proscenium stage, which opens to the audience on only one side. The audience faces that missing wall, and sees the play as a framed picture.

Figure 2.2 A walled set on a proscenium stage, with the fourth wall open to the audience.

taken together with action on stage can result in an "illusion of reality." If the audience is prepared to believe the play and the actors have honed and refined their dialogue and movement, the performance on stage will appear to be a real, spontaneous, unrehearsed event happening for the first time. Then *theatre* is taking place.

The illusion of reality must be understood for what it is—an illusion. Few members of the audience have any problem accepting this convention. It asks them as viewers merely to temper their viewing and their suspension of disbelief with some objectivity and aesthetic distance. When, for example, we watch as Othello is about to kill his wife for a crime she has not committed, we shudder. We are sad as the unsuspecting Desdemona prepares for bed. We watch in horror as he takes the pillow, places it over her face, and snuffs out her life. We are sorry and angry, yet we are able to contain our grief and anger because we can acknowledge that a murder is not actually taking place. It is happening in the play, but only in the play. The play is not reality, but an illusion. Our grief for her death and our anger at her husband are tempered by our awareness that this is only an illusion. If a viewer should lose sight of this convention and believe the action on the stage, then he or she might rush to the stage in a valiant effort to snatch the pillow and prevent the murder. This, of course, would destroy the illusion for other members of the audience.

Empathy

If the illusion of reality is achieved, then it is likely that the audience feels empathy for the characters being played. In the example of Othello and Desdemona, if the viewer is caught up in the emotion of the moment and reacts to it emotionally, then the goal of the actors has been attained. When the audience becomes emotionally involved in the story and the characters, empathy can take place. Empathy is the sharing of an emotion. If you find yourself weeping with Creon at the death of his wife and son in *Antigone*, you are having empathetic response. If you find yourself shocked at Jean's killing of the canary in *Countess Julie*, you have empathy with Julie.

Often, the inexperienced playgoer does not know how much to respond to a play performance, particularly one of great emotional impact. Some people are protective of their emotions and tentative about expressing them. They will not allow themselves to respond empathetically to a play performance. This "hard shell" approach to plays limits the enjoyment that one might have through vicarious experiences in the theatre.

Unlike sympathy, which is an emotion felt "for" someone, empathy is an emotion felt "with" someone. The actor has as his goal to create a character so intensely believable that when he rejoices or grieves, so will the audience. But the extent to which empathetic response will be achieved is directly related to how open an audience member may be to becoming involved.

An actor may have studied, developed, and rehearsed his character thoroughly and may create the illusion of reality in performance. But audience empathy depends not only on these factors but also on the audience members' own preparation, willingness to believe, and emotional vulnerability. Some people have conditioned themselves not to react emotionally to any situation. The inner resources and psychological framework that a viewer brings to a play will influence how much empathy he or she is able to feel with the characters in the play.

Realism versus Stylization

Stylization and realism as theatrical terms may be viewed as opposite ends of a continuum representing the full range of theatrical styles. Realism is a reflection of the real world. Realistic plays deal with some facet of life in the real world. Many realistic plays attempt to show us problems in the world in an attempt to clarify them so that we are better able to handle or solve them. Anton Chekhov said, "To make a man better, you must first show him what he is."[2] For example, Lorraine Hansberry's *A Raisin in the Sun* presents the situation of a black family in the mid-twentieth century trying to improve their lot by moving out of their poverty-level apartment into a house in the suburbs. The chosen house happens to be in a white neighborhood, and here the social problem develops. Shakespeare's *Othello* reveals how devastating uncontrolled jealousy can be. The stark realism of how boring and disappointing a man's life can become when he does not succeed in his job is treated in *Death of a Salesman*. *Countess Julie* deals with sexual and social class conflicts with stark realism.

Realistic plays may be very different in their treatment and interpretation of realism. The producers, designers, and directors attempt to define realism in every aspect of the production. The realistic set is typically a box set with the invisible fourth wall. The interior of the set reflects the interior of any realistic room. Appropriate windows, doors, furniture, and properties are all authentic and "real." That is, most were probably rented or borrowed rather than made in the scene studio. The realism will be reflected in costumes as well. The styles of the clothing will be detailed according to the period of the play and the personality of the characters. Each play will have its particular theme or mood that will be carried out in these set and costume details. *The Glass Menagerie*, a play by Tennessee Williams, for example, gives a painfully realistic version of the frustration brought by the Great Depression. The faded glory of the South, as Amanda Winfield remembers it, is an important theme. This is reflected in the decoration of the set, which contains threadbare and faded furniture and includes a large brass candlebra that, as Amanda explains, was "bent in the Methodist church fire." The faded-glory theme develops further when Amanda entices her son, Tom, to invite home "a nice young man from the factory for your sister," and becomes painfully obvious when Amanda greets the young man wearing a faded formal gown from the days of her "seventeen gentlemen callers."

Moving from realism to stylization in the theatre is to go from one end of the continuum to the other. The stylized play, for whatever reason, has a need to abandon realistic forms in order to invoke a feeling, mood, or interpretation that cannot be achieved through the realistic method. Stylized plays use unrealistic effects. Set design, although it may give the impression of some realistic structure, will obviously and intentionally distort it. Proportions may be disregarded. Walls lean, roofs sag, and unusual angles create startling visual effects. The set designer is interested in the total effect created by the design, not with realistic detail, and may be looking for imbalance, whereas the realistic set designer would strive for balance.

Of course, many plays have been written that fall somewhere between the two extremes. Blendings of these forms in varying ratios are used to achieve the desired effect. In *Our Town*, Thornton Wilder has provided the Stage Manager character who talks directly with the audience in order to provide background data on the town and its people. This unrealistic character introduces the very realistic George and Emily, whose ordinary lives we share in brief moments over thirteen years. Some realistic furniture pieces are used sparingly alongside a ladder to suggest an upstairs room and a picket fence. These are, as the Stage Manager comments, "for those of you who feel you have to have scenery.'' These few pieces are used on a bare stage with no curtain or backdrop. The interrelationship of realistic and stylized elements serves to produce the effect Wilder was trying to achieve: how poignantly beautiful the simple ordinary days of our lives can be if we but take the time to enjoy living them.

The type of play and the set design, lights, and costumes will have some obvious characteristics in common; and each will offer clues to understanding the author's intent. The author is attempting, through a particular style medium, to communicate an idea. (For the inexperienced playgoer, suffice it to say that many before you have had some difficulties in understanding, at least at first, how and why a production is done in a particular fashion. Many a viewer of *Our Town* has come away wondering if the scarcity of set pieces was due to an inadequate theatre budget!) Good advice to follow when viewing an unfamiliar play is to read the program carefully before the curtain rises. Know whether the set is realistic, stylized, or some combination of the two. Pay particular attention to detail in costuming, properties, and set to help you decipher just what this production is striving to accomplish. Try above all to be open-minded and allow yourself to suspend disbelief and participate in the illusion of reality for those magical moments between lights up and final curtain.

Audience Reaction and Feedback

To discuss audience reaction as a theatrical convention may seem unusual at first. ''When a play is over, I clap,'' you may say. ''It's as simple as that.'' It is expected that audience members applaud at the end of a performance to show their enjoyment and approval, but reaction and feedback also occur during the performance. Both actors and the audience are involved in a shared communication during an entire performance.

Audience involvement in and reaction to play performance is an ongoing communication from the play's beginning to its ending. As the communication model points out, the actor and audience are constantly exchanging information. As a play progresses, the audience reacts with laughter, periods of quiet, jeers or cheers for particular characters, or sporadic applause. Actors are attentive to these messages from an audience. In a tense moment of conflict, an actor can ''feel'' the audience's support in its breathless silence. At the conclusion of a comical sequence, the actor is reinforced by the audience's laughter. An actor can tell when the audience is ''with'' him.

Figure 2.3 The wedding scene in Thornton Wilder's *Our Town*, a play that uses costumes but few props.

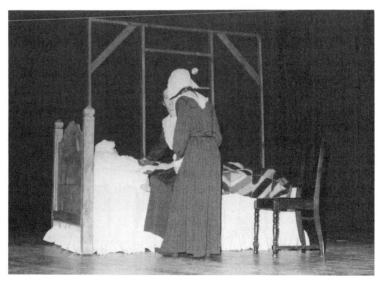

Figure 2.4 The Parris bedroom in Arthur Miller's *The Crucible* is suggestive rather than realistic.

Figure 2.5 Realistic sets are used in *The Rainmaker* by N. Richard Nash.

This ongoing communication cycle is the most exciting element of live theatre. The mutual exchange between audience and actor is the unpredictable variable in every performance situation. It makes each production a nonrepeatable artistic event. The actor can have a powerful influence on the audience, if it is involved in the performance. The audience can help shape and fashion a particular performance by its participation or lack of interest.

Spontaneous behavior from an audience during a play must be appropriate or it can spoil the effect of a scene. An audience may applaud on the exit of an actor who is particularly good. But to interrupt the scene with applause, although well meaning, can serve to disorient the actors and confuse the remainder of the scene. Talking loudly during a performance can divert the attention of the actor and spoil the scene, as well as disturb the rest of the audience.

At the conclusion of a performance, it is generally accepted that spectators communicate their reaction to the piece. As the curtain closes and the lights fade on the final scene, a curtain call generally follows. The cast members come out on the stage, usually in the order of the importance of their parts, to bow to the audience. The audience begins clapping as the lights fade, so as soon as the curtain is closed, it is immediately reopened for the curtain call. To belabor the opening of the curtain is to lose momentum on the curtain call, which could mean embarrassingly little applause for the actors who play the major roles. (Some directors are so sensitive to this that they choose not to do curtain calls at all.) The excitement of the audience at this point can be seen, heard, and felt. A play that has been popular with an audience will be cheered and applauded loudly. A play found to be pleasant entertainment will probably receive moderate applause. And the play deemed not to have met its mark may receive little applause.

Is it ever appropriate not to applaud at all? Applause has a twofold function. First, and most important, it is the audience's way of saying thank you for the effort, the time, and the work. And secondly, it is an audience's method of rating the production. The volume and intensity of the applause will offer clues to the extent of the audience's enjoyment. Actors will know how well or how poorly they did from the audience's reaction.

When a spectator gets up and leaves the house during a scene, not only does it embarrass performers, it distracts other members of the audience. Little emergencies may arise, but usually they can be attended to between scenes or during intermission. It is inappropriate to leave for any reason except a dire emergency during the performance of a scene. (A possible exception might be a scene that a viewer found highly offensive to his or her sense of good taste. But even in this case, the viewer should know enough about the play in advance to ascertain whether or not it would violate a personal code of ethics.)

Although Greek audiences were once inspired to pitch rotting vegetables onto the stage to display their disgust with a play, we have moved into a more enlightened era. Not to applaud or to do so weakly will get the idea of displeasure across to the actor, just as a rousing "bravo" and thunderous applause will let him know he or she did well. But moving about in the house during a scene serves only to communicate bad manners.

Often we take the attitude, "I have paid to be entertained, so entertain me." But there is so much more that we can attain by active (as opposed to passive) attentiveness to a play. For one, there is a vicarious experience. Through the theatre we can encounter and experience many and varied kinds of personalities, situations, and locations. We can become informed of political issues, social conflicts, and problems and solutions in human conflict. As active viewers, we can share emotional experiences with a character if we allow ourselves the empathetic response. If we risk a little emotional involvement, we may find ourselves feeling emotions that may prove reinforcing and therapeutic. If we allow ourselves an open-minded observation of the author's intent and of the technical and directorial interpretation of that intent, we may well broaden our understanding of some new or unfamiliar topic, style, or interpretation.

But we as audience members must be continually aware of the fact that these phenomena do not take place unless we are willing to follow some conventions. We can afford ourselves this unique and powerful experience only if we willingly suspend disbelief and participate in the illusion of reality. Only if we commit ourselves to participating in the conventions of the theatre can we experience it fully. The exciting reward for allowing ourselves this involvement is the heightened appreciation and depth of understanding we can attain.

Suggested Reading

Arnott, Peter. *The Theatre in Its Time*. Boston, Mass.: Little, Brown, 1981.

Hatlen, Theodore W. *Orientation to the Theatre*, 3d. ed. Englewood Cliffs, N.J.: Prentice-Hall, 1981.
Heining, Ruth Beall, and Lyda Stillwell. *Creative Dramatics for the Classroom Teacher*. Englewood Cliffs, N.J.: Prentice-Hall, 1974.
Southern, Richard. *Proscenium and Sight-Lines*. New York: Theatre Arts Books, 1964.

3

The Origins and Development of the Theatre

Where, why, and how did drama begin? Is the desire to express feelings through dance and drama an inherent part of the human psyche? Was drama something devised to fulfill a desire for self-expression and self-fulfillment?

Remnants of past civilizations—pictures on the walls of caves, buried artifacts, pottery decorations, the great pyramids—provide evidence of dramatic forms of expression in which large numbers of people participated. Although information is sketchy, there are indications that dramas were performed in Egypt on the banks of the Nile as long ago as 3200 B.C.

The earliest recorded plays and performances as we know them today occurred in Greece in the sixth and fifth centuries B.C. This dramatic expression, growing primarily out of a desire to worship and praise the gods, particularly Dionysus, developed to the point where competitions were organized, playwrights were rewarded for their efforts, and the state helped to finance productions. Out of this came works like *Antigone* by Sophocles and *Oresteia* by Aeschylus, plays that are discussed and produced today and that rank with the finest works of theatre to be found. From these beginnings, Aristotle formulated and set down certain basic elements of drama in his literary treatise, *Poetics*. The theatre buildings of this period, remains of which can still be seen in such places as Athens and Epidaurus, exhibited fine architectural features, many of which have been incorporated into theatre buildings of the twentieth century.

From these rich beginnings came the first tragic and comic characters, creative use of makeup, painted scenery, costumes, and stage machinery. Historic accounts tell us something of the actors and the playwrights as well as the behavior of the audiences. We can see the Greek influence in every facet of drama as it developed later in Rome, expanded in Europe and England in the medieval and Elizabethan periods, and blossomed in the theatrical expressions of the twentieth century.

Drama: The Beginnings

Pinpointing when and where the first dramatic ritual occurred is not yet possible, though research by historians and anthropologists is ongoing and new information continues to be brought to light. But, for the purposes of this text, it seems desirable to try to determine as nearly as we can the ancient beginnings of drama.

When asked the question, "When did it begin?" many historians and dramatists reply, "With the Golden Age of Greece." However, Egyptologists believe they have far older accounts of the drama. In its embryonic form, drama seems to have been tied to religious ceremonies. Dance-drama rituals performed outdoors served as a method of communicating with and appeasing the gods. Egyptologists have uncovered evidence that such ritualistic dramas occurred in ancient Egypt. Most of the information on early Egyptian drama has been derived from hieroglyphs on the walls of the pyramids and of tombs of the period and in the fifty-five so-called Pyramid texts. According to these inscriptions, the ritual dramas dealt primarily with the theme of death, entombment, and ascent of the soul. The Pyramid texts are believed to be parts of play scripts for these dramas, because not only is dialogue assigned to different characters but technical directions are included as well.

Another type of play apparently performed during this era celebrated the crowning of a new pharaoh and is referred to as a coronation festival play. The earliest known play of this type dates to 3100 B.C. and involves a character named Ptah,[1] who is credited with establishing religion and culture. This drama from the ancient city of Memphis celebrates the claim of Ptah to supreme godhood. Lines in the script state: "Ptah the great is the heart and tongue of the gods."[2] Another possible coronation play, called the Heb Sed, concerns a coronation jubilee celebrating thirty years of a pharaoh's reign and dates to about 2000 B.C.

The Egyptian play that many drama historians think of as the "first" play is the Abdos passion play (sometimes called the

Osiris passion play), which was probably performed sometime between 2500 and 1850 B.C. This play dramatized the death of Osiris, the father of the god Horus and king of the underworld. Later passion plays relate similar celebrations and religious rites. According to Egyptologists, these early plays were performed regularly in places established for that purpose called mortuary temples.[3]

Greek Theatre

Religious expressions also evolved into ritualistic drama in ancient Greece. Here the evidence is fresher and more complete, dating back only as far as the sixth century B.C. Emphasis is given to this period in the history of drama, because it was then that the standards of modern drama were established and championed by several great dramatists. Climaxing with the Dionysian festival plays, this era profoundly influenced drama as it would be written, spoken, and performed for thousands of years to come.

Ritualistic dance-drama probably evolved over many years, occurring whenever groups of people assembled to try to influence the cosmic powers. We can imagine that these early people, overwhelmed by their inability to comprehend weather, disease, or the changing seasons, would feel a need to reach out to those supernatural forces that controlled the universe and their lives. Perhaps they met in a clearing on assigned days or by the exchange of a signal. Speaking, singing, and dancing naturally developed and became parts of the rituals as people sought effective means of communicating with the gods. Perhaps good fortune or good weather followed a certain ritual, and it would be repeated in an effort to please the gods once more.

In pleading for basic needs such as food and healthy children, the people probably began to develop a pattern of ritual that included dialogue. As the group grew larger, the rituals became more sophisticated and stylized, and the places in which they were performed became worn and familiar. Finally, we can envision the pleasure the rituals gave to the participants. Just as we feel satisfaction from singing a familiar song or doing a well-known dance step, so these people probably enjoyed their rituals. They not only fulfilled the desire to communicate with the gods but also alleviated boredom!

Just such an evolution as the one constructed here probably took place in ancient Greece, reaching its zenith in the Dionysian theatres of the fifth century B.C. Worship of Dionysus was intro-

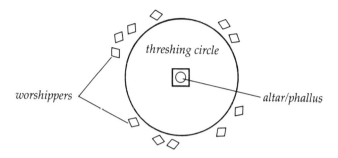

Figure 3.1 Diagram of the earliest Greek theatre.

duced into Greece around the thirteenth century B.C. According to mythology, Dionysus was the son of the Olympian god Zeus and a mortal woman, Semele. He is associated with agriculture, especially the grapes from which wine is made. In one account of his life, he was treacherously killed and later resurrected; thus, he is affiliated with the recurrence of the seasons and the perennial nature of crops. Dionysus was worshipped as the god of wine, merrymaking, and fertility, and through the Golden Age of Greece he was honored at festivals that included dramatic performances.

Archaeological evidence indicates that the earliest Dionysian celebrations took place on a threshing circle, a place where people separated the grain from the chaff. The rituals involved men clad in goatskins dancing and singing around a huge phallic symbol. The phallus symbolized not only human procreation but also the fertility of the land. This ceremony, called the *dithyram* (goat song), consisted of singing narrative songs honoring Dionysus, offering animal sacrifices, and using intoxicating substances such as wine, and there is some indication that in the earliest times human sacrifices were made. The ceremony occurred in early spring before crops were planted.

As the ceremony developed and grew, so did the area in which it was performed. The crowds became larger, and more people participated in the dithyram. Those who gathered for this religious celebration were more than spectators; they were also participants. Everyone who approached the circle joined in a ritualistic and dramatic appeal to Dionysus.

As the crowds grew, it no doubt became difficult for everyone

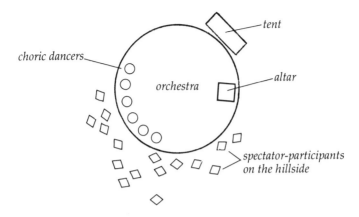

Figure 3.2 Diagram of an early Dionysian theatre.

to see the altar area. Moving the ceremonies to a clearing at the foot of a hill or to a sloping shell of a valley allowed the spectator-participants to sit on the side of the hill and have a clear view of the circle. The effect was much like that of a modern sports arena. The shift in location probably precipitated a change in the performing area. The altar may have been moved to the outer edge of the circle at this time to allow more freedom of movement within the circle. As the dramatic nature of the ceremony expanded, a tent may have been placed near the circle to provide a place for the performers to wait and to prepare themselves. The delineation between performers and audience became clearer, and the chorus emerged as the primary dramatic vehicle for the supplication directed to Dionysus.

The hillside seating came to be called the *theatron*, or "seeing place," and the circle was termed the *orchestra*, or "dancing place." The orchestra, therefore, is probably the oldest existing part of the theatre, tracing its origins to the ancient threshing circle.

By the sixth century B.C., a number of Dionysian festivals had been established. The orgiastic aspects of the worship gradually decreased, and the week-long festivals of drinking, revelry, and phallic worship evolved to become the beginnings of drama.

The Golden Age of Greece

A typical Dionysian festival would be held each year in early spring to commemorate the rebirth of vegetation. The festival began with a long procession of worshippers singing and dancing and carrying a phallus on a pole. This musical procession ended at the altar of Dionysus where a sacrifice was offered.

At the festival in Athens, the competitions were opened with the dithyram contest.[4] Each town or tribe entered a chorus of fifty that presented dances and hymns to Dionysus. Drama contests followed.

The drama began to take shape separately from the dithyramb when Thespis, a member of a chorus, stepped out and spoke lines independent of the rest of the chorus. Up to this point, the chorus had acted as a unit telling stories and relating information about Dionysus. It must have occurred to Thespis that the ceremony would have more meaning if one person spoke the words of Dionysus, that is, pretended to be the god and speak his words. This important move enabled the god to speak to the chorus and the chorus to reply. A dialogue developed, which offered many new possibilities for the theatre. Thespis has come to be known as the first actor, and today, actors and students of acting often refer to themselves as "Thespians." It is believed that the play contest became a viable part of the Dionysian festival when Thespis was brought to Athens as an actor-director in 534 B.C.

The play competitions were carefully organized and highly regarded. Writers who wished to enter their plays in the annual festival would make application to officials in Athens far in advance of the competition. Only citizens could compete, and only three dramatists were chosen to display their work. Each writer was expected to present four plays: three tragedies sharing a common theme (referred to as a trilogy) and a satyr play, a comic take-off on the serious subject of the trilogy. The festival usually lasted five or six days. The dithyramb contests took place during the first two days; the third day was set aside for comedies; and the remaining time was given to the trilogies and satyr plays.

The city-state of Athens and local theatre patrons bore most of the expense of the competitions, including a prize to the winner. Each playwright selected for competition was furnished a lead actor who was paid by the state. (In later years, when the number of actors rose to three, all were paid by the state.) Patrons also helped with the expenses and training of the chorus. Usually, the playwright directed his own work and was in charge of the production. Judging the plays was an elaborate process, and prizes were given jointly to the playwright and his patron. In later years, outstanding actors were also given awards.

Many changes took place in the Dionysian festival as it developed through the years. The original format—three tragedies on a common theme and a satyr play—was somewhat altered, although the basic set of four plays remained. The greatest changes came with the addition of more actors. In the fifth century, the playwright Aeschylus introduced a second actor. The advantages of this innovation are obvious: now the actors could have dialogue. They could exchange ideas, and through their relationship, conflicts could develop. Later, Sophocles added a third actor, allowing even more diversity in situations and dialogue.

The "three actor rule" established by these forefathers of modern theatre proclaimed that a playwright could use only three actors in his competition play. That rule remained in effect for many years. But while only three actors were allowed, the plays could have any number of characters, so each actor might have a number of roles. Only men were allowed to participate in this dramatic festival; all roles, male and female, young and old, were played by male actors. Thespis is credited with making this easier by introducing the mask. With the tragic mask, the actor could change character quickly without changing his costume.

The Dionysian actor was faced with a tremendous challenge. The vast size of the theatres and of the audiences required first and foremost that he be a good speaker. A strong, clear voice was a necessity. The actor's movements had to be broad and sweeping in order to be seen by an audience of fifteen thousand. The nature of the plays required realistic actions, yet the size of the theatre dictated that these movements be stylized or exaggerated. Facial expressions were not important since the actor wore a mask. Most of an actor's training consisted of vocal exercises and practice in gestures that would portray emotion and character properly.

Other changes involved the chorus. Originally, a chorus numbered fifty members. Later, the number was reduced to twelve and then increased to fifteen. In time, the crude, bawdy antics of the early chorus all but disappeared in the tragedies, but continued to be widely used in the satyr plays and comedies. Music was increasingly used in the performances as the years went by. Music had always been a vital part of worship, so it, too, developed and became an integral part of the plays. The flute and the lyre were common instruments used in the dramas, and it seems likely that percussion instruments were also used.

As the form of the plays changed and became more elaborate,

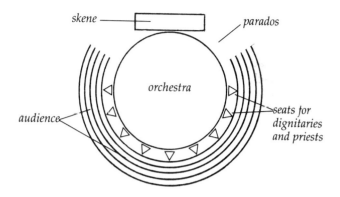

Figure 3.3 Diagram of the Dionysian theatre of the fifth century B.C.

many fine tragedies and several comedies were produced. With the reduced chorus and three tragic actors, intricate plots were devised and hours of entertainment were afforded the Athenian crowds.

The Theatre

As the Dionysian theatre took form, a permanent building called a *skene* was erected behind the circle, or orchestra. This building took the place of the early tent and provided a convenient place for actors to dress and wait. It had doors through which performers could enter and exit and ramps or entryways, called *parados*, on either side. The *skene* was constructed and decorated in various ways according to its geographic location. Playwrights began to use the skene in their plays, for example, as the facade of a home or a public building. In the final development of the theatre, the hillside seating became more permanent. First wooden benches were added; later, stone tiers were built. The elaborate Dionysian theatres, such as the ones in Athens, Delphi, and Epidaurus, had carved stone seating for as many as fifteen thousand persons and ornate carved chairs arranged around the orchestra for dignitaries.

The chorus entered via the parados to begin the play. Their chants and songs provided the prologue, narration, and exposition. Sometimes they spoke to the actors, offering advice and supplying information. At other times they represented the gods or the citizenry—listening, talking, and reacting to the actors.

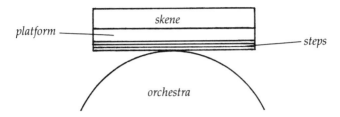

Figure 3.4 Diagram of the stage area of a Dionysian theatre.

Usually, they moved and spoke as a group, although occasionally individual members spoke solo lines. Just as the central focus of the Dionysian theatre was the chorus, so the area where they performed, the orchestra, became the most important part of the performing areas. The round stone floor of the orchestra measured about sixty-five feet in diameter.

Figure 3.5 An artist's rendering of a well-equipped Dionysian theatre, complete with *skene, orchestra,* and *parados.* (Artwork Jackie Copeland)

It is believed that the actors that played character roles performed on a long, narrow platform, two to four feet high, that was attached to the front of the skene and was open to the orchestra and the audience. The actors spoke to the chorus and to the spectators from this elevated and highly visible position. The roof of the skene was also used as an acting area, usually for the appearance of the gods. This physical separation of stage areas (actors on a platform and the chorus in the orchestra) kept a certain distance between the chorus and the actors. Although they could venture out of one area and into another, for the most part they stayed in their defined spaces.

Thousands of people flocked to these open-air theatres and filled them to capacity. But the sloping sides of the hill surrounding the stage served another purpose. As the Dionysian theatres grew larger and the hillside seats were reinforced with carved stones and walkways were constructed, the acoustics improved. In the Dionysian theatre in Athens, which seated fifteen thousand, actors speaking from the platform could be heard clearly by the entire audience. Sunlight provided illumination for the plays, so going to the theatre in the Golden Age of Greece was, of necessity, a daytime activity. Ruins of these useful and effective theatres can still be visited at the sites of the ancient Greek city-states.

Greek Playwrights

According to historical accounts, Thespis was the first actor to be given an award at the Dionysian festivals. In the years that followed, many fine plays were written and performed in the Dionysian theatres in a number of Greek city-states. Some prolific writers wrote plays for the festivals when they were quite young—Aeschylus presented his play at the age of twenty-five; Sophocles at twenty-eight, and Euripides at twenty-six.[5] As play competitions grew in importance, plays became more sophisticated in plot and character.

In a chronology of the most notable Greek playwrights (figure 3.6), Aeschylus appears first; he lived from 525 to 456 B.C. His first production took place about 499 B.C., and his best-known work is a trilogy, the *Oresteia*, performed about 458 B.C. The three plays of the *Oresteia*, are entitled *Agamemnon*, *Libation Bearers*, and *Eumenides*, and make up the only surviving complete Greek trilogy. The common subject of these plays is justice—its principles and concepts.

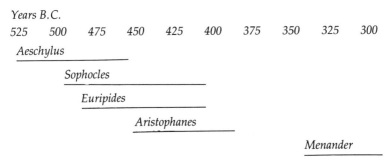

Figure 3.6 Time chart of Greek dramatists.

Living and writing during the same period, Sophocles and Euripides figured prominently in the changing form of the drama. Sophocles lived from 496 to 406 B.C. and produced his most powerful work, *Antigone*, in 441 B.C. Euripides lived from 488 to 406 B.C. and contributed, among other plays, *Medea* and *The Trojan Women*. Aristophanes, the fourth writer in our chronology, gave us one of the finest examples of Greek comedy, *The Birds*, produced in 405 B.C. Aristophanes was born in 450 B.C. and died in 380 B.C. The comedy writer Menander lived at the end of this literary age, from 342 to 292 B.C.

Aeschylus. All of the surviving Greek tragedies have mythological or historical themes. So it is with the plays of Aeschylus. His characters appear almost superhuman in their actions and expectations. In the *Oresteia*, the relationship between men and gods is examined, but references to and reflections on the political situation in Greece at the time are included as well. This trilogy plays out the familiar plot of a curse imposed on a family. Following the requirements for a trilogy, each play is a self-contained story unit, but each also forms one act of a larger drama. The greatness of this work derives not only from its historical importance but also from its universal nature. It deals with common human problems that span time and national boundaries. Through his brilliant use of characters and the chorus, Aeschylus made his play relevant to all times.

Sophocles. Sophocles is considered by many to be the greatest of the Greek dramatists. He is noted for the poetry of his dialogues, the intricacy of his plots, and the depth of his characters. His stories build to a climax that is clear and logical. Whereas the plays of Aeschylus explore lofty themes, the plays of Sophocles deal with more down-to-earth, human problems. His characters are well developed, inhabit the real world, and become involved in human conflicts. Sophocles created characters that are neither all good nor all bad and that have a variety of human strengths and weaknesses.

By giving human qualities to his characters and by streamlining the dialogue, Sophocles greatly refined the drama. As individual characters grew more important, the role of the chorus became peripheral and detached.

Only seven of the more than one hundred twenty plays said to have been written by Sophocles have survived to this day. The three most widely studied and performed are *Electra, Oedipus Rex,* and *Antigone.* In *Oedipus Rex,* the familiar theme of a curse visited on a family is treated. Before Oedipus is born, it is predicted that he will kill his father and marry his mother. Though he takes great pains to avoid it, Oedipus unknowingly carries out the prophecy. When he discovers this, Oedipus gouges out his eyes in remorse. The family curse extends to *Antigone,* who buries her dead brother in spite of her uncle, the king, who has forbidden her to do so. Antigone knows that she will die for her action, yet she makes her decision because she feels it is right. Modern audiences find this play appealing because they admire Antigone's courage.

Sophocles is credited with fixing the size of the chorus at fifteen as well as decreasing its importance. He also added the third actor, contributing even greater versatility to the dramatic form. He was probably the most skillful playwright of his era in the use of dramatic structure, and his plays were frequent winners at the festivals.

Euripides. A contemporary of Sophocles, Euripides also developed characters that were fallible and psychologically complex. He was born in 488 B.C. and died in 406 B.C., within months of Sophocles' death. Euripides, however, was not as popular as Sophocles.

Writers of the Dionysian theatre used familiar themes for their plots, so the audiences usually knew what to expect. While Euripides relied on myth and legend for many of his plays, within this framework he wrote original stories. In creating his plots, Euripides delved deeply into the psychological workings of his characters. His stories often questioned Athenian mores and values and seemed to undermine the status quo. Questioning was unpopular with audiences, so Euripides was not appreciated as much by his contemporaries as he is today.

From Euripides we have the famous play *Medea*, the story of a woman who murders her children in order to wreak revenge on her husband for the wrong he has done her. Medea is drawn as a frustrated woman driven by jealousy. Such psychological honesty in a character had not been seen previously on the Greek stage, and audiences had difficulty accepting it. Few of Euripides's festival entries won prizes. In developing characters, Euripides was no doubt ahead of his time. However, he was not as skillful at structuring plays as his contemporary, Sophocles.

Aristophanes. The first noteworthy attempts at political satire were made by Aristophanes. In a male-dominated society and a very militaristic period, there were subjects aplenty for a political satirist. Devising a form that we now call "old comedy," Aristophanes gave the Dionysian audiences something to laugh about. (Old comedy refers to plays that use sexual suggestion and bawdy jokes to invoke laughter. New comedy plays used clever, humorous language and life situations to get laughs.)

Aristophanes was born in 450 B.C. and died in 380 B.C. His legacy includes *The Frogs* and *Lysistrata*. In his plays, Aristophanes attacked government, education, and philosophy—areas in which he found plenty of material for satire. The targets of his jokes were often lawyers, politicians, and teachers. Though his work may appear frivolous at first glance, like all good comedy it was inspired by a responsible critical spirit. The topic of *Lysistrata*, for example, is women plotting to use their feminine wiles to end a long war. The dialogue was deliciously funny and the theme was popular, but beneath the hilarity was Aristophanes' honest desire for peace in a war-torn country and an argument for a more influential role in society for women. This play is important because it acknowledged women as intelligent decision-makers at a time when they were relegated to the home and denied education. Although women were not allowed to own property, conduct business, or go out of the home alone, they could attend plays.

Aristophanes liked to make fun of his literary predecessors and often made them characters in his plays. In one play he poked fun at the writing accomplishments of Euripides and Sophocles. Aristophanes' plays are unpredictable and always funny; they have a rapid-fire tempo that keeps the audience laughing. While the language of his plays is often bawdy and suggestive, it is also poetic and lyrical. Historians have commented that versatility was probably Aristophanes' greatest attribute.

Menander. The best representative of a "new comedy" play-wright is Menander. Born in 342 B.C., Menander was a great admirer of Euripides. The characters in his plays were finely drawn, and his plots carefully weighed good and evil. The chorus, which had been decreasing in importance for many years, disappeared altogether in Menander's plays.

The new comedy era marks the beginning of the end of the golden age of drama in Greece. Although the architectural splendor of theatres was at its height, the quality of the dramatic works was diminishing.

Tragedy and Comedy

In the early days of the Dionysian festivals, the opening ceremonies included a processional. Some citizens sang and danced to invoke the pleasure of the gods, while others carried phallic symbols and taunted the crowds with bawdy remarks. As the festivals developed into theatrical productions, these two activities seemed to lead the way; the dithyram singers and dancers gave rise to tragedy and the phallus carriers foreshadowed the development of comedy.

Tragedy in the Dionysian theatre served as a method of informing the citizens of important political events. The early tragedies, particularly those of Aeschylus, Sophocles, and Euripides, frequently made reference to political leaders and situations of the period. The plays were highly patriotic. Against a background of politics, the themes of the power and influence of the gods were everpresent. A common theme was the suffering imposed on mankind by the gods, who were often depicted as selfish and cruel, arbitrarily inflicting hardship on groups and individuals. These plays, serving as both instruction and entertainment, were short in length, because most of them were designed to be part of a tetralogy—three tragedies and a satyr play.

The format of the Greek tragedy was fairly uniform. It usually opened with a prologue, which presented information about events that were important to the understanding of the plot. The prologue was followed by the entrance of the chorus; they provided an exposition of the current situation and a description of the characters involved in the play. The action of the play then developed in a series of episodes tied together by choral songs. The episodes were brief and included only the important moments of events. Violent acts occurred offstage, and the news was reported onstage by messengers.

The plays contained many characters. The three-actor rule precluded the use of more than three actors on stage at any one time, so the actors entered and exited, changing costumes and masks to play the different characters. The role of one character was often exchanged among the actors many times during a production. Finally came the exodus, the end of the play when all the actors and the chorus left the stage.

A satyr play followed the three tragedies and had a related political or moral theme, but the subject that had been seriously treated in the tragedies was grossly mocked in this final play. The satyr play took its name from a mythological creature, half goat and half man, who may have been a holdover from the raucous revelry of the early Dionysian ceremonies. A chorus of men dressed in goatskins were included in these plays and were the targets of jokes relating to mythology. The satyr play was an effort at comic relief and probably served to put spectators in a lighter mood after the serious message of the tragedies. The satyr play decreased in significance as drama continued to develop, as did the use of the symbolic phallus as a part of the festivals.

Comedy developed along with tragedy in ancient Greece and was included in the festival competitions. Whereas tragedy dealt with important events and topics and with lofty ideas, comedy dealt with themes that were more secular. Comic writers directed their commentary and sarcasm at politics, art, and society, and they often caricatured popular figures of the times. Aristophanes sometimes made Aeschylus and Sophocles the recipients of his comic attacks, knowing they might be in the audience at the play's performance.

Emphasizing the fertility aspect of the Dionysian festival, comic male characters were sometimes costumed in a short tunic and tights, to which was attached a large phallus, often with giant testicles. Padding was also used to give the actors large bellys and ample derrieres. Sometimes the characters masqueraded as animals; choruses of birds and frogs are found in some of the early comedies.

The action onstage in the comic play was less formal than in the tragedy. Sometimes the chorus was split into parts, each depicting a different side of a question. Eventually, the chorus members took individual roles. Comedy scenes were improvisational in nature and more episodic than those of the tragedies; the story was loosely organized. Humor was often the result of physical interactions of characters, probably like the slapstick comedy we associate today with the Three Stooges. Phallic jokes and obscene language characterized the comic scripts, but the language, while sometimes crude, was also entertaining and even poetic. A fine example of the sophisticated use of language in the early comedies is found in *Lysistrata*.

Comedy was not as highly regarded as tragedy in the festival competitions. It was not considered to be as worthy a literary achievement. Only one day of competition was allotted to comedy, while three days were reserved for the tragedies. As comedy developed, it lost its ribald nature and tended toward more political and social commentary. The sexual aspect of the plays became a less important feature. Originating about 450 B.C. with Aristophanes and lasting about one hundred fifty years, comedy faded with tragedy for a time as the importance of Athens declined.

Technical Innovations

The original Greek theatre, supplied with impressive playwrights and ample physical structures, was equally impressive in costuming its actors and in the technical elements of the play. Elaborate masks, painted scenes, and a number of stage ''machines'' were employed to complete the production.

The costume of the actor was intended primarily to make him more visible and to heighten the visual impact he would have on the audience. The Greek audience was so large, numbering up to twenty thousand persons, that those who sat far back in the seating area had difficulty seeing the action. To give the characters broader visual definition, several special costume elements were designed. The typical costume was a sleeved tunic called a *chiton*, which was sometimes full length and sometimes short. Depending on character portrayed, a cloak might be added. The costumes were colorful, but there was little variety or differentiation between character types. Character delineations were generally made by objects the actor carried rather than by what he wore. A king, for example, carried a scepter; a warrior, a spear or shield. The costumes included boots, called *kothurnos*, with elevated soles to give the actor added height and therefore better visibility.

The most impressive facet of the costume was the mask. One actor might wear several different masks during the performance of a play. It was the mask that defined a specific character. The design of the mask, like the costume, was primarily intended for identification but served to amplify sound as well. Some histo-

Figure 3.7 An artist's rendering of a classical Greek actor with mask
and *chiton* (tunic). (Artwork courtesy Jackie Copeland. From
Navarre, *Le Theatre grec*.)

rians contend that the mask also allowed the actor to hide his true
identity from the gods, since they would be displeased at being
impersonated. It also gave a symbolic characterization to each
role and completely divorced the actor's likeness and personality
from the character. The mask might have a drooping forehead, a
gaping mouth, and other exaggerated facial features that helped

the audience make character differentiations. Masks also defined the sex of the character. Since all roles were played by males, it was important to identify the male from the female characters. The masks were large, covering the entire head, including hair and beard. No masks have survived for study; they were probably made of cork, wood, and linen and have decayed with time.

The technical accoutrements of the stage were also impressive. Historians credit Sophocles with being the first to use painted scenery. It is believed that painted screens were employed as well as scenes painted directly onto the front walls of the skene. Later came the first recorded use of the *periaktoi,* a three-sided structure on which was painted three different scenes, one on each side. Quick scene changes could be made by merely turning the *periaktoi.* The front of the skene had doors through which actors made their entrances and exits. These doors were probably large enough to accommodate scenery that had to be moved on and off the stage.

Two machines were employed in the Dionysian theatre, adaptations of which are still used today. Because violence rarely occurred onstage, a character might be ''killed'' offstage and then rolled onstage on a cart or platform called an *eccylema.* This movable platform was also used to reveal interior scenes. But the most amazing machine was the *deus ex machina,* or god machine, which allowed actors to ''fly'' on and off the stage. It was made up of a series of ropes and pulleys that operated a crane strong enough to carry one or two actors. In one scene, for example, a character died onstage and was carried off by a god; both actors were transported by the *deus ex machina.*

Since no special means of stage lighting were available, night and day in a play were established by props. Torches might identify a night scene; for example, a torch-bearing processional beginning a scene would suggest night. When fog or smoke were needed, something was burned offstage. The ancient Greeks had well-equipped and functional theatres in which they creatively used the equipment they were able to construct.

Audience Reaction

A special bond existed between the performers and the audience in the Greek theatre, because both had come to the theatre to join in a religious celebration in honor of Dionysus. Each audience member was a vital element of the production. Therefore, audiences felt free to participate in and react appropriately to what happened on the stage.

Prior to a performance, the excitement and anticipation of the spectators were at a high pitch. They probably had been treated to a preview of the plays a few days earlier, a practice that was fairly common and that constituted one of the earliest ways to encourage people to come to the theatre. The spectators often arrived at the theatre early in the morning in order to get a seat for the day's performances, for general seating was open to everyone, citizens and slaves alike. The only reserved seats were those next to the stage, which were saved for the priests and other dignitaries and for the authors of the festival plays. Admission at first was free; but in the last half of the fifth century, a small fee was charged. Subsidies existed so that those who could not pay were able to see the performances.[6]

Spectators very likely brought food and cushions or blankets for their day at the theatre, and there was probably much coming and going and eating and drinking. Feeling themselves to be an important part of the creative experience and perhaps also somewhat intoxicated, audience members felt free to comment on the actors' performances and the quality of the production. Good acting would be rewarded with loud clapping. Weak performances would be met with hissing, stamping, jeering, and possibly a barrage of fruit or nuts. However, the crowd was obliged to be somewhat restrained, for this was, after all, a religious observance. Violence in the theatre was punishable by death.[7]

The close proximity of audience and actors contributed to the festive atmosphere. The audience almost surrounded the stage, and this made communication easy and dynamic. This closeness can be appreciated better if we compare the Greek stage with a twentieth century proscenium stage, where the audience is placed at a distance from the stage on only one of four sides. The arrangement of the seating about the stage in the Greek theatre helped to amplify the visual impact of the characters and costumes. It was said that when the grotesquely attired Furies appeared in Aeschylus's production of the *Oresteia*, the effect was so frightening that "women miscarried and some children died."[8]

A festive mood was encouraged by actors as well as audience. Plays were written and produced in such a fashion that the actors or the chorus would sometimes turn to the spectators and address them directly, imploring them to support the government or to give homage to the gods. Such direct communication encouraged a vocal response. Often the spectators were made to feel as if they were an extension of the chorus and therefore of the performance. This festive atmosphere was sometimes aided by theatre patrons who provided refreshments for the entire audience in addition to giving a party for the actors.[9]

Roman Drama

In the third century B.C., the decline of drama in Greece was evident in the lack of new, high quality plays, but the Romans had been absorbing the culture of Greece. The setting for the development of the theatre now shifted to Rome with the gradual ascension of the Roman Empire. The developing Roman theatre gained prominence by the third century B.C.

Early Roman theatres resembled their Greek counterparts. Most, though not all, performers were male and wore the traditional masks. Female performers appeared in mimes, dramatic entertainments that usually portrayed scenes from life but in a ridiculous way. The nature and structure of the Roman tragedies did not depart noticeably from the Greek formula. However, the three-actor rule was no longer followed. Any number of actors could be onstage at one time, but the actors still wore masks.

The years 240 to 75 B.C. are considered the most important to the drama in Rome. During this period, some significant pieces of dramatic writing were produced, although many of them appear to have been modifications of Greek plays.[10] By the time of the birth of Christ, political power in the ancient world had shifted to Rome. The Roman Empire had conquered many of the Greek city-states and adapted the Greek theatre and drama to suit its own needs.

Historical accounts of the excesses of the Roman era tell of sumptuous feasts, orgiastic festivities, and violent competitive events. So it comes as no surprise that excess and self-indulgence appeared in theatrical presentations as well. During the third century A.D., music and dancing, combat, and animal acts were common parts of theatre production, adding spectacle to the performances.

The militaristic nature of Roman civilization was evident in the developing theatre. At official festivals called the *ludi*, entertainment included plays and play competitions. Taking on a circuslike atmosphere, the larger theatres encouraged and showcased chariot races, animal fights, and boxing along with the music, dance, drama, and farce.

Several innovations were made in the Roman drama. Seneca, a noted writer of the period (4 B.C.–A.D. 65), dealt with human passions; his characters were obsessed with revenge or were possessed by other potentially violent emotions. His treatment of characters brought the drama even more into the arena of human emotions and feelings and away from the godlike portrayals of the Greeks. Comedy was popular, and mime developed. One of the more flamboyant and popular diversions of the theatre during the later Roman period was the performance of mock sea battles called *naumachia*. These events were sometimes held in the flooded orchestra of a Roman theatre. Performers could be fatally injured in such dangerous reenactments, and for this reason the sea battles as well as the gladiatorial contests often used condemned criminals and other prisoners as actors.

The architecture of Roman theatre was similar to that of Greek theatres but was adapted for the more active and violent nature of Roman performances. The building of the first permanent Roman theatre building is credited to a general named Pompey in the year 55 B.C. Since it was the tendency of the Romans to honor many gods at one time and not just one, as did the Greeks, it is surprising that this first permanent theatre included a temple honoring Venus, goddess of love and beauty. Historians surmise that this religious symbol helped convince the political establishment of the period that such a theatre building was worthwhile.

In many of the Roman theatre structures, the scene building and the seating area were joined into one unit. This reduced the orchestra circle of the old Greek theatre to a semicircle. The *paradoi*, or passageways for the chorus, were retained, but were roofed as entryways into the auditorium. Three to five doors opened into the scene building through the rear wall of the stage, which was ornately decorated. The width of the stage increased in some theatres to as much as forty feet. Trapdoors were built into the floor of the stage in certain theatres, and the space beneath the building was used for animal cages. During the time of the Roman Empire, more than one hundred permanent theatres were built, and some of these even had efficient cooling systems for the comfort of the spectators. All of them were heavily decorated with marble, gilded wood carvings, and paintings.[11]

Like the Greek theatres before them, the Roman theatres made use of many technical innovations. In addition to the *deus ex ma-*

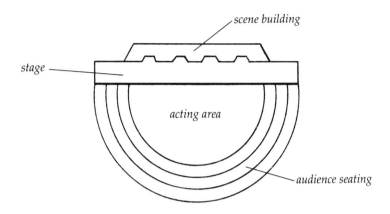

Figure 3.8 Diagram of a Roman theatre.

china and movable scenery, the Romans devised plumbing for flooding the orchestra for naval battles, and the lower levels of the theatre had storage areas for props, scenery, and animals. The Roman Theatre is credited with developing the first drop curtain. Through a long, narrow slot in the front of the stage floor, a curtain could be hoisted on telescoping poles while a set change was made. Then the curtain was quickly dropped to reveal the new setting.

As the Roman Empire began to disintegrate, so did its theatre. Many factors probably contributed to the demise, but one seems certain: a great deal of the theatre had become so obscene and violent that the newly established Christian church would not tolerate it. And the idea that all gods were false except the one Christian God also served to weaken the influence of the theatre. As the Christian church grew in size and strength, the theatre diminished. Dramatic fervor all but died, and dramatic pursuits nearly disappeared.

What is known of the theatre in the next few hundred years is sketchy. The Dark Ages were especially dark for the theatre. However, with the advent of the tenth century, some dramatic stirrings began.

Theatre in the Middle Ages

Though the drama almost disappeared because of the influence of the Christian church, its reinstitution in the tenth century came about within the church. The symbolic sacraments and rituals of

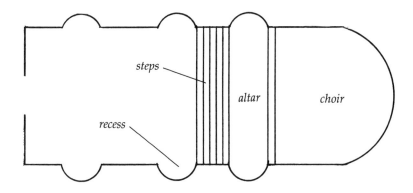

Figure 3.9 Diagram of a medieval church.

the church began to take on dramatic characteristics, and the liturgical celebrations such as the Mass and Hours easily accommodated the performance of short plays. These religious playlets were performed inside the church as a part of the ceremonies, and simple sets and costumes were used. Church interiors were generally long and narrow, and incorporated different levels, steps, a choir loft, and wall recesses. Plays adapted naturally to these performance areas. Scripts still exist from these mid-tenth-century plays, and it is believed that the lines were chanted rather than spoken.

Two hundred years later, in the twelfth century, plays were once again performed outside the church. From A.D. 1200 on, Medieval theatre flourished, reaching a peak from 1350 to 1550. In England, guilds (unions of tradesmen) produced plays in the marketplaces. Some dramas took to the road aboard pageant wagons, and theatre in the round appeared.

The town marketplace became a popular location for the performance of plays. Its large open space placed few restrictions on the number of actors involved, and the plays were assured of a large and eager audience. The plays treated moralistic themes and religious stories, reflecting the earlier liturgical dramas of the church. Morality plays such as *Everyman*, featuring characters that faced mankind's problems, were popular during this era.

Mounds of earth called "rounds" were also popular theatre sites of the period. These outdoor performance areas consisted of a circular mound that functioned as a stage, surrounded by con-

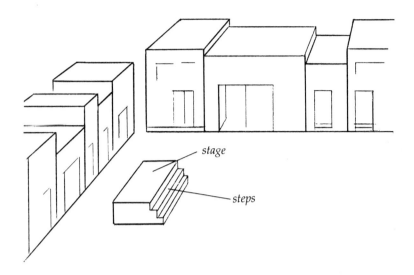

Figure 3.10 Diagram of a marketplace theatre.

centric circles of seats for the audience. According to historians, a ditch encircled the stage and seating area, probably to keep out the nonviewers or to prevent outsiders from disturbing a performance. Scenery structures were used, but little else is known of this theatre type. The remains of one such round still exist in Cornwall, England.[12]

Probably the most familiar of the medieval theatres was the pageant wagon. In those days, it was more sensible to take the

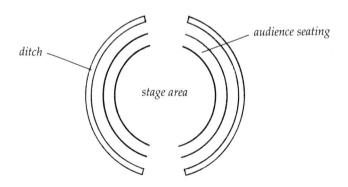

Figure 3.11 Diagram of a Cornish round.

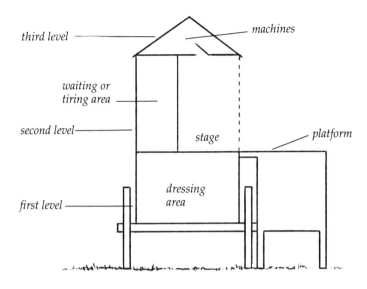

Figure 3.12 Diagram of a pageant wagon with an adjoining platform.

entertainment to the people than to expect people to travel great distances to the theatre. A typical pageant wagon contained a scaffold with two platforms, one over the other, the lower area was used for dressing and storage, and the upper area was the stage. Mounted on wheels, the platforms could be easily transported.[13]

The stage level had a painted backdrop to suggest the setting of the play. As the stage area must have been very small, it is surmised that additional carts or platforms were arranged alongside to give the performers more space and that the ground was also used. Pageant wagons varied in size and style, according to the need of a play and the performing group. Some wagons had a third level for stage machines.

Long plays with several scenes and settings were performed over several days by a caravan of pageant wagons moving from one location to another. Finding a waiting audience at each stop, the performers would begin the play when the first wagon arrived at the first location. Wagon number one then moved on to another town, a second wagon would arrive, and a new group of performers would continue the play. In this fashion, a long play could be performed, and the audience would not have to travel far.

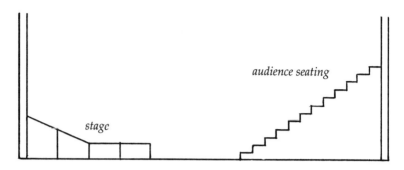

Figure 3.13 Diagram of Serlio's stage and audience seating.

Italian Renaissance Theatre

By the fourteenth century, a new age of artistic and intellectual flowering began, first in Italy and then throughout the rest of Europe. This period, the Renaissance, saw the emergence of sophisticated improvements in the theatre.

Contributing immensely to this period of dramatic growth and invention was an Italian artist, Sebastino Serlio. Although Serlio's perspective drawings did not alter the architecture of theatre buildings (he assumed that plays would be performed in already existing buildings), they did revolutionize the art of scenery painting. Serlio designed settings for a rectangular space that sloped up and away from the audience. His realistic scenes angled toward a vanishing point, creating the illusion of great space and depth. In an effort to complete the illusion, the stage floor was raked, that is, the first few feet of the stage next to the audience were flat, but then the floor rose in elevation at an angle to the back of the stage. Scenery, such as the *periaktoi*, was placed on the raked portion of the stage in a way that would create the desired effect.[14]

Since Serlio's designs were easily adapted to existing buildings, the need for new theatres during this period was slow in arising. However, it was during the Renaissance that the proscenium theatre was born. In a proscenium theatre, the audience views the play through a frame, or proscenium arch, much as one would view a framed picture. The prototype of this modern stage is considered to be the Teatro Farnese in Parma, Italy, first used in 1628. How the proscenium arch came into being is still debated. Perhaps Serlio's drawings gave theatre builders the idea.

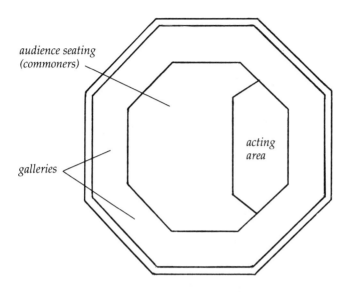

Figure 3.14. Diagram of an Elizabethan theatre.

While the Italian Renaissance produced superb theatre architecture and scene design, little of lasting value was written for the theatre in Italy. But the advances in theatre practices—perspective scenery and indoor performances—were to influence European theatre for years to come.

Elizabethan Theatre

Queen Elizabeth I of England, who reigned from 1558 to 1603, was greatly influenced by the Italian Renaissance and encouraged playwrights and theatre builders. During the Elizabethan era, William Shakespeare lived and worked, and his famous Globe theatre was built (1599).

In Elizabethan England, a theatrical performance was no longer an infrequent occurrence. It became an established part of daily life. No longer did divisions exist between public, court, and church theatre. All the citizens were able to enjoy the contributions of writers such as Shakespeare, Thomas Kyd, and Christopher Marlowe. Sacred themes continued to be used, but playwrights also dealt with real-life situations such as murder, jealousy, greed, and love, and the plays had intricate and finely developed plots.

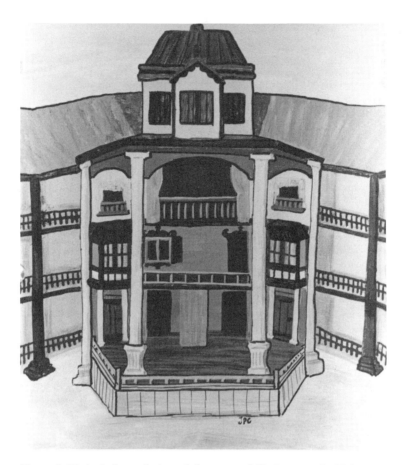

Figure 3.15 Artist's rendering of the stage of Shakespeare's Globe Theatre.   (Artwork courtesy Jackie Copeland)

William Shakespeare is generally acknowledged to be the greatest dramatic writer of all times. He was actively involved in the theatre at every level—actor, playwright, and producer. He managed his own acting troupe and the Globe theatre. He was highly innovative in theatre design and in the use of stage space. Shakespeare's theatre was an imaginative one, requiring great freedom in staging.

The Globe theatre was patterned after an earlier theatre built by an actor named James Burbage in 1576. Called simply The Theatre, Burbage's house was circular in form and had platforms and boxes for the audience.

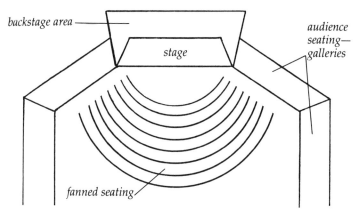

Figure 3.16 Diagram of a Restoration theatre.

The Globe was an eight-sided building open in the center, and the stage projected into the open interior. With its trapdoors, various levels, balconies, curtains, and doors, the stage was a functional and highly versatile performance area. This was important because the settings for Shakespeare's plays changed quickly from intimate interiors to exterior scenes such as open countryside or city street.

The Globe was designed to accommodate a large number of spectators—up to two thousand. The large central open area provided standing room for those not able to afford a seat. Three galleries provided seats that were protected from rain and sun and allowed the occupants to be well away from the lower-class patrons on the lowest level. Private boxes were also available. A flag was raised on the flagstaff on the days of a play performance to signal the townspeople.

The Globe and other similar theatres served the English people until the middle of the seventeenth century, when theatres began to close. Dramatists once held in high regard were now out of favor. The Globe was demolished during this period. Civil war brought the Puritan government of Oliver Cromwell and the official closing of London theatres. But a few inns and taverns managed to keep the theatre alive.

When the monarchy was restored in 1660, the theatre once again began to flourish. New theatres were established, such as Drury Lane (1674) in London, and later, Covent Garden (1732). During the Restoration, the drama and theatre buildings began to change. Theatres became larger, and the seating area was extended back and fanned out on either side, enlarging seating capacity. By the addition of several balconies and wall boxes, seating could be increased, although some of the viewers in the galleries and boxes could not see the stage! These seating arrangements would be copied and used in American theatres.[15]

In the English theatre of this period, the house seating areas included the boxes, two or three galleries, and the pit, or floor level. The pit was raked to improve sight lines (this was an innovation) and was furnished with backless benches. The floor of the small stage was also raked gently upward from the front edge to the back wall.

Theatre in the United States

Pinpointing exactly when and where theatre began in America is difficult. Several Atlantic Coast towns boast of having the "first" theatre, but that honor probably goes to Williamsburg, Virginia, with the Dock Street theatre of Charleston, South Carolina, a close second. American theatre of this period was like its English cousin. Some drama flourished in colleges in the beginning of the eighteenth century, but American puritanism managed to thwart the development of true theatre until the nineteenth century.

Theatre developed along many different avenues in America. Touring companies came from Europe to perform for audiences in major cities and small towns, and riverboats carried performing groups up and down the Mississippi River to many settlements. In the large cities, most notably New York, Boston, and Philadelphia, theatrical enterprises were undertaken with vigor. By the end of the nineteenth century, New York had become the theatre center of the United States.

Theatre buildings in America varied little from those in England. One improvement was gaslight; for the first time the intensity of the stage lights could be controlled. Gaslight provided better illumination than the oil lamps and candles that had been used up to this point. Then, in the 1880s, electric lights made all other kinds of lighting obsolete.

As the country went through various periods in which certain artistic trends were dominant, such as romanticism, realism, and naturalism, the theatre reflected the times. Out of this came the Daly theatre in New York in the late nineteenth century.[16] In Da-

Figure 3.17 The Majestic Theatre, New York City. (Photograph by Byron. Courtesy of The Theatre Collection, Museum of the City of New York.)

ly's theatre, the boxes became circular balconies. A center aisle was established, and the apron of the stage was greatly diminished. This theatrical design is still popular in America today. Steele MacKaye, another noted American figure in theatre architecture, made innovations in his New York theatres. In the late nineteenth century, he opened a theatre with two elevator stages, and he was one of the first to use electric lights.

The twentieth century has added much to the theatre. Lighting can now transform a set instantly and completely. The technological advances in lighting have been phenomenal and have totally revolutionized theatrical performances. The set designs of the

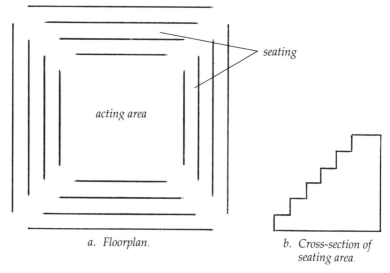

a. Floorplan.

b. Cross-section of seating area.

Figure 3.18 Diagram of the Arena Stage.

Figure 3.19 The Arena Stage production of *Candide*, by Leonard Bernstein. (Photo by Joan Marcus. Courtesy of Arena Stage.)

twentieth century have strayed from the realistic designs of Serlio and may be suggestive and subtle or bold and garish. The modern set may be the shell of one or more rooms, as in Arthur Miller's *The Crucible,* or it may incorporate two or three different sets on a revolving stage. But whatever the design of the modern play set, the theatre in which it is showcased has much in common with theatres of years gone by.

The evolution of the theatre building has taken place slowly since its beginnings in ancient Greece. Although it has changed in many ways over the years, the basic design of the twentieth century theatre is much like the Dionysian theatre. The Arena Stage in Washington, D.C., opened in 1961, is an example of an American contribution to theatre development. Proclaimed as new and innovative, the Arena reminds us of the early "rounds" and the Greek threshing circle. It does not seem so new when one compares it to its ancient predecessors. The Guthrie Theatre in

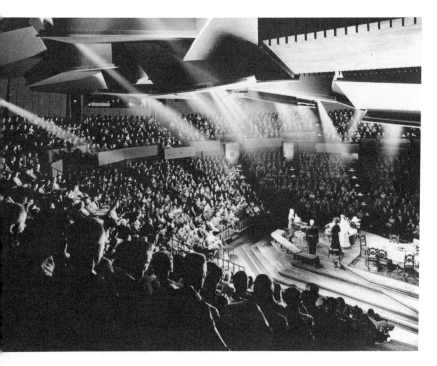

Figure 3.20 A performance at the Guthrie Theatre, Minneapolis, Minnesota. (Courtesy of The Guthrie Theatre.)

Minneapolis has also been hailed as a great accomplishment in modern theatre design. But, again, if we compare it to the Dionysian theatre and to the Globe, we see that they have much in common.

Ease of acting and of scene change are the primary criteria for a theatrical space. The modern stage, although it may vary from one theatre to another, must still meet these criteria.

Suggested Reading

Berthold, Margot. *A History of World Theater*. New York: Frederick Ungar, 1972.

Brockett, Oscar G. *History of the Theatre*, 2d ed. Boston, Mass.: Allyn and Bacon, 1974.

Brockett, Oscar G. *The Essential Theatre*, 2d ed. New York: Holt, Rinehart and Winston, 1980.

Freedley, George, and John A. Reeves. *A History of the Theatre*. New York: Crown, 1941.

Harsh, Philip W. *A Handbook of Classical Drama*. Stanford, Calif.: Stanford Univ. Press, 1944.

Joseph, Stephen. *Theatre in the Round*. New York: Taplinger, 1968.

Kott, Jan. *The Eating of the Gods*. New York: Random House, 1970.

Macgowan, Kenneth, and William Melnitz. *The Living Stage: A History of the World Theatre*. Englewood Cliffs, N.J.: Prentice-Hall, 1955.

Nicoll, Allardyce. *The Development of the Theatre*. New York: Harcourt, Brace, Jovanovich, 1966.

Oates, Whitney J., and Eugene O'Neill, Jr. *The Complete Greek Drama*. Vol. 2. New York: Random House, 1938.

Roberts, Vera M. *On Stage: A History of Theatre*. New York: Harper and Row, 1962.

Rockwood, Jerome. *The Craftsmen of Dionysus*. Glenview, Ill.: Scott, Foresman, 1966.

Webster, Thomas B. L. *Greek Theatre Production*. London: Methuen, 1970.

Part Two

Theatre: Art and Craft

4

The Actor

Any approach to a study of acting begins with an awareness that the actor's only tool for this craft is his or her body and all its attendant faculties. Unlike the teacher who is equipped with blackboard, books, and desks and the painter who uses brushes, paints, and canvas, the actor's only instrument is a finely tuned, well-developed, and responsive body and mind. How well trained and disciplined the body and imaginative the mind will determine the quality of the actor. In addition, every actor needs to acquire or devise (based on study and training) a personal approach to acting and to the portrayal of emotion.

There exist as many acting techniques, theories, and ideas of methodology as there are actors living and working at any one moment. The art of acting is so personal and introspective that many actors claim not to have been influenced by any one technique, but to have devised their own. However, when we look closely at actors who have achieved some degree of success in the theatre, we can identify many commonly held beliefs.

Theories of Acting

Most actors use one of two basic approaches. Jerome Rockwood in *The Craftsmen of Dionysus* refers to these two methods as presentational acting and representational acting.[1] In the first approach the actor "presents" a character to the audience. The actor uses gestures and speech that he or she determines are appropriate for this type of character. In rehearsals, the actor selects and uses gestures and movements that will be used in performance.

The original proponents of this kind of acting technique were William James, an American psychologist and Carl George Lange, a Danish physiologist. These two men, working independently, came up with the same idea. In the early twentieth century, they met, collaborated, and made public what came to be known as the James-Lange theory. Their theory was primarily movement oriented. They taught that, in order for an emotion to be portrayed, the actor must put himself into a physical position he feels coincides with that emotion. For example, for the portrayal of happiness, one should square back the shoulders, lift the chin, and smile. They proposed that putting the body into the proper physical position would result in the appropriate attendant feelings or emotions. This theory, although still utilized occasionally, did not receive the wide-based support or following that its authors had hoped for.

The second approach, representational acting, requires the actor to attempt to portray the character by actually thinking the thoughts and experiencing the feelings of that character. This theory purports that if the proper thoughts and feelings are engendered within the actor, then the appropriate gestures and movement will follow naturally. The presentational actor imitates what he or she has observed in nature; the representational actor attempts to recreate what has been observed or experienced. When viewing an actor in performance, it is difficult to ascertain which approach is being used, because most actors have borrowed from both approaches to create their own technique.

Representational acting and its interpretation and elaboration in the first quarter of this century by Constantin Stanislavski has had great impact on acting and dramatic art as it is known and practiced today. It would be difficult for any actor of the twentieth century to say that he or she has not in some way been affected by the life and teachings of this renowned actor-director from the Moscow Art Theatre. Presentational actors argue that they can imitate life easily and readily simply by repeating what they have seen, but the adherents of the Stanislavski theory maintain that a creative spirit must first be engendered within the actor in order for believable acting to take place. Developing a creative state is the primary focus of the Stanislavski system.

James-Lange Theory

At about the time that Stanislavski was developing his approach to the inner truth of emotion in acting, William James and

Carl George Lange were working on a theory to explain the internal nature of the emotional response. Their explanation of how emotional changes take place was very different from the one advocated and practiced by Stanislavski and the Moscow Art Theatre.

In understanding emotional changes, one must realize that an emotion does not occur instantaneously. That is, a series of steps must occur if one is to experience an emotion. Most people agree that the sequence usually starts with an emotion-provoking situation—a stimulus for the emotion. For example, a frightening situation must occur to begin the sequence of responses felt as fear.[2] It is this sequence that the James-Lange theory addresses.

William James, a turn-of-the-century American psychologist, did extensive work on the stimulus-response relationship in the production of emotion. James and the Danish physiologist Lange coincidentally developed similar, and in many respects related, theories. Although each of these men developed the theory on his own and later collaborated, James usually gets more credit because it was he who published the two-volume *Principles of Psychology* in which this theory is expounded.

James' findings indicated that "bodily changes directly follow our perception of an exciting fact and that our awareness of these bodily changes is the emotion."[3] Accordingly, the James-Lange theory proposed that the order in which the events take place in an emotion is not the same as that ordained by many of the other psychologists of the era. In *Principles of Psychology*, James details this sequence:

> My theory, on the contrary, is that the bodily changes follow directly the perception of the exciting fact, and that our feeling of the same changes as they occur is the emotion. Common sense says, we lose our fortune, are sorry and weep; we meet a bear, are frightened and run; we are insulted by a rival, are angry and strike. The hypothesis here to be defended says that this order of sequence is incorrect, that the one mental state is not immediately induced by the other, that the bodily manifestations must first be interposed between and that the more rational statement is that we feel sorry because we cry, angry because we strike, afraid because we tremble, and not that we cry, strike, or tremble because we are sorry, angry, or fearful, as the case may be. Without the bodily states following on the perception, the latter would be purely cognitive in form, pale, colorless, destitute of emotional warmth. We might then see the bear, and judge it best to run, receive the insult and deem it right to strike, but we should not actually feel afraid or angry.[4]

The James-Lange theory of emotion exerted a strong influence on psychologists and led to a great deal of research on the physiological changes involved in the different emotions. However, further experimental evidence did not support the theory; in fact, several lines of evidence seemed to contradict it. In one experiment, for example, it was established that when humans were injected with adrenalin, they reported feelings of uneasiness, but could not report a specific emotion. When they saw a person angry or joyful, they took on that emotion. The bodily change did not set off a clear, unambiguous emotion, as had been suggested by James.[5] As more studies were made in an effort to corroborate James's findings, they seemed to indicate that the James-Lange theory was incorrect.

As a result, an alternate theory was developed in the late 1920s which maintained that describing what happened in emotional changes would have to take the hypothalmus (midbrain) into consideration. The hypothalmus seemed to control certain emotions such as fear and rage. Ross Stagner states in his book on basic psychology:

> This positive piece of evidence, plus the negative evidence for the James-Lange theory, suggested an alternative theory. When certain stimuli are present, they are perceived, and this leads, in turn, to strong stimulation of the hypothalmus (the emotion) which in turn leads to bodily changes and overt behavior. The sequence now was Stimulus-Perception of Stimulus-Stimulation of Hypothalmus-Bodily Changes and Overt Behavior. The experience of an emotion was not independent of any bodily changes which might ensue.[6]

This theory, in essence, says the sequence of events is: (1) perception of the stimulus (snake); (2) the emotion (fear); and (3) the reaction (running).

Several decades later, researchers proposed a theory stressing the role of learning in shaping one's emotional experiences. They suggested that the James-Lange theory is correct for young infants and lower animals, but that as the individual learns to associate this "primitive" kind of emotion with neutral objects, the later theory proves true.[7]

Although he was aware of the work being done by James and Lange on emotional changes, Stanislavski did not feel their findings contributed in any way to what he was trying to achieve. And indeed, the James-Lange theory was altered and filtered by followers to the point that the resultant findings largely supported Stanislavski's work. Stanislavski believed that if an actor felt an emotion, then his or her movement and voice would develop from or be motivated by that feeling. James and Lange said that the movement prompted the feeling of the emotion. A later theory returned again to the notion that the stimulus elicits the emotion, and the emotion triggers the physical movement.

The Stanislavski System

Volumes have been written on the Stanislavski system, or "The Method" as it has come to be known. What is the Stanislavski system? Some noted actors, directors, and writers of the modern theatre have summed it up as follows:

> Stanislavski's basic point is that his training work is not intended directly for production on the stage. The training work teaches the means by which the actor incites this imagination, this thing that takes place and makes him feel "I think I know what it is. I can't quite put it into words. Let me do it." Then the actor wants to act. He does not quite know what he wants to do, yet he's impelled to go ahead. He is creative. Stanislavski's entire search, the entire purpose of the "Method" or our technique or whatever you want to call it, is to find a way to start in each of us this creative process so that a good deal of the things we know but are not aware of will be used on the stage to create what the author sets for us to do. (Lee Strasberg[8])
>
> He wrote all the stuff down. He tried to systematize it so that you can keep working at it and not just sit and wait for the angel to visit you. After I graduated from Goodman, I assumed—like my fellow students—that I knew all about it. And then to find out that if I studied (the Method) for the next ninety years I'd just be scratching the surface was divine. It's like suddenly being handed a bottomless cup. (Geraldine Page[9])
>
> Perhaps Konstantin Stanislavski was a legend before his death in 1938. He is certainly a legend now. All over the world actors, directors, students, and teachers of acting are quoting his writings and following his teachings. Here in America new words have sprung up in theater language. For years the phrase "Stanislavski's method" was used in theatrical conversations. Now it's simply "the method." We hear phrases like "he's a method actor," "method writing," "method directing." All this, I believe, has stimulated interest in the theater and is producing some great results. (Joshua Logan[10])
>
> Stanislavski's . . . practical wisdom: a . . . legacy he has left behind to carry on his own example and devotion to the theatre which he served so greatly. (Sir John Gielgud[11])

Stanislavski perfected a practical, flexible system for the training of the actor, the building of a character and the analysis of the overall action of the play. Over a period of some thirty years he experimented, testing each formulation of his system in production, revising and discarding in his search for stage truth. In all his work he kept alive the spirit of inquiry and change that had led him in the first decade of the century to question his own creativity as an actor and the very nature of theatre. (Toby Cole[12])

The Stanislavski system has been thought of as a "style" of acting, and one which is primarily suitable for "naturalistic" plays. This is not so at all; it is not a style but an approach to the actor's task, a technique of analyzing a role and of working one's *inner and outer* resources so as to have complete control of one's craft and to be able to offer a fully realized and thoroughly illuminated character. It is an approach which may be applied to any kind of play, from Greek classics to modern farce. (Jerome Rockwood[13])

To understand The Method, let us first look at the reason Stanislavski gave for why his system was devised. He said, "I have groped after a method of work for actors which will enable them to create the image of a character, breathe into it the life of a human spirit and, by natural means, embody it on the stage in a beautiful, artistic form."[14] Responding to inspiration, the painter lays brush to canvas and the musician "hears" a melody and writes it on paper, but the actor cannot wait for creative moments to come. He or she must be able to command inspiration in order to call it forth when the curtain rises for each performance. Achieving an emotional, mental, and spiritual state in which one can be creative is the goal of Stanislavski's teachings. He believed actors could train, study, and discipline themselves to the point that they could control these creative moments. As Stanislavski said:

The concentration of the actor reacts not only on his sight and hearing, but on all the rest of his senses. It embraces his mind, his will, his emotions, his body, his memory and his imagination. The entire physical and spiritual nature of the actor must be concentrated on what is going on in the soul of the person he plays. I perceived that creativeness is first of all the complete concentration of the entire nature of the actor. With this in mind, I began the systematic development of my attention with the help of exercises I invented for that purpose.[15]

Some actors declare that they do not need or use the Stanislavski Method. But the influence of Stanislavski's teachings has been so far-reaching that some may use his system unwittingly. One writer states, "There is no single method which applies to everyone. Stanislavski himself would become very annoyed when anyone spoke of 'his' system. It was not a question of 'his' system or anyone else's system, he maintained; there was only one system, that of creative, organic nature; and all good actors used it whether or not they had ever heard of Stanislavski."[16]

Observation. A good actor must first be an alert observer. The student of acting must see not just with the eye but with the mind and imagination. How lightly and softly does a cat lounge on a chair? How boisterous and awkward are young boys playing ball? How stiffly and slowly do old men stand, sit, and walk? The observations are not only visual, but also tactile and auditory; they use all the sensory faculties. Then they are stored in the mind for future use.

The actor learns from experience, so the more he or she experiences and observes, the more will be learned. Sitting quietly in a public place and watching people as they move and interrelate with others is a learning experience. All manner of vocal variations, hairstyles, postures, expressions, gestures, and mannerisms are there ready to be absorbed by the attentive viewer. Every experience can be a valuable one to the actor. A student of acting does well to become immersed in the activities of living. He or she should visit a bus terminal, a funeral parlor, and a church; attend lectures, concerts, the ballet, and plays; watch athletic events; note a gathering storm; lie in the grass; walk in the rain; and taste varied foods. In other words, the actor must search out and be aggressive about opportunities for observation. The actor who does nothing but study plays will miss greater learning experiences in the world of the living. Stanislavski wrote about the importance of observation:

> An actor should be observant not only on the stage but also in real life. He should concentrate with all his being on whatever attracts his attention. . . . There are people gifted by nature with powers of observation. . . . When you hear such people talk you are struck by the amount that an unobservant person misses. . . . Average people have no conception of how to observe the facial expression, the look of the eye, the tone of the voice, in order to comprehend the state of mind of the persons with whom they talk. . . . If they could do this . . . their creative work would be immeasurably richer, finer and deeper.[17]

Emotion Memory. When the actor observes and experiences life with all its stimuli and stores the memories for future use in acting, he or she is laying the foundation for the use of sensory and emotional recall. Stanislavski referred to this storage of ideas as "emotion memory." His thesis was that every stored image can be brought forth and recreated when new stimuli (such as costumes, makeup, lights, and dialogue) appear in rehearsal or in performance. Once a person has experienced an emotion on a personal level and has retained that event in the mind, then recalling that event enables the actor to feel those emotions and transfer them to an analogous situation in a play. Some actors feel that emotional recall is particularly good for performance situations; others use it only for rehearsals and character study. It was standard practice to use it at the Actors Studio in New York under Lee Strasberg; it was used at the Moscow Art Theatre in rehearsals, but rarely for performances.[18] In both cases, it was effective. The question is not if it works, but how it works most effectively.

Here is an example of how one might use emotion memory and sensory recall to create a role. Suppose an actor is to portray anger toward another character. Julie, for example, in *Countess Julie*, is wild with anger after Jean kills the canary. In order for the actress playing Julie to prepare for this moment and perform it believably, she must delve into her past and draw out some event that caused her to feel rage. The event to be recalled does not have to be the same as that specified in the play, but it must elicit the same response in the actor. For example, one actor may have experienced the loss of a loved one in an automobile accident caused by a drunken driver. Another may have been lied to by a trusted friend. Yet another may have witnessed the wanton vandalism of his property. Each felt anger at the time of the event that could be felt once more through recalling the memory.

Emotion recall has a magical dimension. As one begins to reconstruct some past event, the most minute details may be remembered. As each nuance of the memory is remembered, the vividness of the emotion is increased, so that by the time the climactic moment of the recalled event is reached, the details are so clear and vivid that the person may be sobbing or shouting as he or she feels the emotion again. Note that the goal of the performer using emotion memory is not to recreate how he or she felt in the remembered situation, but rather to recreate the event. Recreating the event vividly will automatically elicit the accompanying emotional response.

Gaining experience with this kind of emotional tuning, an actor becomes more aware of what constitutes believable action. He or she can experience the feelings of a particular character as opposed to "faking it" or forcing the emotion. This kind of exercise in concentration during training and rehearsal periods can better prepare the actor for the performance to come.

Actors should be trained in use of emotional recall and use it carefully. They need a certain amount of distance between themselves and the emotional role they play. To completely and totally relive certain events could prove devastating. An actor always remembers that he or she is acting and is recreating the emotion only for an assumed role.

The Magic "If." When an actor loses control of an emotional situation onstage, the aesthetics of the play and the illusion of reality are destroyed. To achieve the proper balance of emotional recall and aesthetic distance, the actor's concentration and self-discipline must be highly developed. Stanislavski pointed to this important shade of character control when he discussed the magic *"if."*

> From the moment of the appearance of [the magic] *if* the actor passes from the plane of actual reality into the plane of another life, created and imagined by him. In order to be emotionally involved in the imaginary world which the actor builds on the basis of a play, in order to be caught up in the action on the stage, he must believe in it. . . . This does not mean he should give himself up to anything like hallucination . . . quite contrary. . . . He does not forget that he is surrounded by stage scenery and props. . . . He asks himself: "But if this were real, how would I react? What would I do?" . . . And normally, naturally . . . this *if* acts as a lever to lift him into a world . . . of creativity.[19]

The magic "if," according to The Method, asks the actor not to become the character and live the part, but rather to think, "If I were this character, what would I do? How would I behave in this particular circumstance?" Just as the child playing house believes that the dolls are alive and the cups contain real tea, so the actor can believe sincerely in the imagined truth of the play. As the actor steps into the "if" situation, he or she is able to justify how and why the character behaves in a certain way.

If the character being portrayed is to move, dress, talk, or sit in a believable way, justification for these behaviors must be settled. An actor must ask why. In *Countess Julie*, the actor portraying Julie needs to ask, *Why* do I feel so alone and betrayed? *Why* am I reacting so strongly? Answering these questions within the drama's context provides the justification for the character's behavior. Even in the most improbable farce, the actor must believe completely in this justification idea.

Another more modern expression of the same attempt at achieving believability is expressed by a director who asks an actor, "What is your verb in this particular scene?" Again, the action (the verb) is what must be justified and pinpointed. The actor asks the "why" questions. The answer in a given situation defines the action—the verb.

Analysis of the Play. Where does the actor get the clues to a character's personality? On what does the actor base decisions of motivation and justification? How does he or she know where and when emotion memory is needed? The answers to these questions come only from a study of the script. The actor's work begins with an understanding of the character as drawn by the playwright. The written words provide the primary clues for interpreting character and understanding plot.

The actor looks at a script and finds lines of dialogue and occasional blocking instructions (movement instructions for a character). The challenge to the actor is to find the personality and the action that goes with this dialogue. In order to do so, much study and experimentation must be undertaken.

Stanislavski advised that the initial study of the script was most vital to the interpretation of the character and the play as a whole. In his words, "One must be extraordinarily attentive to one's first acquaintance with a part because this is the first stage of creativeness."[20]

One's first impression of something, even if it is later proven mistaken, is usually long lasting and often never forgotten. For this reason the actor and the director must be careful in the early stages of character study and rehearsals that no misinterpretations are made and that any mistake or misinformation is corrected immediately. To allow even the mispronunciation of a word for one rehearsal session might cause the actor to develop a habit that recurs weeks later. Habits are learned behaviors and are difficult to unlearn. So not making a habit of a mistake, whether it be speech, movement, or gesture, is imperative for success.

The author's intent can be discovered and followed by answering several questions: Why did the author write this play? What piece of information, ideology, or psychology is he or she attempting to deal with? What character types are introduced? How complicated are these people? What is the author's attitude toward the subject(s) addressed in the play? Why has the author put this particular set of events into this framework of time and locale? The answers to these and other questions can be found in the script of the play.

To discover and analyze the author's intent, especially in a serious drama or tragedy, is no easy task. It takes hours of reading, sorting, sifting, and discussing the elements of the play, all the while remembering that this is the author's play! The playwright's intent must become the director's intent in directing and the actor's intent in acting. It is their combined responsibility to not veer from the author's purpose. Stanislavski said:

> In the process of analysis searches are made, as it were, in the width, length, and depth of a play and its roles, its separate portions, its component strata, all its planes beginning with the external, more obvious ones, and ending with the innermost, profoundest spiritual levels. For this purpose one must dissect a play and its roles. One must plumb its depths, layer by layer, get down to its essence. Dismember it, examine each portion separately, go over all parts that were not carefully studied before, find the stimuli to creative ardor, plant, so to say, the seed in an actor's heart.[21]

He went on to say that a play must be studied on several planes: literary, psychological, personal, and aesthetic. All of the circumstances that affect the play must be considered, both the external ones involving the given facts (time, place, politics) and the internal ones involving the intellectual and spiritual aspects of the play and of its characters. Nothing appears in the play by accident. Every fact, idea, word, and mood is there because the author considered it to be an important part of a chain of events that culminate in the climax of the play. Finding each piece of this literary puzzle and its relationship to the others is the actor's and director's task.

Actors must then go beyond the lines of dialogue to ferret out the motivations of each character. They must understand not just the text of the play but also its subtext. Stanislavski said that people come to the theatre to see and hear the subtext, because they can read the text at home. The subtext, or meaning, of the play comes to life in the movement and behavior of the actors. A raised eyebrow, a twisted smile, a seductive glance communicates to the audience the motivations behind the lines—this is the subtext.

The lines have little meaning until the subtextual interpretation is added. Then the characters come to life. Each becomes a multi-faceted, colorful personality with different motivations and aspirations. For example, when Julie removes the bit of dust from Jean's eye in the first scene of *Countess Julie*, how she touches him and looks at him reveals far more than the lines she speaks.

Stanislavski called the subtext the life of the spirit that flows beneath the words of the role. Once the actor understands the subtext, it is easier to find or justify the proper movement, voice, posture, and mannerisms for a particular character. As the justification for the decisions of characterization is clearer, the understanding of the subtext will develop even further. One contributes to the understanding of the other. When there is conflict in the action of a play, an actor's understanding of how a character would deal with this conflict also adds dimension to the subtextual portrayal of the character.

The in-depth analysis of a character must deal with every detail. In studying the external characteristics of a role, the actor must know the character's family background, financial status, marital status, age, employment, location, filial relationships, and intelligence level. In studying the internal characteristics, the actor must know the character's mental and emotional stability, spiritual and moral beliefs, and likes and dislikes. In *Basic Drama Projects*, Fran Tanner gives a checklist (of sorts) of questions to be answered about the external and internal characteristics of a role to be played. Her approach attempts to satisfy the playwright's intent and engender audience belief in the performance. Her guidelines for assessment of character are based on the unique experiences of the actor, whose remembered details of encounters with people, vivid sensory and emotional recall, and insight into the role work together to develop a total and believable character.

Character Analysis. The external qualities of a character are those aspects that the audience sees. These outward forms are important because they can communicate inward traits. Externals include a character's physical appearance, costume, facial makeup, movement, and voice. The actor develops these facets carefully so they will be consistent as well as believable. The following is Tanner's checklist of external qualities:

> *Posture:* Is it slumped, stiff, relaxed, attractive? Does it suggest timidity, assuredness, awkwardness, grace?

Movement: Does it convey poise, nervousness, weakness, strength? Does the character walk with a stride, plod, shuffle, bounce? How does his (or her) movement indicate age, health, attitude?

Mannerisms: Does he (or she) bite his nails, clear his throat, keep his hands in his pockets, chew gum, scratch his head when he is thinking, doodle on paper?

Voice: Is it pleasant, high pitched, resonant? Does the character have a twang, a drawl?

Dress: Is his appearance neat, casual, sloppy, prim, clean, dirty? Are his (or her) clothes in good taste, flashy, fashionable?[22]

Tanner offers the following guidelines for assessing the internal qualities of the character:

Background: What can you discover about the character's family, environment, occupation, education, interests, and hobbies?

Mental characteristics: Is he (or she) intelligent, clever, dull, slow, average?

Spiritual qualities: What are his (or her) ideals? What is his (or her) belief, ethical code, religion? What is his (or her) attitude toward other people and toward life?

Emotional characteristics: Is he (or she) confident, outgoing, happy, poised? Is he (or she) sullen, confused, nervous, cynical, timid? What are his (or her) likes and dislikes? How does he (or she) respond to other people? How is his (or her) temperament similar to yours? How is it different?[23]

Answering questions such as those offered by Tanner helps the actor to understand the personality of the character. The actor comes to see the role as a real being with complicated traits and better understands the desires, needs, and motivations of the character. A total picture emerges of not only how the character moves, dresses, and communicates, but also how the character feels, what he or she believes, and what underlies his or her behavior.

In rehearsal, the actor begins the process of selecting, refining, and honing the character's traits. This may entail discarding some of the characteristics thought to be important for ones later deemed to be more in keeping with the character's true personality. As the rehearsals progress toward performance, the character grows and develops into a more complete and believable person.

Creating a vivid, feeling character who comes to life on the stage is an exhilarating accomplishment for an actor. Stanislavski said of the mesh of actor and character:

Living a part helps the artist to carry out one of his main objectives. His job is not to present merely the external life of his character. He must fit his own human qualities to the life of this other person, and pour into it all of his own soul. . . . An artist takes the best that is in him and carries it over on the stage. The form will vary according to the necessities of the play, but the human emotions of the artist will remain alive, and they cannot be replaced by anything else.[24]

Discussing the same topic, Sarah Bernhardt, the famed actress, said:

Unless he can enter into the feelings of his heroes, however violent they may be, however cruel and vindictive they may seem, he will never be anything but a bad actor. . . . How can he convince another of his emotion, of the sincerity of his passions, if he is unable to convince himself to the point of actually becoming the character that he is to impersonate?[25]

Stanislavski believed that the actor should fit "his own human qualities" and pour "his own soul" into the character. Bernhardt wonders how the actor can convince another of his emotion and sincerity if he is unable to convince himself. These two theatrical greats hint at perhaps the most important of the actor's goals—the truthfulness of the portrayal.

Truth in Acting. How can one know what truth in acting is? How does one define it? And is defining it really important? To the representational actor, these questions and their answers are most important. It is at this point that Stanislavski virtually revolutionized attitudes toward acting. In 1923 when he made his first trip to America bringing with him his group of performers, the Moscow Art Theatre became world famous. No one in New York had ever seen such fine acting or such originality and believability of portrayal. Americans were eager to learn the secret of this new technique. Although it was revealed that this method was based on "inner truth,"[26] it was a long time before people came to understand exactly what Stanislavski meant by those words. In *My Life in Art* Stanislavski explains his feelings about truth in acting:

The actor must first of all believe in everything that takes place on the stage, and most of all he must believe in what he himself is doing. And one can believe only in the truth. Therefore it is necessary to feel this truth at all times, to know how to find it, and for this it is unescapable to develop one's artistic sensitivity to truth. It will be said, "But what kind of truth can this be, when all on the

> stage is a lie, an imitation, scenery, cardboard, paint, make-up, properties, wooden goblets, swords and spears. Is all this truth?'' But it is not of this truth I speak. I speak of the truth of emotions, of the truth of inner creative urges which strain forward to find expression, of the truth of the memories of bodily and physical perceptions. I am not interested in a truth that is without myself; I am interested in the truth that is within myself, the truth of my relation to this or that event on the stage, to the properties, the scenery, the other actors who play parts in the drama with me, to their thoughts and emotions.[27]

Finding the "truth of emotions" about which he speaks is no small undertaking. For an actor to clearly understand and deal with his or her own emotions is a feat achieved by few people. To go beyond that understanding and truthfully recreate and aesthetically use those feelings on the stage is a major accomplishment.

When we ask ourselves at the moment when redness is spreading upward from the collar across the face and forehead, "Why am I embarrassed?" there are probably some deep-seated and complicated answers. Do we know ourselves well enough to answer truthfully? Getting to this level of truth is the basic tenet of Method acting as described by Stanislavski. It is an arduous task of looking inward, analyzing feelings, prejudices, likes, and dislikes, and asking, "Why are they there?" Some modern actors who have developed their own personal system of creating believable characters do not feel as strongly about this quest for inner truth as did Stanislavski, although they may, in many other regards, follow much of his teaching. Each actor must decide what constitutes the best regimen to follow in creating believable characters.

Intrusions in the Creative State. Stanislavski said, "The secret of art is that it converts a fiction into a beautiful artistic truth."[28] It was his belief, however, that many intrusions could be made in that conversion that might alter its truth. In a TV interview, a stage and television actress once said that the key to being a good actor or actress (as opposed to settling for mediocrity) is to be able to bare oneself emotionally. She went on to explain that to bare the body meant to remove all of its covering, so to bare the emotions meant to do the same thing—remove the covering. With children, the covering is thin or nonexistent. Their play is uninhibited and full of honest feeling. But with adults, emotional baring is more difficult. Because they have learned socially accepted behaviors, adults sometimes mask real feelings and display more ''acceptable'' ones.

While working with a student actor who was having difficulty displaying anger, I encouraged him to remember a time when he had been angry. His reply was, ''I never get angry.'' I coaxed him to try to recall such a time, but he insisted that he had never been really angry. It is difficult to believe that in nineteen years the young man had never met with circumstances that had elicited anger. Probably he had programmed himself not to feel anger— he had repressed and masked it. Considering anger to be an inappropriate behavior, he had pretended it was not there. If the student actor is so locked into conventional inhibitions that he or she is unable to feel emotions and react with sensitivity and honesty, acting will not hold many thrills.

Another intrusion in the creative state that Stanislavski found diminishing is prejudice. He believed that in order for an actor to be in a ''receptive state of mind,'' he must have ''the emotional concentration without which no creative process is possible. An actor must know how to prepare a mood to incite his artistic feelings, to open his soul. . . . One of the most dangerous obstacles to the receiving of pure and fresh impressions is any kind of prejudice.''[29] He warned the actor repeatedly about allowing outside, extraneous factors or persons to influence or color his or her own interpretation of the character.

Our prejudices may be carryovers from parents or the result of childhood encounters with other's biases. In order to work toward artistic truth, one must be willing to examine and question one's prejudices. Why do I look away, rather than meet the eyes of a person of another race? Why do I believe that some ethnic groups have below-average intellect? Why do I enjoy ethnic jokes so much? Why do I refuse to taste steamed oysters? Why do I sneer when the student next to me repeatedly makes A's on papers? The answers to such questions reveal who we are. Facing the truth is not the easiest task for the actor to undertake, but it is a step toward creating honest, believable characters. Stanislavski said that ''prejudices block up the soul like a cork in the neck of a bottle.''[30] He felt this to be a great deterrent in the search for the inner truth of the character.

Finally, the intrusion that can do the most damage to the creation of the true character is the actor's own ego. In educational theatre, where students are in the theatre today and gone tomorrow, directors see this problem as frequently as in the professional theatrical world. The glamour and applause of the theatre all too often attract persons who need to feel rewarded and powerful. Stanislavski reserves some of his strongest words for this "infection" of theatrical art:

> Meantime do not forget the bad, the dangerous, corrupting bacilli of the theatre. It is not surprising that they thrive there; there are too many temptations in our theatre world.
>
> An actor is on view every day before an audience of a thousand spectators from such and such an hour to such and such an hour. He is surrounded by the magnificent trappings of a production, set against the effective background of painted scenery, dressed often in rich and beautiful clothes. He speaks the soaring lines of geniuses, he makes picturesque gestures, graceful motions, produces impressions of startling beauty—which in large measure are brought about by artful means. Always being in the public eye, displaying his or her best aspects, receiving ovations, accepting extravagant praise, reading glowing criticisms—all these things and many more of the same order constitute immeasurable temptations.
>
> These breed in an actor the sense of craving for constant, uninterrupted titillation of his personal vanity. But if he lives only on that and similar stimuli he is bound to sink low and become trivial. A serious minded person could not be entertained for long by such a life, yet a shallow one is enthralled, debauched, destroyed by it. That is why in our world of the theatre we must learn to hold ourselves well in check. We have to live by rigid discipline.[31]

Being in the public eye spoils actors of small stature. The more their egos are stroked by the applause and the lights, the more they want the stroking and the less attention they give to the character and the goal of the play. They develop a selfish and self-serving desire for attention in which little creativity is likely to develop. All the energy and attention an actor can muster is needed to create and hold a believable character throughout a play production period. Any distractions, such as those provided by inhibitions, prejudices, and ego, serve only to weaken the total performance.

Group Ethics. Ethics in the theatre rank high on a list of priorities. The production of a play is a group effort. It should never be done for the glorification of one ego. It is the combined effort of a group of actors, technicians, and craftsmen to interpret for an audience a script written by a playwright. In her treatise on The Method,

Sonia Moore states: "Ethics, high morale, and stern discipline are indispensable in such a group. The reproduction of life on stage is, for actors, both a challenge and a responsibility toward the people who come to see it."[32]

Maintaining group or team spirit requires self-discipline on the part of the performers and authoritative leadership from the director. Any number of interpersonal problems can develop that may interrupt the creative atmosphere of the group. Individuals who bring personal problems and extraneous concerns to rehearsal will not be able to function creatively. Every ounce of concentration is needed for the job to be done on the stage. Personal concerns must be left behind.

Relationships that develop among group members should strengthen rather than weaken the group's potential for success. The director must be aware of any deterrents that may develop within the group such as personality clashes, romantic liaisons, and egotistical yearnings. Sometimes these can be used for the benefit of the group. Stanislavski warned, however, that sometimes an actor must be sacrificed for the sake of preserving the group. It is the attitude of many directors that even talented actors need to be replaced if they do not contribute to the creative atmosphere and harmony of the play production group. Theatrical people who are striving for creative results have no time to pander to selfish whims; they are interested in a group effort and a successful production.

Using "The Method." Once a commitment is made by a group of actors to try to achieve a state of mind and body in which creativity can take place, they endeavor to search within themselves for the raw materials they need. Study of the script and searching into the character begins and continues as rehearsals progress toward performance. Blocking decisions are made, and the action of the play develops. The rhythm of the play evolves with the growing understanding of the playwright's intent, and tempo becomes a consideration. Emotion and sensory recall are used in applying the experiences (both personal and vicarious) of the actor to the role he or she is playing. The character is refined as movements and gestures are interpreted. With the proper understanding and use of stage fright, all these ingredients come together to form a well-rounded character.

To find the author's intent is the primary goal in the initial script study. The actors and director begin by determining the play *theme*, the thread running through the play that ties all the action together, giving logic and reason to the story. Each facet of the production should contribute to this theme—lighting, costumes, sets, blocking, and tempo, as well as the individual characters. It is the job of the director to see that all the elements of the production mesh effectively to promote the theme.

As rehearsals progress and the characters are realized, decisions are made daily to delete this action or add that one. The director asks, "Does this addition (or deletion) promote the author's theme and the continuity of the total performance?" If the answer is yes, the alteration can be justified.

Once the blocking decisions (movement instructions for a particular character, usually given by the director) and the various character adaptations have been made, the production must achieve a *tempo*, or rhythm, in keeping with the purpose of the play. The elapsed time in which an action is completed can spell the difference between comedy and tragedy. For example, Jean's killing of the canary in *Countess Julie* is an important foreshadowing of her death. To belabor any part of the action unnecessarily or, on the other hand, to treat it too lightly and quickly could elicit giggles rather than empathy from the audience. The violent death of the bird on the chopping block should shock the audience. Only a thorough knowledge of the play and an understanding of its theme can lead to determining the tempo that is right for a particular scene.

Depending on the situation within the play, a decision must be made as to how much time is available in which to execute the particular business. Only a few moments may be available if a deed must be private and other characters will soon return to the stage. More time may be consumed if the scene and mood is leisurely.

The tempo should be felt by the audience, and it should enhance the scene. The audience must feel the imminent tragedy as Othello approaches Desdemona's room and Willy Loman's dread of another day of traveling to sell his wares in *Death of a Salesman*. In *Countess Julie*, the rhythm may change many times within a scene and sometimes within a single speech, for it is motivated by the action or emotions of the characters. Finding the correct tempo for any given scene takes repeated rehearsals in which the actors "feel out" the appropriate tempo, and the director watches and reacts to it.

Once, when I was directing a one-act drama for a competition, tempo became an important issue. The rhythm of the play, which took place in a railway station, changed noticeably several times. An old woman waiting for her son to come home was watching the clock, while another woman was anxious to leave her husband in order to join her lover. After several rehearsals and careful scrutiny of the action, it was ascertained that the best rhythm was achieved when the total play ran for nineteen minutes. Some rehearsals ran for eighteen minutes and others for as much as twenty-two, but the play achieved its best effect when the elapsed time was nineteen minutes. This became the goal—to achieve a playing time of nineteen minutes employing the various tempo changes.

The *movement* of the actor is of paramount importance in interpreting the role. Movement should be graceful, clear, purposeful, and true to the character portrayal. It is the visual manifestation of a character's thoughts and personality and it makes an indelible impression on the viewers. Movement is a primary ingredient of acting and has many facets. For purposes of applying the theories and methods of Stanislavski's system, we will concern ourselves here with control, fluidity, restraint, and motivation of movement.

In Stanislavski's method, the actor tries to establish an internal state or atmosphere in which inspiration and creativity can flourish. Of primary importance in achieving this goal is muscular relaxation and *control*. As Stanislavski said, "This relaxing of the muscles should become a normal phenomenon."[33] Learning to relax is no easy task, but it is a state that can be achieved through practice and concentration. The actor must mentally decide to achieve a physically relaxed state and then set out to do so.

Any number of texts are available that contain exercises ranging from yoga to calisthenics. While training, an actor will use these various approaches and determine which exercises he or she finds most useful in achieving muscular relaxation. Until the actor learns to relax the muscles and make them obey, he or she will not be able to control movement to make it an interpretive asset to a character.

To a member of an audience, the importance of muscular relaxation may be unclear. One may question how vital is the muscular tension of the actor to the role he is playing. Consider for a moment the many postures that varied roles require. Good posture is not an easy goal to attain. Most people give little thought to whether they sway, lean, or slouch, but the actor in a given role has to be consciously aware of whether the character has good or poor posture and why. Placement of the head or the hand should be a conscious and deliberate action that is based on the actor's understanding of the personality of the character. Is the head thrown back in haughty scorn? Is the face held up in wonder? Is the head hanging in disappointment? Are the eyes staring straight ahead in disbelief? Is the hand turned palm up in questioning? Is it limp at the wrist in grandeur? Are the fingers stiff from old age? The answers to these questions are important interpretive keys to the complex personality of the character. Such interpretive movement comes from the actor's relaxed control of his or her body. Jerome Rockwood offers this observation:

> Among our many human peculiarities is the fact that most of us are usually not aware of our tension. Watch people's hands. Though a person is apparently sitting at ease, his hands are clutching the arms of the chair in a death grip. Tell him to relax, and he will bark at you that he is perfectly relaxed; and the tension will travel from his hands all through his body.[34]

The actor must learn to be aware of every part of his or her body and to control it. An actor's movements should be natural and fluid. Technique should never be obvious. Stanislavski often spoke of the "unbroken line" of movement. His point was that the movement of an actor should not be angular, broken into fragments, or separate from and unrelated to the movements of others; rather, it should be a continuous and flowing unbroken line of movement.

The artistic selectivity of the actor determines what gestures should be used and how many. Stanislavski warned of performers who use superfluous gestures in an attempt to cover up bad acting. He commented, "An excessive use of gesture dilutes a part as water does good wine. . . . Gestures per se are the stock-in-trade of actors concerned with showing off their good looks, with posing, with exhibitionism."[35] The trained actor utilizes control and restraint in stage movement. A general rule of thumb is to use just enough movement to send the desired message to the audience. Here again, if the actor is aware of his or her own behaviors and can recall events for use on stage, restraint in kind and number will result.

Ignoring restraint in movement often results in broad cliché gestures that appear deliberate and foolish. The watchful eye of the director is vital in the process of choosing and controlling gestures during rehearsals, because all too often the actor will continue to expand pieces he or she feels are working well. The expansion, however, could prove devastating rather than constructive. We all remember and enjoy the cliché movement of the old melodramas. Mysteries like *Gaslight* and the suspense of Pauline's perils give us hours of enjoyment. But serious actors should strive for more believable movements.

Jean-Louis Barrault, the French actor, said, ''A gesture is not sufficient; it needs to be clothed in thought.''[36] Herein lies the solution to the movement problem: it must be motivated. There must be a reason for it—a purpose behind it. For every movement, the question, Why?, must be asked and answered. Why do I go to the door? Why do I lean forward in the chair? Why do I start suddenly and turn around? The answers to the why questions are found in the psychology of the character. The character must seem to make the movement decisions. The actor studies and concentrates on the role until he or she ''is'' the character for the duration of the play.

No movement onstage should ever be made unless a justifiable purpose for it can be ascertained. Standing still on stage is sometimes difficult for the actor, but if the character is motivated to be still at a particular moment, aimless movement would destroy the interpretation.

Controlling Stage Fright. Of course, tempo, control, restraint, and motivation may be planned and practiced to near perfection and then destroyed in performance by that malady of the performer, stage fright. It may wait until the rise of the curtain to strike, but strike it will. The wise actor is aware of this beforehand and knows how to handle it.

Stage fright is a biological phenomenon caused by the involuntary release of adrenalin into the bloodstream to give extra energy to the body. This energy can be an asset to an actor. It can cause the voice to be clearer and stronger and the body to be more energetic and responsive; but uncontrolled, it can cause the voice to quaver and the knees to shake. In *Building a Character*, Stanislavski warns, ''Every actor should so harness his gestures that he will always be in control of them and not they of him.''[37]

Each of us has at some moment been frozen with the fear of speaking or performing before an audience. We have all felt the sweaty palms, a need to visit a restroom, and a dryness of the throat. The malady is not selective; it is a common one shared by everyone. We have heard stories of superhuman feats performed in emergencies: a car may be lifted or a fallen tree moved by a single person in a moment of crisis. This superhuman energy comes from the overflow of adrenalin triggered by the brain when the body is in an emergency situation and needs additional strength. A performance may be interpreted by the body as just such an emergency. The trained actor is able to harness the extra energy afforded by the adrenalin and use it to heighten and strengthen his or her performance. Those persons who learn to respect, control, and use the adrenalin of stage fright to their advantage develop into fine actors.

When we study Stanislavski's Method, it becomes evident that his approach to acting is an internal one. He sought the mental and emotional understanding of the characters. He charged the actor to study, to observe people, to experience every facet of living, and to store the experiences in the memory. Calling on those memories of events brings forth, in his view, the recreation of emotion. He challenged the actor to find out everything about the character to be played; the character's past, his or her present as presented in the play, and future are all pertinent. Any movement should be a believable physical interpretation of this character. Above all, Stanislavski asked an actor to strive for an honest portrayal by searching for the inner truth of the character and employing it in the portrayal.

But, even if all this advice is taken and followed, there is still the question of how the audience will receive it. When all is said and done, it is only in the performance of a play before an audience that the quality of the play and of the production are revealed. When the audience is there to react and to provide feedback to the actors, then they have some measurement of how effective their performance may be. If the performance still needs work, the actors will know. If the play reaches its mark, the actors will know. For, as the author of The Method wrote, "only true acting can completely absorb an audience, making it not only understand but participate emotionally in all that is transpiring on the stage, thus being enriched by an inner experience which will not be erased by time."[38]

It is always hoped and expected that performers will do well, but that expectation is not always realized. As a matter of fact, it may be realized only rarely. But it takes only a small seed of success to make the acting coach and director satisfied with their efforts. Stanislavski compared his attempts to find and train hardworking actors to those of a miner panning for gold:

When I look back over the roads that I have travelled during my long life in art, I want to compare myself to a gold-seeker who must first make his way through almost impassable jungles in order to find a place where he may discover a streak of gold, and later wash hundreds of tons of sand and stones in order to find at last several grains of the noble metal. And, like the gold-seeker, I cannot will to my heirs my labors, my quests, my losses, my joys and my disappointments, but only the few grains of gold that it has taken me all my life to find.[39]

Whether an actor uses these theories is, of course, a personal choice. Some directors recommend that actors use the Stanislavski Method for drama and tragedy and the James-Lange approach for comedy. Whether or not this is good advice, who can say? But, as suggested earlier in this chapter, most actors have devised their own methods based on their studies and experience. It would be practically impossible to analyze an actor to ascertain how much he or she followed one theory or another. It cannot be overstated that the fine actor is one who has devised and refined a unique artistic system.

The Actor's Instruments

The instruments that the actor uses are the physical body, the voice, and the mind. Keeping these instruments in excellent condition and in constant readiness requires training and conditioning. The perpetuation and practice of the actor's craft demands that maintenance and care of each be careful and continuous. Muscles must be kept flexible, strong, and responsive. The voice must be clear, resonant, and pleasant. Mental concentration abilities must be sharp.

Any regimen undertaken by one actor might be inappropriate for another. Each actor will devise his or her own routine. Very brief sample suggestions are offered here in three areas to introduce some of the interesting and varied activities an actor in training might employ.

The Body

The body is the visible physical tool by which the audience can observe the behavior of the character. An actor's use of his or her body can communicate age, personality, and state of physical, emotional, and mental health. Recent studies reveal that about 73 percent of all communication is visual, that is, 73 percent of the information we have about others, we have gained through observing them. This high percentage of observable communication underscores the importance of the actor's ability to communicate with body language.

The actor's body must be trained to follow the slightest suggestion of the mind. Muscles must be relaxed and controlled. Different parts of the body must move in alignment and with rhythm and grace. The body must be trained and disciplined. Like the dancer, the actor must work patiently every day to keep the body in good working condition.

An actor needs to devise and adapt exercises for warming up and then use them daily. The key to exercising is that no matter what regimen is being used, one should start slowly with a warm-up session. And never overdo.

Some suggested warm-up exercises for the actor might include the following:

Exercise for muscle relaxation.
1. Lie flat on your back, arms by your sides, palms up.
2. Close your eyes, clear your mind, and try to relax.
3. Starting with the feet, tense the muscles of the toes for a count of five and then relax.
4. Repeat several times.
5. Tense the entire foot. Hold for five counts and release.
6. In like fashion add the calves, lower legs, and upper legs. Relax and repeat.
7. Continue to move upward adding the thighs, groin, abdomen, chest, arms, hands, neck, and head. Tense each part for a count of five. Relax, then repeat.
8. Finally, tense your entire body for a count of five and relax. Repeat.
9. Lie still in a relaxed state for several moments, enjoying a completely relaxed body.

Exercise for balance.
1. Lie flat on your back.
2. Raise your legs until they are straight up. Then continue to raise your body so that your weight is resting on your shoulders, placing your hands under your lower back for support. Try to attain balance in a straight line.
3. Touch your toes to the floor above your head.
4. Return legs to an upright position, and maintain balance.
5. Lower your legs to the starting position.
6. Repeat.

Exercise for warming up muscles.
1. Stretching: While standing, stretch each part of the body independently, then stretch the whole body. Extend your hands high overhead, stretching to the left and right. Stretch your abdomen with leg lifts; stretch your neck with head rotation.
2. Swinging: Bend forward at the waist so that your body is bent double. Raise your body stretching to the left, then stretch upward, and then stretch right, and lower your body to the original bent position. Repeat. Swing your arms in circles clockwise and then counterclockwise. Rotate your head in the same fashion to loosen your neck muscles.
3. Shaking: Use small, quick movements to shake out tightness. Shake legs and feet, arms and hands, and your entire body.
4. Collapsing: Give way to complete relaxation, so that you drop to the floor. This can be done with the full body or just waist up. Simply "exhale" all energy as if fainting, and let your body sink into relaxation.

The Voice

The actor's voice, like his or her body, is vital for communication. The personality of the character is more clearly defined as speech is added to the physical character. A well-trained speech mechanism can provide exciting variety to a character. A high-pitched whine may be appropriate for a spoiled teenager. A shaky, throaty hoarseness may be appropriate for a derelict. A forceful, articulate manner may suit the politician. The ability to create such a diversity of character voices is as important as the ability to produce speech that is free of any affectation.

To train the voice, one first needs to understand the body parts used for speaking. No part of the anatomy is designed specifically for speech. Rather, humans have adapted parts designed for other bodily functions (breathing, chewing, swallowing) to produce speech (figure 4.1). The speech mechanism using these adapted organs performs two functions: Vocalization and articulation. Vocalization is a complex process composed of three interrelated operations: (1) breathing, which provides the power for speech; (2) phonation, which is the activity of the vocal folds to produce sounds; and (3) resonance, which is the amplification or reinforcement of tone. When these three operations have produced a sound, it is then shaped by the articulators, and speech is produced. First, we will take a closer look at the three processes involved in vocalization.

Breathing. The normal breathing pattern involves alternate expansion and contraction of the chest as air is drawn into the lungs and then expelled. Inhalation is the result of chest expansion produced by lowering the diaphragm and by muscles of the chest wall lifting the ribs. As the chest cavity increases in size, air flows in and expands the lungs to fill the increased space. In exhalation, the muscles relax, and the chest cavity contracts. When breathing is adapted to voice and speech, the regular alternation of inhalation and exhalation is changed in two ways: (1) inhalation tends to be done more quickly and in somewhat greater volume (this is a response to the speaker's desire to communicate) and (2) exhalation is prolonged—the breath is kept under control and used gradually in order to give adequate power for sustained utterance (pressure of outgoing breath is always necessary to produce the sounds of speech). Breath control is achieved by improving the strength and coordination of the muscles so that they can maintain the expansion of the chest and the reserve supply of air with ease and flexibility. Developing improved breath control is a goal of the actor.

Phonation. The next operation is phonation, producing vocal sounds that make up speech. Inhalation and exhalation force air through the larynx, or voice box. The larynx is a complicated structure of tissues and membranes located at the top of the windpipe. It is open at the top and bottom to allow air to flow to and from the lungs.

Inside the voice box on each side near the top are small muscular folds of tissue extending horizontally like shelves from front to back. These folds, commonly called vocal cords, can be brought toward each other to close the air passageway, and they can be drawn toward the walls on either side so that the air passage is wide open. These muscular folds inside the larynx are the vibrators in voice and therefore are called the true vocal folds or bands. They can be made thin or rounded, tense or lax, and longer or shorter. When breath pressure is maintained against the tensed and adducted folds, they vibrate and give off sound waves. Vocal tone or pitch is the result. Voiceless sounds, such as *p*, *k*, and *t*, do not require the vibration of the vocal folds. To make these sounds, relatively more outflow of air is required and hence a wider opening than for other sounds. Vocal tones, such as *b*, *d*,

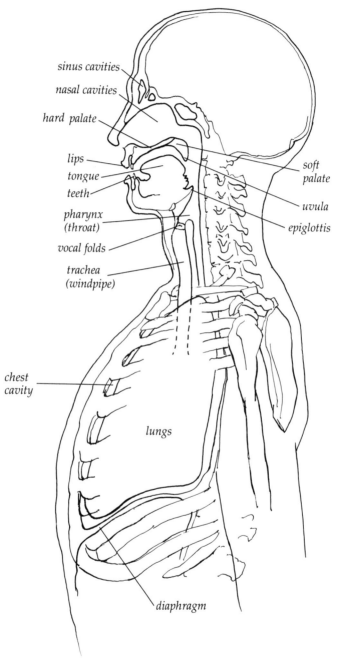

Figure 4.1 Diagram of the speech mechanism.

and *g*, require phonation. They involve less outflow of air, so to produce them the vocal folds are brought close together, making the opening smaller.

Resonance. The principal amplifiers or resonators of vocal tone are the cavities of the mouth, nose, and throat. The mouth and pharynx must be relatively open and adjusted to amplify the vibrations of the sound waves coming from the larynx. To achieve this, the muscles of the tongue, cheeks, lips, soft palate, and pharyngeal walls must be flexible and able to change size and shape rapidly. If sounds are to be clear and accurate, the muscles must be relaxed. Achieving such facile adjustments of mouth and throat so that the cavities are effective amplifiers is called the "open throat."

Resonance produced in an open throat has two primary effects on the vocal tones of speech: amplification for volume and amplification for quality. Amplification of the sound waves originating in the larynx increases their intensity of vibration and, hence, the loudness or tone. Selective amplification of some sounds changes their relative intensity and complexity, resulting in a variety of tones.

Articulation. Once this process of vocalization is complete, articulation takes place in the mouth. Articulation is the process of obstructing and shaping the outgoing stream of breath and tone to produce the sequences of sounds that make up spoken words. To articulate means "to put together in a close-knit fashion," and that is exactly the way speech sounds are made. If we categorize phonemes (sound units or families of variables near enough alike to be recognized as the same sound) in terms of the way the anatomical structures form the obstructions, we have:

1. Bilabial: the obstruction is formed by bringing the two lips firmly together, as in *p*, *b*, and *m*.
2. Labiodental: the lower lip is against the edge of the upper teeth, as in *f*, and *v*.
3. Lingua-dental: the blade of the tongue is against the edge of the upper teeth, as in the *th* sound in *thin* (θ) and in *this* (∂).
4. Lingua-gugal: the tip or front of the tongue is against the upper gums, as in *t*, *d*, *n*, *s*, and *z*.
5. Lingua-palatal: the central part of the tongue is near to or in contact with the front part of the palate or roof of the mouth just behind the gums, as in the words *church* (*t∫*) and *judge* (*d₃*).

6. Lingua-velar: the back of the tongue is against the velum or soft palate, as in *k, g,* and *ng* in the word *sing* (η).

7. Glottal: this is formed by near closure or closure of the vocal bands, as in the breath fricative, *h,* and glottal click of English, but is often heard as a sharp catch or click at the beginnings of vowels in the speech of persons whose voice production is not well coordinated.

Through correct placement of the tongue, teeth, lips, and hard and soft palates, the many sound variables, or phonemes, are made. The number of phonemes or sound units in the English language is between forty and forty-five depending on how finely they are discriminated. For instance, some sounds could be identified in a southern dialect that would not be present in standard American speech. Phonemes may also be categorized according to the manner of release and whether they are voiced or voiceless.

Clear speech is a learned behavior and therefore an attainable goal for anyone who has a normally developed speech apparatus. We learn speech by imitating family members who may have less-than-perfect speech. So the serious actor should study the speech mechanism and practice the proper placement of the articulators (tongue, teeth, lips, hard and soft palates) in order to develop clear, distinct, articulate speech.

Warming up the speech apparatus is an important aspect of the actor's warm-up routine. Throat, mouth, and resonating cavities must be gently coaxed into readiness just as the body muscles must be warmed up before vigorous exercise. Some suggested exercises for vocal warm-ups and proper breathing follow.

Exercise for Controlled Breathing (sometimes called the Cobra).

1. Lie on your stomach, palms down under your shoulders, arms folded against your body, your chin on the floor.

2. Lift your head and begin slow inhalation.

3. Let your head lead the rest of your body until your upper torso is lifted at full arm extension and your pelvis is on the floor.

4. Hold inhalation.

5. Exhale slowly as your body returns to its original position.

6. Repeat.

After a relaxing exercise, lie on your back and do the following vocal warm-ups.

1. Formulate each phonetic vowel sound one at a time. Vocalize it in a low pitch, move into a medium range, and finish in a higher pitch. Make each vocalization one continuous sound on one exhalation of air. For example:

low	medium	high
ah	ah	ah

2. Articulate each consonant sound in repetition. Beginning with *b*, say each consonant sound repeatedly and at a moderate rate for several seconds; then go on to the next consonant. Continue until all consonant sounds are practiced. During practice, exaggerate the movements of facial muscles and articulators in order to get them loosened and relaxed.

3. Choose a phrase and see how many different expression intonations you can give it. For example, say the phrase, "But mother why" expressing pleading, pride, scorn, love, suspicion, anger, and so on.

The Mind

The mind is the master computer of the body and the voice. If the mental self-discipline of the actor is well developed, then the other aspects of his or her performance fall naturally into place. Concentration is essential. Stanislavski believed that the key to creativity lay in the concentration ability of the actor. Each second spent on the stage must be one of concentration.

In order to prepare mentally for a performance, the actor must first prepare physically. Relaxation and warm-up exercises help muscles to work smoothly. As breathing is consciously practiced and sounds are vocalized, the actor's mental state becomes more relaxed and pliable. At this point, with body and voice warmed up and responsive, the actor begins to prepare mentally for the role to be played. Concentration exercises help in this process. One that might be practiced follows:

1. Clear the mind of extraneous thoughts and remove all real-world concerns. What size is the house tonight? and, Was the button replaced on my costume? are questions that cannot be allowed into the consciousness. Concentrate on emptiness, such as an infinite, clear, blue sky.

2. Continue to focus on this idea until it is clear and the picture is uninterrupted. Concentrate on it for a few moments.

3. Then slowly and methodically introduce aspects of the character to be played. This can be done in terms of questions and

answers such as: How old am I? How do I move? What do I believe? How do I feel? What are my likes and dislikes?

4. Recall facets of the character, and piece them together slowly and completely, building a whole and believable character.

5. When the character concentration is finished, begin to move "in character." Speak some lines of dialogue. Walk through the set if possible.

6. Prepare to participate in the play and live the part for the duration of the performance.

Exercises for the training of the professional actor are more highly regimented than the examples included here. However, this gives some insight into the kinds of activities, both physical and mental, that must be practiced in order for an actor to maintain a flexible, responsive body, an articulate voice, and a disciplined mind.

Suggested Reading

Benedetti, Robert L. *The Actor at Work*, 3d ed. Englewood Cliffs, N.J.: Prentice Hall, 1981.

Corrigan, Robert W. *The Making of Theatre*. Glenview, Ill.: Scott, Foresman, 1981.

Corrigan, Robert W. *The World of the Theatre*. Glenview, Ill.: Scott, Foresman, 1979.

King, Nancy R. *A Movement Approach to Acting*. Englewood Cliffs, N.J.: Prentice Hall, 1981.

Moore, Sonia. *The Stanislavski System*. New York: Viking, 1974.

Rizzo, Raymond. *The Total Actor*. Indianapolis, Ind.: Bobbs-Merrill, 1975.

Stanislavski, Constantin. *An Actor Prepares*. New York: Theatre Arts Books, 1948.

Stanislavski, Constantin. *Building a Character*. New York: Theatre Arts Books, 1949.

Stanislavski, Constantin. *Creating a Role*. New York: Theatre Arts Books, 1961.

Stanislavski, Constantin. *My Life in Art*. New York: Theatre Arts Books, 1948.

Tanner, Fran. *Creative Communication*. Pocatello, Id.: Clark Pub. Co., 1973.

5

Play Production

Play production is a technical as well as artistic undertaking. Organizational skills, business sense, and advance planning and thinking must go into the development of a production. Months in advance of a performance, decisions are made regarding script selection and adaptation, arrangements are made for copyright permission and royalty fees, schedules are made, and the technical aspects of the production are initiated. The set designer begins planning a functional set, the costumer begins designing garments and selecting fabrics, the lighting designer begins working on a design plan, and the director plans auditions. Once auditions are held, rehearsals are scheduled. Blocking is done, character interpretations are studied, and movements are refined. As rehearsals continue, the technical elements are added as properties are collected, lights are hung and focused, sets are constructed, and costumes are fitted. Meanwhile, programs are designed and sent to the printers, tickets and posters are printed, and rehearsals move closer to the final dress rehearsal. Actors begin experimenting with makeup and wearing their costumes. Finally, technical features are added and the show is readied for opening night.

Any play production goes through a similar evolutionary process. From the selection of a script to the final curtain on closing night, many people work long hours to see that the best possible performance is achieved. Whether the play is educational theatre, community little theatre, dinner theatre, or the professional stage, the jobs to be done are much the same, varying of course with scripts and interpretations.

The discussion and examples in this chapter will relate primarily to educational theatre. The principles of directing will apply to the production of a standard play on a proscenium stage. Although the problems discussed will be those inherent in educational theatre, similar problems develop in all amateur and professional productions.

Script Selection

The play begins and ends with a script, so the logical starting point for a discussion of play production is the choice of a play. Selecting a script in educational theatre is different from that process in the professional theatre. In the professional arena, a playwright may develop a new play and then seek a producer who is willing to finance its production. Once that producer is found, the machinery is set in motion and a production begins its evolution. In educational theatre (and in many local theatrical endeavors) the producer and director (often the same person) search for a script that will satisfy many variables, ranging from the artistic to the mercenary. The director wants to fulfill many needs with the program of plays he or she will devise in any given year.

First, the director wants to provide opportunities for students of the theatre department to learn and to develop as artists and technicians. A variety of play types are usually selected, including period plays and plays of different genres and interpretations, ranging from highly stylized to purely naturalistic themes. The director strives for this diversity in order to expose both the student actors and the student body audience to the varied types of theatre. The students have a chance to study different styles of costumes and sets, language adaptations and regional accents, authors from around the world, and all manner of physical and vocal requirements. Students, in one year, might create masks and totems of the ancient Inca empire, learn the music of the rock musical *Godspell*, study and fabricate costumes of eighteenth century England, take photographs for screen projections in a set, and construct a set for Shakespeare's *Hamlet*.

The director might also try to see that some money is made during a particular season. Although *Hamlet* and *Mother Courage* are admirable plays, the management knows that, under normal circumstances, those plays will not bring in "standing room only" crowds. An exception might be those performances held in a large metropolitan area. But even then, such a level of attendance is not assured. The theatre may be committed to doing Shakespeare and Brecht for the educational value; however, the budget usually requires that some play be presented that people will find so appealing and entertaining that they will want to pay to see it. Thus, it is fairly common to see two serious classical plays scheduled alternately with comedies like *Arsenic and Old Lace* and *Play It Again Sam* and selections from the box office savior—the musical. Although the musical is rarely acknowledged by directors to be a favorite, it often saves the budget of the small or educational theatre. Audiences enjoy the music and the temporary escape into a world of happy endings. These are the shows that sell out and help pay the bills for the other, more educational productions.

Another financial consideration in play selection is, How much will it cost to stage a particular production? In educational theatre, where money is a constant consideration, plays may be added to or deleted from the program based on their potential cost. A large cast requiring several costume changes may prove to be a burden to the costuming budget. A new, popular play may require expensive royalties.

Numerous intricate set changes might also preclude production of a play from a financial standpoint. Many other financial stumbling blocks thwart the production of some quality plays available to the educational theatre. However, a creative and frugal production team can often find ways to circumvent such prohibitive costs and still produce a worthwhile production of a desired play.

In selecting the program of plays, a producer-director in the educational theatre keeps in mind the available pool of actors—the strengths and weaknesses of the potential auditioners. If a student body is primarily female, a production of *The Front Page* or *Inherit the Wind* would be unwise because those casts are predominantly male. If a large music department is training musicians and vocalists, a musical would seem to be a safe bet. If a large percentage of the student body is black or Puerto Rican, then productions of *The Amen Corner* or *West Side Story* would be appropriate. The director bases artistic goals on the natural resources (people) available. He or she is aware of the available pool of talent and has a fairly good idea, in advance, of students' theatrical experience, expectations, and physical qualifications. It would be folly for a director to attempt a difficult play with inexperienced actors. However, with a pool of both undergraduate and graduate majors in theatre, any number of plays from the simplest to the most difficult can be undertaken with good results.

So the process of play selection in the educational theatre is based on available personnel in artistic and technical areas, cost of production and projected box office income, educational value to students, and perhaps the most important criterion, the literary merit of a play. Hundreds of plays, old and new, are inexpensive, easy to produce, and entertaining, but are often not worth the time of serious students.

Advance Preparation

Once the play is selected, arrangements must be made for acquiring permission to produce it. Agreements must be made for scheduling the production, dividing the labor, and designing the technical aspects. And auditions must be held to select a cast.

Copyright

Once an author has completed the writing of a play, he or she turns it over to a publisher for printing. The publishing company usually controls the rights to the use of the play. A legal agreement or contract between writer and publisher gives that publisher sole rights to publish the play. Copyright laws protect the author from having his or her words plagiarized or fraudulently acquired by others. This law assures that the author's words are legally protected and cannot be used without permission, usually granted in return for a fee or royalty to the author and publishing company.

The publishing company usually rents to production companies (educational theatre and community theatre included) the rights to produce a particular play. The legal requirements for rental of such a play must be prudently followed by both parties. The producing organization, once it has selected a play it wishes to do, requests permission to perform it. The publisher must know the dates of the production, the number of performances planned, and sometimes the seating capacity of the house. Based on this information, an amount will be charged for the play rental. Depending on how long the play has been in print, whether it is a straight play or a musical, and its current popularity, the charge may range from as little as twenty-five dollars to as high as several hundred dollars per performance. A contract between the publisher and the producing organization is then drawn up and signed, and the fees are paid. The producing organization may now advance with its plans for production.

If a publisher denies an organization the right to produce a particular play, for whatever reason, it would be an infringement of the copyright law to advance any further with production plans. Such an infringement could result in fines, lawsuits, and even imprisonment. Copyright laws are designed for the protection of the author and must be followed.

Scheduling

In the weeks prior to auditions, many arrangements need to be made to assure the smooth transformation of a written script into a polished play performance. The dates of the performances are chosen and the number of performances determined. These depend on the available audience and how much experience the director wishes the cast to have.

Setting up a rehearsal schedule is an important preplanning decision. Actors need to know from the beginning when they are expected to be available for rehearsals. The number of rehearsals will vary with play type, length of the play, intricacy of blocking, and depth of understanding required by the actors. One method for conducting rehearsals of a straight play is to use a time block of six weeks. The first two weeks are used primarily for blocking—deciding where and when actors are to move—and working out any unusual movement problems defined in the script, such as choreography, intricate fencing, and so on. The second two weeks are used primarily for character study and development of the plot and subtext. In the final two weeks, the actors refine what has gone before, while integrating the other necessary aspects of production, such as costumes, lights, and props.

Such a six-week schedule might look like the one in figure 5.1 for rehearsals of *The Glass Menagerie* by Tennessee Williams. This play has one act of seven scenes, all taking place in the same set, the living-dining room of an apartment.

This basic six-week time outline is adaptable to any similar straight play. The basic elements of script study, blocking, and technical features are included. Some plays require less time and might be mounted in four weeks. Blocking of longer, more difficult plays, such as Greek or Shakespearean tragedies, could take longer, as would musicals with special choreography and singing rehearsals.

Figure 5.1. Rehearsal schedule for *The Glass Menagerie*.
Read-through and discussion of characters following cast
announcement (TBA refers to rehearsals To Be Announced)

Week	Day	
1	1	Block scenes 1 and 2
	2	Repeat scenes 1 and 2
	3	Block scenes 3 and 4
	4	Repeat scenes 3 and 4
	5	Repeat scenes 1–4
2	1	Block scenes 5 and 6
	2	Repeat scenes 5 and 6
	3	Block scene 7
	4	Repeat scenes 5–7
	5	TBA (work on scenes that seem weak)
3	1	Discussion of characters and action in scenes 1 and 2 Run scenes 1 and 2
	2	Discussion of characters and action in scenes 3 and 4 Run scenes 3 and 4
	3	Discussion of characters and action in scenes 5 and 6 Run scenes 5 and 6
	4	Discussion of characters and action in scene 7 Run scene 7
	5	Run entire play
4	1	Run entire play—no scripts
	2	TBA (discuss weak areas, work on weak scenes)
	3	Run entire play
	4	TBA (discuss and work on weak areas)
	5	Run entire play
5	1	Run entire play using all props
	2	Run entire play using all costumes
	3	Set light cues—sketchy run-through
	4	First full technical rehearsal with makeup
	5	TBA
6	1	Discussion of weak areas—work on weak scenes
	2	Complete dress rehearsal
	3	Complete dress rehearsal
	4	Complete dress rehearsal
	5	Performance

When the rehearsal schedule is being devised, the director must meet with the designers and technical people to be sure they are of one mind in their interpretation of the play and are able to meet the performance deadline. In such meetings, agreements are reached on how the set will look, how it will be constructed, and how the actors will use it. Placement and swing of doors, size of furniture pieces and platforms, and colors in the set and decorations are discussed. Costume designs and details are considered, along with movement problems that relate to costume design. Properties to be collected and made are reviewed and a lighting design plot is drawn. Makeup supplies are inventoried and ordered if needed.

Set construction can begin as soon as the designer and director come to an agreement. In educational theatre, because of budget considerations and the time it takes students to complete actual construction, it is not uncommon for set construction to be started several months, perhaps even a year, in advance of the performance. Lighting crews take inventory of lighting equipment to see if lamps or gels need to be ordered or if maintenance is needed. Costumers begin shopping for fabrics, notions, headdresses, handbags, and so on. Publicity people design logos for programs and playbills, and properties people begin study of the play to see what props need to be built, borrowed, or bought. In fact, much of the technical work is nearly completed before actors begin rehearsal.

The director must have the final say in all of these matters. He or she ultimately must decide if lights are too bright for a particular moment or if a property is too small to be visible or too big to be believable. So many decisions have to be made that the director must stay in close communication with the technical staff.

Casting

Once the rehearsal schedule has been outlined and technical people have been informed of their responsibilities and have begun work, the director is ready to cast the play. Auditions are held at a publicized location and time. Individual directors are as varied in their audition methods as they are in play selection. Depending on the type of play to be cast and the kind of characters the director hopes to see created, any number and variety of requests may be made of the auditioner. Some directors routinely ask actors to read lines from the play in a scene with other readers. Other directors steer away from this method, preferring in-

Figure 5.2 An audition improvisation showing good ensemble playing among participants.

stead to chat with the performer to judge his or her ''spur of the moment'' performance. Often a director will put auditioners through a series of impromptu or improvisational exercises in order to view their creative spontaneity. Sometimes actors are asked to imitate animals and inanimate objects or machines as well as characters like those in the play. Directors may ask that actors come with a prepared audition piece of a defined time limit. Other times directors may ask an actor to read an unfamiliar piece to see how quickly he or she assimilates instructions. A variety of improvisation games as well as pantomime and vocal exercises may be used in an attempt to get the auditioner to display those talents that the director needs for the role positions in the play.

Figure 5.3 A student director coaches an auditioner as he works out a defined situation.

In general, during auditions, the director wants to see how an individual moves, to hear how clearly and distinctly he or she speaks, to be sensitive to the energy level and attitude of the actor, to view the actor's gestures and facial expressions, and to ascertain the level of confidence the actor has on stage. The director is mindful of the actor's mental and emotional understanding of the words and movements. The director also looks for actors who work well together as a group and notices ego involvement and rudeness among actors. He or she will look for what directors call "good chemistry" among actors, that is, working well together, complementing each other's performances and offering mutual support and encouragement. Directors are not impressed by negative, destructive kinds of behavior occurring between actors.

Rehearsals

Once the cast has been selected, the director and actors are ready to begin rehearsal. Initially, the cast and director meet to read and discuss the play. This read-through can probably be handled in one or two sessions. Cast members need a sound understanding of the author's intent and of the director's interpretation. This discussion session can include preliminary analysis of characters and conflicts, explanations of staging techniques to be used, unusual props or set pieces, or any other area needing advance explanation and attention. Changes to be made in the script, such as updating language or dates, can be made in this meeting. Actors are given a copy of the rehearsal schedule. If the director and set designer have agreed on the basic elements of the set, such as the placement of doors, windows, elevations and furniture, the director can begin blocking the play.

From the beginning, the director must be a decision maker and the final authority. He or she stands away from the action and views it objectively. This makes the director a better judge of quality than the actors who are engaged in the action on stage. Although the confident director wants to give the performers a great amount of freedom to block themselves, he or she always has the final say in such matters. It is advantageous throughout rehearsals for a director to encourage the performers to "feel out" their movements and positioning on stage. This is especially true when characters are moving to adjust themselves to the blockings or movements of another character. For example, if two characters facing each other at center stage are engaged in a dialogue and one of them is blocked to cross in front of the other, the second actor must adjust his or her position to the new position of the first actor so that the dialogue can continue believably.

The creative actor often can come up with interesting and justifiable blocking that may not have occurred to the director. The performer may expand pieces already blocked or create entirely new sequences. Such contributions should be encouraged; they give the production variety and flavor and help make it a joint artistic venture rather than the creation of a sole interpreter. But the director must be the final judge as to whether or not the invented piece is included in the blocking.

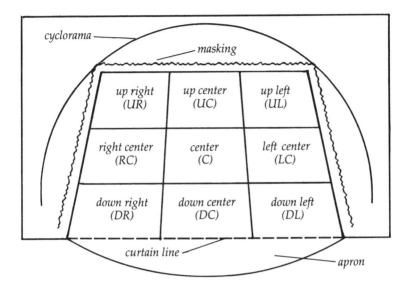

Figure 5.4 Diagram of a typical proscenium stage showing the acting areas.

Blocking

Understanding when and where to move when directed to do so depends on one's knowledge of stage space and how it is identified. Learning the terminology of the stage space, directions of movement, and positions of the body on stage is a necessary prerequisite.

The basic proscenium stage acting area can be envisioned as a rectangle within the larger rectangle of the total stage. The acting area is made up of nine approximately equal-size areas, as shown in figure 5.4. (Some directors may refer to six areas, others to twelve.) The part of the stage extending beyond the curtain line toward the audience is called the apron. On thrust stages, the apron may extend fifteen to thirty feet or more into the audience, or it may simply be a semicircular extension of only a few feet. On the proscenium stage, the front curtain closes at the proscenium arch, separating the nine basic areas from the apron or thrust and, therefore, from the audience. The front curtain is also called the act curtain, because it is opened and closed at the beginning and end of acts.

Usually, the other three sides of the rectangular acting area of the stage are defined by hanging curtains called masking (since they mask backstage areas from the view of the audience) or by a cyclorama. A "cyc" is one continuous semicircular curtain that completely encloses the acting area. Here the "walls" of sets are erected.

The three areas farthest from the audience are called the upstage areas. The three areas nearest the audience are called the downstage areas. This designation of upstage and downstage is historically based, stemming from drawings by Serlio during the Renaissance period when the stage floor rather than the audience seating area was raked, or elevated (see figure 5.5). The stage was slanted upward from front to back to improve the visibility of the actors for the audience. You can imagine the problems this created. Tables needed two legs long and two short. Actors often put down props that subsequently rolled into the audience. The designation of upstage referred to that back part of the stage that was higher, and downstage referred to the lower stage area. The drawbacks of this design were clearly evident, so the rake was transferred instead to the floor of the house to help stage visibility. Although the rake of the stage floor was short lived, the references to upstage and downstage have remained to this day. When a director instructs an actor to move downstage, he or she wants the actor to move toward the audience. Upstage refers to areas away from the audience.

The determination of right stage and left stage is made as the actor faces the audience. This is opposite to the right and left of the seated audience member and because of this often proves confusing. Stage right is the actor's right as he or she faces the audience, and stage left is the actor's left.

Some stage areas are considered weaker and some stronger than others. It is the responsibility of the director to block the play so that important action and those actors needing emphasis are in the strong areas at the proper moment, while less important pieces of business are handled in weaker areas. Stronger areas for playing scenes are downstage, particularly down center and down right. Weak areas are those farthest from the audience. Down right is considered to be a strong area for English-speaking people, who tend to look to the left first. Looking to the left from a seat in the audience is, of course, to look at the down-right area. Down center is a very strong area because of its dominant position of front and center. Although the blocking should never be

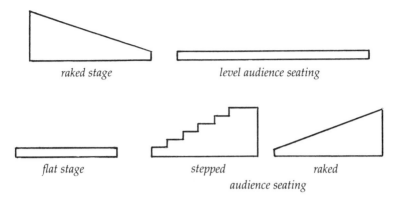

raked stage   *level audience seating*

flat stage   *stepped*   *raked*
audience seating

Figure 5.5 Diagram of audience—stage juxtapositions.

obvious, the chances are that the down-right and down-center areas receive greater use for dominant scenes. In a scene in which two characters are the focal point, they would be located downstage. The other characters in the scene would be located in the upstage areas so that they can focus their attention on the downstage action.

Figure 5.6 Here, attention is focused on the down-center character; other characters watch from upstage positions.

Upstage areas are considered good for mood or dream sequences. Since they are farther from the audience, there is a detached quality about the action there. Violence on stage is usually perpetrated in a weak area; it is such a strong action in itself that getting it away from the audience and even hiding it to some degree adds to its sinister quality. All a director need do in order to bring a character from an immobile or helpless attitude to one of strength and command on the stage is to move the actor from a weak area upstage into a stronger one downstage. Such a move automatically puts the actor into a dominant position, and the attention of the audience focuses there.

Another primary principle of stage blocking is that the moving figure dominates. Whenever there is some small action taking place on stage that must be seen, the director need only ensure that that action is the largest movement taking place at that moment. Our eyes have been trained to follow movement. Even if there are a number of characters on stage, the moving figure will attract the attention of the audience. If the audience must see the potential murderer steal the letter opener from a desk when the room is crowded, the movement to pocket the weapon must be the biggest action onstage at that moment. If it is, the audience will witness the theft. The other characters contribute by making smaller, less conspicuous movements at that moment. A character should have strong movement and stage position when delivering a forceful speech and, conversely, a weaker position and motion when yielding to a stronger character.

In the initial blocking rehearsals, the director gives instructions about when actors are to enter, exit, sit, stand, use particular props, and so on. The actors and director go over the script line by line and speech by speech in order to determine movement that is motivated, believable, and justifiable for a character in that play. Not every word is blocked initially, because it is understood that as the rehearsals develop and progress the creative actor will experiment and develop blocking under the watchful eye of the director.

The instructions given by the director are written by each actor into his or her script in pencil, as any instruction in the early rehearsals is subject to change at a later time. If the acting script being used already contains printed blocking instructions, they for the most part are ignored. Those printed instructions are often ones that were used in the first professional performance of that play and pertain only to that set design, stage, and interpretation. They have little relation to the production in progress.

Figure 5.7. A sample page from an actor's working script including written blocking instructions received from a rehearsal of *Arsenic and Old Lace*.

Martha's Script

MARTHA: (*at door*) Well, now, isn't that nice? (*closes door*) *all men stand*

BROPHY: (*crosses to Martha*) Good afternoon, Miss Brewster.

MARTHA: How do you do, Mr. Brophy?

KLEIN: How are you, Miss Brewster? We dropped in to get the Christmas toys.

MARTHA: Oh, yes, Teddy's Army and Navy. They wear out. They're all packed. (*she turns*) *turn toward stairs*

BROPHY: The Colonel's upstairs after them—it seems the cabinet has to O.K. it. *pat him on shoulder*

MARTHA: Yes, of course. I hope Mrs. Brophy's better.

BROPHY: She's doing fine, ma'am. Your sister's getting some soup for me to take to her.

MARTHA: (*crossing below Brophy to center stage*) Oh, yes, we made it this morning. I just took some to a poor man who broke ever so many bones. (*Abby enters from kitchen carrying a covered pail*)

ABBY: Oh, you're back Martha. How was Mr. Benitzky?

MARTHA: Well dear, it's pretty serious, I'm afraid. The doctor was there. He's going to amputate in the morning. *cross to Abby lead her DS*

ABBY: Can we be present? (*hopefully*)

MARTHA: (*disappointment*) No. I asked him but he says it's against the rules of the hospital. (*Martha goes to sideboard, puts pail down, puts hat and cape on table*) *Harper can't believe what he's hearing*

(*Teddy enters on balcony with large cardboard box and comes downstairs to desk, putting box on stool. Klein crosses to toy box as Harper speaks.*)

HARPER: You couldn't be of any service—and you must spare yourself something.

ABBY: (*to Brophy*) Here's the broth, Mr. Brophy. Be sure it's good and hot.

BROPHY: Yes, ma'am. (*moves upstage*)

KLEIN: This is fine—it'll make a lot of kids happy. (*lifts out toy soldier*) That O'Malley boy is nuts about soldiers.

TEDDY: That's General Miles. I've retired him. (*Klein removes ship*) What's this! The Oregon!

MARTHA: (*crosses to up-left*) Teddy, dear, put it back. *pat his hand*

"Teddy, dear, put it back."

Figure 5.8 The dialogue and blocking in figure 5.7 results in a stage picture like this.

In blocking a play, a director strives for a series of dramatic "still-life pictures" that create emphasis and develop the story lines. Through the spatial relationships between characters, the director tries to reveal one character's feelings for another. Of course, this relies not only on spatial relationships but also on the way the characters deal with each other: their facial expressions, gestures, eye focus, intensity, and so on. Spatial relationships can be defined in different ways, for example, by which characters are standing while others are sitting, by which characters are tense and erect or curved and relaxed, and by which characters look toward or away from each other. Nonverbal communication is all important in this aspect of blocking.

However, when the still-life pictures are transformed by movement into action, the movements become important. Each time a character moves in space, his or her relationship to others is changed. The actors must therefore acknowledge the moves and react or adjust to them. Each actor is constantly moving and adjusting to others' movements, so the spatial composition of the stage is always changing and evolving. As the actors create business for their characters and experiment with movement, they are cognizant of the activity of others. In the midst of all this

Figure 5.9 In this series of photographs from a production of *The Front Page,* character types and relationships can be identified and the progression of events in the plot can be followed.

Figure 5.10 In this early blocking rehearsal, family relationships are established by spatial location in the set; the focal character is in a downstage and right position (this photo shows only half of the stage).

action the director guides the development. He or she weighs and measures each character's movements, making sure they fit the character. Each raised eyebrow or hunched shoulder is observed to be sure that the "picture" created is in keeping with the artistic goals for the performance. The creative, experimental movement of the actors combined with the objective, discerning eye of the director create well-balanced characters and controlled blocking.

No movement on stage should happen by accident. Each move is carefully rehearsed. No movement that has not been tried and tested in rehearsal should be introduced into a performance. That every move an actor makes is reacted to by other cast members explains the importance of this principle. Once blocking is set, it should be adhered to until it is changed by the director with full knowledge of the cast members involved.

Interpreting the Script

During the second phase of play rehearsals, the personal relationships and conflicts of the characters are studied and developed. For those who use The Method, this is a period of "inward looking"—dealing with the personality of the character and meshing it with the personality of the actor. A certain amount of self-analysis takes place during this period as the actor finds out how like or unlike the character he or she is and acknowledges adjustments that need to be made.

The presentational actor uses this time to practice selected movements and to study character types he or she wishes to emulate and adopt for the role. During this interpretive period, the entire cast comes to understand the total play as well as the individual part each plays in its development. Conflicts between characters are discussed and analyzed. All character relationships are developed and explored. Run-through rehearsals, in which the play is rehearsed with little or no interruption, are important in encouraging the development of the proper character relationships during this period. Often, time is set aside when cast members can talk about the characters and their development.

It is during this period that an in-depth look is taken at the playwright's intent, or subtext. The actors must understand not just what the play says, but also what it means. They must search for the inner feeling and motivation behind the lines and then develop business that will convey that subtext to an audience. During this period, blocking is finely developed and polished. Subtle movements and the balance between underplaying and overplaying receive attention. Intricate stage business is refined as the actors experiment with synchronizing particular movements with words. Carefully chosen stage business coordinated with dialogue helps to clarify and enrich characterization.

In-depth character analysis at this point in rehearsals usually includes analysis of each character's emotional and mental state. If a character is wealthy and educated, how can this be revealed through posture and gesture? If a character has a secret or is full of mischief, how can this best be shown? A character's physical traits, identified by the author, need to be integrated into the portrayal. For example, in *The Glass Menagerie,* Tennessee Williams tells us that Laura has a slight limp. Exactly what the deformity is and to what extent it affects her gracefulness is left to the actor to interpret. This period of learning should help actors to understand their characters as less-than-perfect representatives of the human race and therefore a challenge to portray believably.

In some modern plays that emphasize movement and line

rather than character development, more nontraditional movements, gestures, and speech are used. For such plays, this period
of rehearsal would be used for experimenting with body positions, angles, acrobatics, energy level, speed, tensions, and tones
that effectively create the desired mood. Pantomimic movements
are important in these plays. The desired end is a mood or a
theme, rather than a specific characterization and a developed
plot. In *The Leader,* for example, the various members of the Leader's audience parade in and out, which can be done with a variety
of tempos and movements.

During this interpretive period of rehearsal, props and costumes are often used. A character such as Mrs. Bracknell in *The
Importance of Being Earnest* will not be realized fully until the long,
rustling skirts are added. A pipe, a teacup, and a watch and chain
can benefit the actor rehearsing the role of Earnest, helping him
learn the movements and gestures that reveal that particular
character.

The actors' sense of timing and tempo begin to take shape during this period of rehearsal. Performers develop a sense of how
long it takes to say lines and move from one place to another.
With repeated rehearsals, they are better able to pair words or
lines with movement and stage business. They develop a group
sense of timing. They become sensitive to when a scene is playing
well and when it is dragging. The director is especially conscious
of this development of tempo, for the actors may not have the objectivity necessary to set the proper pace. Often, their pace is too
fast because, with repetition, a scene tends to go faster. The director keeps in mind the one-time exposure the audience will have to
this scene and sets a pace that the audience will find understandable and believable.

During this period the director may conduct lengthy discussions with cast members about characterizations. Motivation for
every movement in blocking must be provided by the actors.
They must now be consciously executing business and blocking
"in character."

Polishing for Performance

The final segment of the rehearsal period is devoted to meshing
the various elements of the production into a unified whole. The
actors find that as each of the technical areas is added, it becomes
easier to believe in and to portray their respective characters.
During this final rehearsal period, costumes are finished and

Figure 5.11 The director discusses character relationships during a break in the interpretive period of rehearsals.

Figure 5.12 The cast meets backstage prior to a dress rehearsal in the polishing period of rehearsals.

worn by the actors. Experimentation with makeup begins and continues until the desired face emerges. Lighting cues are integrated so that the mood of a scene and the time of day become evident. All of these technical additions are advantageous to the actors, helping them lose their real-world identities and move into the imagined world of the play. Wearing the face and dress of the character and moving in the detailed set of the play make it easier to create and hold a characterization. Vocal affectations, facial expressions, and gestures magically become more natural and feel more comfortable.

From a technical standpoint, this is the time in rehearsals when all the finishing touches are made. The lighting technician is experimenting with gel colors; the makeup artist is deciding if more blush or fewer age lines are needed; the stage manager is organizing cues and double-checking the accuracy of the prompt book; the costumer is sewing on the buttons and collars and pressing costume pieces; and the director is watching all of this activity to see if the production he or she envisioned months ago is actually emerging in this flurry of activity.

The old adage "bad dress rehearsal—good show" simply doesn't hold true for the polished play performance. By the time a show is in its last two weeks of rehearsal, each rehearsal should show improvement over the one before. The weakest links in the production chain should be detected while there is still enough time to strengthen them. If an actor is weak on some lines, it becomes embarrassingly clear during this time period. If a member of the light crew is unprepared, this will be apparent.

During dress rehearsals, actors usually get a chance to practice "ad-libbing"—filling in when someone forgets a cue or a line. And they may be forced to play a scene without an important prop. The need to improvise will contribute to a better, more polished final performance. What one least expects to happen probably will happen. The test is how the cast and the crews handle it. What does the leading man do if, as he waits to go on, he discovers the zipper of his trousers is broken? What does the leading lady do when she opens the box of roses onstage only to discover that it contains no roses? What does one actor do when his line depends on the entrance of another actor, but that actor doesn't appear? Several final rehearsals may be conducted to give actors experience in handling these kinds of unexpected problems. By performance time, everyone is prepared to handle the unexpected with finesse.

The director watches the tempo during this final set of rehearsals; the actors may accelerate in their increased familiarity with the script or belabor scenes out of a tendency to overplay and dramatize. With repeated rehearsals, the actors may lose their concentration. They have to make a conscious effort to listen to the lines as if they were hearing them for the first time. Maintaining a spontaneous, fresh quality is important.

When a production has evolved from blocking through interpretation to a polished run-through with all technical elements added, then comes the magic of opening night. As the actors wait backstage and the crews are in their assigned places, the rustle of programs and the murmur of voices from the house raise the energy and expectation level of the company to fever pitch. Adrenalin flows and excitement is high as the curtain rises.

Production Responsibilities

While the director and actors prepare for the performance dates, the technical crews are hard at work. The set crew is designing and building a set; lighting technicians are arranging, hanging, and focusing lights; costumers are cutting, sewing, and fitting costumes; publicity staff are preparing news releases, programs, posters, and tickets; makeup personnel are ordering, organizing, and designing character and "straight" makeup; property people are collecting, designing, and making props; and the stage manager is trying to organize and stay in touch with each of these crew areas and keep track of how the total technical production is progressing.

Setting the Stage

The set design for a particular play has to meet several criteria. It must serve to interpret the play genre, that is, its comic, realistic, or tragic nature. In realistic plays, it must reflect the historical period and locale in which the play takes place. It must define the specific areas—drawing room, hospital waiting room, business office, campsite—of the action of the play. The set establishes mood, enhances characterization, and defines socioeconomic conditions. Through color and style, a set can also enhance the mood of the play. For example, in a high comedy, such as *The Importance of Being Earnest*, the set colors might include bright blue, yellow, or orange. In a more dramatic play, such as *The Glass Menagerie*, trim colors would be more subdued—lavender and gray would give a somber feeling appropriate for the serious nature of this play.

Figure 5.13 The stage is a beehive of activity as a set is erected for an upcoming production.

The walls of the set and the furniture and "dressing" that fill it define the socioeconomic level of the characters. The age, wear, and condition of a chair, for example, become just as important as its style. The pictures on the walls, books and memorabilia filling shelves, sofa pillows, rugs, and curtains all serve to reveal to the audience something of the tastes, manners, and personalities of the characters who inhabit this space. Characterization is enhanced by the collection of "things" we associate with particular characters. So, a carefully planned and detailed set helps the audience understand the play, and it provides a proper framework in which the events of the play logically take place. In addition, a set provides a functional area in which actors work. Early in the preplanning for a production, the set designer and director must agree on the interpretation of the play that is to be reflected in the set—what the set will say about the characters and the play as well as the time period in which the play takes place.

In a set for *A Raisin in the Sun,* for example, important information is revealed about the play. The plight of the Younger family is like that of many black American families during the 1960s. The set is a realistic one mirroring the crowded apartment dwellings of blacks in large U.S. cities. The living room–kitchen–dining room combination inhabited by this family is the defined space. The furniture is functional and worn, but it is neat and clean. The sofa doubles as a bed for the younger son, Travis. The kitchen area is furnished with much-used appliances and chairs and a table. The walls of the room might be angular, creating the impression of a building that favored practical use of space over aesthetic beauty. The colors of the walls would convey warmth. Although the set reflects life lived at a low-income level, it also exhibits the love and care given to it over many years by the close-knit family that inhabits the space.

Much warmth and family feeling can be developed in the dressings of the set. Family pictures on the walls, colorful curtains and doilies, a frayed but clean tablecloth, an afghan on the worn sofa—all these personal touches add to the family feeling while also contributing to the visible evidence of the low-income level of the family.

The set design must provide a functional area in which the actors may work. The set must accommodate a large number of characters who make many entrances and exits. Doors are needed to afford access to bedrooms, closets, and the hallway of the apartment building. An adequate number of furniture pieces are needed. In planning the sets the designer acknowledges all these requirements while keeping in mind the various blocking problems to be solved. Large spaces must be left open as traffic areas, and yet the cramped feeling of the apartment must be maintained.

A very different kind of play, *The Leader*, presents an absurdist point of view and is totally unrealistic in design. This play takes place on a street as a parade of fans cheer and follow the Leader. No particular place is identified, so the location of the play, and therefore the set design, is left to the imagination of the director and designer. The function of the set is to provide an interesting space in which the action of the play can take place.

Since no furniture or other set pieces are needed for this play, the "interest" must be provided in other ways. A set designer might create several elevations with platforms, ramps, and obstructions. Since the play is purely theatrical and "unreal," so may be the set. The colors might be as bold as the characterizations. Screen projections or a lighted cyclorama might be used to good effect. The play points to absurdities in hero worship, so the set might in some way use a distortion of this theme. But again, enough space for the movements of the actors is a necessary part of the plan.

Lighting

The stage light is a relative newcomer to theatrical productions in view of the long history of dramatic performance. Early theatrical performances, of necessity, were staged in broad daylight. Later plays were lighted by torches, candles, or oil lamps. But with the invention of electric lighting systems in the late nineteenth and early twentieth century, stage lighting took on new dimensions.

Lighting serves several functions in the production. It defines the period of the play, the time of day, and the source of the light. It establishes shapes and enhances mood, signals the beginning and ending of scenes, and provides special effects. Lights can focus the audience's attention on items or people deemed important by the director and subordinate less important ones. Most importantly, it provides visibility. Characters and scenes must be illuminated in such a way that the audience can see them clearly.

In the initial planning stages of a production, the lighting designer is furnished a drawing or rendering of the set, and a script. When the lighting designer has studied the play and discussed it with the director, he or she can devise lighting that will enhance the production the director has envisioned.

The period in which the play takes place can be expressed through the lighting fixtures used in the set. For example, gaslight fixtures can provide beautiful atmospheric lighting and authentic beauty to a period set. However, designing lighting so that such apparatus appears to be providing all the light is a major undertaking. Time of day is a vital element defined by lights. The white brilliance of high noon is different from the soft ambers of late afternoon or the pale blueness of moonlight in the evening. The angle or direction from which the light comes also helps the audience determine time of day. The long angle of the late-afternoon sun is easily identifiable as is the bright overhead beam of the high-noon sun. Observing the intensity and source of the light also helps the audience locate the play in time and place. It is easy to believe a scene is taking place late at night on a fire escape if the only light provided is moonlight and a flashing neon cafe sign.

The mood of a scene is greatly enhanced by light. Light intensity and color can emphasize fear or joy, rage or sympathy. Bright, warm colors excite us; cool colors have a calming effect. By adding gel, a color medium, to the front of a lighting instrument, a colored light is created. Pure white stage light is harsh; it washes out color from the actors' faces and the set pieces. The colored light softens and defines these features. It adds quality of mood and feeling and guides the attention and understanding of the audience through emotional changes. The lighting designer uses this knowledge to enhance the production. He or she lights a saloon with soft reds and ambers, filters soft white light through a stained-glass window to illuminate a cathedral, and highlights a bedroom at midnight with the soft blues of moonlight.

"General lighting" refers to lighting on the stage that aids visibility of actors. All other lighting used to create effects is referred to as "special lighting." General lighting is fairly routine, but special lighting calls for some ingenuity. Special effects include explosions, fireplaces, lighted lamps, follow spotlights, and so on. They require experimentation in order to appear convincing and can make the difference between a mediocre and a stunning production.

Emphasis on the stage is often accomplished with light. If, in a bedroom scene at midnight, the area needing emphasis is a woman asleep in a bed, then the lighting designer must have light—perhaps moonbeams coming through the window—fall on her. The lighting designer guides the attention of the audience without its awareness. In many modern, nontraditional plays, lights are used to pick up only a face or to create a small pool of light in a sea of darkness. Spotlights sweeping back and forth can create the effect of movement and can move with the actor. Back lighting of doorways or backdrops can be used to create pictures or colors. In most standard plays, the act curtain closes only at the beginning and ending of acts. All other scene changes or passages of time are signaled by the dimming and raising (increasing the intensity) of lights. In plays of many scenes composing only one act, such as *The Glass Menagerie*, lights are used in this fashion to begin and end scenes. The curtain is never closed.

In planning the position of the lights in a particular production, the designer must work with the given stage, and each stage is different. Lights will be hung so that cross lighting (light coming from opposite angles crossing on the target to be lit) is achieved. This avoids unwanted shadows. Lights of different kinds and quality

Figure 5.14 General lighting illuminates actors and the full set.

Figure 5.15 Special lighting isolates the actors in a small pool of light.

are available and some theatres have sophisticated systems that create a wide range of lighting effects. In the educational theatre, adequate lighting is usually available, although probably it is not the best or the most modern. Lights are hung in front, to either side, and above the stage, and special effects are placed offstage right, left, and back. These lights are wired into a central dimming system, so that the intensity of the light is controlled from one location. The settings of the various lights can be changed suddenly and completely or so slowly as to be imperceptible. They can be worked independently or all at once. Computer-controlled lighting systems offer limitless possibilities.

The lighting technicians must be very careful with the equipment. Lighting instruments are expensive and fragile and require careful handling. Using stage lighting equipment requires knowledge of electrical wiring, and the job can be dangerous for the untutored.

As performance time draws near, the lighting crew hangs and focuses lights as the development of the set permits. The light designer begins a list of light cues, and with the director, decides when a light change will take place. Each change of lights is designated to take place on a particular line of dialogue or when a movement or sound occurs on stage. The intensity of the light is also determined. These decisions will be finalized in a technical rehearsal at which actors will be present. On this occasion the play is rehearsed solely for the purpose of setting cues. The cast goes through the script page by page and speech by speech, if necessary, and specific directions are given for every light cue. This information is transcribed onto a light-cue sheet that has cor-

---

Figure 5.16. Light cue sheet.

Godspell Act I

Cue 1: House lights out
Cue 2: Dimmers 1, 2, 5 and 7 up to 7; 3 and 6 up to 5 as actors enter
Cue 3: All stage lights dim to 3 as follow spots pick up John the
        Baptist in rear of house and follow him to stage
Cue 4: All stage lights up to 7 on beginning of chorus ''Prepare Ye''
Cue 5: All stage lights dim to 3 as follow spot picks up Jesus on
        beginning of ''Save the People''
Cue 6: All stage lights up to 7 and spot out as chorus enters on end of
        ''Save the People''

responding dimmer numbers so that the controller knows which dial or lever to operate to get the desired effect. A light cue sheet might look like figure 5.16.

Ideally, during rehearsal and performance, the light controller will be in communication with the stage manager via a headset intercom so that changes in lighting can take place imperceptibly to the audience, but with the full knowledge of the stage crew. Constant communication is necessary between technical people backstage so that if the unexpected takes place, it can be handled without mishap. They all need to exchange information as the production progresses. If problems are developing, everyone needs to be aware of them.

While lighting is important in shaping the mood of the audience and in giving the actors and set needed definition, the most important quality of stage light is illumination. The play must be visible. Designers occasionally go too far with effects so that the audience cannot follow the action or delineate characters. There must be enough light present for the audience to see the action. The designer needs to remember that visibility of the action is the number-one priority.

With carefully planned and executed lighting, the play is transformed into a magical, believable dramatic performance. Lighting effects reveal the energy and emotion of the play as they guide the attention of the audience. Characterization reaches its fullest potential when just the right touch of light falls across an actor's face. If the lighting is done properly, the audience should be so involved with the play that it is totally unaware that its attention is guided by the hand of the person in the light control booth.

Costuming

One of the most challenging tasks in theatre, one requiring much planning and expertise, is that of the costumer. Skill in cutting, fitting, and sewing clothing, along with knowledge of period dress, are essential. An aesthetic sense of how to enhance characterization through the many variables of costume is a vital requirement. The costumer makes a tremendous contribution to the production by designing and fabricating costumes that are appropriate to the characters and reflect the style and period of the play. The costumer is potentially the major contributor to the visual impact of a play. A play with a simple set can be visually dynamic with effective costuming. However, the designer does not think just of individual characters, but rather of character relationships and of the visual interest of the play as a whole.

The addition of a costume to a well-rehearsed performer does more for the visual impact of that specific character and for the development of the characterization than any other facet of technical production. Much about the intent of the play, the mood, and the personality of the character can be revealed through dress. Costuming takes into account the total appearance of the actor—from headwear to footwear and everything in between. Costuming is also the best way to show progression in a play. Through costume changes we watch a cockney girl become a "fair lady." We watch a poor postal clerk become a corporation president. Through costume we witness a character become thinner or heavier; we see a military man progress from recruit to commanding officer. The seasons change visibly as characters go from light pastel clothing in warm weather scenes to heavy sweaters and coats for winter settings.

Although production crews can begin far in advance of rehearsals to build sets, props, and so on, the costumer can begin work only after the show has been cast. Of course, far in advance of the casting, the costumer has studied the play, analyzed its style and characters, and determined the period, fashion, and mood to be interpreted. But the actual construction of the costumes begins after the measurements of the actors have been taken. In preliminary meetings with the director, the costumer displays sketches of the kinds of garments he or she has envisioned for the characters. With input from the director, decisions are made regarding styles and colors. The costumer knows what costumes in stock may be used and how much money has been budgeted for new costumes for a production. If the play is a period piece, research must be done on the style of the particular period. Set specifications are considered in order to determine the freedom of movement characters will have in the finished costumes. The actors must be able to function within the costumes.

The costumer employs the elements of design—line, mass, color, texture, and ornament—in his or her creations. Line, the silhouette outline of the fashion, reveals much about the period of the play. Is the silhouette sleek or bulky? Does the line follow the shape of the body or exaggerate some aspect? Line in period clothing is easily recognizable. For example, the line of Colonial American dress in a production of *1776*, a musical about our Declaration of Independence, is a tight bodice and flowing skirt for women and a fitted jacket and knee breeches for men. The line of Roman costume in *Julius Caesar* is full and flowing for the dress of both sexes. We can easily recognize the period of a play when we see a characteristic style trademark, such as a bustle in a lady's skirt or a toga on a man. This recognition of the line of a costume makes it of great use to the costumer in identifying period.

Line is also used for startling or comic visual effect. The line of Dracula's cape at full arm extension, for example, brings to mind the wings of a bat and adds to the sinister quality of the character. In *Li'l Abner*, a comic musical of Kentucky mountain folk, the silhouette of Marryin' Sam is recognizably rotund. The costume made for Sam accentuates his large belly. The effect sought is comic in this instance, for Marryin' Sam is a chubby, good natured, well-meaning fellow.

The size and shape of a costume, especially in terms of materials, is called mass. Some garments require dozens of yards of material while others need barely one yard. The mass of a Roaring Twenties flapper dress, for example, is small compared to the abundance of material in the dress, petticoats, and outer coverings of a lady of Victorian England. In considering the mass of a garment, all parts of the costume must be taken into consideration. For example, a woman's dress at the time of the American Revolution was full and loose. Lace hung from the cuffs and adorned the collars and pockets. The amount of fabric in such a costume is much greater than that in modern-day dress. There is considerable mass in Elizabethan period dress for both men and women, whereas an American Indian of the seventeenth century wore clothing of less mass.

Color is the most powerful design variable used by the costumer. With color the costumer can reveal the personality of a character and the mood of a scene. Garment colors help identify social or business position and rank or wealth. They make a visual comment on mood and feeling. One immediately identifies a veiled woman in black as someone in mourning and a person wearing a white, crisp uniform and soft-soled, white shoes as a nurse or medical worker. We associate red with danger and adventure, soft beige and white with purity, purple with royalty, and brown with poverty. Mismatched plaids and bright prints are used for comic effect. Somber grays and browns represent the working class, just as silks and satins of blue and lavender represent the upper classes.

The radical or conservative nature of a character can be revealed by the style and color of his or her dress. A character can be set apart by wearing colors not worn by the rest of the cast. The costumer often uses color to highlight a particular character within a scene. Less important characters are usually dressed in softer colors. For example, Miss Julie, by virtue of the character's personality, would be dressed in brighter, more fashionable colors than others in the play in order to be set apart. In *Othello,* the men are generally dressed in heavy, dark costumes, while Desdemona appears frail and feminine in her soft flowing gown as she awaits her husband in the bedroom.

The texture of a costume's material goes hand in hand with color in interpreting character. Heavy, loosely woven fabrics and clothing are associated with the poor, while well-tailored clothing of tightly woven wool, silk, and linen is associated with the rich.

The ornamentation of a costume adds the finishing touches that complete a character's definition. Gold braid on the shoulders tells us the rank of a military man. Wood or brass buttons reveal class and wealth. In costumes as plain as those of the pilgrims in *The Crucible,* white lace at the collar and cuffs and buckles on the black shoes become important accent pieces. A Spanish lady needs her combs; a Southern belle needs her parasol; and an English gentleman must have his monocle. But the costumer is careful in selecting ornamentation, particularly jewelry. Proper balance of ornament creates a tasteful, well-dressed character, while overdoing it can show us a character's lack of taste or disorganized and confused state. The costumer must understand the character well to be able to select the right accessories. The hairstyle or wig, as well as a beard or mustache, are considered with the costume in creating the overall impression.

Finally, the actor must learn to wear the costume comfortably and use it expressively. Facets of a character can be revealed in the use of a costume. Broad, sweeping, majestic turns of a cape can enhance the sense of power of a nobleman. The coquettish flutter of a fan reveals a lady's intentions. A proper Englishman must be able to handle his cane or umbrella, and the medieval king must wear his crown and robe with grandeur. Often a director will ask that an actor dress ''in character'' during the interpretive period of rehearsals in order to aid the development of characterization.

The costumer has a large number of organizational duties. Costumes for each character in a show must be maintained in good condition and remain accessible in a specific location. In prepar-

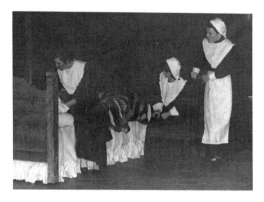

Figure 5.17. Costumes can denote period, . . .

. . . identify characters, . . .

. . . and add comic effect.

ing for a production, the costumer keeps accurate information on all the characters he or she will costume: actors' measurements, height, weight, and other details; how many costumes are needed for each character; and in which scenes of the play costumes are to be worn. Before designing costumes, the costumer considers how much time elapses in the progression of the play. Is it enough that the characters would have changed clothes? How much time an actor has between scenes in order to make a costume change will determine if a complete change can be made or if some item is simply added or deleted to produce the desired effect.

Usually, the costumer keeps a costume chart or file folder as costume pieces are made or acquired and a running tabulation of what is complete and what is still to be done. This sheet contains descriptions of each outfit to be worn and what is to be removed or added for the next scene. Actors use this list during dress rehearsals and performances as they prepare backstage. In the confusion, it is easy to make a mistake, but they have only to refer to the costume sheet to see what needs to be done next. A sample costuming sheet might look like figure 5.18.

Figure 5.18. A sample costume chart.

Don't Drink the Water   Marion Hollander   Costumes

Act I Scene 1: Blue polka-dot pants suit—matching sweater, sneakers, purse
       Scene 2: Remove sweater
       Scene 3: Flowered housecoat, bandanna covering curlers; exit p. 32—return p. 33 having removed housecoat to reveal blue pants suit with sweater, same shoes; curlers removed, hair combed.
       Scene 4: not in this scene
       Scene 5: same outfit as Act I, Scene 1
Act II Scene 1: house dress, bandanna over hair, sneakers
       Scene 2: same outfit as Act I, Scene 3 (blue pants outfit)
       Scene 3: (the party) full length red dress with black pumps
       Scene 4: house dress (same as Act II, Scene 1)

Properties

Handling properties for a play production is primarily an organizational responsibility. Properties, usually called props, are loosely defined as those things used in a production that are not considered sets or costumes. They are primarily items handled and used by the actors. In some plays, such as *The Leader*, few props are required; but in other plays, such as *The Glass Menagerie* and *Countess Julie*, numerous and varied props are needed. Figure 5.19 shows a partial property list for George Bernard Shaw's *Arms and the Man*.

Figure 5.19. Sample property list for *Arms and the Man*.

Divan bed with canopy	candlestick with candle
2 sheets	box of chocolate creams
satin or lace coverlet	2 revolvers
blanket	tablecloth
3 pillows	cigarettes
ivory image of Christ	brandy bottle
wash basin	3 cups and saucers
dressing stool	coins
towel	inkwell and pen

Fortunately, the work of the properties master can begin before rehearsals. He or she carefully studies the script and makes a list of props needed. In discussions with the director, the properties master may find there are items to be added, and some of the items mentioned in the script are not to be used. When the list is accurate, the prop master categorizes it, deciding what objects probably can be found in stock, borrowed, or bought and what will have to be built. The various tasks are delegated to the members of the crew, and the assembling and collecting begins.

The well-organized property master will devise a system for identifying and caring for each item collected. For example, if a silver tea service is borrowed from a theatre patron, the property crew labels it with an identifying name or symbol, stores it in a safe place, and returns it safely to the owner when the show is finished. Properties that belong to the producing organization are also cared for, and as items are purchased or constructed for each new production, the stockpile of props becomes bigger and better.

During a performance, props are kept on a table or on shelves near the stage. Usually they are organized by scene and order of use so that actors can find them easily. After use, the objects are returned to their original location. Carelessness with props by actors and crew members can waste time—and money. The property master oversees the storage, security, and handling of the props between shows.

The property master maintains all props, both perishable and nonperishable. Some props require constant maintenance. Wooden, paper, and fabric items may be broken or torn during the run of a play. Close scrutiny of props following each performance pinpoints those that may need maintenance or replacement before the next show.

Providing food or beverages required in a play is another responsibility of the property crew. They must make provisions for storing the food backstage or bringing it in for each performance. Foods that can be easily handled and that resist spoiling are preferred—for example, colored water for most beverages.

Makeup

Makeup is the final phase in the evolution from actor to character. The magic of stage makeup is nothing short of amazing. With makeup, one can add or take away age, create a lowly servant or a high fashion model, or transform a college student into an Arabian sheik. The art of makeup is the result of detailed planning and trial-and-error experience.

Makeup techniques fall into two categories: straight makeup and character makeup. Straight makeup enhances the actor's face and simply tries to make it look good under stage lights. It does not alter the actor's facial features or appearance. Character makeup is used to change the actor's looks. Antigone, for example, requires only straight makeup if played by a young woman, whereas Grandma in *The American Dream* needs character makeup if played by a young woman. For the character of Grandma, the actor's face would have to be altered to give it the look of age. Of course, any nonhuman character would need character makeup.

Stage makeup ideas emerge as the actor begins to understand the character to be portrayed. Like a costume, the character's face must suit the actor. In realistic plays, makeup should reveal as much as possible about the character. For example, it can reveal age, state of general health, nationality, and psychological state. In nonrealistic plays, makeup can transform an actor into an animal, a robot, or some other nonhuman form. Makeup is necessary to enhance characterization and to reinforce the features that stage light diminishes. Each actor usually applies his or her own

Figure 5.20 A properties crew builds a papier-maché statue for a production of *Li'l Abner*.

Figure 5.21 Students experiment with clown makeup

makeup, but a makeup artist often plans the makeup for the entire cast and assists those who need it.

Many products are used to alter the human visage. The makeup process begins with application of a base color, which may be a cream, lotion, liquid, pancake (which is applied with a wet sponge), or greasepaint. Face and neck are covered with this color medium, which acts as the base for other kinds of makeup that may be applied.

The age of the actor and of the character will determine whether or not age lines are needed. When added, lines follow the actor's natural lines. For example, to make forehead lines, the actor raises his or her eyebrows and, with a lining pencil, fills in the existing grooves. Similar existing lines can be found all over the face and neck when the actor smiles, frowns, and so on. The lines are highlighted with a lighter color blended into the base.

The treatment of the eyes varies with character type, but all actors need some eyeliner, eye color, and highlights. Many need mascara as well. Various shadows can be created with cheek colors and shading. Shadows may give the impression of illness or weight loss, as well as good health and vitality. Cheek rouge helps define the character's state of health.

Crepe hair is used to create realistic beards, mustaches, and hairpieces. Attached with an adhesive, the hair can be fashioned and trimmed to suit the particular character. The shape of facial features can be changed; an actor can create a longer or wider nose as well as a protruding forehead or chin.

The person in charge of makeup formulates and posts in the dressing room a chart displaying the items to be used by each character. This chart describes the makeup colors, lines, hairpieces, and other treatments each character will need. Such a

---

Figure 5.22. Makeup for *Antigone.*

Base pancake 2A face, neck, shoulders
Blue eye shadow #4
Brown cheek shadows
Lip liner and eyeliner, dark brown
Braid crepe hair (brown) around actor's hair
Highlight eyes and nose with clown white
Lipstick red #1
No powder in opening—put powder on hands and arms before
   arrest scene

---

chart proves helpful when many hands are dipping into the makeup box. Items are labelled by color numbers, so keeping a chart is a fairly simple and time-saving device. A chart for the character of Antigone might look like figure 5.22.

The makeup crew lays out items of makeup for each actor. In addition to the necessary stage makeup, the makeup area is supplied with tissues, hairpins, hair sprays, cold creams, and skin lotions or oils.

Stage makeup is removed as carefully as it is applied. Many items of stage makeup may irritate sensitive (and sometimes normal) skin. Because of this, greasepaint, cheek colors, and other makeup items are worn only as long as necessary for the performance. Immediately after the final curtain, actors remove the makeup. They apply theatrical cream, oil, or cold cream, let it set a few minutes to soften and loosen makeup, then wipe away the makeup with tissues. Repeated applications of cream may be required for heavy makeup. When most of the makeup has been removed, wash with mild soap and warm water until the skin is clean.

The Stage Manager

In the flurry of activity that goes on during rehearsals and performances, a level-headed, clear-thinking overseer of the many tasks in progress is needed. Such a position is filled by the stage manager, the ex officio head of all crews who is in charge of everything during a performance, including actors. The stage manager controls the curtain, follows the prompt book to ensure that light, sound, and special-effects cues are properly executed, warns the actors when they are about to go on, and informs the various crew people to be ready for their next function. It is the stage manager who is called on to make decisions about what to do if something goes wrong. If the actors forget lines and skip ahead a few pages, the stage manager must stay with them in the prompt book and warn the other technical people via headset of the adjustments to be made.

In the early rehearsals of a play, the stage manager's duties are varied and haphazard. They may include running errands, taking notes, moving furniture and props, and seeing to it that rehearsals run as smoothly as possible. Once blocking rehearsals are over and sets and props are added, the job becomes more involved. By dress rehearsal, when all elements of the performance are integrated, the stage manager's responsibilities expand to ensuring that the crews have fulfilled their obligations and that all crew areas are ready for performance. If, during the rehearsal or production period, weak links appear in the production chain, the stage manager lets the director know about it and takes steps to improve the situation. The stage manager who does the job well earns the respect and admiration of crew members and actors alike.

The Assistant Director

A student director (or assistant to the director) is a valuable addition to a production team in the educational theatre. This person serves as a communication link (or buffer, as the case may be) between the director and the rest of the production company. The student director performs many important functions as the production period develops from auditions to performance. He or she makes notes, offers suggestions, and helps with paperwork. At auditions, this person might assist the director in handling audition slips and noting who has not yet auditioned, who needs to be called back, and who can be excused. In the blocking segment of rehearsals, the student director maintains the production prompt book, the master script for a production. As actors write their blocking notes into their scripts, the student director documents blocking for all actors in the master script. In later rehearsals, if discrepancies arise between the prompt book and the actor's script, the prompt book is taken as the authority. In the final stage of rehearsals, the prompt book is handed over to the stage manager, who adds notes on the technical aspects, and the student director takes on a new task.

As rehearsals advance to a complete run-through of an act or of the entire play, the director tries not to interrupt with suggestions or criticisms. Instead, without taking his eyes off the stage, the director dictates notes to the assistant, who records them for later discussion with the company. The notes include everything from an actor's misinterpretation of a line, to a missing prop, to a mismatched blouse and skirt, to a late light cue.

The role of the assistant director, because of its importance, must be filled by someone trusted by the director and respected by the company. If this person is reliable and approachable, he or she becomes an important communication link between the director and others in the company. A clever assistant may express to an actor the director's feelings about a scene when the director has failed to communicate. If trouble is brewing among some company members, the assistant is likely to be privy to that information before the director and can troubleshoot a skirmish before it becomes a problem. This person must be someone to whom the director can propose new ideas or make general comments about the production and know that the comments will be confidential. Should the director be called away from a rehearsal for a phone call or brief meeting, the assistant carries on.

The Director

The director is the omniscient presence in all interpretive aspects of the production. Although he or she relies heavily on each member of the company, the director is the final decision maker, exercising artistic control over each facet of the production. The director's constructive criticism, although sometimes feared by the recipients, is usually the springboard to improvement. The director's goal is a finished product that contains the qualities and reaches the heights envisioned from the outset. In order for this goal to be achieved, the director is involved in every decision that is made prior to performance time. Then, when the curtain goes up, the director views the performance as an audience member, entrusting the production to the company.

Business Concerns

In addition to the artistic and technical aspects of a play production, good business management and adequate publicity are needed, so that the production costs are covered and the public is informed of an impending play production.

The business manager keeps a running account of the costs incurred by an ongoing production and sees that tickets are printed and sold. It is his or her responsibility to see that money collected at the box office is used to pay the bills that accumulate during the weeks of production.

Making sure that there will be an audience present to see the play is the job of the publicity crew. They get the word out through the media (that is, newspapers, radio, and TV), with posters and flyers, and by any other means available. Ads are placed in newspapers, articles are written, and pictures of the play in rehearsal are sent out. Flyers or brochures may be mailed to patrons or distributed by hand in public places. Promotional ads on radio and television reach a large audience, and direct contact by letter and telephone with schools, churches, and civic organizations often helps insure good audiences. A welcoming and responsive audience will be waiting when the curtain rises only if the public is aware that a play production is in progress.

A play production is a gigantic undertaking. So many people contribute to the final product that it is truly amazing that out of chaos comes a clearly defined and finely interpreted play performance. And the performance itself is not the only good result. Jobs relating to play production provide valuable experiences. In working together on a common artistic goal, students learn about teamwork, individual effort, and self-discipline. They learn how to cooperate with others in sometimes tense situations in order to attain that artistic goal.

A quality play production is possible only because many people make so many worthwhile and creative contributions. If the director watches and measures each component of the production to ensure that the individual parts are balanced elements of the whole, then the success attained during performance can be shared by every member of the production team.

Suggested Reading

Gassner, John, and Ralph G. Allen. *Theatre and Drama in the Making.* Boston, Mass.: Houghton Mifflin, 1964.

Kernodle, George, and Portia Kernodle. *Invitation to the Theatre.* New York: Harcourt Brace Jovanovich, 1978.

Kirk, John W. and Ralph A. Bellas. *The Art of Directing.* Belmont, Calif.: Wadsworth, 1985.

Tanner, Fran. *Basic Drama Projects.* Pocatello, Id.: Clark Pub. Co. 1977.

Wilson, Edwin. *The Theatre Experience.* New York: McGraw-Hill, 1980.

Part Three

Plays:
The Theatrical
Medium

6

The Elements of Drama

The development of dramas on the hillsides of the Greek city-states established a basis for modern tragedy and comedy. Many play types are now performed in the theatre, ranging from the tragedies of Sophocles to the dramas of August Strindberg to the light musical comedies of Rodgers and Hammerstein to the absurdist plays of Edward Albee and Eugene Ionesco. All of these have grown from basic play forms as outlined by Aristotle in *The Poetics*. Therefore, before we advance into a study of specific plays and genres, it seems fitting that we first examine the elements of drama.

Careful analysis reveals that the modern tragedy is based on an altered Aristotelian definition, but contains the same tragic elements found in plays like *Antigone* written in the sixth century B.C. And comedies such as *The Importance of Being Earnest* are a direct outgrowth of the attempts of early comic writers to satirize serious themes. In the absurdist plays, although structure and plot seem to be erratic, unpredictable, and sometimes nonexistent, one is aware of the tragic-comic nature of the genre. Modern dramas by writers such as Arthur Miller and August Strindberg are excellent examples of the present status of this literary evolution. In Strindberg's *Countess Julie*, for instance, one can see careful development of the elements of drama as they have been refined and developed over the centuries. The unraveling of the character of Julie and her need for the dominating influence of Jean in this play show yet another version of the protagonist and antagonist in subtle conflict.

Aristotle, in his treatment of the structure of drama, said that a play is made of six parts: *plot, character, thought, diction, music,* and *spectacle*. He dictated that the plot of a play needed a beginning, a middle, and an end. By making the second of his elements character, Aristotle sparked a lively debate. Some playwrights and critics have maintained that character is foremost, while others defend the primacy of the plot, or story line. (One way to look at this argument is to consider plot as the "character" of the story.) Thought is the dominant theme or basic purpose of the play. It answers the question, Why did the dramatist write the play? It is also referred to as the playwright's intent. The last three elements of drama—diction, music, and spectacle—serve to enhance and complement plot, character, and thought. They are vehicles for achievement.

Plot

Plot is the superstructure of the play, the organization of events or the common thread that holds the play together. The plot must follow a logical pattern of development. Inherent in a plot's structure are: exposition, discovery, foreshadowing, point of attack, complication, climax, and denouement. These elements may be modified in more contemporary comic and tragic plays, or radically changed, as in the Theatre of the Absurd. These changes, however, will be found to be part of the evolutionary growth of a living art.

The beginning of the play is generally referred to as exposition. This part often is the most tedious, although it is an absolutely essential element of the plot. In the exposition, the audience must be given all the background and introductory information needed to understand the characters and the story that follows. The playwright is challenged in the exposition to whet the audience's appetite for what is to come. Frequently, the characters supply the audience with the necessary background information for understanding the plot and characters. In *Countess Julie*, for example, the exposition begins in the first line with Jean's description of Julie's behavior: "Tonight Miss Julie is crazy again." But in *Antigone*, Sophocles used the chorus and the prologue to provide the necessary exposition.

The discovery of new information about the characters and events in the play is an ongoing adventure for the audience. In "putting the pieces together" as each new revelation is made, we come to understand the plot and characters. As we follow the story of Julie, we discover new information about her valet, Jean, which brings about a reversal or change in our appraisal of him. As we learn that he speaks French, he likes fine wine, and he has lofty ambitions, we tend to think less of his low social state. We experience with him a return to his low-caste state as he shivers at the ringing of a bell and Kristin states: "You have the soul of a servant." Reversal occurs when the fortunes of a character seem to take a turn, and subsequently we alter our image of that character.

The complications of the plot make up the middle of the play. Brought on by point of attack and predetermined in the foreshadowing, the complications build up until a climax is reached. Foreshadowing prepares us for future events in the play, making future action more believable. Foreshadowing serves as a device for building suspense and excitement, thereby holding the audience's interest and giving the plot momentum. In *Othello*, we witness the Moor's jealous rage when he slaps Desdemona in public, so we dread his actions when he believes her to be unfaithful. We are aghast when Jean puts Julie's canary on the chopping block and cuts off its head. Later, because of this, we find it credible that he sends Julie out to take her own life.

A complication is any new element or bit of information that tends to change the direction or development of the plot. Complications may involve a character's discovery of information about himself (such as illness) or another character (he or she is a thief), or about a relationship between characters (an affair between a spouse and a best friend). Each new piece of information further complicates the plot and the condition of the particular character. Complication has been described as a device for keeping the plot "straining forward."

The climax is the culmination of the complications. The climax has been described as the "maximum disturbance of the equilibrium" and the "greatest moment of strain." It is the high point of conflict and upheaval, after which events become less chaotic and people begin to settle into more predictable behavior. Warned of events to come through foreshadowing, we continue to discover new information and witness mounting conflicts and complications. Then, at the moment of greatest turbulence, the climax occurs. Although climax and crisis are sometimes the same, crisis can also be defined as a turning point. In a crisis, a character is faced with a decision or choice, the outcome of which will affect his or her fate. Creon faces a crisis when he learns that Antigone has defied his decree. Deciding to entomb her alive leads ultimately to the death of his own son.

The final portion of the play is that usually brief period of unraveling and resolution referred to as denouement that exists from the moment of climax to the final curtain. The major plot line as well as the various subplots are satisfied, answered, or balanced in such a way that the audience feels the situation is back in a state of equilibrium. This period of denouement marks the closing of the play and the resolution of the different aspects of a complicated plot. For example, in *Countess Julie*, Jean will remain a valet, but Julie may take her own life. The denouement serves to unify the elements of plot, bringing about an orderly, logical resolution.

Character

In his *Poetics*, Aristotle listed character second in importance to plot. However, it seems unnecessary to declare plot more important than character or vice versa, since one is so dependent on the other. The characters are the primary vehicle of the play through which the author speaks. The dialogue spoken by the characters *is* the play. The lines of dialogue spoken by one character and those spoken by other characters about him or her are the primary clues to the character's identity.

The author creates personalities that are differentiated by physical appearance, social and economic status, emotional and mental health, and morality. One or more of these elements will be emphasized in a particular character, depending on the purpose he or she serves in the plot. Although a few clues to characterization may be found in the stage directions and author's notes, much of it must be invented by the actor. This makes each character interpretation unique.

The reader of a play must try to understand and visualize each character through the dialogue. The reader becomes involved with the characterizations to the point that the roles are more than lines. Characters have faces, posture, a mode of dress—and a total personality.

Character is developed in four ways. The first is appearance, a visual image that includes sex, race, build, and general state of health, as well as clues to financial status, occupation, cultural tastes, likeability, and so on. The character's appearance is the single, most powerful element in the audience's impression of that character. The actor must search the script for tidbits of infor mation that will reveal how the character is to look. For example, Kristin in *Countess Julie* is a servant who is happy with her station. The script reveals that she is not concerned with personal beauty or worldly things. This visual impression is created by the actor's face and body and by the use of makeup, costumes, and hairstyle.

Much may be learned about a character through his or her speech. A national or regional accent helps determine a character's place of origin. Cultured, polished speech suggests education and wealth, while broken, ungrammatical speech suggests ignorance or lower class status. In *The Importance of Being Earnest*, for example, the speech pattern of Lady Bracknell is more precise than that of Jack. The playwright may write the lines in a regional dialect or leave it to the actor to add this dimension. Pitch, rate, inflection, and volume of speech say a great deal about a character. A good actor commands a variety of speech patterns and affectations in order to personify many character types.

Much about a character can be expressed through movement. An actor's gait, posture, gestures, and facial expressions all serve to reveal a character. Any deviation from "normal" movement patterns, such as a limp or a twitch, inform the audience of a particular character type. The author's clues to a movement deviation may be vague. For example, in *The Glass Menagerie*, the author does not specify the degree of Laura's limp.

We also learn about a character by the way the other characters react to, talk to, and talk about that character. As in life, we may be misled in a play by one character's appraisal of or reaction to another. We understand a character better when we know how others feel about him or her. We more clearly understand Antigone, for example, when we see her interact with Ismene and Creon.

The dramatic character is multifaceted. He or she has emotional, moral, psychological, and social dimensions. The well-developed character must incorporate all of these dimensions. Most of the clues to a complex personality lie in the lines of dialogue in the play. If a character is disturbed or angry, the lines must contain all the clues to his or her behavior.

Thought

The third Aristotelian element is thought, or ideas. Every play contains the ideas of the author. In order to portray truthfully the author's intent in a particular characterization, the actor must know what the author's thoughts were when he or she wrote the play. The thought is most often implied in subtext. Only rarely does a character blatantly speak the underlying ideas of the play; rather, the ideas are conveyed by the interaction of the characters, the development of the plot, and the evolution of the play production. It is the thought behind the play that elicits discussion and argument after a reading or viewing. We examine characters' motives and the plot resolutions in our attempts to pin down the author's thoughts. *The Leader*, for example, is a series of confusing conversations that, taken together, help us to examine who we choose as heroes. But the hero theme is entirely subtextual.

Diction, Music, and Spectacle

Aristotle's final three elements of drama are the vehicles for accomplishing the first three. Diction, music, and spectacle help the actors attain plot, character, and thought. Diction is heightened and clarified in order to assure that the audience hears every word. Diction does not suggest, however, that formal speech is always appropriate. Depending on the play, regional variations and affectations may be important elements. In his inclusion of music as a primary element, Aristotle must have meant the "music of words" as well as music in its traditional sense. Musical interludes and effects are not often needed in modern dramatic performance, but the rhythmical patterning of pleasant or discordant speech becomes a viable element of the drama. The qualities and rhythms of speech have been essential to the drama since the time when a chorus moved rhythmically around the threshing circle. The general appeal of music has made it a part of theatre throughout its history, from the Dionysian choral odes, to Renaissance church drama, to the Ziegfeld Follies and the American musical.

Spectacle encompasses all the visual technical elements: lighting, scenery, makeup, and so on. These elements heighten dramatic effects. The appearance of the stage set provides the audience with an immediate frame of reference for the action and characters to come. The subtle, varied lighting of costumed characters in the set helps the play come to life. The spectacle nature of plays, which probably reached a zenith in modern times with shows such as the Follies, is still important in dramatic art. But it is not used as frequently as it was in the past.

Modern plays tend to be built around the elements of plot, character, and thought. In these three are found all that is necessary for creating dramatic moments that are believable. The other elements serve to enhance an already sound dramatic work.

Suggested Reading

Beckerman, Bernard. *Dynamics of Drama: Theory of Analysis*. New York: Knopf, 1970.

McKeon, Richard. *Introduction to Aristotle*. New York: Random House, 1947.

Styan, J. L. *The Elements of Drama*. Cambridge: University Press, 1967.

Woodbridge, Elizabeth. *The Drama: Its Law and Its Technique*. Boston, Mass.: Allyn and Bacon, 1898.

7
Tragedy

Throughout the history of drama, playwrights have presented tragic heroes,* both men and women, as persons from whom we can gain insights about our own existence. Early Greek writers gave us Oedipus, Antigone, and Clytemnestra. Shakespeare wrote about Othello, Macbeth, and King Lear. The French playwright Jean Baptiste Racine (1639–1699) presented such tragic protagonists as Phaedra and Andromache. In the nineteenth century, Henrik Ibsen created the tragic hero, Helen Alving, in *Ghosts*.

Aristotle defined tragedy in his *Poetics* as "an imitation of an action that is serious . . . having magnitude . . . with incidents arousing pity and fear, wherefore to accomplish its catharsis of such emotions."[1] This imitation, according to Aristotle, may be of actual people or families familiar to the audiences or of persons "invented" by the artist. Although many of the early Greek tragedies related stories of the familiar houses of Oedipus, Orestes, and others, some of the heroes of tragedy are invented characters. In modern times, Whitney Oates and Eugene O'Neill give three elements or assumptions basic for the creation of tragedy:

*While dictionaries define the word *hero* in masculine terms, students and veterans of the theatre use the term "tragic hero" when referring to a male or a female protagonist in a specific play. In this chapter, the tradition is continued. The reader should consider the statements and documentation within this section that employ "he" not as sexist but as dramatic narration, exposition, and criticism that have lost a specific sexual connotation.

''First, the dignity of man; second, the freedom of his will and his responsibility for the use which he makes of that will; and third, the existence in the universe of a superhuman factor.''[2]

The tragic protagonist in the Aristotelian concept was a good man of higher than ordinary status, but lacking some moral quality or self-knowledge. Although Aristotle's definition of the tragic hero has long been held in reverence, it cannot be considered as a universally true and inflexible definition. For while Aristotle deemed that a tragic hero must be highborn, Tennessee Williams shows us, in *The Glass Menagerie,* that a poor Southern woman can also be a tragic hero.

The Tragic Hero

The tragic hero is a character we can admire and emulate on the one hand and share inadequacies with on the other. We revere the tragic character because by sharing his experiences—both good and bad—we can come to a greater and more complete understanding of ourselves. He is believable because he is neither all good nor all bad, neither idyllic nor repugnant; rather, he is a human displaying strengths and inadequacies symbolic of us all.

Critic R. J. Kaufman defines the tragic hero as a person of noble thought, but lacking common sense. Common sense, Kaufman suggests, often causes us to be shortsighted, to give up on an aspiration for logical and sensical reasons. The individual possessing common sense is prudent, cautious, and undramatic. Kaufman states, ''Tragic heroes tend to be those for whom common sense is either a foreign idiom or only a beginning step. . . . Tragic heroes exist to raise the ceiling of possibility.''[3] The tragic hero has vision beyond that of the common man. He is noble and courageous and may say no when all others say yes. He has personal convictions and adheres to them, even if this means defeat. We admire the hero's stamina in the fight as well as learn from the error causing his inevitable fall. Unlike the chorus of a Greek tragedy that chants the advice and logic of the common man, the tragic hero dares to challenge that logic and test its validity. He is sincere in his efforts to gain truth about himself and the world, even if that truth is destructive.

The audience sees a hero in the tragic protagonist and admires the noble battle he or she wages. Kaufman states:

> If one believes in a dramatic character and the character acts, then there is an experimental opportunity for self-observation. . . . It does draw upon submerged ''if-then'' statements and in-

duces conviction through a combination of direct stimulation of the emotions and indirect testing of life axioms. . . . It shows us what we instinctively know but contrive to forget with regularity, that these relationships between God and man, knowledge and action, virtue and knowledge, life and belief are stabilized only by willful effort.[4]

The glory of the tragic protagonist is his or her willful effort to alter fate, to try to affect the future. Antigone has the courage to bury her brother, even though the result will almost certainly be her death.

The flaw of the tragic hero, highborn or not, involves judgment, decision making or lack of it, and reverence for the gods or revolt against them. The hero represents the universal struggle of mankind for a place of significance and for a feeling of self-worth. A tragic flaw or weakness usually proves to be the downfall of the protagonist. Antigone's stubborn determination to see her brother properly buried leads to her own death, but this is a fate she chooses. She feels her vision of justice for her brother and the spiritual release of his soul is worth the price she must pay. Othello is a man so gripped by blind jealousy that he murders the wife he loves and cherishes. Because he loses reason to the rage of his jealous and wounded pride, he destroys the one thing he loves. We see the inevitability of the fate of a tragic hero, because the flaw in his or her character surfaces and influences the outcome.

Aristotle says that tragedy involves "incidents arousing pity and fear wherefore to accomplish its catharsis." For the audience, this is the beneficial and therapeutic reward of tragedy. Theodore Hatlen says in *Drama: Principles and Plays*, that "tragedy appeals to us because it satisfies our craving to discover, even in moments of utmost suffering and evil, patterns in life which are truly representative of life and therefore just."[5]

The Greek philosopher Socrates said the unexamined life is not worth living. Tragedy helps us to examine our own lives. Tragic drama allows us an opportunity to see into the life of the tragic hero and in so doing, we see ourselves more clearly. As our self-knowledge is gradually and more positively increased, we undergo a gradual catharsis or purifying. This catharsis, if it is to be therapeutic and educational, must be an experience that is genuinely felt as well as intelligently understood. We need to feel and to understand the conviction that motivates the protagonist. Aristotle used the words "fear and pity"; we may fear for the hero as we anticipate his approaching doom, and we pity him in retrospect. But through our empathy with the hero—our kindred spirit—we vicariously share his ambition and defeat. We share the hero's wonder, conviction, frustration, and doom. Thus, we feel relieved or purged of all of this emotion when the play is ended, and the hero has met his just fate.

The Elements of Tragedy

The elements of tragedy were first set down by Aristotle in his *Poetics*. And over the years, they have been altered little from the initial guidelines he set down, owing perhaps to his depth of understanding of the literary forms.

According to Aristotle, plot is the most important element of tragedy. He said that plot needed to be of a length that could be easily held in the mind of the observer. That was taken to mean the amount of time it took for one revolution of the sun and became the definition of the unity of time. The arrangement of the plot, he went on, must allow the hero to pass through "a series of probable or necessary stages from happiness to misfortune."[6] This does not mean that a tragedy must be only one character's story. In *Antigone*, for example, we are moved by Antigone's bravery but we are also impressed by Creon's behavior as king.

Aristotle held that the plot must be tied together in a logical sequence of events leading to a final conclusion. He advised not to try to stretch the plot beyond its capabilities. Plots, he said, were at the same time both simple and complex, happening unexpectedly and yet in an apparent design. There should be no scene included except of necessity. A well-developed plot was one that revealed "a man not pre-eminently virtuous and just, whose misfortune . . . is brought upon him not by vice and depravity but by some error of judgment."[7] The single identifying element is a hero whose fortune changes from happiness to misery because of some fault within himself. Of the "fear and pity" element of tragedy, Aristotle required that "the plot in fact should be so framed that, even without seeing the things take place, he who simply hears the account of them shall be filled with horror."[8] And, indeed, we are disquieted when we hear that Antigone has hanged herself in the cavern.

Development of the characters was the second most important element of the Aristotelian tragedy. Four criteria were established in the *Poetics*. First, characters must be good—revealing moral purpose. Second, they must be appropriate. Third, they must reflect reality, and fourth, the behavior of each character should be consistent throughout the play. Much of our discovery of the plot is through the development of the characters in the natural progression of the play.

In the development of a character, Aristotle admonishes us to take a lesson from the artist who paints a portrait and is able, without altering the likeness, to make the subject more handsome than he is in life. This goal of having the protagonist be a noble character was carefully followed in all the tragedies of the Greek period. As playwriting blossomed in Elizabethan England, more variety appeared in the personality of the tragic protagonist, as we see in Hamlet and Othello. And in the twentieth century, with our desire to understand the inner psychology of our ''heroes,'' we find the Willy Loman-type protagonist. No effort is made to have him appear more handsome than he is. That character or force opposing the protagonist and thereby contributing to his downfall is labelled the antagonist.

Aristotle goes on to discuss diction and elocution, the use of spectacle in the productions, and other elements of the actor's preparation, but it is clear that he knew that the strength of the tragedy lay in the structure of the plot and the development of the characters.

Aristotle's guidelines form our frame of reference for tragedy, but as the plays in this book attest, from *Antigone* to *Othello* to *Countess Julie*, there is no one true pattern for the tragedy or the tragic hero. They are unique to the time period they represent and depend on the playwright's construction of a set of circumstances. We do find, however, repeated reflection on and adherence to the Aristotelian ideas: A protagonist is caught in a series of events leading from fortune to misfortune. This misfortune is brought on, to some degree, by inadequacies or misjudgments on the part of that protagonist. Often the events find the hero pitted against supernatural forces or at least factors beyond his control. The protagonist is basically a good person, although we may find he has certain psychological or emotional weaknesses. Because of these human weaknesses, we are able to empathize with and to share the burden of the protagonist and participate in the therapeutic benefits of the catharsis.

A Misconception about Tragedy

A widely held misconception is that tragedy is inherently pessimistic. Many people think of a tragedy only as a story with a sad ending. Yet if one understands tragedy, nothing could be farther from the truth. Arthur Miller, in addressing this question, said that there may indeed be more optimism in tragedy than in comedy, because in tragedy there exists the possibility of triumph. Even in the end, when our hero is dead, hope may live on—brighter and stronger than ever. Antigone loses her life, but only after she has attained the goal of putting her brother's soul to rest. It is not so important in tragedy whether a man or woman dies; what is important is the reason the character dies. Miller says this motivation in the modern protagonist may be his tragic flaw: "The flaw, or crack, in the character is really nothing—and need be nothing but his inherent unwillingness to remain passive in the face of what he conceives to be a challenge to his dignity, his image of his rightful status."[9] Miller goes on to say that this is why we continue to revere the tragedy above other play forms. It reinforces our belief in the "perfectibility" of man. How can it be sad or pessimistic that man dares to tempt his fate in the hope that he can improve it or that he dares to question tradition when time has proven the tradition outmoded? Perhaps the radical demonstrator is our modern protagonist. Perhaps the hunger striker, though he or she may starve to death, will make some lasting change in the political system.

Many scholars contend that a great tragedy cannot be written in modern times because "nobility" is no more and because the skepticism of science has caused us to hold nothing in unquestioned reverence. But doesn't the working-class salesman claim some nobility, as Miller suggests? Even in the face of unending scientific inquiry, are we not constantly reminded of the smallness of man in comparison to the immensity of the universe? In admitting our small, yet noble, position in this universe, are we not capable of great joy and great pain—and therefore, great tragedy?

Greek Tragedy: *Antigone*

In the tradition of the Greek tragedy, *Antigone* begins with a prologue that serves as an introduction. In the opening conversation between Antigone and Ismene, we learn of Antigone's dilemma. This is followed by the appearance of the chorus chanting and moving in rhythms appropriate to the words they speak concerning the gods. After a choral song, the episodes of the plot begin.

Two brothers have been killed in a civil war—Eteocles while fighting for the king, and Polyneices while fighting against him.

The king, Creon, Antigone's uncle, announces that anyone who died opposing him shall not be given a burial but will be left for birds and dogs to feed on. Religious law decrees that the spirit cannot rest until the body is properly buried, so Antigone, sister of the dead brothers, feels it her obligation to bury Polyneices. She has a decision to make: Will she obey man's law or the law of the gods?

The performance traditions of the Dionysian Theatre in this period should be remembered when reading this play. No more than three actors are allowed on the stage at one time, and the chorus is composed of fifteen members. Violent deeds (such as the death of a character) take place offstage and are related in dialogue onstage. (Perhaps the *eccylema* was used to roll out the bodies.)

Antigone is a relatively short play, since it would have been one of three or four plays performed in one day. It is the third play in a trilogy; therefore, it is the climax of the trilogy as well as a complete story in itself.

Antigone
Sophocles

Characters

    ANTIGONE, daughter of dead King Oedipus
    ISMENE, her sister
    CHORUS of Theban elders
    CREON, uncle of ANTIGONE and ISMENE, King of Thebes
    GUARD
    HAEMON, son of CREON, betrothed to ANTIGONE
    TEIRESIAS, a blind prophet
    FIRST MESSENGER
    EURYDICE, wife of CREON
    SECOND MESSENGER
    ATTENDANTS

Scene

    Before the palace of CREON in Thebes

    (*Enter* ANTIGONE *and* ISMENE)
    ANTIGONE: Ismene, my dear, my mother's child, my sister,
      What part of Oedipus' sad legacy

From *Sophocles: Oedipus the King and Antigone,* translated and edited by Peter D. Arnott, © 1960 by Harlan Davidson, Inc., Arlington Heights, IL, pp. 57–105. Reprinted by permission of Harlan Davidson, Inc.

Figure 7.1 A stage production of Sophocles' *Antigone*. (Courtesy of Department of Communications and Theatre, University of North Carolina in Greensboro.)

Has Zeus not laid in full on us who live?
There is nothing bitter, nothing of disaster,
No shame, no humiliation I have not seen
In the number of your sufferings and mine.
And now what is this order which they say
Our leader has announced throughout the city?
Do you know? Have you heard? Or do I have to tell you   10
That what has happened to our enemies
Is threatening to fall upon our friends?
ISMENE: I have heard no word of friends, Antigone,
  To bring me comfort or to bring me pain
  Since the time we two were robbed of our two brothers,
  Dead in one day, and by each other's hand.
  And now the Argive army overnight
  Has disappeared, I am no nearer knowing
  Whether my luck has changed for good or bad.
ANTIGONE: I know, too well. That is why I wanted to bring you   20
  Outside the courtyard, to talk to you alone.
ISMENE: What is it? Trouble, you do not need to tell me.
ANTIGONE: What else, when Creon singles out one brother
  For a hero's grave, and lets the other rot?
  They are saying he has laid Eteocles in the ground
  With every rite and custom that is fitting
  To give him honor with the dead below.
  But Polyneices' body, that was killed
  So pitifully, they say he has commanded
  Should not be mourned or given burial   30
  But lie unburied and unwept, a feast
  For passing birds to gorge on at their pleasure.
  And so, the rumor runs, has our good Creon
  Decreed for you and me—for me, I say!
  And is on his way here now, to spell it out
  To those who have not heard. He does not take
  This matter lightly. Anyone who disobeys
  In any way will die by public stoning.
  So there you have it. Now we shall soon find out
  If you are a true-born daughter of your line,   40
  Or if you will disgrace your noble blood!
ISMENE: But, my poor sister, if things are as you say,
  What ways and means have I to set them straight?
ANTIGONE: Ask yourself, will you work with me, help me do it?
ISMENE: What adventure is this? What do you have in mind?
ANTIGONE: Will you help this hand of mine to lift the dead?
ISMENE: You mean to bury him? Against the law?
ANTIGONE: Bury my brother? Yes—and bury yours,
  If you will not. No-one shall call me faithless.

ISMENE: You would not dare, when Creon has forbidden it!   *50*
ANTIGONE: He has no right to keep me from my own.
ISMENE: Oh sister, think of how our father died,
  Hated, despised, and driven by the sins
  He had himself laid bare, to turn his hand
  Against himself, and strike out both his eyes.
  And then his mother, wife—which shall I call her?
  Knotted a noose, and took away her life.
  Then the final blow, two brothers in one day,
  Unhappy pair, each shedding kinsman's blood,
  Lay hands on each other, and made one in death.   *60*
  Now we two are alone. Think how much worse
  Our deaths will be, if in despite of law
  We brave the king's commandment and his power.
  Let us not forget two things—that we were born
  Women, and so not meant to fight with men;
  And then, that we must do what our masters tell us—
  Obey in this, and other things far worse.
  I, then, will ask the kingdom of the dead
  To pardon me; since I am no free agent,
  I will yield to the powers that be. There is no sense   *70*
  In meddling in things outside our sphere.
ANTIGONE: I shall not persuade you. You would not be welcome
  To help me now, even if you wanted to.
  Be what you want to be; but I intend
  To bury him. It is a noble way to die.
  I shall lie with him for love, as he loved me,
  A criminal, but guiltless; for the dead
  Have longer claims upon me than the living.
  There is my lasting home. If you think fit
  To dishonor the gods' commandments, then you may.   *80*
ISMENE: I mean them no dishonor; but when it means
  Defying the state—I am not strong enough.
ANTIGONE: Let that be your excuse. Now I shall go
  To heap the earth on my beloved brother.
ISMENE: Antigone, no! I am so afraid for you!
ANTIGONE: You need not fear for me. Look after yourself.
ISMENE: At least tell no-one what you mean to do.
  Keep it a secret, I shall do the same.
ANTIGONE: Oh no, denounce me! You will be in far worse
    trouble   *90*
  For keeping silence, if you do not tell the world.
ISMENE: You have a hot heart where you should be shivering.
ANTIGONE: I know I am giving pleasure where I should.
ISMENE: Yes, if you can. But you ask too much of yourself.
ANTIGONE: When I have no more strength, then I shall stop.

ISMENE: No point in starting, when the cause is hopeless.
ANTIGONE: Go on like this and you will make me hate you,
    And the dead will hate you too; you give him cause.
    Leave me alone with my stupidity
    To face this dread unknown; whatever it is,   100
    Anything is better than to die a coward!
ISMENE: Then if your mind is made up, go. You are a fool,
    And yet your own will love you for it.

(*Exit* ANTIGONE; ISMENE *retires within the palace.*
    Enter CHORUS *of Theban elders.*)

CHORUS: Light of the morning sun, brightest that ever yet
    Dawned upon the seven gates of Thebes;
    Eye of the golden day, at last we see you   110
    Rising over Dirke's streams,
    Turning to rout the white-shielded warrior
    That came from Argos in his array,
    Winging his feet, and sending him flying home.

    Polyneices' contentious quarrel
    Was the cause of his coming here,
    Winging over our country
    Like an eagle clamoring,
    Sheathed in snow-white feathers   120
    With mail-clad men and waving plumes.

    Over the housetops hovering, howling before
    Our seven gates for blood to slake his spears;
    But before he could suck his fill of Theban
    Blood, before the Fire-god's flame
    Leapt from the logs to embrace our ramparts,
    He left, so loud the roaring of the war-cry
    Behind him, as he fought the Theban dragon.
                                    130
    Zeus hates nothing more than a boastful tongue.
    When he saw them coming, a mighty stream
    Arrogant in their clanging gold
    He brandished his thunderbolt and felled the man
    Who had scaled our ramparts, and stood at his goal
    With the cry of victory on his lips.

    And over he tumbled, torch in hand,
    He who a moment before
    Had come at us like a man possessed,   140
    Running berserk, with the hot breath of hatred.
    Earth rang with his fall, and his threats went wide.
    Then the God of War, our good yoke-fellow,

Lashed out, and assigned
To each of the rest their several deaths.

Seven captains stood before seven gates,
Matched against seven, and left their armor
In homage to Zeus, the arbiter of battles,
All but the ill-starred pair, who, born   150
Of one father and mother, leveled their spears
At each other; both won, and both fell dead.

But now the glorious name of Victory
Enters our chariot-proud
City, to laugh with us in our joy,
Let us put all memory of past war behind us
And visit the temples of the gods with song
And with nightlong dances; Bacchus, whose steps
Set the meadows dancing,   160
Come down to lead the procession!

(*Enter* CREON)

But here comes our country's ruler
Creon, Menoeceus' son, our new lord
By the gods' new dispensations.
What counsel can he be pondering
To summon the elders by general decree
To meet in special conference together?   170
CREON: Gentlemen, the state has been in troubled waters,
But now the gods have set us back on course.
My summons came to you, of all the people,
To meet here privately, because I knew
Your constant reverence for Laius' throne,
And then, when Oedipus became our king,
After his death, I saw their children
Secure in your unswerving loyalty.
And now this double blow has taken both
His sons in one day, each struck down by the other,   180
Each with his brother's blood upon his hands,
The throne and all its powers come to me
As next of kin in order of succession.
But you can never know what a man is made of,
His character or powers of intellect,
Until you have seen him tried in rule and office.
A man who holds the reins of government
And does not follow the wisest policies
But lets something scare him from saying what he thinks,
I hold despicable, and always have done.   190
Nor have I time for anyone who puts

His popularity before his country.
As Zeus the omnipotent will be my witness,
If I saw our welfare threatened; if I saw
One danger-signal, I would speak my mind,
And never count an enemy of my country
To be a friend of mine. This I believe:
The state keeps us afloat. While she holds an even keel,
Then, and then only, can we make real friends.
By this creed I shall make Thebes prosperous;   200
And in accordance with it, I have published
My edict on the sons of Oedipus,
That Eteocles, who died a hero's death
While fighting to defend his fatherland
Should be entombed with every solemn rite
With which the glorious dead are sent to rest.
But his brother Polyneices, who returned
From exile, with intent to devastate
The country of his fathers, and to burn
The temples of his fathers' gods, to taste   210
His brother's blood, and make the rest his slaves,
Concerning him, it is proclaimed as follows:
That nobody shall mourn or bury him,
But let his body lie for dogs and birds
To make their meal, so men may look and shudder.
Such is my policy; foul play shall never
Triumph over honest merit, if I can help it,
But the man who loves his city shall receive
Honor from me, in his life and in his death.
CHORUS: Such is your pleasure, Creon, son of Menoeceus,   220
    Concerning our city's friend and enemy,
    And you have the power to order as you wish,
    Not only the dead, but the living too.
CREON: Then see to it my orders are obeyed.
CHORUS: Lay this responsibility on someone younger!
CREON: No, not to guard the corpse; that has been seen to.
CHORUS: Then what else are you asking me to do?
CREON: Not to side with anyone who disobeys me.
CHORUS: No man is fool enough to ask for death.
CREON: That is what you would get. But hope of gain   230
    Has often led men on to their destruction.

(*Enter* GUARD)

GUARD: My lord, I won't say that I'm out of breath
    From hurrying, or that I've run here all the way,
    For several times my thoughts pulled me up short
    And made me turn round to go back again.

There was a voice inside me kept on saying
"Why go, you fool? You're certain to be punished."   *240*
"Idiot, why hang about? If Creon hears
The news from someone else, you'll smart for it."
Arguing like this I went at snail's pace,
And so a short road turned into a long one.
But in the end, go forward won the day.
There's nothing to say, but all the same I'll say it.
I'm certain of one thing, at any rate,
That I can only get what's coming to me.
CREON: What is it that has put such fear in you?
GUARD: First let me say a word on my own account.   *250*
    I didn't do it, nor did I see who did,
    And it isn't right that I should take the blame for it.
CREON: A well-placed shot. You have covered yourself
    Well against attack. I see you mean to surprise me.
GUARD: A man thinks twice before he tells bad news.
CREON: Then tell me, will you, and be on your way.
GUARD: Well, here it is: the corpse—someone has buried it.
    And gone away; he sprinkled dry dust over
    The flesh, and did whatever else was fitting.
CREON: What are you saying? What man has dared to do this?   *260*
GUARD: I don't know. There was no mark of a pickaxe,
    No spade had been at work; the ground was hard,
    Dry and unbroken; we could find no tracks
    Of wheels; he left no trace, whoever did it.
    And when the man who took the morning watch
    Showed us, nobody knew what to make of it.
    The corpse was out of sight—not in a tomb
    But sprinkled with dust, as though someone had thrown it
    To avoid bad luck. There was no sign of wild beasts
    Or dogs around; the corpse was in one piece.   *270*
    Then we all started cursing each other at once,
    One sentry blaming the next; it would have come
    To blows in the end, there was no-one there to stop us,
    First one had done it, then the next man, then the next,
    But we couldn't pin it down, all pleaded ignorance.
    We were ready to take red-hot irons in our hands,
    To walk through fire, to swear an oath to heaven
    That we were innocent, had no idea
    Of who had planned it all, or done the work.
    In the end, when there was no more point in searching,   *280*
    One man said something which made every one of us
    Shiver, and hang our heads; we didn't see
    How we could argue with him, or if we listened
    How we could save our necks. He said we couldn't

Keep the thing dark, but we must come and tell you.
So we did; and I was the unlucky one.
The lot picked me to receive the prize.
So here I am—about as pleased to be here
As I know you are to see me. Nobody
Has any love for the one who brings bad news.   290
CHORUS: My lord, since he began, I have been wondering
   Could this perhaps have been the work of heaven?
CREON: Be quiet, before you make me lose my temper.
   Do you want to look like fools in your old age?
   What you suggest is intolerable,
   That the gods would give this corpse a second thought.
   Why should they try to hide his nakedness?
   In reward for services rendered? When he came
   To burn their marble halls and treasuries,
   To burn their land, make havoc of its laws?   300
   Or can you see the gods rewarding sinners?
   Never. No, there were people in this town
   Who took it hard from the first, and grumbled at me,
   Furtively tossing their heads, not submitting
   To the yoke as in duty bound, like contented men.
   It was these people—of that I am convinced—
   Who bribed the guards and urged them on to do it.
   Of all the institutions of mankind
   The greatest curse is money. It destroys
   Our cities, it takes men away from home,   310
   Corrupts men's honest minds, and teaches them
   To enter on disreputable courses.
   It shows them how to lead immoral lives
   And flout the gods in everything they do.
   But every one of the bribers will be caught
   Sooner or later, they may be sure of that.
   But by the reverence I owe to Zeus,
   I tell you this upon my solemn oath,
   That if you do not find the author of
   This burial, and produce him before my eyes,   320
   Death alone will be too good for you; you will be
   Left hanging, till you tell about this outrage.
   Then, when you next go stealing, you will know
   What you may take, and learn for once and all
   Not to love money without asking where
   It comes from. You will find ill-gotten gains
   Have ruined many more than they have saved.
GUARD: May I speak? Or shall I just turn round and go?
CREON: Do you still need telling that your voice annoys me?
GUARD: Where does it hurt? In your ears or in your heart?   330

CREON: Is there any call for you to define my pain?
GUARD: The criminal troubles your mind, and I your ears.
CREON: Oh, you were born with a loose tongue, I can see.
GUARD: Maybe I was, but this I didn't do.
CREON: You did, and worse. You sold your life for money.
GUARD: How dreadful to judge by appearances, then be wrong.
CREON: Moralize as you please; but if you do not show me
   The men who did this thing, you will bear witness
   That dishonest winnings bring you into trouble.

(*Exit* CREON *to the palace*)   340

GUARD: Well, I only hope he's caught; but whether he is
   Or not—it's in the hands of fortune now—
   You won't see me coming this way again.
   I never thought I'd get away with this.
   It's more than I hoped—the gods be praised for it.

(*Exit*)   350

CHORUS: The world is full of wonderful things
   But none more so than man,
   This prodigy who sails before the storm-winds,
   Cutting a path across the sea's gray face
   Beneath the towering menace of the waves.
   And Earth, the oldest, the primeval god,
   Immortal, inexhaustible Earth,
   She too has felt the weight of his hand
   As year after year the mules are harnessed
   And plows go back and forwards in the fields.   360

   Merry birds and forest beasts,
   Fish that swim in the deep waters,
   Are gathered into the woven nets
   Of man the crafty hunter.
   He conquers with his arts
   The beasts that roam in the wild hill-country
   He tames the horses with their shaggy manes
   Throwing a harness around their necks,
   And the tireless mountain bull.   370

   Speech he has made his own, and thought
   That travels swift as the wind,
   And how to live in harmony with others
   In cities, and how to shelter himself
   From the piercing frost, cold rain, when the open
   Fields can offer but a poor night's lodging.
   He is ever-resourceful; nothing that comes
   Will find him unready, save Death alone.

Then he will call for help and call in vain,   *380*
Though often, where cure was despaired of, he has found one.

The wit of man surpasses belief,
It works for good and evil too;
When he honors his country's laws, and the right
He is pledged to uphold, then city
Hold up your head; but the man
Who yields to temptation and brings evil home
Is a man without a city; he has
No place in the circle of my hearth,   *390*
Nor any part in my counsels.

(*Enter* GUARD, *leading* ANTIGONE *prisoner*)

But what is this? The gods alone know.
Is it Antigone? She and no other.
Oh unhappy daughter of
Your wretched father Oedipus,
What is it? Have they arrested you?
Have you broken the royal commandment?   *400*
Has your foolishness brought you to this?
GUARD: Here she is! This is the girl who did it!
    We caught her burying him. But where is Creon?
CHORUS: Here, coming from the palace, just in time.

(*Enter from the palace* CREON *with* ATTENDANTS)

CREON: Coming in time for what? What is it now?
GUARD: My lord, a man should never swear to anything.   *410*
    Second thoughts belie the first. I could have sworn
    I wouldn't have come back here again in a hurry
    After the tongue-lashing you gave me last time.
    But there's no pleasure like the one that comes
    As a surprise, the last thing you expected.
    So here I am, breaking my solemn oath,
    Bringing this girl, who was caught performing
    The final rites. We didn't draw lots this time.
    This piece of luck belongs to me, and no-one else.
    So now, my lord, she's yours, for you to examine   *420*
    And question as you wish. I've done my duty;
    It's someone else's problem from now on.
CREON: This girl? Where did you take her? What was she doing?
GUARD: Burying the man. That's all there is to know.
CREON: Are you serious? Do you know what you are saying?
GUARD: I saw her burying the corpse, the thing
    You had forbidden. What could be clearer than that?
CREON: You saw her? Captured her redhanded? How?

GUARD: It happened this way. When we returned to our posts
   With your dreadful threats still ringing in our ears   430
   We swept off every bit of dust that covered
   The corpse, and left the rotting carcass bare,
   Then sat down on the brow of a hill to windward
   Where the stench couldn't reach us. We kept ourselves lively
   By threatening each other with what would happen
   If anyone were careless in his duty.
   And so time passed, until the sun's bright disk
   Stood midway in the heavens, and the heat
   Began to burn us. Suddenly a whirlwind
   Raised a dust storm, a black blot on the sky,   440
   Which filled the plain, played havoc with the leaves
   Of every tree in sight, and choked the air.
   We shut our eyes and bore it; heaven sends
   These things to try us. When it had gone at last
   There was the girl; she gave a shrill sharp cry
   Like a bird in distress when it sees its bed
   Stripped of its young ones and the nest deserted.
   So she cried, when she saw the corpse left bare,
   Raising her voice in grief, and calling down
   Curses on the men who had done this thing.   450
   Then at once she brought handfuls of dry dust,
   Lifted a handsome vase, and poured from it
   The three drink-offerings to crown the dead.
   When we see it, out we run and close around her
   In a moment. She was not at all put out.
   We taxed her with what she had done, both then
   And earlier; she admitted everything,
   Which made me gald, but miserable too.
   Nothing makes you happier than to get yourself
   Out of trouble; but it's quite another thing   460
   To get friends into it. But there's nothing
   I wouldn't do, to keep myself from harm.
CREON: You there; yes, you, who dare not look me in the face;
   Do you admit this accusation or deny it?
ANTIGONE: Oh, I admit it. I make no denial.
CREON:(*to the* GUARD) Take yourself off, wherever you want to
     go,
   A free man. You are cleared of a serious charge.
   (*to* ANTIGONE) Now tell me, you, and keep your answers brief
   Did you know there was an order forbidding this?   470
ANTIGONE: Yes. How could I help it? Everybody knew.
CREON: And yet you dared to go against the law?
ANTIGONE: Why not? It was not Zeus who gave the order,
   And Justice living with the dead below

Has never given men a law like this.
Nor did I think that your pronouncements were
So powerful that mere man could override
The unwritten and unfailing laws of heaven.
These live, not for today and yesterday
But for all time; they came, no man knows whence.   *480*
There is no man's resolve I fear enough
To answer to the gods for breaking these.
I knew that I must die—how could I help it?
Even without your edict; but if I die
Before my time is up, I count it gain.
For when a person lives as I do, in the midst
Of evils, what can death be but gain?
And so for me to happen on this fate
Is grief not worth a thought; but if I had left
My mother's son to lie a homeless corpse,   *490*
Then had I grieved. I do not grieve for this.
If what I do seems foolish in your sight
It may be that a fool condemns my folly.
CHORUS: This is her father's willful spirit in her,
    Not knowing how to bend before the storm.
CREON: Come, you must learn that over-stubborn spirits
    Are those most often humbled. Iron that has
    Been hardened in the fire and cannot bend
    You will find the first to snap and fly in pieces.
    I have known high-mettled horses brought to order   *500*
    By a touch on the bridle. Pride is not for those
    Who live their lives at their neighbour's beck and call.
    This girl was already schooled in insolence
    When she disobeyed the official proclamation,
    And now she adds insult to injury
    By boasting of it, glorying in her crime.
    I swear, she is the man and I the woman
    If she keeps her victory and goes unpunished.
    No! Even though she be my sister's child,
    If she were bound to me by ties more close   *510*
    Than anyone who shares our household prayers
    She and that sister of hers will not escape
    The ultimate fate; for I accuse her too
    Of equal guilt in plotting this burial.
    So go and call her. I saw her indoors just now
    Delirious, not knowing what she was saying.

(*Exit* ATTENDANTS *to the palace*)

A guilty mind betrays itself beforehand
When men go plotting mischief in the dark.   *520*

But no less do I hate the criminal
Who is caught, and tries to glorify his crime.
ANTIGONE: What more would you take from me than my life?
CREON: Not a thing. When I have that, I have all I want.
ANTIGONE: Then what are you waiting for? Your arguments
Fall on deaf ears; I pray they always will.
My loyalties are meaningless to you.
Yet, in the world's eyes, what could I have done
To earn me greater glory, than to give
My brother burial? Everybody here   530
Would cheer me, if they were not dumb with fear.
But royalty, among so many blessings,
Has power to say and do whatever it likes.
CREON: These Thebans take a different view from yours.
ANTIGONE: Not they. They only curb their tongues for your sake.
CREON: Then why be different? Are you not ashamed?
ANTIGONE: Ashamed? Of paying homage to a brother?
CREON: Was not the man he killed your brother too?
ANTIGONE: My brother, by one mother, by one father.
CREON: Then why pay honors hateful in his eyes?   540
ANTIGONE: The dead man will not say he finds them hateful.
CREON: When you honor him no higher than a traitor?
ANTIGONE: It was his brother died, and not his slave.
CREON: Destroying Thebes; while he died to protect it.
ANTIGONE: It makes no difference. Death asks these rites.
CREON: But a hero asks more honor than a traitor.
ANTIGONE: Who knows? The dead may find no harm in this.
CREON: Even death cannot change hatred into love.
ANTIGONE: But I was born for love, and not for hate!
CREON: Then if you have to love, go down and love   550
The dead; while I live, no woman shall rule me!

(*Enter* ATTENDANTS *from the palace with* ISMENE)

CHORUS: Look, the gates open and Ismene comes
Weeping for love and sisterhood.
Her brows are clouded, shadowing
Her face flushed red, and teardrops
Fall on her lovely cheek.
CREON: And you, a viper lurking in my house,   560
Were sucking my life's blood, while I, unknowing,
Raised a twin scourge to drive me from my throne.
Come, answer me. Will you confess your share
In this burial, or deny all knowledge of it?
ISMENE: I did it—if my sister will allow me.
Half the blame is mine. I take it on myself.

ANTIGONE: No! Justice will not let you! You refused,
  And I denied you any part in it.
ISMENE: But now you are in trouble. I am not
  Ashamed to ride the storm out at your side.   *570*
ANTIGONE: Who did it, Hades and the dead can witness.
  I love not those who only talk of love.
ISMENE: No, sister, do not reject me. Let
  Me die with you and sanctify the dead.
ANTIGONE: You shall not share my death. You had no hand in this.
  Do not say you had. My death will be enough.
ISMENE: What joy have I in life when you are gone?
ANTIGONE: Ask Creon. All your care has been for him.
ISMENE: Why do you want to hurt me? It does no good.
ANTIGONE: You are right. If I mock you it is for my pain.   *580*
ISMENE: Then tell me how I can help you, even now.
ANTIGONE: Save yourself. I do not grudge you your escape.
ISMENE: Then is poor Ismene not to share your fate?
ANTIGONE: It was you who chose to live, and I to die.
ISMENE: At least I tried to move you from your choice.
ANTIGONE: One side approved your wisdom, the other mine.
ISMENE: And yet the offence is the same for both of us.
ANTIGONE: Be of good heart. You live; but I have been
  Dead for a long time now, to serve the dead.
CREON: Here are two fools, one lately come to folly,   *590*
  The other since the day that she was born.
ISMENE: Indeed, my lord, such sense as nature gives us
  Is not for ever. It goes in time of trouble.
CREON: Like yours, when you chose bad friends and evil ways.
ISMENE: How can I bear to live without my sister?
CREON: Sister? You have no sister. She is dead.
ISMENE: But will you kill your son's appointed bride?
CREON: I will. My son has other fields to plow.
ISMENE: He will never love another as he loved her.
CREON: No son of mine will wed an evil woman.   *600*
ISMENE: Haemon, my dearest! How your father wrongs you!
CREON: Let us have no further talk of marriages.
CHORUS: You will do it, then? You will rob your son of his bride?
CREON: Not I, but Death; yes, Death will break the match.
CHORUS: The decision stands, then, that the girl must die?
CREON: For you, and me. Let us have no more delay.
  Servants, take them inside. From this time on
  They must be women, not let out alone.
  Even the boldest of us turns and runs
  The moment he can see death closing in.   *610*

(*Exit* ATTENDANTS *with* ANTIGONE *and* ISMENE)

CHORUS: Blessed are those whose days have not tasted evil,
    For once the gods have set a house tottering
    The curse will never fade, but continues
    From generation unto generation,
    Like a storm rolling over the dark waters
    Driven by the howling Thracian gales,
    Stirring black mud from the bottom of the sea;   *620*
    And the wind-torn headlands answer back
    In a sullen roar, as the storm breaks over them.

    I look on the house of Labdacus
    And see how, from time immemorial,
    The sorrows of the living have been heaped upon
    The sorrows of those that died before them.
    One generation does not set another
    Free, but some god strikes them down
    And they have no means of deliverance.   *630*
    Over the last root of the house of Oedipus
    Shone a ray of hope; but now this too has been
    Laid low by a handful of bloody dust
    Demanded by the gods of the underworld,
    By unthinking words, and the heart's delirium.

    Zeus, what man's transgression can restrain your power,
    When neither Sleep, that encompasses all things,
    Nor the months' unwearied and god-ordered march
    Can arrest it? You do not grow old with the years   *640*
    But rule in shining splendor as Olympus' king.
    As it was in the past, this law will hold
    Tomorrow and until the end of time:
    That mortal life has a limited capacity.
    When it aims too high, then the curse will fall.

    For Hope, whose territory is unbounded,
    Brings comfort to many, but to many others
    Insane desires and false encouragement.
    A man may go blindly on his way   *650*
    Then walk into the fire and burn himself,
    And so disillusion comes.
    In his wisdom, someone coined the famous saying
    That when a god leads a man's mind on
    To destruction, sooner or later he comes
    To believe that evil is good, good evil,
    And then his days of happiness are numbered.

(*Enter* HAEMON)

    But here is Haemon, your youngest son.   *660*
    Does he come to grieve for the doom that has fallen

Upon Antigone, his promised bride,
To complain of the marriage that is taken from him?
CREON: We shall not need second sight to tell us that.
My son, have you heard that sentence has been passed
On your betrothed? Are you here to storm at me?
Or have I your good will, whatever I do?
HAEMON: Father, I am in your hands. You in your wisdom
Lay down for me the paths I am to follow.
There is no marriage in the world   670
That I would put before my good advisor.
CREON: Yes, keep this always in your heart, my son:
Accept your father's word as law in all things.
For that is why men pray to have
Dutiful children growing up at home,
To repay their father's enemies in kind
And honor those he loves no less than he does.
But a man is sowing troubles for himself
And enemies' delight—what else?—when he
Sires sons who bring no profit to their father.   680
So, my son, do not be led by passing fancy
To lose your head for a woman's sake. You know,
The warmth goes out of such embraces, when
An evil woman shares your home and bed.
False friends are deadlier than a festered wound.
So turn from her with loathing; let her find
A husband for herself among the dead.
For now that I have caught her, the only one
Of all the city to disobey me openly,
My people shall not see me break my word.   690
I shall kill her. Let her plead the sacred ties
Of kinship! If I bring up my own family
To flout me, there will be no holding others.
A man who sees his family obey him
Will have authority in public matters.
But if anyone offends, or violates the laws,
No word of praise shall he ever have from me.
Whoever the state appoints must be obeyed,
In little things or great things, right or wrong.
I should have confidence that such a man   700
Would be as good a ruler as a subject
And in a hail of spears would stand his ground
Where he was put, a comrade you could trust.
But disobedience is the worst of evils;
It is this that ruins cities, it is this
That makes homes desolate, turns brothers in arms
To headlong rout. But those who are preserved

Owe their lives, the greater part of them, to discipline.
And so we must stand up for law and order,
Not let ourselves be worsted by a woman.   710
If yield we must, then let us yield to a man.
Let no-one call us woman's underlings.
CHORUS: Unless the years have robbed me of my wits
    You seem to have sound sense in what you say.
HAEMON: Father, the gods endow mankind with reason,
    The highest quality that we possess.
    It is not for me to criticize your words.
    I could not do it, and would hate to try.
    And yet, two heads are sometimes better than one;
    At least, it is my place to watch, on your behalf,   720
    All that men do and say and criticize.
    Fear of your frown prevents the common man
    From saying anything that would displease you,
    But I can hear these murmurs in the dark,
    The feeling in the city for this girl.
    "No woman" they say "has ever deserved death less,
    Or died so shamefully in a noble cause.
    When her brother fell in the slaughter, she would not
    Leave him unburied, to provide a meal
    For carrion dogs or passing birds of prey.   730
    Is she not, then, deserving golden honors?"
    This is what men are whispering to each other.
    Father, there is nothing dearer to my heart
    Than your continuing prosperity.
    What finer ornament could children have
    Than a father's proud success—or he, than theirs?
    So wear an open mind; do not suppose
    That you are right, and everyone else is wrong.
    A man who thinks he has monopoly
    Of wisdom, no rival in speech or intellect,   740
    Will turn out hollow when you look inside him.
    However wise he is, it is no disgrace
    To learn, and give way gracefully.
    You see how trees that bend to winter floods
    Preserve themselves, save every twig unbroken,
    But those that stand rigid perish root and branch,
    And also how the man who keeps his sails
    Stretched taut, and never slackens them, overturns
    And finishes his voyage upside down.
    Let your anger rest; allow us to persuade you.   750
    If a young man may be permitted his opinion
    I should say it would be best for everyone
    To be born omniscient; but otherwise—

And things have a habit of falling out differently—
It is also good to learn from good advice.
CHORUS: My lord, if he speaks to the point you ought to listen,
And Haemon, you to him. There is sense on both sides.
CREON: And is a man of my age to be taught
What I should think by one so young as this?
HAEMON: Nothing that is not right; young though I may be,   *760*
You should judge by my behavior, not my age.
CREON: What sort of behavior is it to honor rebels?
HAEMON: I would never suggest that the guilty should be honored.
CREON: And is she not infected with this disease?
HAEMON: The people of Thebes unanimously deny it.
CREON: Will the city tell me how I am to rule?
HAEMON: Listen to that! Who is being childish now?
CREON: Is the state to listen to any voice but mine?
HAEMON: There is no state, when one man is its master.
CREON: Is not the state supposed to be the ruler's?   *770*
HAEMON: You would do well as the monarch of a desert.
CREON: It seems the woman has a champion here.
HAEMON: Then you are the woman! It is you I care about!
CREON: Insolent cub! Will you argue with your father?
HAEMON: I will, when I see you falling into error.
CREON: Am I wrong to respect my own prerogatives?
HAEMON: It is no respect, when you offend the gods.
CREON: How contemptible, to give way to a woman!
HAEMON: At least I do not give way to temptation.
CREON: But every word you say is a plea for her.   *780*
HAEMON: And for you, and for me, and for the gods below.
CREON: You will never marry her this side of the grave.
HAEMON: Then she will die—and take somebody with her.
CREON: So! Do you dare to go so far? Are you threatening me?
HAEMON: Is it threatening, to protest a wrong decision?
CREON: You shall pay for this. A fine one to teach wisdom!
HAEMON: If you were not my father, I should call you a fool.
CREON: You woman's slave; do not try to wheedle me!
HAEMON: Would you stop everyone from speaking but yourself?
CREON: Indeed! I tell you, by the gods above us,   *790*
You shall pay for using such language to your father.

(*to the* ATTENDANTS)

Bring this abomination out, and let her die
Here, in his presence, at her bridegroom's side.
HAEMON: No, she will never perish at my side,
So do not think it. From this moment on
Your eyes will never see my face again,
So rave away, to those who have more patience!

(Exit)   *800*

CHORUS: My lord, he has gone away in angry haste.
    Young tempers are fierce when anything provokes them.
CREON: Let him do or dream all men can do and more.
    He shall never save those girls from punishment.
CHORUS: Do you mean to put the two of them to death?
CREON: You are right to ask. Not her whose hands are clean.
CHORUS: And how do you intend to kill the other?
CREON: I shall take her where nobody ever comes
    And shut her in a rocky vault alive,   *810*
    With the minimum of food that is permitted
    To stop pollution falling on the city.
    There she may pray to Death, the only god
    She worships, and perhaps he may forgive her.
    If not, she will learn—but when it is too late—
    That honoring the dead is wasted effort.

(Exit)

CHORUS: Love, whom we fight but never conquer,   *820*
    Love, the ravager of proud possessions
    Who keep eternal vigilance
    In the softness of a young girl's cheek,
    You go wherever the wide seas go
    And among the cottages of country-dwellers.
    None of the immortal gods can escape you,
    Nor man, whose life is as a single day,
    And, to whoever takes you in, comes madness.

    The minds of honest men you lead   *830*
    Out of the paths of virtue to destruction.
    Father is at odds with son
    And it is you who set this quarrel in their hearts.
    One glance from the eyes of a ready bride
    Bright with desire, and a man is enslaved.
    On the throne of the eternal laws
    Love has a place, for there the goddess Aphrodite
    Decides men's fates, and there is no withstanding her.

(Enter ATTENDANTS *with* ANTIGONE *bound)*   *840*

    It is my turn now; at a sight like this
    The voice of the laws cannot hold me back
    Or stop the tears from pouring down my cheeks.
    Here comes Antigone, on her way
    To the bridal-chamber where all must go to rest.
ANTIGONE: See me, citizens of my fatherland, as I go out

On my last journey; as I look my last on the sunlight,
Never to see it again; Death, who puts all to sleep,
Takes me as I am,   850
With life still in me, to the shores of the midnight lake,
A bride with no choir to accompany her way,
With no serenade at the bedroom door;
I am to marry with the King of Darkness!
CHORUS: And so you go with honor and praise
Below to the caverns of the dead;
No sickness has wasted you away,
You do not pay the wages of the sword,
But will go to death a law unto yourself
As no human being has done before you.   860
ANTIGONE: I have heard of one, a stranger among us from
Phrygia,
Tantalus' daughter, and her sad end on Mount Sipylus,
Growing slowly into stone as a tree is wrapped with ivy.
And the story goes
That her body pines in unceasing snow and rain
And tears from her streaming eyes pour upon her breast.
Her fate is mine; like her I go to rest.
CHORUS: But she was a goddess, born of gods,
And we are mortals, mortal born.   870
When a woman has to die, it is
A great distinction, for her to share
The lot of those who are one removed from gods,
Both here, and in the manner of her death.
ANTIGONE: Oh, you make fun of me! Gods of my fathers!
Must you laugh in my face? Can you not wait till I am gone?
Oh, my city; Thebans, proud in your possessions;
Chariot-thundering plain, you at least will bear witness
How no friends mourn for my passing, by what laws
I go to my rock-barred prison, my novel tomb.   880
Luckless Antigone, an alien in both worlds,
Among the living and among the dead!
CHORUS: You have driven yourself to the furthest limit of daring
And run, my child, against the high throne
Where justice sits; and great has been your fall.
Perhaps you are paying the price of your father's sin.
ANTIGONE: You have touched the memory bitterest in my mind,
The dirge for my father that is never finished,
For the fate of us all, the famous house of Labdacus.
Oh, the curse born   890
In a mother's bed; doomed mother, sleeping with her son,
My father. Poor Antigone, what parents brought you
Into this world! Now I go to join them, accursed, unwed.

Oh, my brother, how ill-fated was your marriage.
Your dead hand has reached out to destroy the living.
CHORUS: Pious actions are a sort of piety.
  But a man who has authority in his keeping
  Can permit no offence against authority.
  Your own willful temper has destroyed you.
ANTIGONE: Friendless, unwept, without a wedding song,   900
  They call for me, and I must tread my road.
  Eye of heaven, light of the holy sun,
  I may look on you no longer.
  There is no friend to lament my fate,
  No-one to shed a tear for me.

(*Enter* CREON)

CREON: Let me tell you, if songs and dirges before dying
  Did any good, we should never hear the end of them.   910
  Take her, and be quick about it. Lock her up
  In her cavern tomb, as I have ordered you,
  And leave her alone—to die, if she prefers,
  Or live in her tomb, for that will be her home.
  Whatever becomes of her our hands are clean.
  But in this world she has a place no longer.
ANTIGONE: Tomb, bridal-chamber, my eternal home
  Hewn from the rock, where I must go to meet
  My own, those many who have died, and been
  Made welcome by Persephone in the shadow-world.   920
  I am the last, my death the worst of all
  Before my allotted span of years has run.
  But as I go I have this hope in heart,
  That my coming may be welcome to my father,
  My mother; welcome, dearest brother, to you.
  For when you died, with my own hands I washed
  And robed your bodies, and poured offerings
  Over your graves. Now this is my reward,
  Polyneices, for rendering such services to you.
  Yet wisdom would approve my honoring you.   930
  If I were a mother; if my husband's corpse
  Were left to rot, I never should have dared
  Defy the state to do what I have done.
  What principle can justify such words?
  Why, if my husband died I could take another;
  Someone else could give me a child if I lost the first;
  But Death has hidden my mother and father from me.
  No brother can be born to me again.
  Such was the principle by which I chose
  To honor you; and for this Creon judges me guilty   940

Of outrage and transgression, brother mine!
And now he seizes me to lead me off,
Robbed of my bride-bed and my marriage song.
I shall never marry, never be a mother.
And so, in misery, without a friend,
I go still living to the pit of death.
Which one of heaven's commandments have I broken?
Why should I look to the gods any longer
After this? To whom am I to turn for help
When doing right has branded me a sinner?   950
If the gods approve what is happening to me,
After the punishment I shall know my fault,
But if my judges are wrong, I wish them no worse
Than what they have unjustly done to me.
CHORUS: Still the same tempestuous spirit
  Carrying her along.
CREON: Then those who are charged with taking her
  Shall have cause to repent their slowness.
ANTIGONE: Oh, that word has brought me
  Very near my death.   960
CREON: I can offer you no hope.
  Your punishment stands unchanged.
ANTIGONE: City of my father in the land of Thebes,
  The time has come, they take me away.
  Look, princes of Thebes; this is the last
  Daughter of the house of your kings.
  See what I suffer, and at whose hands,
  For doing no less than heaven bids us do.

(*Exit* ATTENDANTS, *leading off* ANTIGONE)   970

CHORUS: So Danae in her beauty endured the change
  From the bright sky to the brazen cell,
  And there she was hidden, lost to the living world.
  Yet she was of proud birth too, my daughter,
  And the seed of Zeus was trusted to her keeping
  That fell in golden rain.
  But the power of fate is terrible.
  Wealth cannot keep you from its reach, nor war,
  Nor city walls, nor the dark sea-beaten ships.   980

  And the king of the Edonians, the fiery-tempered
  Son of Dryas, was held in bondage
  For his savage taunts, at Dionysus' will,
  Clapped in a rocky cell; and so the full
  Flowering of his madness passed from him gradually
  And he came to recognize

The god he had insulted in his frenzy.
He had sought to stop the women when the god was in them
And the Bacchic torches, and enraged the piping Muses.   *990*

And by the Dark Rocks at the meeting of two waters
Lie the shores of Bosporos and Thracian Salmydessos.
Here was a sight for the eyes
Of the city's neighbour, Ares—
The two sons of Phineus, blinded
By stepmother's fury, their sightless eyes
Appealing for vengeance, calling down a curse
On her bloody hands and the shuttle turned dagger.
        1000
Pining in grief they bewailed their cruel fate.
How sad their mother's marriage; but her line
Went back to the ancient family
Of Erechtheus—she was a child
Of the North Wind, nursed in distant caves,
Who played with her father's storms, a child of the gods
Running swift as a steed upon the high hills.
Yet on her too the gray Fates laid their hand, my daughter.

(*Enter* TEIRESIAS, *led by a boy*)   *1010*

TEIRESIAS: Princes of Thebes, we have come here side by side,
    One pair of eyes for both of us. That is how
    Blind men must walk, supported by a guide.
CREON: What news have you for us, old Teiresias?
TEIRESIAS: I will tell you. Listen when the prophet speaks.
CREON: I have never yet disregarded your advice.
TEIRESIAS: And so have kept Thebes safely on her course.
CREON: I know my debt to you, and acknowledge it.
TEIRESIAS: Then listen. Once more you stand on the verge of   *1020*
    doom.
CREON: What do you mean? I shudder at your words.
TEIRESIAS: You will know, when you hear the warnings of my
    art.
  As I took my place upon my ancient seat
  Of augury, where all the birds come flocking,
  I heard a noise I had never heard before,
  Their cries distorted in a scream of fury,
  And I knew that they were clawing, killing each other;
  The whirring of wings told a tale too clear.   *1030*
  I was frightened, and went at once to light the altar
  And offer sacrifice; but from my offerings
  No flame sprang up. Fat melted on the thighs
  And oozed in slow drops down to quench the embers

And smoked and spluttered; and the gall was scattered
Into the air. The streaming thighs were raw,
Bare of the fat which once enfolded them.
And so my rites had failed. I asked a sign
And none was given, as I learnt from this boy here.
He is my guide, as I am guide to others.   1040
Your counsels brought this sickness on our state.
The altars of our city and our homes
All are defiled by dogs and birds of prey
Who feed on Oedipus' unhappy son.
And so the gods no longer accept our prayers,
Our sacrifices, our burnt offerings.
The birds no longer warn us with their cries;
They have drunk the fat blood of a slaughtered man.
Think on these things, my son. To err is human,
But when we err, then happy is the man   1050
Who is not stubborn, and has sense enough
To remedy the fault he has committed.
Give the dead his due, and do not stab a man
When he is down. What good to kill him twice?
I have your interests at heart, and speak
To help you. No advisor is more welcome
Than when you profit from his good advice.
CREON: You circle me like archers, all of you,
And I am made your target! Even the prophets
Conspire against me. They have long been using me   1060
As merchandise, a thing to buy and sell!
If profit is what you seek, go look abroad!
There is silver in Sardis, gold in India.
But you will not bury this man in his grave,
No, not if the eagles of great Zeus himself
Should lay his flesh before their master's throne.
Not even that defilement frightens me
Enough to bury him, for well I know
No human being can defile the gods.
The wisest of us, old Teiresias,   1070
Sink to the depths, when they hide their evil thoughts
In fair-phrased speeches for the sake of money.
TEIRESIAS: If men only knew, would only realize—
CREON: Knew what? Another pronouncement! Let us hear!
TEIRESIAS: Good counsel is worth more than worldly riches.
CREON: Just as stupidity is the greatest harm.
TEIRESIAS: Yet that is the sickness that has tainted you.
CREON: I do not want to call a prophet names.
TEIRESIAS: But you do, when you say my prophecies are false.
CREON: Men of your tribe were always moneyseekers.   1080

TEIRESIAS: And men of yours have always been dictators.
CREON: Have you forgotten you are speaking to your king?
TEIRESIAS: No. It was because of me that you saved Thebes.
CREON: You are a wise prophet but in love with evil.
TEIRESIAS: You will move me to tell the unutterable secret.
CREON: Tell it—as long as there is no profit in it!
TEIRESIAS: I do not think so—as far as you are concerned.
CREON: You will make no money out of my decision.
TEIRESIAS: Then listen well. Before the sun's swift wheels
  Have numbered many more days of your life,   1090
  You will surrender corpse for corpses, one
  Begotten from the seed of your own loins,
  Because you have sent this world to join the next
  And cruelly lodged the living in the grave,
  But keep Death's property on earth, unburied,
  Robbed of its honor, an unhallowed corpse.
  This is not for you to say, nor for the gods
  In heaven, but in doing this you wrong them.
  And so the Avengers, Furies sent by Death
  And by the gods, lie in waiting to destroy you   1100
  And snare you in the evils you have worked.
  So watch, and you will see if I am bribed
  To say these things. Before much time is out
  The cries of men and womenfolk will fill your house.
  And hatred rises against you in every city
  Whose mangled sons were left for burial
  To dogs, or beasts, or birds of prey, who bore
  Their stinking breath to every soldier's home.
  Archer you call me; then these are the arrows
  I send into your heart, since you provoke me,   1110
  Sure arrows; you will not escape their sting.
  Boy, take me to my home again, and leave him
  To vent his fury on some younger man,
  And learn to moderate his tongue, and bear
  A better spirit in his breast than now.

(*Exit*)

CHORUS: He has gone, my lord; his prophecies were fearful.
  As long as I remember, since my hair   1120
  Has turned from black to white, this man has never
  Made one false prophecy about our city.
CREON: I know it as well as you. My mind is troubled.
  To yield is fatal; but to resist and bring
  A curse on my proud spirit—that too is hard.
CHORUS: Son of Menoeceus, you must listen to good advice.
CREON: What's to be done? Tell me and I will do it.

CHORUS: Go free the girl from her prison in the rocks
  And give the corpse an honorable tomb.
CREON: Is this your advice? You think that I should yield?   *1130*
CHORUS: Yes, lord, as quickly as you can. The gods
  Move fast to cut short man's stupidity.
CREON: It is hard; but I resign my dear resolve.
  We cannot fight against necessity.
CHORUS: Go do it now; do not leave it to another.
CREON: I will go as I am. Servants, be off with you,
  Each and every one; take axes in your hands
  And go to the hill you can see over there.
  Now that my judgment has been reversed
  I shall be there to free her, as I imprisoned her.   *1140*
  Perhaps after all the gods' ways are the best
  And we should keep them till our lives are done.

(*Exit*)

CHORUS: You who are known by many names,
  Who blessed the union of Cadmus' daughter,
  Begotten by Zeus the Thunderer, guarding
  The land of Italy famed in story,
  King of Eleusis, in the land-locked plain   *1150*
  Of Deo where the wanderer finds welcome,
  Bacchus whose home is Thebes, mother-city of Bacchanals,
  By Ismenus' tranquil waters where the fierce dragon's teeth
    were sown.

The fitful gleam of the torchlight finds you
Amid the smoke on the slopes of the forked mountains
Where tread your worshippers, the nymphs
Of Corycia, by Castalia's stream.
From Nysa's ivy-mantled slopes,   *1160*
From the green shore carpeted with vines
You come, and they are no human lips that cry
Your name, as you make your progress through the ways of
  Thebes.

For it is she you honor above all other cities,
And your mother too, who died by a bolt from heaven.
And now the whole city labors under
This grievous malady, come with healing feet
Down from the slopes of Parnassus or the sounding sea.   *1170*

Conductor of the stars, whose breath is made of fire,
Lord of the voices that cry aloud in the night,
Son born of Zeus, appear to us, oh lord,

With the Thyiads your servants who in nightly abandon
Dance before you, Iacchus, the bringer of all blessings.

(*Enter* MESSENGER)

MESSENGER: You who live by Amphion's and Cadmus' walls,   1180
　No man's estate is ever so assured
　That I would set it down as good or bad.
　Fortune can raise us, fortune cast us down,
　Depending on our luck, from day to day,
　But for how long? No man can see the future.
　For Creon was once blessed, as I count blessings;
　He saved the land of Cadmus from its enemies,
　Became its sole and undisputed king
　And ruled, proud father of a princely line.
　Now everything is gone. A man who forfeits   1190
　All of life's pleasures I can count no longer
　Among the living, but as dead in life.
　So stack your house with treasures as you will
　And live in royal pomp; when joy is absent
　I would not give the shadow of a breath
　For all the rest, compared with joy alone.
CHORUS: What is this new grief you come to tell us?
MESSENGER: Death; and the living must answer to the dead.
CHORUS: Who killed? And who has been killed? Tell us.
MESSENGER: Haemon, and by a hand he knew too well.   1200
CHORUS: By his father's hand? Or was it by his own?
MESSENGER: His own, in anger for his father's murder.
CHORUS: Oh prophet, how much truth was in your words.
MESSENGER: That is how things are. For the rest you must
　　decide.

(*Enter* EURYDICE)

CHORUS: And here is Eurydice, the unhappy wife
　Of Creon; she is coming from the palace.   1210
EURYDICE: People of Thebes, I heard what you were saying
　As I was going from my house to offer
　Devotions at the goddess Pallas' shrine.
　I stood there with my hand about to draw
　The bolt, and my ears were greeted by this tale
　Of family disaster. Terrified,
　I fell back swooning in my servants' arms.
　But tell again what you were telling then.
　The first grief is over. I shall listen now.
MESSENGER: Dear lady, I shall tell you what I saw   1220
　Omitting nothing, exactly as it happened.
　Why should I give false comfort? You would soon

Know I was lying? Truth is always best.
I attended on your husband to direct his way
Across the plain, where Polyneices' corpse,
Mangled by dogs, still lay unburied.
We prayed the goddess of the roads, and Pluto,
To have mercy on us and restrain their wrath,
Performed the ritual washing of the corpse,
Cut branches and cremated what was left of him   1230
And raised a hillock of his native soil
Above him; then made for the cavern, where the girl
Waited for Death to share her rocky bed.
Far off, one of us heard a piercing cry
Coming from that unholy bridal chamber
And came to report it to our master Creon.
As he approached, a cry of anguish came
To greet him, half-heard words; he groaned aloud
And in his grief said "Creon, you are doomed;
Can my fear be true? Is the path I tread today   1240
To be the bitterest path I ever trod?
The voice that greets me is my son's; men, run ahead,
Make for the tomb; there is an opening
Where someone has wrenched the stones away. Squeeze
    inside
To the cell-mouth, see if it is Haemon's voice
I hear, or if the gods are mocking me."
And so, at our despairing master's bidding,
We made the search, and in the farthest corner
Of the tomb we saw her, hanged by the neck   1250
In a noose of twisted linen, soft as silk,
While Haemon stood with his arms clasped round her waist
Weeping for his bride now with the dead,
For his father's actions and his foredoomed marriage.
When he saw him his father gave a fearful cry
And went to him and called to him through his tears
"Oh Haemon, what is this that you have done?
What has possessed you? Have you gone insane?
Come out, my son, I beg you, I implore you."
But the boy glared back at him wild-eyed,   1260
Spat in his face, and without a word of answer
Drew his cross-hilted sword and thrust at him
But missed, as he jumped aside. Then in wild remorse
The poor wretch threw his weight upon the point
And drove it half into his side. As long as sense
Was left him, he clasped the girl in a limp embrace
And as his breath came hard, a jet of blood
Spurted from his lips, and ran down her pallid cheek,

The bodies lie in each others arms. He has
Claimed his bride—in the next world, not in this—   1270
And he has given proof to all mankind
That of all human ills, bad counsel is the worst.

(*Exit* EURYDICE *to the palace*)

CHORUS: What would you make of this? Eurydice
   Has vanished without a word, good or bad.
MESSENGER: It alarms me too. Yet I nourish the hope
   That now she knows her loss she does not think it proper
   To mourn in public, but has gone inside   1280
   To set her maids to mourn for her bereavement,
   She has learnt discretion and will not be foolish.
CHORUS: I am not so sure. To me this unnatural silence
   Is as ominous as the wildest excess of grief.
MESSENGER: Well, I shall go in and see, in case
   She is keeping some dark purpose hidden from us
   In her grief-torn heart. You are right to be concerned.
   It is just as dangerous to be too quiet.

(*Exit*)   1290

CHORUS: But here is Creon coming himself
   Bringing testimony all too plain,
   The work of his and no other's madness,
   If I may speak out, and his own wrongdoing.

(*Enter* CREON *with servants bearing the body of* HAEMON)

CREON: Oh deadly end of stubborn sins
   Born in the blindness of understanding!   1300
   See here, a son dead, a father who killed him.
   Oh the fatal workings of my mind;
   My son, to die so young
   So soon to be taken from me
   By my folly, not by yours.
CHORUS: Perhaps you see now too late what was best.
CREON: Yes, I have learned my bitter lesson.
   Some god must have chosen that moment
   To crush me under his heavy hand
   And hurl me into cruelty's ways,   1310
   Riding roughshod over all I held dear.
   Oh, mankind, you were born to suffer!

(*Enter* SECOND MESSENGER *from the palace*)

MESSENGER: Master, you do not come empty-handed; but there
     is
   More in store for you. You bear one load of grief
   But soon you will see another, in your home.

CREON: My grief is here; is any worse to come?   1320
MESSENGER: Your wife is dead—true mother to her son
  To the last, poor lady—by a wound still fresh.
CREON: Oh Death, ever-open door,
  Do you have no mercy on me?
  You who bring this tale of death and sorrow
  What is this you are saying to me?
  What news is this, my boy?
  My wife is dead? One more
  To add to the pile of corpses?
MESSENGER: See for yourself. It is no longer hidden.   1330

(*The body of* EURYDICE *is brought out*)

CREON: Oh, here is another, a second blow.
  What has fate in store for me after this?
  I have but this moment lifted
  My child in my arms, and again
  I see a corpse brought out to greet me.
  Oh wretched mother; oh my child.
MESSENGER: There she lies at the altar, knife-point in her heart.
  She mourned the noble fate of Megareus,   1340
  The first to die, then his; then closed her eyes
  For ever, and with her dying breath called down
  A curse on you for murdering her sons.
CREON: I am shaken with fear. Will nobody take
  His two-edged sword and run me through?
  For, oh, I am sick at heart.
  Sorrow has made me his own.
MESSENGER: Yes, she whose body you see lying here
  Laid the deaths of both sons at your door.
CREON: And what was the violent manner of her leaving?   1350
MESSENGER: Her own hand drove the knife into her heart
  When she had heard them singing her son's dirge.
CREON: Nobody else can bear the guilt,
  No-one can take the blame from me.
  I killed you, I, your unhappy father,
  This is the truth.
  Servants, take me away from this place.
  Let me stay not a moment longer.
  Creon has ceased to exist.
CHORUS: Good advice, if there can be any good in evil.   1360
  In present trouble the shortest way is best.
CREON: Let it come. What better fate could I ask
  Than the fate which ushers in my life's last day?
  Let it come, the best of all;
  Let me never see tomorrow's dawn.

CHORUS: All in its proper time. We have things to see to
    Here and now. The future is in other hands.
CREON: But everything I want was in that prayer.
CHORUS: Save your prayers. Whatever is going to happen
    Is already fated. Nobody can change it.   1370
CREON: Come, take this hot-headed fool away,
    A fool who killed you, my son, in my blindness,
    And you too, who are lying here; poor fool.
    I do not know
    Which way I am to take, where to lean;
    My hands can do nothing right;
    I am crushed beneath my fate.

(*Exit*)
                                                                1380
CHORUS: To be happy it is first of all necessary
    To be wise, and always remember
    To give the gods their due,
    The measure of a proud man's boasting
    Shall be the measure of his punishment
    And teach him late in life
    The nature of true wisdom.

Understanding *Antigone*

The characters of Antigone and Creon developed by Sophocles are charismatic and believable. Creon, on the one hand, is a new king who needs to establish a reputation. Being new in so demanding a role, it is understandable that he is a bit tentative about his public image and is looking for an opportunity to establish his authority. Wanting to shake off the scourge of civil war, he hopes to unify the country and get everything back to normal as soon as possible. In so doing, he proclaims a death penalty for anyone defying his burial decree. Little does he suspect that the first law breaker will be Antigone. Once he learns that Polyneices' body has been buried and that Antigone is the guilty party, we see that he is as stubborn as Antigone. He has many opportunities to change her fate and therefore alter his own destiny, but he holds fast to his decree, thus ensuring a tragic conclusion.

Antigone is young and boldly moralistic. After deciding she will bury her brother, she is proudly defiant as she realizes the full weight of her decision. Knowing that she faces certain death, she is satisfied because she has obeyed the law of the gods. When her sister offers to share her guilt, she adamantly refuses. Antigone decides she will risk death at the hands of the king in order to do what is morally right for her brother. She is young, strong willed, and brave, and she refuses to share her deed with anyone. She is satisfied with her decision, and once the chain of events is set in motion, she makes no effort to hide or to disclaim her actions.

Sophocles dealt at great length with the Oedipus curse in three plays called the Theban Trilogy. *Antigone* is the final play of that set. The curse of Oedipus—that he would murder his father and marry his mother—taints each of the plays. In *Antigone,* several allusions are made to the bad blood in the house of Oedipus. The chorus warns us early in the play that "once the gods have set a house tottering, the curse will never fade, but continues from generation unto generation." And later they chide, "Perhaps you are paying the price of your father's sin." In this trilogy, Oedipus must play out his fate. He tries to avoid it, but only turns back to face it. He is an inherently good man, yet a tragic character who must suffer for his sins. That suffering continues with his daughter, Antigone, and Creon as well.

We cannot help but admire the responsibility Antigone feels for her brother's soul. She says, "I intend to bury him. It is a noble way to die. I shall lie with him for love, as he loved me, a criminal, but guiltless; for the dead have longer claims upon me than the living." She knows from the outset that she is choosing death for herself, but she feels guiltless. She feels her responsibility is to fulfill the ritual expectations of her religious belief. She holds this duty above that of obedience to an earthly king. She says of Creon's law, "It was not Zeus who gave the order." She feels her decision is right and just. Antigone anticipates that she will die a glorious death and that her death will be remembered and hailed as a great feat by the people. And indeed, the chorus reflects that this is so. Haemon, Creon's son and Antigone's betrothed, reports that the people say, "No woman . . . has ever deserved death less, or died so shamefully in a noble cause." But once Antigone sets this chain of events in motion, the inevitable will take place. As she is led away to the tomb, she says, "Death . . . take me as I am." She is ready to die. Indeed she seems satisfied, perhaps even victorious, to be claiming a fate she deserves.

As we watch Creon's handling of this potentially explosive situation, we are aware of his lack of experience in matters of state. His desire to be a good king is probably a genuine and well-founded ambition, yet we can't help but wish he would bend the rules a little. He says unequivocally, however, that he has no time "for anyone who puts his popularity before his country." He feels justified in punishing a treasonous act by denial of burial, although he is aware of the spiritual implications of his act. We sense that Creon is taken aback when he learns that Antigone has defied him. He sends the guard away before he speaks to her so that he may deal with her in private. We hope that he may reconsider his threat. With his decision to entomb Antigone alive, we hope that she may survive. A second glimmer of hope for a reprieve for Antigone comes with Tieresias's advice to Creon, "To err is human, but when we err, then happy is the man who is not stubborn, and has sense enough to remedy the fault he has committed."

At this point we are more aware than ever of the two strong wills at war here. Who can we justify as being "right"? Civil law and moral law have come into conflict, and tragedy will result. So the blind sage's advice falls on deaf ears. And Creon's stubborn determination to see Antigone dead reaps for Creon two more corpses—those of his son and wife. he begs for the knife to be driven into his ribs to end the pain of his own guilt.

The Dionysian theatre and, concurrently, the genius of Sophocles developed during a period of religious stirring in which people sought ways to please and to appease the gods. This helps us appreciate the tragic and heroic story of *Antigone*. Sophocles' play is held in high regard for many reasons, not the least of which is the bravado and spirit of a young girl committed to an ideal. Yet we must also give King Creon his due. He, too, is a member of the house of Oedipus. He wishes to be a good king and a wise counselor. The play shows us how problematic it can be when two strong-willed individuals come into conflict and it attempts to deal fairly and equally with the strife created when religious law comes into direct conflict with civil law.

In acknowledging the similarity of the characters of Antigone and Creon, it is difficult to determine who is the protagonist. In Aristotle's classic definition, three elements are required: the protagonist must be highborn, aspire to lofty ambitions, and yet be hindered by some flaw of character. Both Creon and Antigone possess these characteristics. Both are highborn members of the family of Oedipus. Both have lofty ambitions: Creon aspires to be a good king and unify the country; Antigone desires proper spiritual rest for her brother. Both characters suffer because of their strong-willed personalities. One writer has said, "Creon's tragedy is dwelt upon at such length not because Creon is the main character of the play—he is vastly overshadowed by Antigone—

but because the dreadfulness of his fate is the final justification of Antigone.''[10] Another author has stated:

> Sophocles . . . shows us again what happens when the ostensibly good man succumbs to pride. . . . Creon, who is the protagonist rather than Antigone, and who is a kind of second Oedipus in his ruthless pursuit of what he thinks is right, brings final ruin to the House of Oedipus, destroying not only himself, his wife, his son, the love of these for him, but the very person his son is going to marry and the one who is most dedicated to the right— Antigone.[11]

In this play, Sophocles has created two of the most tragic characters of all time. His skillful development of the story around Antigone in the beginning and then its obvious shift to Creon typifies the basic theme conflict of the play: Should we follow divine law or secular law? Antigone is an admirable character who fulfills her moral obligation. Creon is the strong ruler who enforces the civil law. Both are destroyed. But it is Creon who lives on to suffer in this destruction as Oedipus did before him. Antigone is at rest.

From a careful, line-by-line analysis, we can appreciate the craftsmanship of the author. We can see how finely developed a character can be with only a few carefully chosen, detailed lines of dialogue. We can compare and attempt to balance the two protagonistic characters Sophocles gives us. Best of all, we can experience and benefit from the catharsis of its protagonists. In the wrenching agony of Creon's self-knowledge at the end of the play, we feel that justice has been done. In the best tradition of Greek tragedy, there is hope in the end that good may outweigh evil.

Elizabethan Tragedy: *Othello*

With the defeat of the Spanish Armada and the ascension to the throne of a brilliant and thrifty queen, England prepared the way for the greatest period of dramatic excellence the world has seen. Elizabeth I was a charismatic queen. She not only reigned, she governed. She took an active part in the life of the country and encouraged the development of the arts. So long as it cost her no money, she was an earnest patron of the theatre.

The plays of Elizabethan England reflected the greatness of the monarchy. Prior to Elizabeth's ascension, England had experienced the reign of ''bloody'' Mary, the weakness of Edward VI, and the excesses of Henry VIII. As the national life of a country determines its achievements in the arts, those years of English history passed without artistic moment. But with the Elizabethan period came a renewed zest for the arts. Elizabeth's name has become synonymous with a glorious period of dramatic history.

It was during this time of renewed and refreshed spirit of artistic endeavor that the famous dramatist William Shakespeare created his dramatic literature. Shakespeare, born and reared in Stratford-on-Avon, thought of himself as a dramatist of sorts, but was an actor before he tried his hand at writing. During his lifetime, he filled many of the positions in the theatre, including manager, director, actor, and of course writer. With Elizabethan England as a stimulus for his vivid imagination and the colorful families of royal lineages as subjects, Shakespeare created some of the finest dramatic writing of all time.

The plays of Shakespeare offer us characters and themes more believably human than those that preceded them. Aristotle's dramatic protagonists are highborn personifying lofty ambition. Sophocles' Theban Trilogy revolves around the destinies of characters who live out a predestined and often horrible fate. Inherent in this ancient drama is a mystical obeisance to unknown and feared gods. The plays present a sense of the powerlessness of man in comparison to the forces of the cosmos. But in the sixteenth century, we see a different kind of tragedy evolving. Shakespeare's dramatic figures deal more directly with the mind and spirit of man. They find their strength or weakness within themselves. The base characters seem inherently evil and do not, as their Greek predecessors, anticipate divine intervention. George Freedly says, "The importance of Shakespeare to us lies in his universality of thought, his comprehension of human motives and the frailties of the flesh, his masterly depiction of character through his majestic lines and economical use of words."[12]

Shakespeare wrote tragedies of persons of "high degree." This does not necessarily correspond to Aristotle's "highborn." While the Greek protagonist was always of royal blood, the Elizabethan protagonist tended to be a public figure held in high regard. Julius Caesar was a Roman statesman held in great favor. Romeo and Juliet represented noted families of their period. Othello, although a Moor, was a converted Christian, a wealthy merchant, and a valuable man in the military.

Shakespeare created a kind of tragedy that affected not just a family, but often the fate of a government or nation. In his plays, one person's behavior could have great bearing on the lives of others. And while there is a sense of fate at work, we always feel as if the protagonist reserves the right to make choices in order to alter that fate. In the words of A. C. Bradley, "The centre of the Shakespearean tragedy . . . lies in action issuing from character."[13] We see in Shakespeare's tragedies the disintegration of great men of state, because of inherent flaws that cause them to have poor judgment.

Shakespeare sometimes introduces abnormalities or supernatural influences, as in *Macbeth, Hamlet,* and *King Lear*. We remember the witches and illusions, but these influences are secondary to the behavior of the characters themselves. There is also some element of fate or well-placed accident in Shakespearean plays. Romeo never gets the Friar's message. Desdemona loses the fated handkerchief. Yet these events are believable; we do not doubt their validity for a moment.

So our definition of tragedy for Shakespeare is slightly different from Aristotle's. The story is based on human actions. A character (the protagonist) of high degree or public importance makes a hasty or imprudent decision and may experience exceptional disappointment, disillusionment, and chaos resulting in the death of that character. The tragic flaw in such a character is some aspect of his or her personality, some passion or ideal or ambition that, when taken to extreme or full realization, results in death. An example is Othello. Here is a man of public importance and an inherently good character, but his passionate love for his wife is marred by jealousy. In Shakespeare's protagonists, such as Othello, we may see ourselves. The tendency to give in to our baser urgings, although we may be inherently "good," is often our tragic error. When such a tragic character dies, we feel a sense of relief and release. In the recognition of the tragic flaw and the protagonist's submission to it, we know there must follow some retribution and justification of the action. Thus, the Shakespearean tragedy ends not with sadness but with hope for the human spirit and a belief in the innate goodness of all mankind.

Shakespeare wrote *Othello* near the end of his play-writing years, around 1604. Perhaps because it was written after many of the other plays, this one seems the most carefully drawn and expertly crafted of the tragedies. It is reported that the English poet, Samuel Taylor Coleridge, said, "*Lear* is the most tremendous effort of Shakespeare as a poet, *Hamlet* as a philosopher or meditator; and *Othello* is the union of the two."[14] While many hold *Hamlet* to be Shakespeare's greatest tragedy, most will agree that

Othello is his most compact and compelling story of love and the jealousies that destroy it.

Othello is perhaps Shakespeare's greatest dramatic triumph, for while it is the story of love between a man and woman, it also reveals the destruction and disintegration of a friendship between two men. The tragedy *Othello* includes a range of human emotions. Othello is a foreigner, a Moor, who has achieved status as a soldier and is a faithful servant to his country. Desdemona is beautiful; a more chaste and loving wife could not be found. Iago is bright, scheming, and suspicious. Perhaps Shakespeare chose to have a symbolic contrast in Othello's dark, fierce countenance and Desdemona's fairness to signify that the two are separated by race and custom.[15] Othello, as an outsider, is filled with self-doubt and suspicion. He allows his suspicions to be fed by Iago's tales of misdeeds.

This play is about romantic love's splendid moments as well as its suspicions, about its expectations and its shortcomings. And especially, it is about the evil hidden, but always present, in the world. In *Othello* and other dramas, Shakespeare revised the ancient definition of tragedy, giving it human qualities and enhancing its universality.

Othello
The Moor of Venice

William Shakespeare

Characters

DUKE OF VENICE
BRABANTIO, a senator
GRATIANO, brother to Brabantio
LODOVICO, kinsman to Brabantio
OTHELLO, a noble Moor; in the service of the Venetian State
CASSIO, his lieutenant
IAGO, his ancient
RODERIGO, a Venetian gentleman
MONTANO, Othello's predecessor in the government of Cyprus
CLOWN, servant to Othello
DESDEMONA, daughter to Brabantio; and wife to Othello
EMILIA, wife to Iago
BIANCA, mistress to Cassio

Small Parts and Extra Characters

SENATORS
SAILOR
OFFICERS
MESSENGER
FOUR GENTLEMEN
HERALD
GALLANTS
ATTENDANTS
MUSICIANS
CLOWN

Vocabulary

ancient: an old and trusted friend
assays: proves or attests
bawd: indecent
beseech: to beg, entreat
beshrew: to curse
caitiff: evil, mean, cowardly
castigate: to purify, chastise
chide: to scold, blame, rebuke
chrysolite: a semiprecious stone
clamour: (clamor) a noisy demand
coxcomb: a silly, vain fellow
cozening: cheating
cuckold: a man whose wife has committed adultery
cudgel: to beat with a stick or club
dilatory: causing delay
disembark: to put ashore from a ship
disport: to play, to amuse
dotage: a doting, foolish, childish state
filche: to steal
fitchew: European polecat
Florentine: of Florence, Italy
grange: a farm with dwelling houses and barns
haggard: an evil woman
horologe: a timepiece, clock
humour: fluids responsible for one's health; a person's
    temperament
imputation: attributing a fault or crime
incontinent: without self-restraint, especially in sexual activity
ingraft (engraft): to insert
jesses: straps for fastening
knave: a man of humble birth; a dishonest person

languish: to lose vitality, become weak
lewd: lustful
mettle: quality of character; courage
minion: a favorite, especially one who is a follower
minx: a pert, saucy girl
Moor: a Spaniard of mixed Arab and Berber descent, originally
     from northwest Africa
nether: lower or under
parley: to speak; a conference
pernicious: causing injury or destruction
pish: an exclamation of disgust
prate: to talk on and on foolishly
prithee: I pray thee; please
provender: dry food for livestock
sequestration: seclusion
signore: Italian title of respect; a gentleman
strumpet: a prostitute
sup: to eat
tup: to copulate with (said of a ram and ewe)
veritable: true, real, actual
wanton: senseless, unrestrained
warrant: to state with confidence
woo: to try to get, to entreat, to make love to

Act I

Scene 1
Venice. A street.

(The curtains of the inner stage are full open. Enter RODERIGO *and*
    IAGO)
RODERIGO: Tush, never tell me; I take it much unkindly
  That thou, Iago, who hast had my purse
  As if the strings were thine, shouldst know of this—
IAGO: S'blood.
  But you'll not hear me. If ever I did dream
  Of such a matter, abhor me.
RODERIGO: Thou told'st me, thou did'st hold him in thy hate.
IAGO: Despise me, if I do not. Three great ones of the city,   *10*
  In personal suit to make me his lieutenant,
  Off-capp'd to him: and, by the faith of man,
  I know my price, I am worth no worse a place:
  But he, as loving his own pride and purposes,
  Evades them, with a bombast circumstance,
  Horribly stuff'd with epithets of war;
  And in conclusion,

Nonsuits my mediators. For, ''Certës,'' says he,
''I have already chose my officer,''
And what was he?   *20*
Forsooth, a great arithmetician,
One Michael Cassio, a Florentine,
A fellow almost damn'd in a fair wife,
That never set a squadron in the field,
Nor the division of a battle knows
More than a spinster; unless the bookish theorick,
Wherein the toged consuls can propose
As masterly as he: mere prattle, without practice,
Is all his soldiership. But he, sir, had the election:
And I,—of whom his eyes had seen the proof   *30*
At Rhodes, at Cyprus, and on other grounds
Christian and heathen,—must be be'-lee'd and calm'd
By debitor and creditor: this counter castor.
He, in good time, must his lieutenant be,
And I,—God bless the mark! his moor-ship's ancient.
RODERIGO: By heaven, I rather would have been his hangman.
IAGO: Why, there's no remedy, 't is the curse of service;
    Preferment goes by letter and affection,
    And not by old gradation, where each second
    Stood heir to the first. Now, sir, be judge yourself,   *40*
    Whether I in any just term am affin'd
    To love the Moor.
RODERIGO: I would not follow him then.
IAGO: O sir, content you;
    I follow him to serve my turn upon him:
    We cannot all be masters, nor all masters
    Cannot be truly follow'd. You shall mark
    Many a duteous and knee-crooking knave,
    That, doting on his own obsequious bondage,
    Wears out his time, much like his master's ass,   *50*
    For nought but provender; and when he's old, cashier'd;
    Whip me such honest knaves: Others there are
    Who trimm'd in forms and visages of duty,
    Keep yet their hearts attending on themselves;
    And, throwing but shows of service on their lords,
    Do well thrive by them, and, when th' ave lin'd their coats,
    Do themselves homage: these fellows have some soul;
    And such a one do I profess myself. For, sir,
    It is as sure as you are Roderigo,
    Were I the Moor I would not be Iago.   *60*
    In following him I follow but myself;
    Heaven is my judge, not I for love and duty,

But seeming so, for my peculiar end:
For when my outward action doth demonstrate
The native act and figure of my heart
In complement extern, 't is not long after
But I will wear my heart upon my sleeve
For daws to peck at; I am not what I am.
RODERIGO: What a fall Fortune does the Thick-lips owe,
  If he can carry 't thus!   70
IAGO: Call up her father,
  Rouse him: make after him, poison his delight,
  Proclaim him in the streets; incense her kinsmen,
  And though he in a fertile climate dwell,
  Plague him with flies: though that his joy be joy,
  Yet throw such chances of vexation on 't,
  As it may lose some colour.
RODERIGO: Here is her father's house; I'll call aloud.
IAGO: Do; with like timorous accent, and dire yell,
  As when—by night and negligence—the fire   80
  Is spied in populous cities.
RODERIGO: What, ho! Brabantio! signior Brabantio, ho!
IAGO: Awake! what, ho! Brabantio! thieves! thieves!
  Look to your house, your daughter, and your bags?
  Thieves! thieves!

(*Enter* BRABANTIO, *above. He appears in the window.*)

BRABANTIO: What is the reason of this terrible summons?
  What is the matter there?
RODERIGO: Signior, is all your family within?   90
IAGO: Are your doors lock'd?
BRABANTIO: Why, wherefore ask you this?
IAGO: Sir, y'are robb'd; for shame put on your gown;
  Your heart is burst, you have lost half your soul;
  Even now, now, very now, an old black ram
  Is tupping your white ewe. Arise! arise!
  Awake the snorting citizens with the bell,
  Or else the devil will make a grandsire of you:
  Arise! I say!
BRABANTIO: What, have you lost your wits?   100
RODERIGO: Most reverend signior, do you know my voice?
BRABANTIO: Not I; what are you?
RODERIGO: My name is Roderigo.
BRABANTIO: The worser welcome:
  I have charg'd thee not to haunt about my doors:
  In honest plainness thou hast heard me say
  My daughter is not for thee; and now, in madness,

Being full of supper and distempering draughts,
Upon malicious bravery, dost thou come
To start my quiet.   110
RODERIGO: Sir, sir, sir,—
BRABANTIO: But thou must needs be sure,
  My spirits and my place have in their power
  To make this bitter to thee.
RODERIGO: Patience good sir.
BRABANTIO: What tell'st thou me of robbing? this is Venice;
  My house is not a grange.
RODERIGO: Most grave Brabantio,
  In simple and pure soul I come to you.
IAGO: Sir, you are one of those that will not serve heaven, if the   120
  devil bid you. Because we come to do you service, and you
  think we are ruffians, you'll have your daughter cover'd
  with a Barbary horse; you'll have your nephews neigh to
  you; you'll have coursers for cousins and 'gennets for
  germans.
BRABANTIO: What profane wretch art thou?
IAGO: I am one, sir, that comes to tell you your daughter and the
  Moor are making the beast with two backs.
BRABANTIO: Thou art a villain.
IAGO: You are— a senator.   130
BRABANTIO: This thou shalt answer. I know thee Roderigo.
RODERIGO: Sir,
  I'll answer anything. But I b'seech you
  If 't be your pleasure and most wise consent,
  As partly I find it is, that your fair daughter,
  At this odd-even, and dull watch o' th' night,
  Transported with no worse nor better guard,
  But with a knave of common hire, a gondolier,
  To the gross clasps of a lascivious Moor:
  If this be known to you, and your allowance,   140
  We then have done you bold and saucy wrongs;
  But if you know not this, my manners tell me
  We have your wrong rebuke. Do not believe
  That, from the sense of all civility,
  I thus would play and trifle with your reverence:
  Your daughter,—if you have not given her leave,—
  I say again, hath made a gross revolt;
  Tying her duty, beauty, wit and fortunes,
  In an extravagant and wheeling stranger,
  Of here and every where: Straight satisfy yourself: 150
  If she be in her chamber, or your house,
  Let loose on me the justice of the state
  For thus deluding you.

BRABANTIO: Strike on the tinder, ho!
  Give me a taper; call up all my people:
  This accident is not unlike my dream;
  Belief of it oppresses me already:
  Light, I say! light!

(*Exit from the upper stage*)   160

IAGO: Farewell; for I must leave you:
  It seems not meet, nor wholesome to my place,
  To be produc'd—as, if I stay, I shall—
  Against the Moor; For I do know, the state,
  —However this may gall him with some check—
  Cannot with safety cast him. For he's embark'd
  With such loud reason to the Cyprus' wars,
  —Which e'en now stand in act,—that for their souls,
  Another of his fathom they have none   170
  To lead their business: in which regard,
  Though I do hate him as I do hell pains,
  Yet, for necessity of present life,
  I must show out a flag and sign of love,
  Which is indeed but sign. That you shall surely find him,
  Lead to the Sagitt'ry the raised search;
  And there will I be with him. So, farewell. (Exit)

(*Enter* BRABANTIO, *and three* SERVANTS *with torches*)
                                                          180

BRABANTIO: It is too true an evil: gone she is,
  And what's to come of my despised time
  Is nought but bitterness. Now, Roderigo,
  Where didst thou see her?—O, unhappy girl!
  With the Moor, say'st thou?— Who would be a father?—
  How didst thou know't was she?—O, she deceives me
  Past thought!—What said she to you?—Get more tapers;
  Raise all my kindred.—Are they marri'd, think you?
RODERIGO: Truly, I think they are.
BRABANTIO: O heaven!—How got she out?—O treason of the   190
    blood!—
  Fathers, from hence trust not your daughters' minds
  By what you see them act.—Are there not charms
  By which the property of youth and maidhood
  May be abus'd? Have you not read, Roderigo,
  Of some such thing?
RODERIGO: Yes, sir; I have indeed.
BRABANTIO: Call up my brother.—O, would you had had her!—
  Some one way, some another.—Do you know
  Where we may apprehend her and the Moor?   200

RODERIGO: I think I can discover him, if you please
  To get good guard, and go along with me.
BRABANTIO: Pray you, lead on. At every house I'll call;
  I may command at most;—Get weapons, ho!
  And raise some special officers of night.—
  On, good Roderigo. I'll deserve your pains. (Exit)

Scene 2

(*Enter* OTHELLO, IAGO *and* ATTENDANTS)

IAGO: Though in the trade of war I have slain men,
  Yet do I hold it very stuff o' the conscience,   210
  To do no contriv'd murder: I lack iniquity
  Sometime to do me service: Nine or ten times
  I'd thought t' have yerk'd him here under the ribs.
OTHELLO: 'T is better as it is.
IAGO: Nay, but he prated
  And spoke such scurvy and provoking terms
  Against your honour,
  That, with the little godliness I have,
  I did full hard forbear him. But I pray you, sir,
  Are you fast marri'd? Be assur'd of this,   220
  That the magnifico is much belov'd,
  And hath, in his effect, a voice potential,
  As double as the duke's: he will divorce you;
  Or put upon you what restraint and grievance
  The law—with all his might to enforce it on—
  Will give him cable.
OTHELLO: Let him do his spite:
  My services, which I've done the signi'ry,
  Shall out-tongue his complaints. 'T is yet to know,—
  Which, when I know that boasting is an honour,   230
  I shall promulgate—I fetch my life and being
  From men of royal siege; and my demerits
  May speak, unbonneted, t'as proud a fortune
  As this that I have reach'd: For know, Iago,
  But that I love the gentle Desdemona,
  I would not my unhoused free condition
  Put into circumscription and confine
  For the sea's worth. But, look! what lights come yond?
IAGO: Those are the raised father and his friends:
  You're best go in.   240
OTHELLO: Not I: I must be found;
  My parts, my title, and my perfect soul,
  Shall manifest me rightly. Is it they?

IAGO: By Janus, I think no.

(*Enter two* SOLDIERS *wearing the* DUKE's *livery preceded by a* TORCHBEARER *and followed by* CASSIO, *behind whom are two more* SOLDIERS *each carrying torches.*)

OTHELLO: The servants of the duke!—and my lieutenant!   250
   The goodness of the night upon you, friends!
   What is the news?
CASSIO: The duke does greet you, general;
   And he requires your haste-post-haste appearance,
   Even on the instant.
OTHELLO: What is the matter, think you?
CASSIO: Something from Cyprus, as I may divine:
   It is a business of some heat. The galleys
   Have sent a dozen sequent messengers
   This very night, at one another's heels;   260
   And many of the consuls rais'd and met,
   Are at the duke's already:
   You have been hotly call'd for;
   When, being not at your lodging to be found,
   The senate hath sent about three several quests,
   To search you out.
OTHELLO: 'T is well I am found by you.
   I will but spend a word here in the house,
   And go with you. (Exit)
CASSIO: Ancient, what makes he here?   270
IAGO: 'Faith, he to-night hath boarded a land carack;
   If 't prove lawful prize he's made for ever.
CASSIO: I do not understand.
IAGO: He's marri'd.
CASSIO: To who?

(*Re-enter* OTHELLO)

IAGO: Marry, to—Come, captain, will you go?
OTHELLO: Have with you.   280
CASSIO: Here comes another troop to seek for you.

(*Enter* RODERIGO, *preceded by a* TORCHBEARER *and followed by* BRABANTIO)

IAGO: It is Brabantio:—general, be advis'd;
   He comes to bad intent.
OTHELLO: Hola! stand there!
RODERIGO: Signior, it is the Moor.
BRABANTIO: Down with him, thief!   290

(*Swords are drawn on both sides and by* SOLDIERS *as well as principals*)

IAGO: You, Roderigo! Come, sir, I am for you.

OTHELLO: Keep up your bright swords, for the dew will rust
    them.
  Good signior, you shall more command with years
  Than with your weapons.
BRABANTIO: O thou foul thief, where hast thou stow'd my
    daughter?   300
  Damn'd as thou art, thou hast enchanted her:
  For I'll refer me to all things of sense,
  If she in chains of magic were not bound,
  Whether a maid so tender, fair and happy,
  So opposite to marriage, that she shunn'd
  The wealthy curled darlings of our nation,
  Would ever have, t' incur a general mock,
  Run from her guardage to the sooty bosom
  Of such a thing as thou,—to fear, not to delight.
  Judge me the world, if 't is not gross in sense,   310
  That thou hast practis'd on her with foul charms:
  Abus'd her delicate youth with drugs, or minerals,
  That weaken motion:—I'll have 't disputed on:
  'T is probable, and palpable to thinking.
  I therefore apprehend and do attach thee,
  For an abuser of the world, a practiser
  Of arts inhibited and out of warrant:
  Lay hold upon him; if he do resist,
  Subdue him at his peril.
OTHELLO: Hold your hands,   320
  Both you of my inclining, and the rest:
  Were it my cue to fight, I should have known 't,
  Without a prompter.—Where will you that I go
  To answer this your charge?
BRABANTIO: To prison: till fit time
  Of law, and course of direct session,
  Call thee to answer.
OTHELLO: What if I do obey?
  How may the duke be therewith satisfi'd;
  Whose messengers are here about my side,   330
  Upon some present business of the state,
  To bring me to him?
CASSIO: 'T is true, most worthy signior,
  The duke's in council; and your noble self,
  I am sure is sent for.
BRABANTIO: How! the duke in council?
  In this time of the night?—Bring him away:
  Mine's not an idle cause: the duke himself,
  Or any of my brothers of the state,

Cannot but feel this wrong as 't were their own: *340*
For if such actions may have passage free,
Bond-slaves and pagans shall our statemen be.

(*Exit*)

Scene 3

The same. A council chamber.

(*The* DUKE *and* SENATORS *sit at a table;* OFFICERS *attending*)

DUKE: There is no composition in this news,
  That gives them credit.
FIRST SENATOR: Indeed, th' are disproportion'd;
  My letters say, a hundred and seven galleys.   *350*
DUKE: And mine, a hundred and forty.
SECOND SENATOR: And mine, two hundred:
  But though they jump not on a just account,
  —As in these cases where the aim reports,
  'T is oft with diff'rence,—yet do they all confirm
  A Turkish fleet, and bearing up to Cyprus.
DUKE: Nay, 't is possible enough to judgment.
  I do not so secure me in the error,
  But the main article I do approve
  In fearful sense.   *360*
SAILOR within: What ho! what ho! what ho!

(*Enter* SAILOR)

THIRD SENATOR: A messenger from the galleys.
DUKE: Now? the business?
SAILOR: The Turkish preparation makes for Rhodes;
  So was I bid report here to the state,
  By signior Angelo.
DUKE: How say you by this change?   *370*
FIRST SENATOR: This cannot be.
  By no assay of reason; 't is a pageant,
  To keep us in false gaze: When we consider
  Th' importancy of Cyprus to the Turk;
  And let ourselves again but understand
  That, as it more concerns the Turk than Rhodes,
  So may he with more facile question bear it,
  For that it stands not in such warlike brace,
  But altogether lacks th' abilities
  That Rhodes is dress'd in: if we make thought of this,   *380*
  We must not think the Turk is so unskilful

To leave that latest which concerns him first,
Neglecting an attempt of ease and gain,
To wake and wage a danger profitless.
DUKE: Nay, in all confidence, he's not for Rhodes.
OFFICER: Here is more news.

(*Enter a* MESSENGER)

MESSENGER: The Ottomites, reverend and gracious,   390
Steering with due course toward the isle of Rhodes,
Have there injointed them with an after fleet.
FIRST SENATOR: Ay, so I thought:—How many, as you guess?
MESSENGER: Of thirty sail: and now they do re-stem
Their backward course, bearing with frank appearance
Their purposes to'ard Cyprus. Signior Montano,
Your trusty and most valiant servitor,
With his free duty, recommends you thus,
And prays you to believe him.
DUKE: 'T is certain then for Crypus.   400
Marcus Luccicos, is he not in town?
FIRST SENATOR: He's now in Florence.
DUKE: Write from us to him, post—post-haste, despatch.
FIRST SENATOR: Here comes Brabantio—and the valiant Moor.

(*Enter* BRABANTIO, OTHELLO, IAGO, RODERIGO, *and* OFFICERS)

DUKE: Valiant Othello, we must straight employ you
Against the general enemy Ottoman.
I did not see you; welcome gentle signior.   410
We lack'd your counsel and your help to-night.
BRABANTIO: So did I yours: Good your grace, pardon me;
Neither my place nor aught I heard of business,
Hath rais'd me from my bed; nor doth the general care
Take hold on me; for my particular grief
Is of so flood-gate and o'erbearing nature,
That it engluts and swallows other sorrows,
And it is still itself.
DUKE: Why, what's the matter?
BRABANTIO: My daughter! O, my daughter!   420
SENATOR: Dead?
BRABANTIO: Ay, to me;
She is abus'd, stol'n from me, and corrupted
By spells and medicines, bought of mountebanks
For nature so preposterously to err,
Being not deficient, blind, or lame of sense,
Sans witchcraft could not.
DUKE: Who'er he be, that in this foul proceeding
Hath thus beguil'd your daughter of herself,

And you of her, the bloody book of law   *430*
You shall yourself read in the bitter letter,
After your own sense; yea though our proper son
Stood in your action.
BRABANTIO: Humbly I thank your grace.
  Here is the man, this Moor; whom now, it seems,
  Your special mandate, for the state affairs,
  Hath hither brought.
DUKE: We are very sorry for 't.
  (*To* OTHELLO) What, in your own part, can you say to this?
BRABANTIO: Nothing, but this is so.   *440*
OTHELLO: Most potent, grave, and reverend signiors,
  My very noble and approv'd good masters,—
  That I have ta'en away this old man's daughter,
  It is most true; true I have marri'd her;—
  The very head and front of my offending
  Hath this extent, no more. Rude am I in my speech,
  And little bless'd with the soft phrase of peace;
  For since these arms of mine had seven years' pith,—
  Till now some nine moons wasted,—they have us'd
  Their dearest action in the tented field;   *450*
  And little of this great world can I speak,
  More than pertains to feats of broil and battle;
  And therefore little shall I grace my cause,
  In speaking for myself: Yet, by your gracious patience,
  I will a round, unvarnish'd tale deliver
  Of my whole course of love: what drugs, what charms,
  What conjuration, and what mighty magic,
  For such proceeding I am charg'd withal,—
  I won his daughter.
BRABANTIO: A maiden never bold;   *460*
  Of spirit so still and quiët, that her motion
  Blush'd at herself: And she, in spite of nature,
  Of years, of country, credit, every thing,
  To fall in love with what she fear'd to look on—
  It is a judgment maim'd, and most imperfect,
  That will confess perfection so could err
  Against all rules of nature; and must be driven
  To find out practices of cunning hell,
  Why this should be. I therefore vouch again,
  That with some mixtures powerful o'er the blood,   *470*
  Or with some dram conjur'd to this efffect,
  He wrought upon her.
DUKE: To vouch this is no proof;
  Without more wider and more overt test,
  Than these thin habits, and poor likelihoods

Of modern seeming do prefer against him.

FIRST SENATOR: But, Othello, speak;
Did you by indirect and forced courses
Subdue and poison this young maid's affections?
Or came it by request, and such fair question   *480*
As soul to soul affordeth?

OTHELLO: I do beseech you,
Send for the lady to the Sagitt'ry,
And let her speak of me before her father:
If you do find me foul in her report,
The trust, the office, I do hold of you,
Not only take away, but let your sentence
Even fall upon my life.

DUKE: Fetch Desdemona hither.

OTHELLO: Ancient, conduct them: you best know the place.   *490*

(*Exit* IAGO)

And, till she come, as truly as to heaven
I do confess the vices of my blood.
So justly to your grave ears I'll present
How I did thrive in this fair lady's love,
And she in mine.

DUKE: Say it, Othello.

OTHELLO: Her father lov'd me; oft invited me;   *500*
Still question'd me the story of my life,
From year to year; the battles, sieges, fortunes,
That I have pass'd.
I ran it through, even from my boyish days,
To th' very moment that he bade me tell it.
Wherein I spoke of most disastrous chances;
Of moving accidents by flood and field;
Of hair-breadth 'scapes i' th' imminent-deadly breach;
Of being taken by the insolent foe
And sold to slavery; of my redemption thence,   *510*
And portance in my traveller's history,
Wherein of antres vast and deserts idle,
Rough quarries, rocks, and hills whose heads touch heaven,
It was my hint to speak,—such was my process,—
And of the Cannibals that each other eat,
The Anthropophagi, and men whose heads
Do grow beneath their shoulders. These things to hear
Would Desdemona seriously incline;
But still the house affairs would draw her thence:
Which ever as she could with haste despatch,   *520*
She'd come again, and with a greedy ear
Devour up my discourse: Which I observing,

Took once a pliant hour; and found good means
To draw from her a prayer of earnest heart,
That I would all my pilgrimage dilate,
Whereof by parcels she had something heard,
But not intentively: I did consent;
And often did beguile her of her tears,
When I did speak of some distressful stroke
That my youth suffer'd. My story being done,   530
She gave me for my pains a world of sighs:
She swore,—In faith, 't was strange, 't was passing strange;
'T was pitiful; 't was wondrous-pitiful:
She wish'd she had not heard it; yet she wish'd
That heav'n had made her such a man: she thank'd me;
And bade me, if I had a friend that lov'd her,
I should but teach him how to tell my story,
And that would woo her. Upon this hint I spake:
She lov'd me for the dangers I had pass'd;
And I lov'd her that she did pity them.   540
This only is the witchcraft I have us'd;

(IAGO *re-enters leading in* DESDEMONA)

Here comes the lady, let her witness it.
DUKE: I think this tale would win my daughter too.
  Good Brabantio,
  Take up this mangl'd matter at the best:
  Men do their broken weapons rather use,
  Than their bare hands.   550
BRABANTIO: I pray you, hear her speak;
  If she confess that she was half the wooer,
  Destruction on my head if my bad blame
  Light on the man!—Come hither, gentle mistress;
  Do you perceive in all this noble company
  Where most you owe obedience?
DESDEMONA: My noble father,
  I do perceive here a divided duty:
  To you, I am bound for life and education;
  My life and education both do learn me   560
  How to respect you; you are the lord of duty;—
  I'm hitherto your daughter: But here's my husband;
  And so much duty as my mother show'd
  To you, preferring you before her father,
  So much I challenge, that I may profess
  Due to the Moor, my lord.
BRABANTIO: God be with you! I have done:—
  Please it your grace, on to the state affairs.
  I had rather to adopt a child than get it.

Come hither, Moor: 570
I here do give thee that with all my heart
Which, but thou hast already, with all my heart
I would keep from thee.—For your sake, jewel,
I am glad at soul I have no other child;
For thy escape would teach me tyranny,
To hang clogs on them.—I have done, my lord.
DUKE: Let me speak like yourself; and lay a sentence.
Which, as a grise or step, may help these lovers
Into your favour.
When remedies are past, the griefs are ended,   580
By seeing the worst, which late on hopes depended.
To mourn a mischief that is past and gone
Is the next way to draw new mischief on.
What cannot be preserv'd when fortunes take,
Patience her injury a mockery makes.
The robb'd that smiles steals something from the thief;
He robs himself that spends a bootless grief.
BRABANTIO: So let the Turk of Cyprus us beguile;
We lose it not so long as we can smile.
He bears the sentence well that nothing bears   590
But the free comfort which from thence he hears:
But he bears both the sentence and the sorrow
That, to pay grief, must of poor patience borrow.
These sentences, to sugar, or to gall,
Being strong on both sides, are equivocal:
But words are words; I never yet did hear
That the bruis'd heart was pierced through the ear.
I humbly beseech you, proceed to th' affairs of state.
DUKE: The Turk with a most mighty preparation makes for
Cyprus:—Othello, the fortitude of the place is best known to   600
you: And though we have there a substitute of most
allowed sufficiency, yet opinion, a sovereign mistress of
effects, throws a more safer voice on you: you must
therefore be content to slubber the gloss of your new
fortunes with this more stubborn and boisterous
expedition.
OTHELLO: The tyrant custom, most grave senators,
Hath made the flinty and steel couch of war
My thrice-driven bed of down; I do agnize
A natural and prompt alacrity   610
I find in hardness; and do undertake
These present wars against the Ottomites.
Most humbly, therefore, bending to your state,
I crave fit disposition for my wife;

Due reference of place, and exhibition;
With such accommodation and besort,
As levels with her breeding.
DUKE: If you please,
   Be 't at her father's.
BRABANTIO: I will not have it so.   *620*
OTHELLO: Nor I.
DESDEMONA: Nor I, I would not there reside,
   To put my father in impatient thoughts,
   By being in his eye. Most gracious duke,
   To my unfolding lend your prosperous ear;
   And let me find a charter in your voice
   To assist my simpleness.
DUKE: What would you, Desdemona?
DESDEMONA: That I did love the Moor to live with him,
   My downright violence and storm of fortunes   *630*
   May trumpet to the world: my heart's subdued
   Even to the very quality of my lord:
   I saw Othello's visage in his mind;
   And to his honours and his valiant parts
   Did I my soul and fortunes consecrate.
   So that, dear lords, if I be left behind,
   A moth of peace, and he go to the war,
   The rites for which I love him are bereft me,
   And I a heavy interim shall support
   By his dear absence: Let me go with him.   *640*
OTHELLO: Let her have your voices.
   Vouch with me, heaven, I therefore beg it not,
   To please the palate of my appetite;
   Nor to comply with heat, the young affects
   In me defunct, and proper satisfaction;
   But to be free and bounteous to her mind:
   And heaven defend your good souls that you think
   I will your serious and great business scant,
   When she is with me: No, when light-wing'd toys
   Of feather'd Cupid seel with wanton dullness   *650*
   My speculative and offic'd instrument,
   That my disports corrupt and taint my business,
   Let housewifes make a skillett of my helm,
   And all indign and base adversities
   Make head against my estimation.
DUKE: Be it as you shall privately determine,
   Either for her stay or going; th' affair cries haste,
   And speed must answer it. You must hence to-night.
DESDEMONA: To-night, my lord?

DUKE: This night.   660
OTHELLO: With all my heart.
DUKE: At nine i' the morning here we'll meet again.
  Othello, leave some officer behind,
  And he shall our commission bring to you;
  With such things else of quality and respect
  As doth import you.
OTHELLO: So please your grace my ancient;
  A man he is of honesty and trust:
  To his conveyance I assign my wife,
  With what else needful your good grace shall think   670
  To be sent after me.
DUKE: Let it be so.
  Good night to every one.—And, noble signior,
  If virtue no delighted beauty lack,
  Your son-in-law is far more fair than black.
FIRST SENATOR: Adieu, brave Moor! use Desdemona well.
BRABANTIO: Look to her, Moor, have a quick eye to see;
  She has deceiv'd her father, and may thee.
OTHELLO: My life upon her faith! Honest Iago,
  My Desdemona must I leave to thee;   680
  I prithee let thy wife attend on her;
  And bring them after in the best advantage.
  Come Desdemona, I have but an hour
  Of love, of worldly matter and direction,
  To spend with thee: we must obey the time.

(*Exit* OTHELLO *and* DESDEMONA)

RODERIGO: Iago.
IAGO: What say'st thou, noble heart?   690
RODERIGO: What will I do, think'st thou?
IAGO: Why, go to bed and sleep.
RODERIGO: I will incontinently drown myself.
IAGO: If thou dost I shall never love thee after.
  Why thou silly gentleman!
RODERIGO: It is silliness to live when to live is torment: and then
      have we a prescription to die when death is our physician.
IAGO: O villainous! I have looked upon the world for four times
      seven years; and since I could distinguish betwixt a benefit
      and an injury, I never found man that knew how to love   700
      himself.
    Ere I would say I would drown myself for the love of a
      Guineahen, I would change my humanity with a baboon.
RODERIGO: What should I do? I confess it is my shame to be so
      fond; but it is not in my virtue to amend it.

IAGO: Virtue? a fig! 't is in ourselves that we are thus, or thus.
Our bodies are our gardens; to the which our wills are
    gardeners: so that if we plant nettles, or sow lettuce; set
    hyssop, and weed up thyme; supply it with one gender of
    herbs, or distract it with many; either to have it steril with   710
    idleness, or manured with industry; why, the power and
    corrigible authority of this lies in our wills. If the balance of
    our lives had not one scale of reason to poise another of
    sensuality, the blood and baseness of our natures would
    conduct us to most preposterous conclusions: But we have
    reason to cool our raging motions, our carnal stings, our
    unbitted lusts; whereof I take this, that you call love, to be
    a sect or scion.
RODERIGO: It cannot be.
IAGO: It is merely a lust of the blood, and a permission of the   720
    will.
Come, be a man: Drown thyself? drown cats and blind
    puppies. I have professed me thy friend, and I confess me
    knit to thy deserving with cables of perdurable toughness.
    I could never better stead thee than now. Put money in thy
    purse; follow thou the wars; defeat thy favour with an
    usurped beard; I say put money in thy purse. It cannot be
    that Desdemona should long continue her love to the
    Moor,—put money in thy purse;—nor he his to her: it was
    a violent commencement, and thou shalt see an   730
    answerable sequestration: but put money in thy
    purse.—These Moors are changeable in their wills;—fill thy
    purse with money: the food that to him now is as luscious
    as locusts, shall be to him shortly as bitter as coloquintida.
    She must change for youth: when she is sated with his
    body she will find the error of her choice. Therefore put
    money in thy purse.—if thou wilt needs damn thyself, do
    it a more delicate way than drowning. Make all the money
    thou canst: If sanctimony and a frail vow, betwixt an
    erring barbarian and super-subtle Venetian, be not too   740
    hard for my wits and all the tribe of hell, thou shalt enjoy
    her; therefore make money. A plague of drowning thyself!
    it is clean out of the way: seek thou rather to be hanged in
    compassing thy joy, than to be drowned and go without
    her.
RODERIGO: Wilt thou be fast to my hopes, if I depend on the
    issue?
IAGO: Thou art sure of me,—Go, make money: I have told thee
    often, and I re-tell thee again and again, I hate the Moor:
    My cause is hearted: thine hath no less reason: Let us be   750

conjunctive in our revenge against him: if thou canst
cuckold him, thou dost thyself a pleasure, me a sport.
There are many events in the womb of time which will be
delivered. Traverse; go; provide thy money. We will have
more of this to-morrow. Adieu.

RODERIGO: Where shall we meet i' the morning?

IAGO: At my lodging.

RODERIGO: I'll be with thee betimes.

IAGO: Go to; Farewell. Do you hear, Roderigo?

RODERIGO: What say you?   760

IAGO: No more of drowning, do you hear?

RODERIGO: I am changed. I'll go sell all my land.

(*Exit* RODERIGO)

IAGO: Thus do I ever make my fool my purse:
For I mine own gain'd knowledge should profane,
If I would time expend with such a snipe,
But for my sport and profit.—I hate the Moor;
And it is thought abroad, that 'twixt my sheets   770
He has done my office: I know not if 't be true;
But I, for mere suspicion in that kind,
Will do, as if for surety. He holds me well;
The better shall my purpose work on him.
Cassio's a proper man: Let me see now;
To get his place, and to plume up my will
In double knavery,—How? how?—Let's see:—
After some time, to abuse Othello's ear
That he is too familiar with his wife:
He hath a person, and a smooth dispose,   780
To be suspected; fram'd to make women false.
The Moor is of a free and open nature,
That thinks men honest that but seem to be so;
And will as tenderly be led by the nose,
As asses are—
I have't;—it is engender'd:—Hell and night
Must bring this monstrous birth to the world's light. (*Exit*)

Act II

Scene 1
A Seaport Town in Cyprus.

(*Enter* MONTANO, *between* TWO GENTLEMEN)

MONTANO: What from the cape can you discern at sea?

FIRST GENTLEMAN: Nothing at all: it is a high-wrought flood;
 I cannot, 'twixt the heaven and the main,
 Descry a sail.
MONTANO: Methinks the wind hath spoke aloud at land;
 A fuller blast ne'er shook our battlements:
 If it hath ruffian'd so upon the sea,
 What ribs of oak, when mountains melt on them,   *10*
 Can hold the mortice? what shall we hear of this?
SECOND GENTLEMAN: A segregation of the Turkish fleet:
 For do but stand upon the foaming shore,
 The chidden billow seems to pelt the clouds;
 The wind-shak'd surge, with high and monstrous mane,
 Seems to cast water on the burning bear,
 And quench the guards of th' ever fixed pole:
 I never did like molestation view
 On th' enchaf'd flood.
MONTANO: If that the Turkish fleet   *20*
 Be not enshelter'd and embay'd, they 're drown'd.
 It is impossible to bear it out.

(*Enter a* THIRD GENTLEMAN *from c. opening*)

THIRD GENTLEMAN: News, lads! our wars are done:
 The desperate tempest hath so bang'd the Turks,
 That their designment halts: A noble ship of Venice
 Hath seen a grievous wrack and sufferance
 On most part of their fleet.   *30*
MONTANO: How, is this true?
THIRD GENTLEMAN: The ship is here put in,
 A Veronessa: Michael Cassio,
 Lieutenant to the warlike Moor, Othello,
 Is come on shore: the Moor himself's at sea,
 And is in full commission here for Cyprus.
MONTANO: I am glad on 't; 't is a worthy governor.
THIRD GENTLEMAN: But this same Cassio,—though he speak of
  comfort,
 Touching the Turkish loss,—yet he looks sadly,   *40*
 And prays the Moor be safe; for they were parted
 With foul and violent tempest.
MONTANO: Pray heaven he be:
 For I have serv'd him, and the man commands
 Like a full soldier. Let's to the sea-side,—ho!
 As well to see the vessel that's come in
 As to throw out our eyes for brave Othello;
 Even till we make the main, and th' aerial blue,
 An indistinct regard.

THIRD GENTLEMAN: Come, let's do so.   *50*
  For every minute is expectancy
  Of more arrivance.

(*Enter* CASSIO *c.*)

CASSIO: Thanks, you the valiant of this warlike isle,
  That so approve the Moor! O, let the heavens
  Give him defence against the elements,
  For I have lost him on a dangerous sea!
MONTANO: Is he well shipp'd?   *60*
CASSIO: His bark is stoutly timber'd, and his pilot
  Of very expert and approv'd allowance;
  Therefore my hopes, not surfeited to death,
  Stand in bold cure.

(*Within c.*) A sail, a sail, a sail!

(*Enter a* FOURTH GENTLEMAN *c.*)

CASSIO: What noise?   *70*
FOURTH GENTLEMAN: The town is empty; on the brow o' the sea
  Stand ranks of people, and they cry—a sail.
CASSIO: My hopes do shape him for the governor.
SECOND GENTLEMAN: They do discharge their shot of courtesy:

(*Guns heard off c.*)

  Our friends at least.
CASSIO: I pray you, sir, go forth,
  And give us truth who 't is that is arriv'd.   *80*
FOURTH GENTLEMAN: I shall. (*Exit c.*)
MONTANO: But, good lieutenant, is your general wiv'd?
CASSIO: Most fortunately: he hath achiev'd a maid
  That paragons description and wild fame;
  One that excels the quirks of blazoning pens,
  And in the essential vesture of creation
  Does tire the ingener.—How now? who has put in?

(*Re-enter the* FOURTH GENTLEMAN)

                                               90
GENTLEMAN: 'T is one Iago, ancient to the general.
CASSIO: H' 'as had most favourable and happy speed:
  Tempests themselves, high seas, and howling winds,
  The gutter'd rocks, and congregated sands,
  Traitors ensteep'd to clog the guiltless keel,
  As having sense of beauty do omit
  Their mortal natures, letting go safely by
  The divine Desdemona.
MONTANO: What is she?

CASSIO: She that I spake of, our great captain's captain,   100
    Left in the conduct of the bold Iago;
    Whose footing here anticipates our thoughts,
    A se'nnight's speed.—Great Jove, Othello guard,
    And swell his sail with thine own powerful breath;
    That he may bless this bay with his tall ship,
    Make love's quick pants in Desdemona's arms,
    Give renew'd fire to our extincted spirits,
    And bring all Cyprus comfort!—O, behold,

(*Enter* DESDEMONA, EMILIA, IAGO, RODERIGO, *and* ATTENDANTS)   110

    The riches of the ship is come on shore!
    You men of Cyprus, let her have your knees:
    Hail to thee, lady! and the grace of heaven,
    Before, behind thee, and on every hand,
    Enwheel thee round!
DESDEMONA: I thank you, valiant Cassio,
    What tidings can you tell me of my lord?
CASSIO: He is not yet arriv'd; nor know I aught
    But that he 's well, and will be shortly here.   120
DESDEMONA: O, but I fear,—How lost you company?
CASSIO: The great contention of the sea and skies
    Parted our fellowship:

(*Cry within,* "A sail! a sail!" *Then guns heard.*)

    But hark! a sail.
GENTLEMAN: They give their greeting to the citadel;
    This likewise is a friend.
CASSIO: See for the news.—   130
    Good Ancient, you are welcome;—Welcome, mistress:—

(*To* EMILIA *and kissing her*)

    Let it not gall your patience, good Iago,
    That I extend my manners; 't is my breeding
    That gives me this bold show of courtesy.
IAGO: Sir, would she give you so much of her lips
    As of her tongue she oft bestows on me,
    You'd have enough.   140
DESDEMONA: Alas, she has no speech.
IAGO: In faith, too much;
    I find it still when I have list to sleep:
    Marry, before your ladyship, I grant
    She puts her tongue a little in her heart,
    And chides with thinking.
EMILIA: You have little cause to say so.

IAGO: Come on, come on: you are pictures—out of doors;
  Bells—in your parlours, wild cats in your kitchens;
  Saints in your injuries; devils being offended;   *150*
  Players in your huswifery; and huswives in your beds.
DESDEMONA: O, fye upon thee, slanderer!
IAGO: Nay, it is true, or else I am a Turk.
  You rise to play and go to bed to work.
EMILIA: You shall not write my praise.
IAGO: No, let me not.
DESDEMONA: What wouldst thou write of me if thou shouldst
    praise me?
IAGO: O gentle lady, do not put me to 't;
  For I am nothing if not critical.   *160*
DESDEMONA: Come on, essay:—There's one gone to the
    harbour?
IAGO: Ay, madam.
DESDEMONA: I am not merry; but I do beguile
  The thing I am, by seeming otherwise.
  Come, how wouldst thou praise me?
IAGO: I am about it; but, indeed, my invention
  Comes from my pate as birdlime does from frize,—
  It plucks out brains and all: But my muse labours,
  And thus she is deliver'd.   *170*
  If she be fair and wise,—fairness and wit,
  The one's for use, the other useth it.
DESDEMONA: Well prais'd! How if she be black and witty?
IAGO: If she be black, and thereto have a wit,
  She'll find a white that shall her blackness fit.
DESDEMONA: Worse and worse.
EMILIA: How if fair and foolish?
IAGO: She never yet was foolish that was fair:
  For even her folly help'd her to an heir.
DESDEMONA: These are old fond paradoxes, to make fools laugh *180*
    i' the alehouse. What miserable praise hast thou for her
    that's foul and foolish?
IAGO: There's none so foul and foolish thereunto,
  But does foul pranks which fair and wise ones do.
DESDEMONA: O heavy ignorance!—thou praisest the worst best.
  But what praise couldst thou bestow on a deserving woman
    indeed? one, that in the authority of the merit, did justly
    put on the vouch of very malice itself?
IAGO: She that was ever fair, and never proud;
  Had tongue at will, and yet was never loud;   *190*
  Never lack'd gold, and yet went never gay;
  Fled from her wish, and yet said,—now—I may;

She that, being anger'd, her revenge being nigh,
Bade her wrong stay and her displeasure fly;
She that in wisdom never was so frail,
To change the cod's head for the salmon's tail;
She that could think, and ne'er disclose her mind,
See suitors following and not look behind:
She was a wight—if ever such wight were—

DESDEMONA: To do what?   200

IAGO: To suckle fools, and chronicle small beer.

DESDEMONA: O most lame and impotent conclusion!—Do not
    learn of him, Emilia, though he be thy husband.—How say
    you, Cassio? is he not a most profane and liberal
    councillor?

CASSIO: He speaks home, madam, you may relish him more in
    the soldier than in the scholar.

IAGO: He takes her by the palm: Ay, well said, whisper: with as
    little a web as this will I ensnare as great a fly as Cassio.
    Ay, smile upon her, do; I will gyve thee in thine own   210
    courtship.

    You say true; 't is so, indeed: if such tricks as these strip you
    out of your lieutenantry, it had been better you had not
    kissed your three fingers so oft, which now again you are
    most apt to play the sir in. Very good! well kissed, and
    excellent courtesy! 't is so, indeed. Yet again your fingers
    to your lips? Would they were cluster-pipes for your sake.
    (IAGO *makes his next line a general announcement Trumpet off*
    c.) The Moor, I know his trumpet.

CASSIO: 'T is truly so.   220

DESDEMONA: Let's meet him and receive him.

CASSIO: Lo, where he comes!

(*Enter* OTHELLO *and* ATTENDANTS)

OTHELLO: O my fair warriör!

DESDEMONA: My dear Othello!

OTHELLO: It gives me wonder great as my content,
    To see you here before me. O my soul's joy!
    If after every tempest comes such calms,   230
    May the winds blow till they have waken'd death!
    And let the labouring bark climb hills of seas,
    Olympus-high; and duck again as low
    As hell's from heav'n! If it were now to die,
    'T were now to be most happy; for, I fear
    My soul hath her content so absolute,
    That not another comfort like to this
    Succeeds in unknown fate.

DESDEMONA: The heavens forbid
  But that our loves and comforts should increase,   240
  Even as our days do grow!
OTHELLO: Amen to that, sweet Powers!
  I cannot speak enough of this content,
  It stops me here; it is too much of joy;
  And this, and this, the greatest discord be
  That e'er our hearts shall make!
IAGO: O, you are well tun'd now!
  But I'll set down the pegs that make this music,
  As honest as I am.
OTHELLO: Come; let 's to the castle.—   250
  News, friends; our wars are done, the Turks are drown'd.
  How does my old acquaintance of this isle?
  Honey, you shall be well desir'd in Cyprus,
  I've found great love amongst them. O my sweet,
  I prattle out of fashion, and I dote
  In mine own comforts.—I prithee, good Iago,
  Go to the bay, and disembark my coffers:
  Bring thou the master to the citadel;
  He is a good one, and his worthiness
  Does challenge much respect.—Come, Desdemona,   260
  Once more well met at Cyprus.

(*Exit* OTHELLO, DESDEMONA, *followed by* EMILIA *and* MONTANO,
DESDEMONA'S ATTENDANTS, *and* OTHELLO'S *staff*)

IAGO: Do thou meet me presently at the harbour. Come hither.
  If thou be'st valiant,—as they say, base men being in love have
    then a nobility in their natures more than is native to
    them—list me.
  The lieutenant to-night watches on the court of guard:—First, I
    must tell thee this—Desdemona is directly in love with   270
    him.
RODERIGO: With him! why, 't is not possible.
IAGO: Lay thy finger thus, and let thy soul be instructed. Mark
  me with what violence she first loved the Moor, but for
  bragging and telling her fantastical lies: Will she love him
  still for prating? let not thy discreet heart think it. Her eye
  must be fed; and what delight shall she have to look on the
  devil?
  When the blood is made dull with the act of sport, there
    should be, again to inflame it and to give satiety a fresh   280
    appetite, loveliness in favour; sympathy in years,
    manners, and beauties; all which the Moor is defective in:
    Now for want of these required conveniences, her delicate
    tenderness will find itself abused, begin to heave the

gorge, disrelish and abhor the Moor; very nature will
instruct her in it, and compel her to some second choice.
Now, sir, this granted,—as it is a most pregnant and
unforced position—who stands so eminent in the degree of
this fortune as Cassio does?—a knave very voluble; no
further conscionable than in putting on the mere form of   290
civil and humane seeming, for the better compassing of his
salt and most hidden loose affection? why none; why
none: A slipper and subtle knave; a finder of occasions;
that has an eye can stamp and counterfeit advantages
though true advantage never present itself: A devilish
knave! besides, the knave is handsome, young; and hath
all those requisites in him that folly and green minds look
after: A pestilent-complete knave; and the woman hath
found him already.

RODERIGO: I cannot believe that in her; she is full of most bless'd 300
condition.

IAGO: Bless'd fig's end! the wine she drinks is made of grapes: if
she had been bless'd, she would never have loved the
Moor: Bless'd pudding! Didst thou not see her paddle
with the palm of his hand? Didst not mark that?

RODERIGO: Yes, that I did; but that was but courtesy.

IAGO: Lechery, by this hand; an index and obscure prologue to
the history of lust and foul thoughts. They met so near
with their lips that their breaths embraced together.
Villainous thoughts, Roderigo! When these mutualities so   310
marshall the way, hard at hand comes the master and
main exercise, the incorporate conclusion: Pish!—But, sir,
be you ruled by me: I have brought you from Venice.
Watch you to-night; for the command, I'll lay 't upon you:
Cassio knows you not;—I'll not be far from you: Do you
find some occasion to—anger—Cassio, either by speaking
too loud, or tainting his discipline, or from what other
cause you please, which the time shall more favourably
minister.

RODERIGO: Well.   320

IAGO: Sir, he's rash, and very sudden in choler; and, haply, may
strike at you: Provoke him that he may: for even out of
that will I cause these of Cyprus to mutiny; whose
qualification shall come into no true taste again, but by the
displanting of Cassio. So shall you have a shorter journey
to your desires, by the means I shall then have to prefer
them; and the impediment most profitably removed,
without the which there were no expectation of our
prosperity.

RODERIGO: I will do this, if you can bring it to any opportunity.   330

IAGO: I warrant thee. Meet me by and by at the citadel. I must
        fetch his necessaries ashore. Farewell.
RODERIGO: Adieu. (*Exit*)
IAGO: That Cassio loves her, I do well believe it;
   That she loves him, 't is apt, and of great credit:
   The Moor—howbeit that I endure him not,—
   Is of a constant-loving, noble nature;
   And, I dare think, he'll prove to Desdemona
   A most dear husband. Now I do love her too;
   Not out of absolute lust—though peradventure,   340
   I stand accountant for as great a sin,—
   But partly led to diet my revenge,
   For that I do suspect the lusty Moor
   Hath leap'd into my seat: the thought whereof
   Doth, like a poisonous mineral, gnaw my inwards,
   And nothing can or shall content my soul,
   Till I am even'd with him, wife for wife;
   Or, failing so, yet that I put the Moor
   At least into a jealousy so strong
   That judgment cannot cure. Which thing to do,—   350
   If this poor trash of Venice, whom I trace
   For his quick hunting, stand the putting on,
   I'll have our Michael Cassio on the hip;
   Abuse him to the Moor in the right garb,—
   For I fear Cassio with my night-cap too;—
   Make the Moor thank me, love me, and reward me,
   For making him egregiously an ass,
   And practising upon his peace and quiet
   Even to madness. 'Tis here, but yet confus'd;
   Knavery's plain face is never seen till us'd.   360

(*Exit Curtain falls*)

Scene 2
A Street

(*Enter the* HERALD, *who unrolls his proclamation*)

HERALD: It is Othello's pleasure, our noble and valiant general,
        that upon certain tidings now arrived, importing the mere
        perdition of the Turkish fleet, every man put himself into
        triumph: some to dance, some to make bonfires, each man
        to what sport and revels his addiction leads him; for,
        besides these beneficial news, it is the celebration of his   370
        nuptial: so much was his pleasure should be proclaimed.

All offices are open; and there is full liberty of feasting,
from this present hour of five till the bell hath told eleven.
Bless the isle of Cyprus, and our noble general, Othello.

Scene 3
A Hall in the Castle.

(*Enter* OTHELLO, DESDEMONA, *and* CASSIO)

OTHELLO: Good Michael, look you to the guard to-night:
  Let's teach ourselves that honourable stop,
  Not to outsport discretion.
CASSIO: Iago hath direction what to do;   *380*
  But, notwithstanding, with my personal eye
  Will I look to 't.
OTHELLO: Iago is most honest.
  Michael, good night: To-morrow, with your earliest,
  Let me have speech with you.—Come, my dear love,
  The purchase made, the fruits are to ensue;
  That profit's yet to come 'tween me and you.—
  Good night.

(*Exit* OTHELLO *and* DESDEMONA. *enter* IAGO)   *390*

CASSIO: Welcome, Iago: We must to the watch.
IAGO: Not this hour, lieutenant; 't is not yet ten o' th' clock:
  Our general cast us thus early for the love of his Desdemona,
    who let us not therefore blame: he hath not yet made
    wanton the night with her; and she is sport for Jove.
CASSIO: She's a most exquisite lady.
IAGO: And I'll warrant her full of game.
CASSIO: Indeed, she 's a most fresh and delicate creature.
IAGO: What an eye she has! methinks it sounds a parley to   *400*
    provocation.
CASSIO: An inviting eye; and yet methinks right modest.
IAGO: And when she speaks is it not an alarum to love?
CASSIO: She is, indeed, perfection.
IAGO: Well, happiness to their sheets! Come, lieutenant, I have a
    stoop of wine: and here without are a brace of Cyprus
    gallants, that would fain have a measure to the health of
    black Othello.
CASSIO: Not to-night, good Iago; I have very poor and unhappy
    brains for drinking: I could well wish courtesy would   *410*
    invent some other custom of entertainment.
IAGO: O, they are our friends; but one cup: I'll drink for you.

CASSIO: I have drunk but one cup to-night, and that was craftily
    qualified too—and, behold, what innovation, it makes
    here: I am unfortunate in the infirmity, and dare not task
    my weakness with any more.
IAGO: What, man! 't is a night of revels; the gallants desire it.
CASSIO: Where are they?
IAGO: Here at the door; I pray you call them in.
CASSIO: I'll do 't; but it dislikes me. (*Exit*)   *420*
IAGO: If I can fasten but one cup upon him,
  With that which he hath drunk to-night already,
  He'll be as full of quarrel and offence,
  As my young mistress' dog. Now, my sick fool Roderigo,
  Whom love hath turn'd almost the wrong side out,
  To Desdemona hath to-night carous'd
  Potations pottle deep—and he's to watch:
  Three lads of Cyprus,—noble, swelling spirits,
  That hold their honours in a wary distance,
  The very elements of this warlike isle,—   *430*
  Have I to-night fluster'd with flowing cups,
  And they watch too! Now, 'mongst this flock of drunkards,
  Am I to put our Cassio in some action
  That may offend the isle:—But here they come:
  If consequence do but approve my dream,
  My boat sails freely, both with wind and stream.

(*Re-enter* CASSIO, *with him* MONTANO *and* GENTLEMEN)

CASSIO: 'Fore heaven, they have given me a rouse already.   *440*
MONTANO: Good faith, a little one; not past a pint, as I am a
    soldier.
IAGO: Some wine, ho! (*Sings*)

           And let me the canakin clink, clink,
           And let me the canakin clink,
         A soldier's a man; A life's but a span;
           Why then let a soldier drink.

  Some wine, boys!   *450*
CASSIO: 'Fore heaven, an excellent song.
IAGO: I learned it in England, where indeed they are most potent
    in potting: your Dane, your German, and your
    swag-bellied Hollander,—Drink, ho!—are nothing to your
    English.
CASSIO: Is your Englishman so exquisite in his drinking?
IAGO: Why, he drinks you, with facility, your Dane dead drunk;
    he sweats not to overthrow your Almain; he gives your
    Hollander a vomit, ere the next pottle can be filled.

CASSIO: To the health of our general.   460
MONTANO: I am for it, lieutenant; and I'll do you justice.
IAGO: O sweet England!

> King Stephen was a worthy peer,
> His breeches cost him but a crown;
> He held them sixpence all too dear,
> With that he call'd the tailor lown.

> He was a wight of high renown,
> And thou art but of low degree: 470
> 'Tis pride that pulls the country down,
> And take thy old cloak about thee.

Some wine, ho!
CASSIO: Why this is a more exquisite song than the other.
IAGO: Will you hear it again?
CASSIO: No; for I hold him to be unworthy of his place that does
        those things.—Well,—Heaven 's above all; and there be
        souls must be saved, and there be souls must not be
        saved.   480
IAGO: It 's true, good lieutenant.
CASSIO: For mine own part,—no offence to the general, nor any
        man of quality,—I hope to be saved.
IAGO: And so do I too, lieutenant.
CASSIO: Ay, but by your leave, not before me; the lieutenant is
        to be saved before the ancient. Let's have no more of this:
        let's to our affairs.—Forgive us our sins!—Gentlemen, let
        's look to our business. Do not think, gentlemen, I am
        drunk: this is my ancient; this is my right hand, and this is
        my left:—I am not drunk now; I can stand well enough,   490
        and speak well enough—
BOTH GALLANTS: Excellent well.
CASSIO: Why, very well then: you must not think then that I am
        drunk. (*Exit*)
MONTANO: To the platform, masters; come, let's set the watch.
IAGO: You see this fellow that is gone before;—
    He is a soldier fit to stand by Caesar
    And give direction: and do but see his vice;
    'T is to his virtue a just equinox,
    The one as long as the other: 't is pity of him.   500
    I fear, the trust Othello puts him in,
    On some odd time of his infirmity,
    Will shake this island.
MONTANO: But is he often thus?
IAGO: 'T is evermore the prologue to his sleep:

He 'll watch the horologe a double set,
If drink rock not his cradle.
MONTANO: It were well
　The general were put in mind of it.
　Perhaps he sees it not; or his good nature   510
　Prizes the virtue that appears in Cassio,
　And looks not on his evils Is not this true?

(*Enter* RODERIGO)

IAGO: How, now, Roderigo?
　I pray you, after the lieutenant; go.

(*Exit* RODERIGO)
                                                                            520
MONTANO: And 't is great pity, that the noble Moor
　Should hazard such a place, as his own second,
　With one of an ingraft infirmity:
　It were an honest action, to say so
　To the Moor.
IAGO: Not I, for this fair island:
　I do love Cassio well, and would do much
　To cure him of this evil. But hark! what noise?

(*Enter* CASSIO, *pursuing* RODERIGO)   530

CASSIO: You rogue! you rascal!
MONTANO: What's the matter, lieutenant?
CASSIO: A knave—teach me my duty!
　I'll beat the knave into a twiggen bottle.
RODERIGO: Beat me!
CASSIO: Dost thou prate, rogue?
MONTANO: Nay, good lieutenant;
　I pray you, sir, hold your hand.
CASSIO: Let me go, sir,   540
　Or I'll knock you o'er the mazzard.
MONTANO: Come, come, you're drunk.
CASSIO: Drunk!
IAGO: Away, I say! go out, and cry—a mutiny.
　Nay, good lieutenant,—alas, gentlemen,—
　Help, ho!—Lieutenant, sir Montano,—
　Help, masters:—Here's a goodly watch indeed!
　Who's that that rings the bell?—Diablo, ho!
　The town will rise: Fie, fie, lieutenant hold;
　You will be sham'd for ever.   550

(*Enter* OTHELLO, *and* TWO ATTENDANTS)

OTHELLO: What is the matter here?
MONTANO: I bleed still; I am hurt to the death.
OTHELLO: Hold, for your lives.

IAGO: Hold, ho! Lieutenant,—sir Montano,—gentlemen,—
   Have you forgot all sense of place and duty?
   Hold! the general speaks to you; hold, hold, for shame!
OTHELLO: Why, how now? ho! from whence ariseth this?   *560*
   Are we turn'd Turks, and to ourselves do that
   Which heaven hath forbid the Ottomites?
   For Christian shame, put by this barbarous brawl:
   He that stirs next to carve for his own rage,
   Holds his soul light; he dies upon his motion.
   Silence that dreadful bell! it frights the isle
   From her propriety.—What is the matter, masters?—
   Honest Iago, that look'st dead with grieving,
   Speak, who began this? on thy love, I charge thee.
IAGO: I do not know:—friends all but now, e'en now,   *570*
   In quarter, and in terms like bride and groom
   Divesting them for bed: and then, but now,
   As if some planet had unwitted men,
   Swords out, and tilting one at other's breast,
   In opposition bloody. I cannot speak
   Any beginning to this peevish odds;
   And, would in action glorious I had lost
   Those legs, that brought me to a part of it!
OTHELLO: How comes it, Michael, you are thus forgot?
CASSIO: I pray you, pardon me; I cannot speak.   *580*
OTHELLO: Worthy Montano, you were wont be civil;
   The gravity and stillness of your youth
   The world hath noted, and your name is great
   In mouths of wisest censure: What's the matter
   That you unlace your reputation thus,
   And spend your rich opinion, for the name
   Of a night-brawler? give me answer to 't.
MONTANO: Worthy Othello, I am hurt to danger;
   Your officer, Iago, can inform you—
   While I spare speech, which something now offends me,—   *590*
   Of all that I do know: nor know I aught
   By me that's said or done amiss this night;
   Unless self-charity be sometimes a vice,
   And to defend ourselves it be a sin
   When violence assails us.
OTHELLO: Now, by heaven,
   My blood begins my safer guides to rule;
   And passion, having my best judgment colli'd,
   Assays to lead the way: If I once stir
   Or do but lift this arm, the best of you   *600*
   Shall sink in my rebuke. Give me to know
   How this foul rout began, who set it on;

And he that is approv'd in this offence,
Though he had twinn'd with me, both at a birth,
Shall loose me.—What! in a town of war,
Yet wild, the people's hearts brimful of fear,
To manage private and domestic quarrel,
In night, and on the court and guard of safety!
'T is monstrous.—Iago, who began 't?

MONTANO: If—partially affin'd, or leagu'd in office,—   *610*
Thou dost deliver more or less than truth,
Thou art no soldier.

IAGO: Touch me not so near:
I had rather have this tongue cut from my mouth,
Than it should do offence to Michael Cassio;
Yet, I persuade myself, to speak the truth
Shall nothing wrong him.—Thus it is, general.
Montano and myself being in speech,
There comes a fellow crying out for help;
And Cassio foll'wing him with determin'd sword,   *620*
To execute upon him: Sir, this gentleman
Steps in to Cassio, and entreats his pause;
Myself the crying fellow did pursue,
Lest, by his clamour,—as it so fell out,—
The town might fall in fright: he, swift of foot,
Outran my purpose; and I return'd the rather
For that I heard the clink and fall of swords,
And Cassio—high in oath; which, till to-night,
I ne'er might say before: When I came back,
—For this was brief,—I found them close together,   *630*
At blow, and thrust; even as again they were
When you yourself did part them.
More of this matter cannot I report:—
But men are men: the best sometimes forget:—
Though Cassio did some little wrong to him,—
As men in rage strike those that wish them best,—
Yet surely Cassio, I believe, receiv'd
From him that fled some strange indignity,
Which patience could not pass.

OTHELLO: I know, Iago,   *640*
Thy honesty and love doth mince this matter,
Making it light to Cassio:—Cassio, I love thee;
But never more be officer of mine.

(*Enter* DESDEMONA *attended*)

Look, if my gentle love be not rais'd up;—
I'll make thee an example.

DESDEMONA: What is the matter, dear?

OTHELLO: All's well, sweeting.   *650*
   Come away to bed. Sir for your hurts,
   Myself will be your surgeon: Lead him off.

(*To* MONTANO, *who is led off*)

   Iago, look with care about the town;
   And silence those whom this vile brawl distracted.
   Come, Desdemona, 't is the soldier's life
   To have their balmy slumbers wak'd with strife.

(*Exit all but* IAGO *and* CASSIO)   *660*

IAGO: What, are you hurt, lieutenant?

CASSIO: Ay, past all surgery.

IAGO: Marry, heaven forbid!

CASSIO: Reputation, reputation, reputation! O, I have lost my
   reputation! I have lost the immortal part of myself, and
   what remains is bestial.—My reputation, Iago, my
   reputation.

IAGO: As I am an honest man I had thought you had received
   some bodily wound; there is more sense in that than in
   reputation. Reputation is an idle and most false   *670*
   imposition; oft got without merit, and lost without
   deserving: You have lost no reputation at all, unless you
   repute yourself such a loser. What, man! there are ways to
   recover the general again: You are but now cast in his
   mood, a punishment more in policy than in malice; even
   so as one would beat his offenceless dog to affright an
   imperious lion: sue to him again, and he's yours.

CASSIO: I will rather sue to be despised, than to deceive so good
   a commander with so slight, so drunken, and so indiscreet
   an officer. Drunk? and speak parrot? and squabble?   *680*
   swagger? swear? and discourse fustian with one's own
   shadow?—O thou invisible spirit of wine, if thou hast no
   name to be known by, let us call thee devil!

IAGO: What was he that you followed with your sword? What
   had he done to you?

CASSIO: I know not.

IAGO: Is 't possible?

CASSIO: I remember a mass of things, but nothing distinctly; a
   quarrel, but nothing wherefore.—O God that men should
   put an enemy in their mouths to steal away their brains!   *690*
   that we should with joy, pleasance, revel, and applause
   transform ourselves into beasts!

IAGO: Why, but you are now well enough: how came you thus
   recovered?

CASSIO: It hath pleased the devil drunkenness, to give place to

the devil wrath: one unperfectness shows me another, to
make me frankly despise myself.

IAGO: Come, you are too severe a moraler: As the time, the
place, and the condition of this country stands, I could
heartily wish this had not befallen; but, since it is as it is   *700*
mend it for your own good.

CASSIO: I will ask him for my place again; he shall tell me I am a
drunkard! Had I as many mouths as Hydra such an
answer would stop them all. To be now a sensible man, by
and by a fool, and presently a beast! O strange!—Every
inordinate cup is unbless'd, and the ingredient is a devil.

IAGO: Come, come, good wine is a good familiar creature, if it be
well used; exclaim no more against it. And good
lieutenant, I think you think I love you.

CASSIO: I have well approv'd it, sir.—I drunk!   *710*

IAGO: You, or any man living, may be drunk at some time, man.
I'll tell you what you shall do. Our general's wife is now the
general:—I may say so in this respect, for that he hath
devoted and given up himself to the
contemplation,—mark,—and denotement of her parts and
graces:—confess yourself freely to her; importune her help
to put you in your place again: she is of so free, so kind, so
apt, so blessed a disposition, she holds it a vice in her
goodness not to do more than she is requested: This
broken joint, between you and her husband, entreat her to *720*
splinter; and, my fortunes against any lay worth naming,
this crack of your love shall grow stronger than it was
before.

CASSIO: You advise me well.

IAGO: I protest, in the sincerity of love and honest kindness.

CASSIO: I think it freely; and, betimes in the morning, I will
beseech the virtuous Desdemona to undertake for me: I
am desperate, of my fortunes if they check me here.

IAGO: You are in the right. Good night, lieutenant; I must to the
watch.   *730*

CASSIO: Good night, honest Iago.

(*Exit* CASSIO)

IAGO: And what's he then that says I play the villain?
When this advice is free, I give, and honest,
Probal to thinking, and indeed the course
To win the Moor again? For 't is most easy
The inclining Desdemona to subdue
In any honest suit; she's fram'd as fruitful
As the free elements. And then for her   *740*
To win the Moor,—were 't to renounce his baptism

All seals and symbols of redeemed sin,—
His soul is so enfetter'd to her love,
That she may make, unmake, do what she list,
Even as her appetite shall play the god
With his weak function. How am I then a villain,
To counsel Cassio to this parallel course,
Directly to his good? Divinity of hell!
When devils will the blackest sins put on,
They do suggest at first with heavenly shows,   750
As I do now: For whiles this honest fool
Plies Desdemona to repair his fortune
And she for him pleads strongly to the Moor,
I'll pour this pestilence into his ear,—
That she repeals him for her body's lust;
And by how much she strives to do him good,
She shall undo her credit with the Moor.
So will I turn her virtue into pitch;
And out of her own goodness make the net
That shall enmesh them all.—   760

(*Enter* Roderigo)
How now, Roderigo?

Roderigo: I do follow here in the chase, not like a hound that
          hunts, but one that fills up the cry. My money is almost
          spent; I have been to-night exceedingly well cudgelled;
          and, I think, the issue will be I shall have so much
          experience for my pains: and so, with no money at all, and
          a little more wit, return to Venice.   770
Iago: How poor are they that have not patience!
      What wound did ever heal but by degrees?
      Thou know'st, we work by wit and not by witchcraft;
      And wit depends on dilatory time.
      Does 't not go well? Cassio hath beaten thee,
      And thou, by that small hurt, hast cashier'd Cassio:
      Though other things grow fair against the sun,
      Yet fruits that blossom first will first be ripe:
      Content thyself a while.—In troth, 't is morning;
      Pleasure, and action, make the hours seem short   780
      Retire thee: go where thou art billeted:
      Away, I say, thou shalt know more hereafter:
      Nay—get thee gone.

(*Exit* Roderigo)

Two things are to be done,—
My wife must move for Cassio to her mistress,
I'll set her on;

Myself, the while, to draw the Moor apart,   *790*
And bring him jump when he may Cassio find
Soliciting his wife:—Ay, that's the way;
Dull not device by coldness and delay.

(*The curtain falls*)

Act III

Scene 1
Before the castle.

(*Enter* Cassio *and some* Musicians)

Cassio: Masters, play here, I will content your pains,
    Something that's brief: and bid, Good-morrow, general.

(*Enter* Clown. *He comes down to the* Musicians)   *10*

Clown: Why, masters, have your instruments been in Naples,
    that they speak i' the nose thus?
First Musician: How, sir, how?
Clown: Are these, I pray you, wind instruments?
First Musician: Ay, marry, are they, sir.
Clown: O, thereby hangs a tale. But masters, here's money for
    you: and the general so likes your music that he desires
    you, for love's sake, to make no more noise with it.
First Musician: Well, sir, we will not.   *20*
Clown: If you have any music that may not be heard, to 't
    again: but, as they say, to hear music the general does not
    greatly care.
First Musician: We have none such, sir.
Clown: Then put up your pipes in your bag, for I'll away: Go:
    vanish into air; away. (*Exeunt* Musicians)
Cassio: Dost thou hear, my honest friend?
Clown: No, I hear not your honest friend; I hear you.
Cassio: Prithee, keep up thy quillets. There's a poor piece of
    gold for thee: if the gentlewoman that attends the   *30*
    general's wife be stirring, tell her there's one Cassio
    entreats her a little favour of speech: wilt thou do this?
Clown: She is stirring, sir; if she will stir hither I shall seem to
    notify unto her. (*Exit*)

(*Enter* Iago)

Cassio: Do, good my friend.—In happy time, Iago.
Iago: You have not been a-bed then?
Cassio: Why, no; the day had broke   *40*
    Before we parted. I have made bold, Iago,

To send into your wife: My suit to her
Is, that she will to virtuous Desdemona
Procure me some access.
IAGO: I'll send her to you presently;
  And I'll devise a mean to draw the Moor
  Out of the way, that your converse and business
  May be more free.
CASSIO: I humbly thank you for 't. I never knew
  A Florentine more kind and honest.   *50*

(*Enter* EMILIA)

EMILIA: Good morrow, good lieutenant, I am sorry
  For your displeasure; but all will sure be well.
  The general and his wife are talking of it,
  And she speaks for you stoutly: The Moor replies,
  That he you hurt is of great fame in Cyprus,
  And great affinity; and that, in wholesome wisdom,
  He might not but refuse you: but he protests he loves you,   *60*
  And needs no other suitor, but his likings,
  To take the saf'st occasion by the front,
  To bring you in again.
CASSIO: Yet, I beseech you,—
  if you think fit, or that it may be done,—
  Give me the advantage of some brief discourse
  With Desdemona alone.
EMILIA: Pray you, come in;
  I will bestow you where you shall have time
  To speak your bosom freely.   *70*
CASSIO: I am much bound to you.

(*Exit*)

Scene 2
Beyond the castle

(*Enter* OTHELLO, IAGO, *and* GENTLEMEN)

OTHELLO: These letters give, Iago, to the pilot;
  And, by him, do my duties to the senate:
  That done, I will be walking on the works,—
  Repair thou to me.
IAGO: Well, my good lord, I'll do 't.— (*Exit*)   *80*
OTHELLO: This fortification, gentlemen, shall we see 't?
GENTLEMEN: We'll wait upon your lordship. (*Exeunt*)

Scene 3
Within the castle

(*Enter* DESDEMONA, CASSIO, *and* EMILIA)

DESDEMONA: Be thou assur'd, good Cassio, I will do
  All my abilities in thy behalf.
EMILIA: Good madam, do; I warrant it grieves my husband
  As if the case were his.
DESDEMONA: O, that's an honest fellow.—Do not doubt Cassio,
  But I will have my lord and you again   90
  As friendly as you were.
CASSIO: Bounteous madam,
  Whatever shall become of Michael Cassio,
  He's never any thing but your true servant.
DESDEMONA: I know't,—I thank you: you do love my lord:
  Y'ave known him long: and be you well assur'd
  He shall in strangeness stand no farther off
  Than in a politic distance.
CASSIO: Ay, but lady,
  That policy may either last so long,   100
  Or feed upon such nice and waterish diet,
  Or breed itself so out of circumstance,
  That I, being absent, and my place supplied,
  My general will forget my love and service.
DESDEMONA: Do not doubt that; before Emilia here,
  I give thee warrant of thy place: assure thee,
  If I do vow a friendship I'll perform it
  To the last article: my lord shall never rest;
  I'll watch him tame, and talk him out of patience;
  His bed shall seem a school, his board a shrift.   110
  I'll intermingle every thing he does
  With Cassio's suit: Therefore be merry, Cassio,
  For thy solicitor shall rather die
  Than give thy cause away.

(*Enter* OTHELLO *and* IAGO)

EMILIA: Madam, here comes my lord.
CASSIO: Madam, I'll take my leave.
DESDEMONA: Nay, stay, and hear me speak.   120
CASSIO: Madam, not now, I'm very ill at ease,
  Unfit for mine own purpose.
DESDEMONA: Well, do your discretion.

(*Exit* CASSIO)

IAGO: Ha! I like not that.
OTHELLO: What do'st thou say?

IAGO: Nothing, my lord: or if—I know not what.

OTHELLO: Was not that Cassio parted from my wife?   130

IAGO: Cassio, my lord? No, sure, I cannot think it.
   That he would steal away so guilty-like,
   Seeing you coming.

OTHELLO: I do believe 't was he.

DESDEMONA: How, now, my lord?
   I have been talking with a suitor here,
   A man that languishes in your displeasure.

OTHELLO: Who is 't you mean?

DESDEMONA: Why, your lieutenant Cassio. Good my lord,
   If I have any grace, or power to move you,   140
   His present reconciliation take,
   For, if he be not one that truly loves you,
   That errs in ignorance and not in cunning,
   I have no judgment in an honest face:
   I prithee call him back.

OTHELLO: Went he hence now?

DESDEMONA: Ay, sooth, so humbled,
   That he hath left part of his grief with me,
   To suffer with him. Good love, call him back.

OTHELLO: Not now, sweet Desdemona; some other time.   150

DESDEMONA: But shall 't be shortly?

OTHELLO: The sooner, sweet, for you.

DESDEMONA: Shall 't be to-night at supper?

OTHELLO: No, not to-night.

DESDEMONA: To-morrow dinner then?

OTHELLO: I shall not dine at home;
   I meet the captains at the citadel.

DESDEMONA: Why, then, to-morrow night; or Tuesday morn,
   Or Tuesday noon, or night; or Wednesday morn;—
   I prithee name the time; but let it not   160
   Exceed three days: in faith he's penitent;
   And yet his trespass, in our common reason,
   —Save that, they say, the wars must make example
   Out of their best,—is not almost a fault
   To incur a private check: When shall he come?
   Tell me, Othello. I wonder in my soul,
   What you would ask me that I should deny,
   Or stand so mammering on. What! Michael Cassio,
   That came a wooing with you; and so many a time,
   When I have spoke of you dispraisingly,   170
   Hath ta'en your part; to have so much to do
   To bring him in! Trust me, I could do much,—

OTHELLO: Prithee, no more: let him come when he will;
   I will deny thee nothing.

DESDEMONA: Why, this is not a boon;
    'T is as I should entreat you wear your gloves,
    Or feed on nourishing dishes, or keep you warm;
    Or sue to you to do a peculiar profit
    To your own person: Nay, when I have a suit
    Wherein I mean to touch your love indeed,   180
    It shall be full of poise and difficult weight,
    And fearful to be granted.
OTHELLO: I will deny thee nothing:
    Whereon, I do beseech thee, grant me this,
    To leave me but a little to myself.
DESDEMONA: Shall I deny you? no: farewell, my lord.
OTHELLO: Farewell, my Desdemona: I'll come to thee straight.
DESDEMONA: Emilia, come:—Be as your fancies teach you;
    Whate'er you be, I am obedient. (*Exit followed by* EMILIA.)
OTHELLO: Excellent wretch! Perdition catch my soul   190
    But I do love thee! and, when I love thee not,
    Chaos is come again.
IAGO: My noble lord,—
OTHELLO: What doest thou say, Iago?
IAGO: Did Michael Cassio, when you woo'd my lady,
    Know of your love?
OTHELLO: He did, from first to last; Why dost thou ask?
IAGO: But for a satisfaction of my thought;
    No farther harm.
OTHELLO: Why of thy thought, Iago?   200
IAGO: I did not think he had been acquainted with her.
OTHELLO: O, yes; and went between us very oft.
IAGO: Indeed?
OTHELLO: Indeed? ay, indeed:—Discern'st thou aught in that?
    Is he not honest?
IAGO: Honest, my lord?
OTHELLO: Honest? Ay, honest.
IAGO: My lord, for aught I know.
OTHELLO: What dost thou think?
IAGO: Think, my lord?   210
OTHELLO: Think, my lord? By heaven, he echoes me
    As if there were some monster in his thought
    Too hideous to be shown.—Thou dost mean something:
    I heard thee say but now,—thou lik'dst not that,
    When Cassio left my wife: What didst not like?
    And, when I told thee he was of my counsel
    In my whole course of wooing, thou cry'dst, Indeed?
    And didst contract and purse thy brow together,
    As if thou then hadst shut up in thy brain

Some horrible conceit: If thou dost love me   *220*
   Show me thy thought.
IAGO: My lord, you know I love you.
OTHELLO: I think thou dost;
   And, for I know thou 'rt full of love and honesty,
   And weigh'st thy words before thou giv'st them breath,
   Therefore these stops of thine fright me the more:
   For such things in a false, disloyal knave
   Are tricks of custom; but in a man that's just,
   They're close delations, working from the heart,
   That passion cannot rule.   *230*
IAGO: For Michael Cassio,—
   I dare be sworn I think that he is honest.
OTHELLO: I think so too.
IAGO: Men should be what they seem;
   Or, those that be not 'would they might seem none!
OTHELLO: Certain, men should be what they seem.
IAGO: Why then, I think Cassio's an honest man.
IAGO: Nay, yet there's more in this.
   I prithee speak to me, as to thy thinkings,
   As thou dost ruminate; and give thy worst of thoughts   *240*
   The worst of words.
IAGO: Good my lord, pardon me;
   Though I am bound to every act of duty,
   I am not bound to that all slaves are free to.
   Utter my thoughts? Why, say, they are vile and false,—
   As where's that palace whereinto foul things
   Sometimes intrude not?—who has a breast so pure,
   But some uncleanly apprehensions
   Keep leets and law-days, and in sessions sit
   With medications lawful?   *250*
OTHELLO: Thou dost conspire against thy friend, Iago,
   If thou but think'st him wrong'd, and mak'st his ear
   A stranger to thy thoughts.
IAGO: I do beseech you,—
   Though I perchance, am vicious in my guess,
   —As I confess it is my nature's plague
   To spy into abuses, and oft my jealousy
   Shapes faults that are not,—that your wisdom yet,
   From one that so imperfectly conceits,
   Would take no notice; nor build yourself a trouble   *260*
   Out of his scatt'ring and unsure observance:
   It were not for your quiët, nor your good,
   Nor for my manhood, honesty, and wisdom,
   To let you know my thoughts.

OTHELLO: What does thou mean?
IAGO: Good name in man and woman, dear my lord,
  Is the immediate jewel of their souls;
  Who steals my purse steals trash; 't is something-nothing;
  'T was mine, 't is his, and has been slave to thousands;
  But he that filches from me my good name,   270
  Robs me of that which not enriches him,
  And makes me poor indeed.
OTHELLO: By Heaven I'll know thy thoughts.
IAGO: You cannot, if my heart were in your hand;
  Nor shall not, whilst 't is in my custody.
OTHELLO: Ha!
IAGO: O, beware, my lord, of jealousy;
  It is the green-ey'd monster, which doth mock
  The meat it feeds on: That cuckold lives in bliss
  Who, certain of his fate, loves not his wronger;   280
  But, O, what damned minutes tells he o'er,
  Who dotes, yet doubts; suspects, yet strongly loves!
OTHELLO: O misery!
IAGO: Poor, and content, is rich, and rich enough;
  But riches, fineless, is as poor as winter,
  To him that ever fears he shall be poor:
  Good heaven, the souls of all my tribe defend
  From jealousy!
OTHELLO: Why! why is this?
  Think'st thou, I'd make a life of jealousy,   290
  To follow still the changes of the moon
  With fresh suspicions? No: to be once in doubt,
  Is once to be resolv'd: Exchange me for a goat,
  When I shall turn the business of my soul
  To such exufflicate and blow'd surmises,
  Matching thy inference. 'T is not to make me jealous,
  To say my wife is fair, feeds well, loves company,
  Is free of speech, sings, plays, and dances well;
  Where virtue is, these are more virtuous;
  Nor from mine own weak merits will I draw   300
  The smallest fear, or doubt of her revolt;
  For she had eyes, and chose me: No, Iago;
  I'll see before I doubt; when I doubt, prove;
  And, on the proof, there is no more but this,—
  Away at once with love, or jealousy.
IAGO: I'm glad of it; for now I shall have reason
  To show the love and duty that I bear you
  With franker spirit: therefore, as I am bound,
  Receive it from me:—I speak not yet of proof.

Look to your wife; observe her well with Cassio;   310
Wear your eye thus—not jealous, nor secure;
I would not have your free and noble nature,
Out of self-bounty, be abus'd; look to 't;
I know our country disposition well;
In Venice they do let heaven see the pranks
They dare not show their husbands; their best conscience
Is not to leave 't undone, but keep 't unknown.
OTHELLO: Dost thou say so?
IAGO: She did deceive her father, marrying you;
And when she seem'd to shake and fear your looks,   320
She lov'd them most.
OTHELLO: And so she did.
IAGO: Why, go to, then;
She that so young could give out such a seeming,
To seel her father's eyes up, close as oak,
He thought 't was witchcraft:—But I am much to blame;
I humbly do beseech you of your pardon,
For too much loving you.
OTHELLO: I am bound to thee for ever.
IAGO: I see, this hath a little dash'd your spirits.   330
OTHELLO: Not a jot, not a jot.
IAGO: Trust me, I fear it has.
I hope you will consider what is spoke
Comes from my love:—But I do see y'are mov'd:—
I am to pray you not to strain my speech
To grosser issues, nor to larger reach
Than to suspicion.
OTHELLO: I will not.
IAGO: Should you do so, my lord,
My speech should fall into such vile success   340
As my thoughts aim not at. Cassio's my worthy friend:—
My lord, I see y'are mov'd.
OTHELLO: No, not much mov'd:—
I do not think but Desdemona's honest.
IAGO: Long live she so! and long live you to think so!
OTHELLO: And yet, how nature erring from itself,—
IAGO: Ay, there's the point:—As,—to be bold with you,—
Not to affect many proposed matches
Of her own clime, complexion and degree;
Whereto, we see, in all things nature tends;   350
Foh! one may smell in such a will most rank,
Foul disproportions, thoughts unnatural,—
But, pardon me: I do not in position
Distinctly speak of her: though I may fear,

Her will, recoiling to her better judgment,
May fall to match you with her country forms,
And haply, repent.
OTHELLO: Farewell, farewell:
  If more thou dost perceive let me know more;
  Set on thy wife to observe: Leave me, Iago.   *360*
IAGO: My lord, I take my leave.
OTHELLO: Why did I marry?—This honest creature, doubtless,
  Sees and knows more, much more, than he unfolds.
IAGO: My lord, I would I might entreat your honour
  To scan this thing no farther; leave it to time:
  Although 't is fit that Cassio have his place,—
  For, sure, he fills it up with great ability,—
  Yet, if you please to hold him off awhile,
  You shall by that perceive him and his means:
  Note, if your lady strain his entertainment   *370*
  With any strong or vehement importun'ty;
  Much will be seen in that. In the mean time,
  Let me be thought too busy in my fears,—
  As worthy cause I have to fear I am,—
  And hold her free, I do beseech your honour,
OTHELLO: Fear not my government.
IAGO: I once more take my leave.

(*Exit* IAGO)

OTHELLO: This fellow's of exceeding honesty,   *380*
  And knows all qual'ties, with a learned spirit
  Of human dealings: If I do prove her haggard,
  Though that her jesses were my dear heart-strings,
  I'd whistle her off, and let her down the wind,
  To prey at fortune. Haply, for I am black;
  And have not those soft parts of conversation
  That chamberers have: Or, for I am declin'd
  Into the vale of years;—yet that 's not much:—
  She's gone; I am abus'd; and my relief
  Must be to loath her. O curse of marriage,   *390*
  That we can call these delicate creatures ours,
  And not their appetites! I'd rather be a toad,
  And live upon the vapour of a dungeon,
  Than keep a corner in the thing I love,
  For other's uses. Yet 't is the plague of great ones;
  Prerogativ'd are they less than the base;
  'T is destiny unshunnable, like death;
  Even then this forked plague is fated to us,
  When we do quicken. Desdemona comes.

If she be false, O, then heaven mocks itself!   *400*
  I'll not believe 't.

(*Enter* DESDEMONA *and* EMILIA)

DESDEMONA: How, now, my dear Othello?
  Your dinner, and the generous islanders
  By you invited, do attend your presence.
OTHELLO: I am to blame.
DESDEMONA: Why do you speak so faintly?
  Are you not well?   *410*
OTHELLO: I have a pain upon my forehead here.
DESDEMONA: Why, that's with watching; 't will away again:
  Let me but bind it hard, within this hour
  It will be well.
OTHELLO: Your napkin is too little;
  Let it alone. Come, I'll go in with you.
DESDEMONA: I am very sorry that you are not well.
EMILIA: I am glad I have found this napkin;
  This was her first remembrance from the Moor:
  My wayward husband hath a hundred times   *420*
  Woo'd me steal it: but she so loves the token,—
  For he conjur'd her she should ever keep it,—
  That she reserves it evermore about her,
  To kiss, and talk to. I'll have the work ta'en out,
  And give 't Iago; what he will do with it,
  Heaven knows, not I:
  I nothing, but to please his fantasy.

(*Enter* IAGO)

IAGO: How, now! What do you here alone?   *430*
EMILIA: Do not you chide; I have a thing for you.
IAGO: A thing for me?—it is a common thing—
EMILIA: Ha?
IAGO: To have a foolish wife.
EMILIA: O, is that all? What will you give me now
  For that same handkerchief?
IAGO: What handkerchief?
EMILIA: What handkerchief?
  Why, that the Moor first gave to Desdemona;
  That which so often you did bid me steal.   *440*
IAGO: Hast stolen it from her?
EMILIA: No; faith she let it drop by negligence:
  And, to the advantage, I being there, took 't up.
  Look, here it is.
IAGO: A good wench; give it me.

EMILIA: What will you do with 't, that you have been so earnest
    To have me filch it?
IAGO: Why, what's that to you?
EMILIA: If 't be not for some purpose of import,
    Give 't me again: Poor lady! she'll run mad   450
    When she shall lack it.
IAGO: Be not acknown on 't: I have use for it.
    Go, leave me.
    I will in Cassio's lodging lose this napkin,
    And let him find it: Trifles, light as air,
    Are to the jealous confirmations strong
    As proofs of holy writ. This may do something.
    The Moor already changes with my poison:
    Dangerous conceits are, in their natures, poisons,
    Which, at the first, are scarce found to distaste;   460
    But, with a little act upon the blood,
    Burn like the mines of sulphur.—I did say so—
    Look, where he comes! Not poppy, nor mandragora,
    Nor all the drowsy syrups of the world,
    Shall ever medicine thee to that sweet sleep
    Which thou ow'dst yesterday.

(*Enter* OTHELLO)

OTHELLO: Ha! ha! false to me?
IAGO: Why, how now, general? no more of that.   470
OTHELLO: Avaunt! be gone! th'ast set me on the rack:—
    I swear, 't is better to be much abus'd,
    Than but to know 't a little.
IAGO: Now now, my lord?
OTHELLO: What sense had I of her stolen hours of lust?
    I saw 't not, thought it not; it harm'd not me:
    I slept the next night well, was free and merry;
    I found not Cassio's kisses on her lips:
    He that is robb'd, not wanting what is stolen,
    Let him not know 't, and he's not robb'd at all.   480
IAGO: I am sorry to hear this.
OTHELLO: I had been happy if the general camp,
    Pioners and all, had tasted her sweet body,
    So I had nothing known: O now, for ever,
    Farewell the tranquil mind! farewell content!
    Farewell the plumed troops, and the big wars,
    That makes ambition virtue! O, farewell!
    Farewell the neighing steed, and the shrill trump;
    The spirit-stirring drum—the ear-piercing fife,—
    The royal banner—and all quality,   490
    Pride, pomp, and circumstance of glorious war!

And O you mortal engines, whose rude throats
Th' immortal Jove's dread clamours counterfeit,
Farewell! Othello's occupation's gone!
IAGO: Is 't possible?—My lord?—
OTHELLO: Villain, be sure thou prove my love a whore,
  Be sure of it; give me the ocular proof;
  Or, by the worth of mine eternal soul,
  Thou hadst been better have been born a dog
  Than answer my wak'd wrath.   500
IAGO: Is 't come to this?
OTHELLO: Make me to see 't; or, at the least, so prove it,
  That the probation bear no hinge, nor loop,
  To hang a doubt on: or woe upon they life!
IAGO: My noble lord,—
OTHELLO: If thou dost slander her, and torture me,
  Never pray more: abandon all remorse;
  On horror's head horrors accumulate:
  Do deeds to make heaven weep, all earth amaz'd,
  For nothing canst thou to damnation add,   510
  Greater than that.
IAGO: O grace! O heaven defend me;
  Are you a man? have you a soul, or sense?—
  God b' wi' you; take mine office.—O wretched fool,
  That liv'st to make thine honesty a vice.—
  O monstrous world! Take note, take note, O world,
  To be direct and honest is not safe.
  I thank you for this profit; and, from hence,
  I'll love no friend, sith love breeds such offence.
OTHELLO: Nay, stay:—Thou shouldst be honest.   520
IAGO: I should be wise; for honesty's a fool,
  And loses that it works for.
OTHELLO: By the world,
  I think my wife be honest, and think she 's not;
  I think that thou art just, and think th' art not;
  I'll have some proof: Her name, that was as fresh
  As Dian's visage, is now begrim'd and black
  As mine own face.—If there be cords, or knives,
  Poison, or fire, or suffocating streams,
  I'll not endure 't.—Would I were satisfied!   530
IAGO: I see, sir, you are eaten up with passion:
  I do repent me that I put it to you.
  'You would be satisfi'd?
OTHELLO: Would? nay, I will.
IAGO: And may: But how? how satisfi'd, my lord?
  Would you the supervisor grossly gape on?
  Behold her tupped?

OTHELLO: Death and damnation! O!

IAGO: It were a tedious difficulty, I think,
    To bring them to that prospect:—Damn them then,   540
    If ever mortal eyes do see their guilt,
    More than their own! What then? how then?
    What shall I say? Where's satisfaction?
    It is impossible you should see this,
    Were they as prime as goats, as hot as monkeys,
    As salt as wolves in pride, and fools as gross
    As ignorance made drunk. But yet, I say,
    If imputation, and strong circumstances,
    Which lead directly to the door of truth,
    Will give you satisfaction, you may have't.   550

OTHELLO: Give me a living reason she's disloyal.

IAGO: I do not like the office:
    But, sith I 'm enter'd in this cause so far,
    Prick'd to 't by foolish honesty and love,
    I will go on. I lay with Cassio lately;
    And, being troubled with a raging tooth,
    I could not sleep.
    There are a kind of men so loose of soul,
    That in their sleep will mutter their affairs;
    One of this kind is Cassio: 560
    In sleep I heard him say,—Sweet Desdemona,
    Let us be wary, let us hide our loves!
    And then, sir, would he gripe and wring my hand,
    Cry,—O sweet creature! then kiss me hard,
    As if he pluck'd up kisses by the roots,
    That grew upon my lips; and then laid his leg
    Over my thigh, and sigh'd, and kiss'd; and then
    Cry,—Cursed fate that gave thee to the Moor!

OTHELLO: O monstrous! monstrous!

IAGO: Nay, this was but his dream.   570

OTHELLO: But this denoted a foregone conclusion;
    'T is a shrewd doubt, though it be but a dream.

IAGO: And this may help to thicken other proofs,
    That do demonstrate thinly.

OTHELLO: I'll tear her all to pieces.

IAGO: Nay, but be wise; yet we see nothing done;
    She may be honest yet. Tell me but this,—
    Have you not sometimes seen a handkerchief,
    Spotted with straw-ber-ries, in your wife's hand?

OTHELLO: I gave her such a one: 't was my first gift.   580

IAGO: I know not that: but such a handkerchief,—
    I'm sure it was your wife's,—did I to-day
    See Cassio—wipe his beard with.

OTHELLO: If it be that,—
IAGO: If it be that or any, that was her's,
  It speaks against her, with the other proofs.
OTHELLO: O, that the slave had forty thousand lives;
  One is too poor, too weak for my revenge!
  Now do I see 't is true.—Look here, Iago;
  All my fond love thus do I blow to heaven: 590
  'T is gone!—
  Arise, black vengeance, from thy hollow hell!
  Yield up, O love, they crown, and hearted throne,
  To tyrannous hate! swell, bosom, with thy fraught,
  For 't is of aspicks' tongues!
IAGO: Yet, be content.
OTHELLO: O, blood, blood, blood!
IAGO: Patience, I say; your mind perhaps may change.
OTHELLO: Never, Iago. Like to the Pontick sea,
  Whose icy current and compulsive course   600
  Ne'er feels retiring ebb, but keeps due on
  To the Propontick and the Hellespont:
  Ev'n so my bloody thoughts, with violent pace,
  Shall ne'er look back, ne'er ebb to humble love,
  Till that a capable and wide revenge
  Swallow them up.—Now, by yond' marble heaven,
  In the due reverence of a sacred vow
  I here engage my words.
IAGO: Do not rise yet.—
  Witness, ye ever-burning lights above!   610
  You elements that clip us round about!
  Witness, that here Iago doth give up
  The execution of his wit, hands, heart,
  To wrong'd Othello's service! let him command,
  And to obey shall be in me remorse,
  What bloody business ever—
OTHELLO: I greet thy love,
  Not with vain thanks, but with acceptance bounteous,
  And will upon the instant put thee to 't:
  Within these three days let me hear thee say   620
  That Cassio's not alive.
IAGO: My friend is dead; 't is done, at your request:
  But let her live.
OTHELLO: Damn her, lewd minx! O, damn her!
  Come, go with me apart; I will withdraw,
  To furnish me with some swift means of death
  For the fair devil. Now art thou my lieutenant.
IAGO: I am your own for ever.

Scene 4
The same

(*Enter* DESDEMONA, EMILIA, *and* CLOWN)

DESDEMONA: Do you know, sirah, where lieutenant Cassio lies? *630*
CLOWN: I dare not say he lies anywhere.
DESDEMONA: Why, man?
CLOWN: He is a soldier; and for me to say a soldier lies 't is
    stabbing.
DESDEMONA: Go to. Where lodges he?
CLOWN: To tell you where he lodges is to tell you where I lie.
DESDEMONA: Can anything be made of this?
CLOWN: I know not where he lodges; and for me to devise a
    lodging, and say he lies here, or he lies there, were to lie in
    mine own throat. *640*
DESDEMONA: Can you enquire him out, and be edified by report?
CLOWN: I will catechize the world for him; that is, make
    questions, and by them answer.
DESDEMONA: Seek him, bid him come hither; tell him, I have
    moved my lord in his behalf, and hope all will be well.
CLOWN: To do this is within the compass of man's wit; and
    therefore I will attempt the doing it. (*Exit*)
DESDEMONA: Where should I lose that handkerchief, Emilia?
EMILIA: I know not, madam.
DESDEMONA: Believe me, I had rather have lost my purse *650*
    Full of cruzadoes. And, but my noble Moor
    Is true of mind, and made of no such baseness
    As jealous creatures are, it were enough
    To put him to ill thinking.
EMILIA: Is he not jealous?
DESDEMONA: Who, he? I think the sun, where he was born,
    Drew all such humours from him.
EMILIA: Look where he comes.

(*Enter* OTHELLO)
660
DESDEMONA: I will not leave him now till Cassio
    Be call'd to him.—How is 't with you—my lord?
OTHELLO: Well,—my good lady;—(*Aside.*) O, hardness to
    dissemble!—
    How do you, Desdemona?
DESDEMONA: Well,—my good lord.
OTHELLO: Give me your hand: This hand is moist, my lady.
DESDEMONA: It yet has felt no age, nor known no sorrow.
OTHELLO: This argues fruitfulness, and liberal heart;
    Hot, hot,—and moist: This hand of yours requires *670*
    A sequester from liberty, fasting and prayer,

Much castigation, exercise devout;
For here's a young and sweating devil here,
That commonly rebels. 'T is a good hand,
A frank one.
DESDEMONA: You may, indeed, say so;
For 't was that hand that gave away my heart.
OTHELLO: A liberal hand: The hearts of old gave hands:
But our new heraldry is—hands, not hearts.
DESDEMONA: I cannot speak of this. Come now, your promise.   *680*
OTHELLO: What promise, chuck?
DESDEMONA: I have sent to bid Cassio come speak with you.
OTHELLO: I have a salt and sorry rheum offends me;
Lend me thy handkerchief.
DESDEMONA: Here, my lord.
OTHELLO: That which I gave you.
DESDEMONA: I have it not about me.
OTHELLO: Not?
DESDEMONA: No, indeed, my lord.
OTHELLO: That is a fault: That handkerchief   *690*
Did an Egyptian to my mother give;
She was a charmer, and could almost read
The thoughts of people: she told her, while she kept it,
'T would make her amiable, and subdue my father
Entirely to her love; but if she lost it,
Or made a gift of it, my father's eye
Should hold her loathed, and his spirit should hunt
After new fancies: She, dying, gave it me;
And bid me, when my fate would have me wive,
To give it her. I did so, and take heed on 't,   *700*
Make it a darling like your precious eye;
To lose 't or—to give 't away were such perdition
As nothing else could match.
DESDEMONA: Is 't possible?
OTHELLO: 'T is true: There's magic in the web of it,
A sybil, that had number'd in the world
The sun to course two hundred compasses,
In her prophetic fury sew'd the work:
The worms were hallow'd that did breed the silk,
And it was dy'd in mummy, which the skilful   *710*
Conserv'd of maidens' hearts.
DESDEMONA: Indeed; is 't true?
OTHELLO: Most veritable; therefore look to 't well.
DESDEMONA: Then 'would to heaven that I had never seen it.
OTHELLO: Ha! wherefore?
DESDEMONA: Why do you speak so startingly and rash?
OTHELLO: Is 't lost? is 't gone? speak, is 't out of the way?

DESDEMONA: Heaven bless us!
OTHELLO: Say you?
DESDEMONA: It is not lost: but what and if it were?   720
OTHELLO: How?
DESDEMONA: I say, it is not lost.
OTHELLO: Fetch 't, let me see it,
DESDEMONA: Why, so I can, sir, but I will not now.
   This is a trick, to put me from my suit;
   Pray you, let Cassio be receiv'd again.
OTHELLO: Fetch me the handkerchief: my mind misgives.
DESDEMONA: Come, come;
   You'll never meet a more sufficient man.
OTHELLO: The handkerchief,—   730
DESDEMONA: I pray, talk me of Cassio.
OTHELLO: The handkerchief,—
DESDEMONA: A man that, all his time,
   Hath founded his good fortunes on your love,
   Shar'd dangers with you;—
OTHELLO: The handkerchief,—
DESDEMONA: In sooth, you are to blame.
OTHELLO: Away!

(*Exit* OTHELLO)
                                                           740
EMILIA: Is not this man jealous?
DESDEMONA: I ne'er saw this before.
   Sure, there's some wonder in this handkerchief;
   I'm most unhappy in the loss of it.
EMILIA: 'T is not a year or two shows us a man:
   They are all but stomachs, and we all but food;
   They eat us hungerly, and when they are full
   They belch us. Look you! Cassio, and my husband.

(*Enter* IAGO *and* CASSIO)
                                                           750
IAGO: There is no other way; 't is she must do 't;
   And, lo, the happiness! go, and importune her.
DESDEMONA: Now now, good Cassio? what's the news with
      you?
CASSIO: Madam, my former suit: I do beseech you,
   That, by your virtuous means, I may again
   Exist, and be a member of his love,
   Whom I, with all the office of my heart,
   Entirely honour; I would not be delay'd;
   If my offence be of such mortal kind,   760
   That nor my service past, nor present sorrows,
   Nor purpos'd merit in futurity
   Can ransom me into his love again,

But to know so must be my benefit;
So shall I clothe me in a forc'd content,
And shut myself up in some other course,
To fortune's alms.
DESDEMONA: Alas! thrice-gentle Cassio,
My advocation is not now in tune;
My lord—is not my lord; nor should I know him,   770
Were he in favour, as in humour alter'd.
So help me every spirit sanctifi'd,
As I have spoken for you all my best,
And stood within the blank of his displeasure,
For my free speech! You must awhile be patient:
What can I do I will; and more I will,
Than for myself I dare: let that suffice you.
IAGO: Is my lord angry?
EMILIA: He went hence but now,
And, certainly, in strange unquiëtness.   780
IAGO: Can he be angry? I have seen the cannon,
When it hath blown his ranks into the air;
And, like the devil, from his very arm
Puff'd his own brother—And can he be angry?
Something of moment, then: I will go meet him;
There 's matter in 't indeed, if he be angry.
DESDEMONA: I prithee, do so.—Something, sure, of state,

(*Exit* IAGO)

Either from Venice; or some unhatch'd practice   790
Made demonstrable here in Cyprus to him,
Hath puddled his clear spirit; and, in such cases,
Men's natures wrangle with inferior things,
Though great ones are their object. 'T is even so;
For let our finger ache, and it indues
Our other healthful members e'en to a sense
Of pain: Nay, we must think men are not gods;
Nor of them look for such observancy
As fits the bridal.—Beshrew me much, Emilia,
I was—unhandsome warrior as I am—   800
Arraigning his unkindness with my soul;
But now I find I have suborn'd the witness,
And he's indicted falsely.
EMILIA: Pray heaven it be state matters, as you think;
And no conception, nor no jealous toy,
Concerning you.
DESDEMONA: Alas, the day! I never gave him cause.
EMILIA: But jealous souls will not be answer'd so;
They are not ever jealous for the cause.

But jealous for they're jealous: It is a monster,   810
  Begot upon itself, born on itself.
DESDEMONA: Heaven keep that monster from Othello's mind!
EMILIA: Lady,—amen.
DESDEMONA: I will go seek him.—Cassio, walk here about:
  If I do find him fit, I'll move your suit,
  And seek t' effect it to my uttermost.
CASSIO: I humbly thank you ladyship.

(*Exit* DESDEMONA *and* EMILIA)

(*Enter* BIANCA)   820

BIANCA: Save you, friend Cassio!
CASSIO: What make you from home?
  How is it with you, my most fair Bianca?
  Indeed, sweet love, I was coming to your house.
BIANCA: And I was going to your lodging Cassio.
  What! keep a week away? seven days and nights?
  Eight score eight hours? and lovers' absent hours,
  More tedious than the diäl eight score times?
  O weary reckoning!   830
CASSIO: Pardon me, Bianca?
  I have this while with leaden thoughts been press'd;
  But I shall, in a more continuate time,
  Strike off this score of absence. Sweet Bianca. (*Giving her*
    DESDEMONA's *handkerchief*)
  Take me this work out.
BIANCA: O, Cassio, whence came this?
  This is some token from a newer friend.
  To the felt absence now I feel a cause.
  Is 't come to this? Well, well.   840
CASSIO: Go to, woman!
  Throw your vile guesses in the devil's teeth,
  From whence you have them. You are jealous now
  That is from some mistress, some remembrance:
  No, in good troth, Bianca.
BIANCA: Why, whose is it?
CASSIO: I know not, neither: I found it in my chamber.
  I like the work well: ere it be demanded,
  —As like enough it will,—I'd have it copied:
  Take it, and do 't; and leave me for this time.   850
BIANCA: Leave you! wherefore?
CASSIO: I do attend here on the general;
  And think it no addition, nor my wish,
  To have him see me woman'd.

BIANCA: Why, I pray you?
CASSIO: Not that I love you not.
BIANCA: But that you do not love me.
  I pray you bring me on the way a little;
  And say, if I shall see you soon at night.
CASSIO: 'Tis but a little way that I can bring you,   860
  For I attend here: but I'll see you soon.
BIANCA: 'T is very good: I must be circumstanc'd.

Act IV

Scene 1
Another room in the castle

(OTHELLO *is discovered seated in the chair,* IAGO *standing above him.*)

IAGO: Will you think so?
OTHELLO: Think so, Iago?
IAGO: What,
  To kiss in private?
OTHELLO: An unauthoriz'd kiss?
IAGO: Or to be naked with her friend in bed
  An hour, or more, not meaning any harm?
OTHELLO: Naked in bed, Iago, and not mean harm?   10
  It is hypocrisy against the devil.
  They that mean virtuously, and yet do so,
  The devil their virtue tempts, and they tempt heaven.
IAGO: If they do nothing, 'tis a venial slip:
  But if I give my wife a handkerchief,—
OTHELLO: What then?
IAGO: Why then 't is hers, my lord; and, being hers,
  She may, I think, bestow 't on any man.
OTHELLO: She is protectress of her honour too;
  May she give that?   20
IAGO: Her honour is an essence that's not seen,
  They have it very oft that have it not:
  But, for the handkerchief,—
OTHELLO: By heaven, I would most gladly have forgot it:—
  Thou said'st,—O, it comes o'er my memory,
  As doth the raven o'er the infected house,
  Boding to all,—he had my handkerchief.
IAGO: Ay, what of that?
OTHELLO: That's not so good, now.
IAGO: What, if I had said I had seen him do you wrong?   30
  Or heard him say,—as knaves be such abroad,
  Who, having by their own importunate suit,

Or voluntary dotage of some mistress,
Convinced or suppli'd them, cannot choose
But they must blab,—
OTHELLO: Hath he said anything?
IAGO: He hath, my lord; but be you well assur'd,
No more than he'll unswear.
OTHELLO: What hath he said?
IAGO: Why, that he did,—I know not what he did.   40
OTHELLO: What? what?
IAGO: Lie—
OTHELLO: With her?
IAGO: With her? On her—what you will.
OTHELLO: Lie with her, lie on her? We say lie on her, when they
      belie her. Lie with her, that's
      fulsome.—Handkerchief,—confessions,—handkerchief.—To
      confess, and be hanged for his labour.—First, to be
      hanged, and then to confess:—I tremble at it.
      Nature would not invest herself in such shadowing passion,   50
      without some instruction. It is not words that shake me
      thus:—Pish!—Noses, ears, and lips:—Is 't
      possible?—Confess!—Handkerchief!—O devil.
IAGO: Work on.
   My medicine, work! Thus credulous fools are caught;
   And many worthy and chaste dames, ev'n thus,
   All guiltless, meet reproach.—What, ho! my lord!

(*Enter* CASSIO. *He comes to* OTHELLO's *head*)

   My lord! I say! Othello!—How now, Cassio?   60
CASSIO: What is the matter?
IAGO: My lord is fall'n into an epilepsy;
   This is his second fit; he had one yesterday.
CASSIO: Rub him about the temples.
IAGO: No, forbear;
   The lethargy must have his quiet course:
   If not, he foams at mouth; and, by and by,
   Breaks out to savage madness. Look, he stirs:
   Do you withdraw yourself a little while,
   He will recover straight: when he is gone,   70
   I would on great occasion speak with you.—

(*Exit* CASSIO. IAGO *returns to above* OTHELLO *and raises his head
on to his knee.*)

   How is it, general; have you not hurt your head?
OTHELLO: Dost thou mock me?
IAGO: I mock you! no, by heaven:
   Would you would bear your fortune like a man.

OTHELLO: A horned man's a monster, and a beast.

IAGO: There's many a beast then in a populous city,   *80*
  And many a civil monster.

OTHELLO: Did he confess it?

IAGO: Good sir, be a man;
  Think, every bearded fellow that's but yok'd
  May draw with you. There's millions now alive,
  That nightly lie in their unproper beds,
  Which they dare swear peculiar. Your case is better.
  O, 't is the spite of hell, the fiend's arch-mock,
  To lip a wanton in a secure couch,
  And to suppose her chaste! No, let me know;   *90*
  And, knowing what I am, I know what she shall be.

OTHELLO: O, thou art wise; 't is certain.

IAGO: Stand you awhile apart;
  Confine yourself but in a patient list.
  Whilst you were here, o'erwhelmed with your grief,—
  A passion most unsuiting such a man,—
  Cassio came hither: I shifted him away,
  And laid good 'scuse upon your ecstacy;
  Bade him anon return and here speak with me;
  The which he promis'd. Do but encave yourself,   *100*
  And mark the fleers, the gibes, and notable scorns,
  That dwell in every region of his face;
  For I will make him tell the tale anew,—
  Where, how, how oft, how long ago, and when
  He hath, and is again to meet your wife;
  I say, but mark his gesture. Marry, patience;
  Or I shall say, y'are all-in-all in spleen,
  And nothing of a man.

OTHELLO: Dost thou hear, Iago?
  I will be found most cunning in my patience;   *110*
  But—dost thou hear?—most bloody.

IAGO: That's not amiss;
  But yet keep time in all. Will you withdraw?

(OTHELLO *withdraws and conceals himself behind the curtain*)

  Now will I question Cassio of Bianca,
  A housewife, that by selling her desires
  Buys herself bread and clothes: it is a creature
  That dotes on Cassio,—as 't is the strumpet's plague,
  To beguile many, and be beguil'd by one;—   *120*
  He, when he hears of her, cannot refrain
  From the excess of laughter:—Here he comes:—
  As he shall smile, Othello shall go mad;
  And his unbookish jealousy must construe

Poor Cassio's smiles, gestures, and light behaviour,   *130*
Quite in the wrong.—

(*Enter* Cassio)

How do you now, lieutenant?
Cassio: The worser, that you give me the addition,
  Whose want even kills me.
Iago: Ply Desdemona well, and y' are sure on 't.
  Now, if this suit lay in Bianca's power,
  How quickly should you speed?
Cassio: Alas, poor caitiff.   *140*
Othello: Look, how he laughs already!
Iago: I never knew woman love man so.
Cassio: Alas, poor rogue! I think indeed she loves me.
Othello: Now he denies it faintly, and laughs it out.
Iago: Do you hear, Cassio?
Othello: Now he importunes him
  To tell it o'er: Go to: well said, well said.
Iago: She gives it out, that you shall marry her:
  Do you intend it?
Cassio: Ha, ha, ha!   *150*
Othello: Do you triumph, Roman? do you triumph?
Cassio: I marry her?—what? a customer! Prithee bear some
    charity to my wit; do not think it so unwholesome. Ha, ha,
    ha!
Othello: So, so, so, so: They laugh that win.
Iago: Why, the cry goes, that you marry her.
Cassio: Prithee, say true.
Iago: I am a very villain else.
Othello: Have you scored me? Well.
Cassio: This is the monkey's own giving out: she is persuaded I *160*
    will marry her, out of her own love and flattery, not out of
    my promise.
Othello: Iago beckons me; now he begins the story.
Cassio: She was here even now; she haunts me in every place. I
    was, the other day, talking on the sea-bank with certain
    Venetians; and thither comes the bauble, and falls me thus
    about my neck;—
Othello: Crying, O dear Cassio! as it were: his gesture imports
    it.
Cassio: So hangs, and lolls, and weeps upon me; so shakes and *170*
    pulls me: ha, ha, ha!—
Othello: Now he tells how she plucked him to my chamber: O,
    I see that nose of yours, but not that dog I shall throw it to
Cassio: Well, I must leave her company.
Iago: Before me! look, where she comes.

(*Enter* BIANCA)

CASSIO: 'T is such another fitchew! marry, a perfumed one.—
What do you mean by this haunting of me?
BIANCA: Let the devil and his dam haunt you! What did you   180
mean by that same handkerchief you gave me even now? I
was a fine fool to take it. I must take out the work!—A
likely piece of work that you should find it in your
chamber, and know not who left it there! This is some
minx's token, and I must take out the work! There—give it
to your hobby horse: wheresoever you had it I'll take out
no work on 't.
CASSIO: How now, my sweet Bianca? how now, how now?
OTHELLO: By heaven, that should be my handkerchief!
BIANCA: If you'll come to supper to-night you may, if you will   190
not, come when you are next prepared for. (Exit)
IAGO: After her, after her.
CASSIO: I must; she'll rail in the street else.
IAGO: Will you sup there?
CASSIO: Yes, I intend so.
IAGO: Well, I may chance to see you; for I would very fain speak
with you.
CASSIO: Prithee, come: Will you?
IAGO: Go to; say no more. (*Exit* CASSIO)
OTHELLO: How shall I murder him, Iago?   200
IAGO: Did you perceive how he laughed at his vice?
OTHELLO: O, Iago!
IAGO: And did you see the handkerchief?
OTHELLO: Was that mine?
IAGO: Yours, by this hand: and to see how he prizes the foolish
woman, your wife! she gave it him, and he hath given it
his mistress.
OTHELLO: I would have him nine years a killing:—A fine woman!
a fair woman! a sweet woman!
IAGO: Nay, you must forget that.   210
OTHELLO: Ay, let her rot, and perish, and be damned to-night;
for she shall not live: No, my heart is turned to stone; I
strike it, and it hurts my hand. O, the world hath not a
sweeter creature: she might lie by an emperor's side, and
command him tasks.
IAGO: Nay, that's not your way.
OTHELLO: Hang her! I do but say what she is:—So delicate with
her needle!—An admirable musician! O, she will sing the
savageness out of a bear!—Of so high and plenteous wit
and invention!   220
IAGO: She's the worse for all this.

OTHELLO: O, a thousand times:—And then, of so gentle a
    condition!
IAGO: Ay, too gentle.
OTHELLO: Nay, that's certain: But yet the pity of it, Iago!—O,
    Iago, the pity of it, Iago!
IAGO: If you are so fond over her iniquity, give her patent to
    offend; for, if it touch not you it comes near nobody.
OTHELLO: I will chop her into messes:—Cuckold me!
IAGO: O, 't is foul in her.   230
OTHELLO: With mine officer!
IAGO: That's fouler.
OTHELLO: Get me some poison, Iago; this night:—I'll not
    expostulate with her, lest her body and beauty unprovide
    my mind again:—this night, Iago.
IAGO: Do it not with poison; strangle her in her bed, even the
    bed she hath contaminated.
OTHELLO: Good, good; the justice of it pleases; very good.
IAGO: And, for Cassio,—let me be his undertaker; You shall hear
    more by midnight.   240
OTHELLO: Excellent good.—What trumpet is that same?
IAGO: Something from Venice, sure. 'T is Lodovico,
  Come from the duke; and see, your wife is with him.

(*Enter* LODOVICO *and* DESDEMONA)

LODOVICO: Save you worthy general!
OTHELLO: With all my heart, sir.
LODOVICO: The duke and senators of Venice greet you. (*Gives
    him a sealed letter*)
OTHELLO: I kiss the instrument of their pleasures. (*Opens the   250
    letter and reads*)
DESDEMONA: And what's the news, good cousin Lodovico?
IAGO: I'm very glad to see you, sig-ni-or;
  Welcome to Cyprus.
LODOVICO: I thank you: how does lieutenant Cassio?
IAGO: Lives, sir.
DESDEMONA: Cousin, there's fall'n between him and my lord
  An unkind breech: but you shall make all well.
OTHELLO: Are you sure of that?
DESDEMONA: My lord?   260
OTHELLO: (*Reads*) ''This fail you not to do, as you will''—
LODOVICO: He did not call: he's busy in the paper.
  Is there division 'twixt my lord and Cassio?
DESDEMONA: A most unhappy one; I would do much
  T' atone them, for the love I bear to Cassio.
OTHELLO: Fire and brimstone!
DESDEMONA: My lord?

OTHELLO: Are you wise?

DESDEMONA: What, is he angry?

LODOVICO: 'May be, the letter mov'd him;   270
  For, as I think, they do command him home,
  Deputing Cassio in his government.

DESDEMONA: By my troth, I'm glad on 't.

OTHELLO: Indeed?

DESDEMONA: My lord?

OTHELLO: I am glad to see you mad.

DESDEMONA: Why, sweet Othello?

OTHELLO: Devil! (*He strikes her*)

DESDEMONA: I have not deserv'd this.

LODOVICO: My lord, this would not be believ'd in Venice,   280
  Though I should swear I saw 't: 'T is very much;
  Make her amends, she weeps.

OTHELLO: O devil, devil!
  If that the earth could teem with woman's tears,
  Each drop she falls would prove a crocodile:—
  Out of my sight!

DESDEMONA: I will not stay t' offend you.

LODOVICO: Truly, an obedient lady:—
  I do beseech your lordship, call her back.

OTHELLO: Mistress—   290

DESDEMONA: My lord?

OTHELLO: What would you with her, sir?

LODOVICO: Who, I, my lord?

OTHELLO: Ay; you did wish that I would make her turn;
  Sir, she can turn, and turn, and yet go on,
  And turn again; and she can weep, sir, weep;
  And she's obedient, as you say,—obedient,—
  Very obedient:—Proceed you in your tears.—
  Concerning this, sir,—O well-painted passion!
  I am commanded home:—Get you away;   300
  I'll send for you anon.—Sir, I obey the mandate,
  And will return to Venice:—Hence—avaunt!
  Cassio shall have my place. And, sir, to-night,
  I do entreat that we may sup together.
  Y' are welcome, sir, to Cyprus.—Goats and monkeys! (*Exit.*)

LODOVICO: Is this the noble Moor whom our full senate
  Call all-in-all suffcent?—Is this the nature
  Whom passion could not shake? whose solid virtue
  The shot of accident, nor dart of chance,
  Could neither graze, nor pierce?   310

IAGO: He is much chang'd.

LODOVICO: Are his wits safe? is he not light of brain?

IAGO: He's that he is; I may not breathe my censure.

What he might be,—if, what he might, he's not,—
I would to heaven, he were.
LODOVICO: What! strike his wife?
IAGO: 'Faith, that was not so well; yet 'would I knew
That stroke would prove the worst.
LODOVICO: Is it his use?
Or did the letters work upon his blood,   320
And new-create this fault?
IAGO: Alas, alas!
It is not honesty in me, to speak
What I have seen and known. You shall observe him;
And his own courses will denote him so,
That I may save my speech: Do but go after,
And mark how he continues.
LODOVICO: I am sorry that I am deceiv'd in him.

Scene 2
Another room in the castle

(OTHELLO *is standing facing front with his arms folded*)

OTHELLO: Y'ave seen nothing then?   330
EMILIA: Nor ever heard; nor ever did suspect.
OTHELLO: Yes, you have seen Cassio and she together.
EMILIA: But then I saw no harm; and then I heard
Each syllable that breath made up between them.
OTHELLO: What, did they never whisper?
EMILIA: Never, my lord.
OTHELLO: Nor send you out o' the way?
EMILIA: Never.
OTHELLO: To fetch her fan, her gloves, her mask, nor nothing?
EMILIA: Never, my lord.   340
OTHELLO: That's strange.
EMILIA: I durst, my lord, to wager she is honest,
Lay down my soul at stake: if you think other,
Remove your thought; it doth abuse your bosom.
If any wretch have put this in your head,
Let heaven requite it with the serpent's curse!
For, if she be not honest, chaste, and true,
There's no man happy; the purest of their wives
Is foul as slander.
OTHELLO: Bid her come hither:—go.—   350
She says enough;—yet she's a simple bawd
That cannot say as much. This is a subtle whore,
A closet lock-and-key of villainous secrets:
And yct she'll kneel, and pray; I have seen her do 't.

(*Re-enter* EMILIA, *with* DESDEMONA)

DESDEMONA: My lord, what is your will?
OTHELLO: Pray, chuck, come hither.
DESDEMONA: What is your pleasure?
OTHELLO: Let me see your eyes;   360
  Look in my face.
DESDEMONA: What horrible fancy's this?
OTHELLO: Some of your function, mistress;
  Leave procreants alone, and shut the door;
  Cough, or cry hem, if any body come:
  Your mystery, your mystery;—nay, despatch.
DESDEMONA: Upon my knees what doth your speech import?
  I understand a fury in your words,
  But not the words.
OTHELLO: Why, what art thou?   370
DESDEMONA: Your wife, my lord; your true and loyal wife.
OTHELLO: Come, swear it, damn thyself;
  Lest, being like one of heaven, the devils themselves
  Should fear to seize thee: therefore be double-damn'd,
  Swear—thou art honest.
DESDEMONA: Heaven doth truly know it.
OTHELLO: Heaven truly knows that thou art false as hell.
DESDEMONA: To whom, my lord? with whom? How am I false?
OTHELLO: O Desdemona!—away! away! away!
DESDEMONA: Alas the heavy day!—Why do you weep?   380
  Am I the motive of these tears, my lord?
  If, haply, you my father do suspect
  An instrument of this your calling back,
  Lay not your blame on me; if you have lost him,
  Why I have lost him too.
OTHELLO: Had it pleas'd heaven
  To try me with affliction; had they rain'd
  All kinds of sores, and shames, on my bare head:
  Steep'd me in poverty to the very lips;
  Given to captivity me and my utmost hopes;   390
  I should have found in some place of my soul
  A drop of patience: but, alas! to make me
  A fixed figure for the time of scorn
  To point his slow and moving finger at,—
  Yet could I bear that too; well, very well:
  But there, where I have garner'd up my heart;
  Where either I must live, or bear no life;
  The fountain from the which my current runs,
  Or else dries up; to be discarded thence!
  Or keep it as a cistern, for foul toads   400

To knot and gender in!—turn thy complexion there,
Patience, thou young and rose-lipp'd cherubim!
Ay, there, look grim as hell!

DESDEMONA: I hope my noble lord esteems me honest.

OTHELLO: O, ay; as summer flies are in the shambles,
That quicken even with blowing. O thou weed,
Who art so lovely fair, and smell'st so sweet,
That the sense aches at thee,—'would thou had'st ne'er been
born!

DESDEMONA: Alas! what ignorant sin have I committed?   410

OTHELLO: Was this fair paper, this most goodly book,
Made to write whore upon? What committed?
Committed?—O thou public commoner?
I should make very forges of my cheeks,
That would to cinders burn up modesty,
Did I but speak thy deeds.—What committed?
Heaven stops the nose at it, and the moon winks;
The bawdy wind, that kisses all it meets,
Is hush'd within the hollow mine of earth,
And will not hear it: What committed?   420
Impudent strumpet.

DESDEMONA: By heaven, you do me wrong?

OTHELLO: Are you not a strumpet?

DESDEMONA: No, as I am a Christian.
If to preserve this vessel for my lord
From any other foul unlawful touch
Be not to be a strumpet, I am none.

OTHELLO: What, not a whore?

DESDEMONA: No, as I shall be saved.

OTHELLO: Is 't possible?   430

DESDEMONA: O, heaven forgive us!

OTHELLO: I cry you mercy, then;
I took you for that cunning whore of Venice,
That marri'd with Othello.—You, mistress,
That have the office opposite to Saint Peter,
And keep the gate of hell; You! you! ay, you!
We have done our course; there's money for your pains;
I pray you turn the key and keep our counsel. (*Exit*)

EMILIA: Alas, what does this gentleman conceive?—
How do you, madam? how do you, my good lady?   440

DESDEMONA: 'Faith, half asleep.

EMILIA: Good madam, what's the matter with my lord?

DESDEMONA: With who?

EMILIA: Why, with my lord, madam.

DESDEMONA: Who is thy lord?

EMILIA: He that is yours, sweet lady.

DESDEMONA: I have none: Do not talk to me, Emilia;
  I cannot weep; nor answer have I none,
  But what should go by water. Prithee, to-night
  Lay on my bed my wedding sheets,—remember;—   450
  And call thy husband hither.
EMILIA: Here's a change, indeed! (*Exit*)
DESDEMONA: 'T is meet I should be us'd so, very meet.
  How have I been behav'd, that he might stick
  The small'st opinion on my least misuse?

(*Enter* IAGO *followed by* EMILIA)

IAGO: What is your pleasure, madam? How is 't with you?
DESDEMONA: I cannot tell. Those that do teach young babes,
  Do it with gentle means and easy tasks: 460
  He might have chid me so; for, in good faith,
  I am a child to chiding.
IAGO: What is the matter, lady?
EMILIA: Alas, Iago, my lord hath so bewhor'd her,
  Thrown such despite and heavy terms upon her,
  As true hearts cannot bear.
DESDEMONA: Am I—that name, Iago?
IAGO: What name, fair lady?
DESDEMONA: Such as she said my lord did say I was.
EMILIA: He call'd her whore; a beggar, in his drink,   470
  Could not have laid such terms upon his callet.
IAGO: Why did he so?
DESDEMONA: I do not know; I am sure I am none such.
IAGO: Do not weep, do not weep; Alas the day!
EMILIA: Has she forsook so many noble matches,
  Her father, and her country, and her friends,
  To be called whore? would it not make one weep?
DESDEMONA: It is my wretched fortune.
IAGO: Beshrew him for 't!
  How comes this trick upon him?   480
DESDEMONA: Nay, heaven doth know.
EMILIA: I will be hang'd, if some eternal villain,
  Some busy and insinuating rogue,
  Some cogging, cozening slave, to get some office,
  Have not devis'd this slander: I will be hang'd else.
IAGO: Fie, there is no such man; it is impossible.
DESDEMONA: If any such there be, heaven pardon him!
EMILIA: A halter pardon him! and hell gnaw his bones!
  Why should he call her whore? who keeps her company?
  What place? what time? what form? what likelihood?   490
  The Moor's abus'd by some most villainous knave,
  Some base, notorious knave, some scurvy fellow:—

O, heaven, that such companions thou 'dst unfold,
And put in every honest hand a whip,
To lash the rascals naked through the world,
Even from the east to the west!
IAGO: Speak within door.
EMILIA: O, fie upon them! some such squire he was
   That turn'd your wit the seamy side without,
   And made you to suspect me with the Moor.   500
IAGO: You are a fool; go to.
DESDEMONA: O good Iago,
   What shall I do to win my lord again?
   Good friend, go to him; for, by this light of heaven,
   I know not how I lost him. Here I kneel;
   If e'er my will did trespass 'gainst his love,
   Either in discourse of thought, or actual deed;
   Or that mine eyes, mine ears, or any sense,
   Delighted them in any other form;
   Or that I do not yet, and ever did,   510
   And ever will,—though he do shake me off
   To beggarly divorcement,—love him dearly,
   Comfort forswear me! Unkindness may do much;
   And his unkindness may defeat my life,
   But never taint my love. I cannot say 'whore':
   It does abhor me, now I speak the word;
   To do the act that might the addition earn,
   Not the world's mass of vanity could make me.
IAGO: I pray you, be content; 't is but his humour;
   The business of the state does him offence.   520
   And he does chide with you.
DESDEMONA: If 't were no other!
IAGO: It is but so, I warrant.

(*Trumpets heard off* L. EMILIA *turns and composes herself*)

   Hark, how these instruments summon to supper;
   The messengers of Venice stay the meat.
   Go in, and weep not: all things shall be well.

(*Exit* DESDEMONA *and* EMILIA)   530

(*Enter* RODERIGO)

   How now, Roderigo?
RODERIGO: I do not find that thou deal'st justly with me.
IAGO: What in the contrary?
RODERIGO: Every day thou dafts me with some device, Iago; and
      rather, as it seems to me now, keep'st from me all
      conveniency, than suppliest me with the least advantage

of hope. I will, indeed, no longer indure it: Nor am I yet   *540*
persuaded to put up in peace what already I have foolishly
suffered.

IAGO: Will you hear me, Roderigo?

RODERIGO: I have heard too much, and your words and
performances are no kin together.

IAGO: You charge me most unjustly.

RODERIGO: With naught but truth. I have wasted myself out of
my means. The jewels you have had from me, to deliver to
Desdemona, would half have corrupted a votarist: You
have told me she hath received them, and returned me   *550*
expectations and comforts of sudden respect and
acquaintance: but I find none.

IAGO: Well; go to; very well.

RODERIGO: Very well! go to! I cannot go to, man; nor 't is not
very well. Nay, I think, it is very scurvy; and begin to find
myself fobbed in it.

IAGO: Very well.

RODERIGO: I tell you, 't is not very well. I will make myself
known to Desdemona: If she will return me my jewels I
will give over my suit, and repent my unlawful   *560*
solicitation; if not assure yourself I will seek satisfaction of
you.

IAGO: You have said now.

RODERIGO: Ay, and said nothing but what I protest intendment
of doing.

IAGO: Why, now I see there's mettle in thee; and even, from this
instant, do build on thee a better opinion than ever before.
Give me thy hand, Roderigo: Thou hast taken against me a
most just conception; but yet, I protest, I have dealt most
directly in thy affair.   *570*

RODERIGO: It hath not appeared.

IAGO: I grant, indeed, it hath not appeared; and your suspicion
is not without wit and judgment. But, Roderigo, if thou
hast that in thee indeed, which I have greater reason to
believe now than ever,—I mean, purpose, courage, and
valour,—this night show it: if thou the next night following
enjoy not Desdemona, take me from this world with
treachery, and devise engines for my life.

RODERIGO: Well, what is it? is it within reason and compass?

IAGO: Sir, there is especial commission come from Venice, to   *580*
depute Cassio in Othello's place.

RODERIGO: Is that true? why then Othello and Desdemona return
again to Venice.

IAGO: O, no; he goes into Mauritania, and takes away with him
the fair Desdemona, unless his abode be lingered here by

some accident; wherein none can be so determinate
as—the removing of Cassio.
RODERIGO: How do you mean—removing him?
IAGO: Why by making him uncapable of Othello's place;
knocking out his brains.   590
RODERIGO: And that you would have me to do.
IAGO: Ay; if you dare do yourself a profit, and a right. He sups
to-night with a harlotry, and thither will I go to him;—he
knows not yet of his honourable fortune: if you will watch
his going thence, which I will fashion to fall out between
twelve and one, you may take him at your pleasure; I will
be near to second your attempt and he shall fall between
us. Come, stand not amazed at it, but go along with me; I
will show you such a necessity in his death, that you shall
think yourself bound to put it on him. It is now   600
high-supper time, and the night grows to waste: about it.
RODERIGO: I will hear further reason for this.
IAGO: And you shall be satisfied

(*Exit*)

Scene 3
Another room in the castle

(*Enter* OTHELLO, LODOVICO, DESDEMONA, EMILIA *and*
ATTENDANTS)

LODOVICO: I do beseech you, sir, trouble yourself no further.
OTHELLO: O pardon me; 't will do me good to walk.   610
LODOVICO: Madam, good night; I humbly thank your ladyship.
DESDEMONA: Your honour is most welcome.
OTHELLO: Will you walk, sir?
  O, Desdemona.
DESDEMONA: My lord?
OTHELLO: Get you to bed on the instant; I will be returned
    forthwith; dismiss your attendant there; look it be done.
DESDEMONA: I will, my lord.

(*Exit* OTHELLO, LODOVICO, *and* ATTENDANTS)
                                                            620
EMILIA: How goes it now? he looks gentler than he did.
DESDEMONA: He says he will return incontinent;
  And hath commanded me to go to bed,
  And bade me to dismiss you.
EMILIA: Dismiss me!
DESDEMONA: It was his bidding; therefore, good Emilia,
  Give me my nightly wearing, and adieu;
  We must not now displease him.

EMILIA: I would you had never seen him!

DESDEMONA: So would not I; my love doth so approve him,   *630*
  That even his stubbornness, his checks, his frowns,—
  Prithee, unpin me,—have grace and favour in them.

EMILIA: I have laid those sheets you bade me on the bed.

DESDEMONA: All's one:—Good father! how foolish are our
     minds!—
  If I do die before thee, prithee, shroud me
  In one of those same sheets.

EMILIA: Come, come, you talk.

DESDEMONA: My mother had a maid call'd Barbara;
  She was in love; and he she lov'd prov'd mad,   *640*
  And did forsake her: she had a song of "willow,"
  An old thing 't was, but it express'd her fortune,
  And she died singing it: That song, to-night,
  Will not go from my mind: I have much to do,
  But to go hang my head all at one side,
  And sing it, like poor Barbara. Prithee, dispatch.

EMILIA: Shall I go fetch your night-gown?

DESDEMONA: No,—unpin me here.—
  This Lodovico is a proper man.

EMILIA: A very handsome man.   *650*

DESDEMONA: He speaks well.

EMILIA: I know a lady in Venice would have walked barefoot to
    Palestine, for a touch of his nether lip.

DESDEMONA:
     The poor soul sat singing by a sycamore tree,
        Sing all a green willow;
    Her hand on her bosom, her head on her knee,
        Sing willow, willow, willow:
  The fresh streams ran by her, and murmur'd her moans;
        Sing willow, willow, willow;   *660*
    Her salt tears fell from her, and soften'd the stones.
  Lay by these—
        Sing willow, willow, willow,—
  Prithee, hie thee: he'll come anon.—
      Sing all a green willow must be my garland.
      Let nobody blame him, his scorn I approve,—
  Nay, that's not next.—Hark! who is 't that knocks?

EMILIA: It's the wind.

DESDEMONA:
     I call'd my love, false love; but what said he then?   *670*
        Sing willow, willow, willow;
    If I court no women you'll couch with no men.
  So get thee gone; good night. Mine eyes do itch;
  Doth that bode weeping?

EMILIA: 'Tis neither here nor there.

DESDEMONA: I have heard it said so.—O these men, these
    men!—

Dost thou in conscience think,—tell me, Emilia,—

That there be women do abuse their husbands

In such gross kind?   680

EMILIA: There be some such, no question.

DESDEMONA: Wouldst thou do such a deed for all the world?

EMILIA: Why, would not you?

DESDEMONA: No, by this heavenly light!

EMILIA: Nor I neither by this heavenly light;
  I might do 't as well i' the dark.

DESDEMONA: Wouldst thou do such a deed for all the world?

EMILIA: The world's a huge thing: 'T is a great price for a small
    vice.

DESDEMONA: In troth, I think thou wouldst not.   690

EMILIA: In troth, I think I should; and undo 't, when I had done.
    Marry, I would not do such a thing for a joint ring; nor for
    measures of lawn; nor for gowns, petticoats, nor caps, nor
    any petty exhibition; but, for all the whole world; why
    who would not make her husband a cuckold to make him
    a monarch? I should venture purgatory for 't.

DESDEMONA: Beshrew me, if I would do such a wrong for the
    whole world.

EMILIA: Why, the wrong, is but a wrong i' the world; and having
    the world for your labour, 't is a wrong in your own world 700
    and you might quickly make it right.

DESDEMONA: I do not think there is any such woman.

EMILIA: Yes, a dozen; and as many to the vantage, as would
  store the world they play'd for.

But I do think it is their husbands' faults

If wives do fall: Say, that they slack their duties,

And pour our treasures into foreign laps;

Or else break out in peevish jealousies,

Throwing restraint upon us; or, say, they strike us,

Or scant our former having in despite;   710

Why, we have galls; and though we have some grace,

Yet have we some revenge. Let husbands know

Their wives have sense like them: they see, and smell,

And have their palates both for sweet and sour,

As husbands have. What is it that they do,

When they change us for others? Is it sport?

I think it is: And doth affection breed it?

I think it doth: Is 't frailty that thus errs?

It is so too: And have not we affections?

Desires for sport? and frailty, as men have?   720

Then, let them use us well: else, let them know
The ills we do their ills instruct us so.
DESDEMONA: Good night, good night: Heaven me such uses
      send,
Not to pick bad from bad; but, by bad, mend!

(*Exit*)

Act V

Scene 1
A street

(*Enter* IAGO, *followed by* RODERIGO)

IAGO: Here, stand behind this bulk; straight will he come:
    Wear thy good rapier bare, and put it home;
    Quick, quick—fear nothing; I'll be at thy elbow;
    It makes us, or it mars us; think on that,
    And fix most firm thy resolu-ti-on.
RODERIGO: Be near at hand; I may miscarry in 't.
IAGO: Here, at thy hand; be bold, and take thy stand.
RODERIGO: I have no great devotion to the deed!
    And yet he hath given me satisfying reasons:—   10
    'T is but a man gone:—forth, my sword; he dies.
IAGO: I have rubb'd this young quat almost to the sense,
    And he grows angry. Now whether he kill Cassio,
    Or Cassio him, or each do kill the other,
    Every way makes my gain: Live Roderigo,
    He calls me to a restitution large
    Of gold, and jewels, that I bobb'd from him
    As gifts to Desdemona;
    It must not be: if Cassio do remain,
    He hath a daily beauty in his life   20
    That makes me ugly; and, besides, the Moor
    May unfold me to him; there stand I in much peril:

(*Enter* CASSIO)

    No, he must die:—But so, I hear him coming.
RODERIGO: I know his gait,—'t is he:—Villain, thou diest.
CASSIO: That thrust had been mine enemy indeed,
    But that my coat is better than thou know'st;
    I will make proof of thine.
RODERIGO: O, I am slain!   30
CASSIO: I am maim'd for ever:—Help, ho! murder! murder!

(*Enter* OTHELLO)

OTHELLO: The voice of Cassio;—Iago keeps his word.

RODERIGO: O, villain that I am!

OTHELLO: 'T is even so.

CASSIO: O, help! ho! light! a surgeon!

OTHELLO: 'T is he:—O brave Iago, honest, and just.
  That hast such noble sense of thy friend's wrong!
  Thou teachest me;—Minion, your dear lies dead,   40
  And your unblest fate hies;—Strumpet, I come;
  Forth of my heart those charms, thine eyes, are blotted:
  Thy bed, lust-stain'd, shall with lust's blood be spotted.

(*He withdraws and exits*)

CASSIO: What, ho! no watch? no passage: murder! murder!

(*Enter* LODOVICO *and* GRATIANO)

GRATIANO: 'T is some mischance; the cry is very direful.

CASSIO: O, help!   50

LODOVICO: Hark!

RODERIGO: O wretched villain!

LODOVICO: Two or three groan;—'t is a heavy night:
  These may be counterfeits; let's think 't unsafe
  To come into the cry without more help.

RODERIGO: Nobody come? then shall I bleed to death.

(*Re-enter* IAGO, *without his doublet*)

LODOVICO: Hark!   60

GRATIANO: Here's one comes in his shirt, with light and
       weapons.

IAGO: Who's there? whose noise is this that cries on murder?

LODOVICO: We do not know.

IAGO: Do not you hear a cry?

CASSIO: Here, here; for heaven's sake, help me.

IAGO: What's the matter?

GRATIANO: This is Othello's ancient as I take it.

LODOVICO: The same, indeed: a very valiant fellow.

IAGO: What are you here that cry so grievously?   70

CASSIO: Iago? O, I am spoil'd, undone by villains!
  Give me some help.

IAGO: O me, lieutenant! what villains have done this?

CASSIO: I think that one of them is hereabout,
  And cannot make away.

IAGO: O treacherous villains!—
  What are you there? come in, and give some help.

(*To* LODOVICO *and* GRATIANO)

RODERIGO: O, help me here!   80

CASSIO: That's one of them.

IAGO: O murderous slave! O villain!

RODERIGO: O damn'd Iago! O inhuman dog:—
IAGO: Kill men i' the dark!—Where be these bloody thieves?
  How silent is this town! Ho! murder! murder!
  What may you be? are you of good or evil?
LODOVICO: As you shall prove us, praise us.
IAGO: Signior Lodovico?
LODOVICO: He, sir.
IAGO: I cry you mercy; Here's Cassio hurt by villains.   *90*
GRATIANO: Cassio?
IAGO: How is 't, brother?
CASSIO: My leg is cut in two.
IAGO: Marry, heaven forbid!
  Light, gentlemen: I'll bind it with my shirt.

(*Enter* BIANCA)

BIANCA: What is the matter, ho? who is 't that cry'd?
IAGO: Who is 't that cry'd?
BIANCA: O my dear Cassio! my sweet Cassio! O Cassio! Cassio, *100*
    Cassio!
IAGO: O notable strumpet!—Cassio, may you suspect
  Who should they be that have thus mangled you?
CASSIO: No.
GRATIANO: I am sorry to find you thus; I have been to seek you,
IAGO: Lend me a garter: So,—O, for a chair
  To bear him easily hence!
BIANCA: Alas, he faints: O Cassio! Cassio! Cassio!
IAGO: Gentlemen all, I do suspect this trash
  To be a party in this injury.—   *110*
  Patience awhile, good Cassio.—Come, come:
  Lend me a light.—Know we this face, or no?
  Alas! my friend, and my dear countryman,
  Roderigo? no:—Yes, sure; yes; 't is Roderigo.
GRATIANO: What, of Venice?
IAGO: Even he, sir: did you know him?
GRATIANO: Know him? ay.
IAGO: Signior Gratiano? I cry your gentle pardon:
  These bloody accidents must excuse my manners,
  That so neglected you.   *120*
GRATIANO: I am glad to see you.
IAGO: How do you, Cassio? O, a chair, a chair!
GRATIANO: Roderigo!
IAGO: He, he, 't is he;—O, that's well said: the chair;—

(*A chair brought in*)

  Some good man bear him carefully from hence:
  I'll fetch the general's surgeon.—For you mistress, (*To* BIANCA)

Save you your labour.—He that lies slain here, Cassio,   130
  Was my dear friend: What malice was between you?
CASSIO: None in the world: nor do I know the man.
IAGO: (*To* BIANCA): What, look you pale?—O bear him out o' the
  air.

(CASSIO *and* RODERIGO *are borne off*)

Stay you, good gentlemen.—Look you pale, mistress?
Do you perceive the ghastness of her eye?
Nay, if you stare we shall hear more anon: 140
Behold her well: I pray you look upon her;
Do you see, gentlemen? nay, guiltiness will speak,
Though tongues were out of use.

(*Enter* EMILIA)

EMILIA: Alas, what is the matter? what is the matter, husband?
IAGO: Cassio hath here been set on in the dark,
  By Roderigo, and fellows that are scap'd;
  He's almost slain, and Roderigo dead.   150
EMILIA: Alas, good gentleman! alas, good Cassio!
IAGO: This is the fruits of vice.—Prithee Emilia,
  Go, know of Cassio where he supp'd to-night:—
  What, do you shake at that?
BIANCA: He supp'd at my house: but I therefore shake not.
IAGO: O, did he so? I charge you go with me.
EMILIA: O, fie upon thee, strumpet!
BIANCA: I am no strumpet: but of life as honest
  As you that thus abuse me.
EMILIA: As I? fie upon thee!   160
IAGO: Kind gentlemen, let's go see poor Cassio dress'd:—
  Come, mistress, you must tell us another tale.
  Emilia, run you to the citadel,
  And tell my lord and lady what hath happ'd.—
  Will you go on I pray? This is the night,
  That either makes me or fordoes me quite.

Scene 2
A bedchamber: DESDEMONA in bed asleep

(OTHELLO *enters*)

OTHELLO: It is the cause, it is the cause, my soul,—   170
  Let me not name it to you, you chaste stars!—
  It is the cause.—Yet I'll not shed her blood;
  Nor scar that whiter skin of hers than snow,
  And smooth as monumental alabaster.
  Yet she must die, else she'll betray more men.

Put out the light, and then—Put out the light!
If I quench thee, thou flaming minister!
I can again thy former light restore,
Should I repent me:—but once put out thy light,
Thou cunning'st pattern of excelling nature,   *180*
I know not where is that Promethean heat
That can thy light relume. When I have pluck'd the rose,
I cannot give it vital growth again,
It needs must wither:—I'll smell it on the tree.—
O balmy breath, that doth almost persuade
Justice to break her sword!—One more, one more.—
Be thus when thou art dead, and I will kill thee,
And love thee after:—One more, and that's the last:
So sweet was ne'er so fatal. I must weep,
But they are cruel tears: This sorrow's heavenly;   *190*
It strikes where it doth love.—She wakes—
DESDEMONA: Who's there? Othello?
OTHELLO: Ay, Desdemona.
DESDEMONA: Will you come to bed, my lord?
OTHELLO: Have you pray'd to-night, Desdemona?
DESDEMONA: Ay, my lord.
OTHELLO: If you bethink yourself of any crime
  Unreconcil'd as yet to heaven and grace,
  Solicit for it straight.
DESDEMONA: Alas, my lord, what may you mean by that?   *200*
OTHELLO: Well, do it, and be brief; I will walk by:
  I would not kill thy unprepared spirit;
  No; heaven forfend.—I would not kill thy soul.
DESDEMONA: Talk you of killing?
OTHELLO: Ay, I do.
DESDEMONA: Then heaven
  Have mercy on me!
OTHELLO: Amen, with all my heart!
DESDEMONA: If you say so, I hope you will not kill me.
OTHELLO: Hum!   *210*
DESDEMONA: And yet I fear you; for you are fatal then
  When your eyes roll so: Why I should fear I know not,
  Since guiltiness I know not; but yet,—I feel,—I fear.
OTHELLO: Think on thy sins.
DESDEMONA: They are loves I bear to you.
OTHELLO: Ay, and for that thou diest.
DESDEMONA: That death's unnatural that kills for loving.—
  Alas, why gnaw you so your nether lip?
  Some bloody passion shakes your very frame:
  These are portents; but yet I hope, I hope,   *220*
  They do not point on me.

OTHELLO: Peace, and be still!

DESDEMONA: I will—so—: What's the matter?

OTHELLO: That handkerchief, which I so lov'd and gave thee,
  Thou gav'st to Cassio.

DESDEMONA: No, by my life and soul;
  Send for the man and ask him.

OTHELLO: Sweet soul, take heed,
  Take heed of perjury; thou 'rt on thy death-bed.

DESDEMONA: Ay, but not yet to die.   230

OTHELLO: Yes, presently,
  Therefore confess thee freely of thy sin;
  For to deny each article with oath
  Cannot remove, nor choke, the strong conception,
  That I do groan withal. Thou art to die.

DESDEMONA: O, heaven have mercy on me!

OTHELLO: I say, amen.

DESDEMONA: And have you mercy too!—I never did
  Offend you in my life: never lov'd Cassio,
  But with such general warranty of heaven   240
  As I might love: I never gave him token.

OTHELLO: By heaven, I saw my handkerchief in 's hand.
  O perjur'd woman! thou dost stone my heart,
  And mak'st me call what I intend to do,
  A murder, which I thought a sacrifice:
  I saw the handkerchief.

DESDEMONA: He found it then;
  I never gave it him:—Send for him hither;
  Let him confess a truth.

OTHELLO: He hath confess'd.   250

DESDEMONA: What, my lord?

OTHELLO: That he hath us'd thee.

DESDEMONA: How?—unlawfully?

OTHELLO: Ay.

DESDEMONA: He will not say so.

OTHELLO: No, his mouth is stopp'd;
  Honest Iago hath ta'en order for 't.

DESDEMONA: O, my fear interprets,—What is he dead?

OTHELLO: Had all his hairs been lives, my great revenge
  Had stomach for them all.   260

DESDEMONA: Alas! he is betray'd, and I undone.

OTHELLO: Out, strumpet! weep'st thou for him to my face?

DESDEMONA: O banish me, my lord, but kill me not.

OTHELLO: Down, strumpet!

DESDEMONA: Kill me to-morrow, let me live to-night.

OTHELLO: Nay, if you strive.—

DESDEMONA: But half an hour.

OTHELLO: Being done,
  There is no pause.
DESDEMONA: But while I say one prayer.   *270*
OTHELLO: It is too late. (*He smothers her*)
EMILIA: My lord! my lord! what ho! my lord! my lord!
OTHELLO: What noise is this?—Not dead! not yet quite dead?
  I, that am cruel, am yet merciful;
  I would not have thee linger in thy pain.—
  So, so.
EMILIA: What ho, my lord! my lord!
OTHELLO: Who's there?
EMILIA: O, good my lord, I would speak a word with you.
OTHELLO: Yes;—'t is Emilia;—by and by:—She's dead.   *280*
  'T is like she comes to speak of Cassio's death,
  The noise was high. Ha! no more moving?
  Still as the grave. Shall she come in? Were 't good?
  I think she stirs again:—No.—What's best to do?
  If she come in she'll sure speak to my wife:
  My wife! my wife! what wife!—I have no wife:
  O, insupportable! O heavy hour!
  Methinks it should be now a huge eclipse
  Of sun and moon, and that the affrighted globe
  Should yawn at alteration.   *290*
EMILIA: I do beseech you that I may speak with you,
  O, good my lord!
OTHELLO: I had forgot thee: O, come in, Emilia:—
  Soft,—by and by:—Let me the curtains draw.—
  Where art thou? What's the matter with thee now?

(*Enter* EMILIA)

EMILIA: O, my good lord, yonder's foul murders done.
OTHELLO: What? now?
EMILIA: But now, my lord!   *300*
OTHELLO: It is the very error of the moon;
  She comes more nearer earth than she was wont,
  And makes men mad.
EMILIA: Cassio, my lord, hath kill'd a young Venetian,
  Call'd Roderigo.
OTHELLO: Roderigo kill'd?!
  And Cassio kill'd!
EMILIA: No, Cassio is not kill'd.
OTHELLO: Not Cassio kill'd? Then murder's out of tune,
  And sweet revenge grows harsh.   *310*
DESDEMONA: O falsely, falsely murder'd!
EMILIA: Alas; what cry is that?
OTHELLO: That! what?

EMILIA: Out, and alas! that was my lady's voice:—
   Help! help! ho! help!—O lady, speak again!
   Sweet Desdemona! O, sweet mistress, speak!
DESDEMONA: A guiltless death I die.
EMILIA: O, who hath done this deed?
DESDEMONA: Nobody; I myself; farewell:
   Commend me to my kind lord. O, farewell.   *320*
OTHELLO: Why, how should she be murder'd?
EMILIA: Alas, who knows?
OTHELLO: You heard her say herself, it was not I.
EMILIA: She said so: I must needs report the truth.
OTHELLO: She's like a liar, gone to burning hell;
   'T was I that kill'd her.
EMILIA: O, the more angel she,
   And you the blacker devil?
OTHELLO: She turn'd to folly, and she was a whore.
EMILIA: Thou dost belie her, and thou art a devil.   *330*
OTHELLO: She was false as water.
EMILIA: Th' art rash as fire, to say
   That she was false; O, she was heavenly true!
OTHELLO: Cassio did tup her; ask thy husband else.
   O, I were damn'd beneath all depth in hell,
   But that I did proceed upon just grounds
   To this extremity: Thy husband knew it all.
EMILIA: My husband?
OTHELLO: Thy husband.
EMILIA: That she was false to wedlock?   *340*
OTHELLO: Ay, with Cassio. Nay, had she been true,
   If heaven would make me such another world
   Of one entire and perfect chrysolite,
   I'd not have sold her for it.
EMILIA: My husband?
OTHELLO: Ay, 't was he that told me on her first;
   An honest man he is, and hates the slime
   That sticks on filthy deeds.
EMILIA: My husband?
OTHELLO: What needs this iterance, woman? I say thy husband *350*
EMILIA: O mistress, villainy hath made mocks with love!—
   My husband say that she was false?
OTHELLO: He woman;
   I say, thy husband: Dost understand the word?
   My friend, thy husband, honest, honest, Iago.
EMILIA: If he say so, may his pernicious soul
   Rot half a grain a day! he lies to the heart;
   She was too fond of her most filthy bargain.
OTHELLO: Ha!

EMILIA: Do thy worst;   360
  This deed of thine is no more worthy heaven,
  Than thou wast worthy her.
OTHELLO: Peace you were best.
EMILIA: Thou hast not half that power to do me harm,
  As I have to be hurt. O gull! O dolt!
  As ignorant as dirt! thou hast done a deed,—
  I care not for thy sword; I'll make thee known,
  Though I lost twenty lives:—Help! help! ho! help!
  The Moor hath kill'd my mistress. Murder! murder!

(*Enter* MONTANO, *followed by* GRATIANO *with* IAGO *appearing*   370
after a slight pause)

MONTANO: What is the matter!—How now, general?
EMILIA: O, are you come, Iago? you have done well,
  That men must lay their murders on your neck.
GRATIANO: What is the matter?
EMILIA: Disprove this villain, if thou be'st a man:
  He says, thou toldst him that his wife was false:
  I know thou didst not, thou 'rt not such a villain:
  Speak, for my heart is full.   380
IAGO: I told him what I thought; and told no more
  Than what he found himself was apt and true.
EMILIA: But did you ever tell him she was false?
IAGO: I did.
EMILIA: You told—a lie; an odious,—damned lie;
  Upon my soul, a lie; a wicked lie:
  She—false with Cassio!—Did you say with Cassio?
IAGO: With Cassio, mistress: Go to, charm your tongue.
EMILIA: I will not charm my tongue; I am bound to speak;
  My mistress here lies murder'd in her bed.   390
GRATIANO: O heavens forfend!
EMILIA: And your reports have set the murder on.
OTHELLO: Nay, stare not, masters; it is true indeed.
GRATIANO: 'T is a strange truth.
MONTANO: O monstrous act!
EMILIA: Villainy, villainy, villainy!
  I think upon 't,—I think,—I smell 't—O villainy!—
  I thought so then;—I'll kill myself for grief.
  O villainy, villainy!
IAGO: What, are you mad? I charge you, get you home.   400
EMILIA: Good gentlemen, let me have leave to speak;
  'T is proper I obey him, but not now:
  Perchance, Iago, I will ne'er go home.
OTHELLO: Oh! Oh! Oh?
EMILIA: Nay, lay thee down, and roar:

For thou hast kill'd the sweetest innocent,
That ere did lift up eye.—
OTHELLO: O, she was foul!—
I scarce did know you, uncle: there lies your niece,
Whose breath, indeed, these hands have newly stopp'd: 410
I know this act shows horrible and grim.
GRATIANO: Poor Desdemona! I am glad thy father's dead!
Thy match was mortal to him, and pure grief
Shore his old thread in twain: did he live now,
This sight would make him do a desperate turn,
Yea, curse his better angel from his side,
And fall to reprobation.
OTHELLO: 'T is pitiful; but yet Iago knows,
That she with Cassio hath the act of shame
A thousand times committed; Cassio confess'd it: 420
And she did gratify his amorous works
With that recognizance and pledge of love
Which I first gave her; I saw it in his hand;
It was a handkerchief, an antique token
My father gave my mother.
EMILIA: O heaven! O heavenly powers!
IAGO: Come, hold your peace.
EMILIA: 'T will out, 't will out!—I hold my peace, sir? no:
No, I will speak as liberal as the north:
Let heaven, and men, and devils, let them all,   430
All, all, cry shame against me, yet I'll speak.
IAGO: Be wise, and get you home (*reaching for his sword*)
EMILIA: I will not.
GRATIANO: Fie!
Your sword upon a woman?
EMILIA: O thou dull Moor! that handkerchief thou speak'st of
I found by fortune, and did give my husband,
For often with a solemn earnestness,
More than, indeed, belong'd to such a trifle,
He begg'd of me to steal it.   440
IAGO: Villainous drab!
EMILIA: She give it Cassio! no, alas, I found it,
And I did give 't my husband.
IAGO: Filth, thou liest.
EMILIA: By heaven, I do not; I do not, gentlemen:
O murderous coxcomb; what should such a fool
Do with so good a wife?

(IAGO *places his hand on his dagger as she addresses* OTHELLO. *Here
he swiftly draws it and stabs* EMILIA *in the back and runs out*)
                                                                              450
OTHELLO: Are there no stones in heaven,

But what serve for the thunder?—Precious villain!

GRATIANO: The woman falls; sure he has kill'd his wife.

EMILIA: Ay, ay; O, lay me by my mistress' side!

GRATIANO: He's gone, but his wife's kill'd.

MONTANO: 'T is a notorious villain. Take you this weapon,
  Which I have here recovered from the Moor:
  Come, guard the door without: let him not pass,
  But kill him rather; I'll after that same villain,
  For 't is a damned slave.   460

(*Exit quickly followed by* GRATIANO)

OTHELLO: I am not valiant neither,
  But every puny whipster gets my sword:—
  But why should honour outlive honesty?
  Let it go—all.

EMILIA: What did thy song bode, lady?
  Hark, can'st thou hear me? I will play the swan,
  And die in music;—''Willow, willow, willow.''—   470
  Moor she was chaste; she lov'd thee, cruel Moor;
  So come my soul to bliss, as I speak true—
  So speaking as I think,—alas—I die.

OTHELLO: I have another weapon in this chamber.
  It is a sword of Spain, the ice-brook's temper;—
  O, here it is:—Uncle, I must come forth.

GRATIANO: If thou attempt it, it will cost thee dear;
  Thou hast no weapon, and perforce must suffer.

OTHELLO: Look in upon me then, and speak with me,
  Or, naked as I am, I will assault thee.   480

(*Re-enter* GRATIANO)

GRATIANO: What is the matter?

OTHELLO: Behold! I have a weapon:
  A better never did itself sustain
  Upon a soldier's thigh: I have seen the day,
  That with this little arm, and this good sword,
  I have made my way through more impediments
  Than twenty times your stop:—But, O vain boast!   490
  Who can control his fate? 't is not so now.—
  Be not afraid though you do see me weapon'd;
  Here is my journey's end, here is my butt,
  And very sea-mark of my utmost sail.
  Do you go back dismay'd? 't is a lost fear;
  Man but a rush against Othello's breast,
  And he retires;—Where should Othello go?—

(*Exit* GRATIANO)

Now, how dost thou look now? O ill-starr'd wench!   500
Pale as thy smock! When we shall meet at compt,
This look of thine will hurl my soul from heaven,
And fiends will snatch at it. Cold, cold, my girl?
E'en like thy chastity.—O cursed, slave!
Whip me, ye devils,
From the possession of this heavenly sight!
Blow me about in winds! roast me in sulphur!
Wash me in steep-down gulfs of liquid fire!—
O Desdemona! Desdemona! dead. Oh, oh, oh.

(*Enter* LODOVICO *and* MONTANO *bearing* CASSIO *between them with*   510
his leg bound. His arms are round their necks and they slowly bear hin
to the seat. Enter OFFICERS *with* IAGO. GRATIANO *enters and stands*
above the entrance with his drawn sword)

LODOVICO: Where is this rash and most unfortunate man?
OTHELLO: That's he that was Othello; here I am.
LODOVICO: Where is that viper? bring the villain forth.
OTHELLO: I look down towards his feet;—but that's a fable,
    If that thou be'st a devil I cannot kill thee.
LODOVICO: Wrench his sword from him.   520
IAGO: I bleed, sir; but not kill'd.
OTHELLO: I am not sorry, neither; I'd have thee live;
    For, in my sense, 't is happiness to die.
LODOVICO: O thou Othello, that wert once so good,
    Fall'n in the practice of a damned slave,
    What shall be said to thee?
OTHELLO: Why, any thing:
    An honourable murderer, if you will;
    For nought did I in hate, but all in honour.
LODOVICO: This wretch hath part confess'd his villainy: 530
    Did you and he consent in Cassio's death?
OTHELLO: Ay.
CASSIO: Dear general, I never gave you cause.
OTHELLO: I do believe it, and I ask your pardon.
    Will you, I pray, demand that demi-devil,
    Why he hath thus ensnar'd my soul and body?
IAGO: Demand me nothing: what you know, you know:
    From this time forth I never will speak word.
LODOVICO: What? not to pray?
GRATIANO: Torments will ope your lips.   540
OTHELLO: Well—thou dost best.
LODOVICO: Sir, you shall understand what hath befall'n
    Which, as I think, you know not: Here is a letter,
    Found in the pocket of the slain Rod'rigo;
    And here, another: the one of them imports

The death of Cassio to be undertook
  By Roderigo.
OTHELLO: O villainy!
CASSIO: Most heathenish and most gross!
LODOVICO: Now here's another discontented paper,   550
  Found in his pocket too; and this, it seems,
  Roderigo meant to have sent this damned villain;
  But that, belike, Iago in the interim
  Came in and satisfi'd him.
OTHELLO: O, the pernicious caitiff!—
  How came you, Cassio, by that handkerchief
  That was my wife's?
CASSIO: I found it in my chamber;
  And he himself confess'd, but even now,
  That there he dropp'd it, for a special purpose,   560
  Which wrought to his desire.
OTHELLO: O fool! fool! fool!
CASSIO: There is, besides, in Roderigo's letter,
  How he upbraids Iago, that he made him
  Brave me upon the watch; whereon it came
  That I was cast: And even but now he spake,
  After long seeming dead,—Iago hurt him,
  Iago set him on.
LODOVICO: You must forsake this room, and go with us:
  Your power and your command is taken off,   570
  And Cassio rules in Cyprus. For this slave,—
  If there by any cunning cruelty,
  That can torment him much, and hold him long,
  It shall be his: You shall close prisoner rest,
  Till that the nature of your fault be known
  To the Venetian state.—Come, bring away.

> "Be thus when thou art dead, and I will kill thee,
>   And love thee after."

Had he not have loved her, would he not have whistled her off 580

>   "and let her down the wind
>   To prey at Fortune"?

And at the last does not the dagger only anticipate what
  nature would soon have done herself?
OTHELLO: Soft you; a word or two, before you go.
  I have done the state some service, and they know 't;
  No more of that:—I pray you, in your letters,
  When you shall these unlucky deeds relate,
  Speak of me as I am; nothing extenuate,   590
  Nor set down aught in malice: then must you speak

Of one that lov'd not wisely, but too well;
Of one, not easily jealous, but, being wrought,
Perplex'd in the extreme; of one, whose hand,
Like the base Judean, threw a pearl away,
Richer than all his tribe; of one, whose subdu'd eyes,
Albeit, unused to the melting mood,
Drop tears as fast as the Arabian trees
Their med'cinable gum: Set you down this:
And say, besides,—that in Aleppo once,   600
Where a malignant and a turban'd Turk
Beat a Venetian, and traduc'd the state,
I took by the throat the circumcised dog,
And smote him—thus. (*stabs himself*)
LODOVICO: O bloody period!
GRATIANO: All that is spoke is marr'd.
OTHELLO: I kiss'd thee, ere I kill'd thee;—No way but this,
  Killing myself to die upon a kiss. (*falls on* DESDEMONA)
CASSIO: This did I fear, but thought he had no weapon:
  For he was great of heart.   610
LODOVICO: O spartan dog!
  More fell than anguish, hunger or the sea!
  Look on the tragic loading of this bed:
  This is thy work; the object poisons sight;—
  Let it be hid.—Gratiano, keep the house,
  And seize upon the fortunes of the Moor,
  For they succeed on you.—To you, lord governor,
  Remains the censure of this hellish villain:
  The time, the place, the torture,—O enforce it!
  Myself will straight aboard; and, to the State,   620
  This heavy act with heavy heart relate.

Understanding *Othello*

In constructing the tragedy of *Othello*, Shakespeare was dealing
not with a moral lesson or a justification of God's ways to man,
but with the tragic relationship of three characters. This play rec-
ognizes that in a world constantly struggling for improvement
and the recognition of good, evil is everpresent. If evil is allowed
to gain control, it will bring damage and destruction.

Othello's tragedy is painful for several reasons. His best
friend's love turns to hatred. His wife's obedience and chastity is
twisted into ugliness. His own self-doubt eats at his soul. Yet, the
evil and the good of the play are so compellingly realistic that we
cannot turn away; we must suffer through it with Othello to see
how it ends. Larry Champion comments that "the action is sim-

ple, yet just such economy of design permits the playwright to focus the audience's attention intensely on the lack of self-knowledge which renders Othello woefully susceptible to jealousy concerning his new wife; the important thing is not what in fact happens, but what Othello thinks happens.[16] Through Shakespeare's artistic and powerful use of language, we understand the Moor's "powerful powerlessness."

We are easily deceived by Iago in the opening scene of the play when he appears to be a dutiful servant and faithful friend to Othello. But because he has been passed over for a promotion which was given to Cassio, his vile nature surfaces. The spiteful nature of his personality is apparent as he hopes to turn Brabantio, Desdemona's father, against Othello. He arouses Brabantio to inform him that "an old black ram is tupping your white ewe." However, the two lovers are wed. Othello does not recognize the ill humor in his friend Iago, and even refers to him as a man "of honesty and trust." Othello is called away to attend to matters of state. Iago immediately busies himself planting seeds of desire for Desdemona in the mind of Roderigo, but Othello returns to a warm reunion with his wife.

Iago continues to weave his plot, plying Cassio with wine and feeding Roderigo tales of Desdemona's longing. Othello believes Iago's lies, and the drunken Cassio is removed from his position. Iago is delighted, for now he can make it appear that Cassio is wooing Desdemona. Then, as Cassio seeks Othello's favor through Desdemona, Iago tells Othello that the two are together. Iago, cool as always, warns his master to beware of "the green-eyed monster," thus sowing the seeds of jealousy. Emilia unknowingly aids her husband in his wicked plot when she gives him Desdemona's handkerchief, which she has found. Iago plants it on Cassio in order to convince Othello of his guilt. When Othello asks Desdemona for the favorite handkerchief, she cannot produce it. He is further angered and entangled in Iago's web. When Othello slaps her publicly over a minor incident, we are shown the violent potential of his jealousy. And after Iago accuses Desdemona of being unfaithful, Othello goes into her bedchamber to "put out the light." Only when it is too late does Emilia recognize that the master mind behind all the evil doings is her own husband. When Othello sees his dead Desdemona, he wails, "It should be now a huge eclipse of sun and moon," falls on his sword, and dies "upon a kiss." In the denouement, Cassio is reinstated and Iago is imprisoned. So ends the tragedy of *Othello*.

The characters are the most dynamic element of *Othello*. Shakespeare has so adeptly balanced the good of Desdemona, the evil of Iago, and the confusion of the Moor that our attention is riveted on their actions throughout the play. Othello is the most painful and the most exciting character. He is a large and commanding personage, a barbarian who has become civilized. Though he is a converted Christian, we are constantly reminded of the "savage" blood flowing in his veins. His tragedy lies in the fact that he trusts too much, too completely. He trusts his wife's fidelity and Iago's friendship. This leaves him open to deception because he questions no one. He is not given to suspicions or second guessing. When fed lies by his companion Iago concerning his wife, his thoughts are clouded and his heart is heavy. He stirs within us admiration for his ability to trust without questioning but, at the same time, pity for having foolishly done so. We can understand his frustration on hearing the rumor of Desdemona's infidelity, having known her so briefly before their marriage. He knows little of the habits of Venetian women. Perhaps Iago is speaking the truth, but he does not want to believe it. "If she be false, oh then Heaven mocks itself." Then he says, "O Iago, the pity of it, Iago!" In those awful moments when he puts the pillow to Desdemona's face and later the knife to his own chest, we cannot help but feel this is not so much murder as an act to save his honor. There is no more anger, only sorrow. The man who appears the essence of self-control in the beginning ends as the man who has yielded to hateful gossip and savagely killed the true love and "good light" of his life. As Othello falls on his sword, he begs us to remember him as one who "lov'd not wisely, but too well" and who "threw away a pearl, richer than all his tribe."

All who know Iago refer to him as "honest Iago." He is respected and admired, especially by his idol, Othello. But Othello, unaware of Iago's feelings, gives Cassio a promotion. From that slight, the wrath of one of the most evil characters in Shakespearean tragedy is born. Iago is dangerous because he is so shrewd and cunning. Iago is Othello's ancient—not only his assistant, but also his close friend and companion. This association has taught Iago that to get the better of Othello, one need deal blow after blow, never allowing him to recover from a shock. Once Iago's plan is set in motion, he does just that! One critic reminds us to "constantly remember not to believe a syllable that Iago utters on any subject, including himself."[17]

Iago is good at his knavery. Not even his wife suspects his evil intentions until it is too late, and Desdemona is dead. Iago never slips and makes a mistake. His intrigue does not make him nervous or unsure. Every move is cold and calculated and achieves his desired end. He holds everyone in contempt. Although Cassio's new position is the excuse Iago gives for his behavior, we cannot believe that he cares so much for a simple promotion. In subjecting his victims to pain, he enforces his feeling of power. He is evil for no apparent reason. Coleridge used the term "motive hunting" to describe Iago, who ponders his behavior and searches for some way to justify it.[18] "Iago stands supreme among Shakespeare's evil characters because the greatest intensity and subtlety of imagination have gone to his making."[19]

Because of the caprice of Iago and the self-doubt of Othello, the fair Desdemona is doomed. Othello relates, "She loved me for the dangers I had passed, and I loved her that she did pity them." He is her hero—he has braved the sea while she stayed safe at home. She is sweet, innocent, and trusting; and for this, she suffers greatly. She is unable to alter the events in which she finds herself trapped. She is at once both beautiful and pathetic. When she is challenged by Othello, she is so taken off guard that she cannot find the words to answer. This makes her guilt seem even more certain. Editor and critic Alvin Kernan comments, "In Desdemona alone do the heart and the hand go together: she is what she seems to be. Ironically, she alone is accused of pretending to be what she is not."[20]

Suggested Reading

Bradley, Andrew C. *Shakespearean Tragedy*. New York: Macmillan, 1960.

Champion, Larry S. *Shakespeare's Tragic Perspective*. Athens: University of Georgia Press, 1976.

Fitts, Dudley, and Robert Fitzgerald. *Sophocles: The Oedipus Cycle*. New York: Harcourt, Brace and World, 1949.

Frye, Northrop. *Fools of Time: Studies in Shakespearean Tragedy*. Toronto: University of Toronto Press, 1967.

Lesky, Albin. *A History of Greek Literature*. New York: Crowell, 1963.

McKeon, Richard P. *Aristoteles: The Basic Works of Aristotle*. New York: Random House, 1941.

McKeon, Richard. *The Basic Works Of Aristotle*. New York: Random House, 1941.

Olson, Elder. *Aristotle's "Poetics" and English Literature.* Chicago, Ill.: University of Chicago Press, 1965.

Parker, Douglas (translator). *Aristophanes' Lysistrata.* New York: New American Library, 1964.

Spatz, Lois. *Aristophanes.* Boston, Mass.: Twayne Pub., 1978.

8

Comedy

Laughter is a necessary emotional release from the stresses and seriousness of everyday life. Theatrical comedy is a form of entertainment at which people are encouraged to do just that—laugh! Franklin Delano Roosevelt once said, "I doubt if there is among us a more useful citizen than the one who holds the secret of banishing gloom, of making tears give way to laughter, of supplanting desolation and despair with hope and courage, for hope and courage always go with a light heart."[1] And English novelist George Meredith said, "One excellent test of the civilization of a country . . . I take to be the flourishing of the comic idea and comedy; and the test of true comedy is that it shall awaken thoughtful laughter."[2]

How do we elicit laughter through comedy? What benefits can we reap from the comic mode? This chapter, through a look at the amazing similarity comedy bears to tragedy and the comic elements, structure, and characters, will attempt to analyze and to define the ways comedy can unleash the mirthful smile, the bubbly giggle, and the hearty belly laugh.

Defining comedy is no easy task. Writers and critics have examined the comic elements and comic characters, but few agree on what basic ingredients produce laughter. Athene Seyler, in her collection of letters entitled *The Craft of Comedy*, says comedy is "the sparkle on the water, not the depths beneath the gay surface . . . but note, the waters must run deep underneath."[3] Her view treats comedy as a light, superficial look at life but also indicates the depth of thought on which it is based. For example, many comedies deal with serious and important political or social issues.

Another provocative definition of comedy comes from English playwright Christopher Fry, who said, "Comedy is an escape, not from truth but from despair, a narrow escape into faith. It believes in a universal cause for delight, even though knowledge of the cause is always twitched away from under us, which leaves us to rest on our own bouyancy. In tragedy we suffer pain; in comedy, pain is a fool, suffered gladly."[4] In his treatise on comedy entitled *The Divine Average*, William McCollom offers this definition, "Comedy is an amusing, relatively discontinuous action concerning success and failure in social relations and culminating in a judgment whereby the 'divine average' triumphs over the exceptional or peculiar. The movements toward success and failure are arranged in a pattern of inevitability and chance: The freedom of the will is not stressed. The total work, therefore, presents life as a product of natural law and erratic fortune."[5] He goes on to say that the "amusing and discontinuous" nature of the comedy tends to be a reinforcement or justification for the "divine average."

Last, but not least, in the brief accounts we have of Aristotle's comments on comedy in the *Poetics*, we find the following definition: "Comedy is an artistic imitation of men of an inferior bent; faulty, . . . it may be described as that kind of shortcoming and deformity which does not strike us as painful, and causes no harm to others."[6] It is obvious from these definitions that comedy can be almost tragic; it can approximate life or it can make life appear absurd; it can be an escape from life or a method of meeting life head on; it can amuse or serve as a corrective.

One way to define comedy, then, is to compare and contrast it with tragedy. In his writings on the imitative nature of drama, Aristotle said that tragedy dealt with men as "better than they are" and comedy deals with men as "worse than they are." This may be compared to McCollom's notion of the "divine average." McCollom believes comedy to be a more realistic reflection of man in his day-to-day behavior than tragedy. Tragedy portrays the noble rebelliousness of man, while comedy deals with the mundane routine of success and failure. While the tragic character has one great and noble goal, and succeeds or fails to achieve it, the comic hero has many encounters in which he fails, then pulls himself together again to go on. While the tragic hero deals with the event of a lifetime, the comic hero deals with the daily difficulties of existence.

In tragedy, the typical hero lacks common sense. Conversely, we find the comic hero to be, in the words of George Meredith, "the first born of common sense."[7] The tragic hero is too noble for his or her own good; the comic hero is too ordinary and enraptured with the mundane to achieve anything but the "divine average." Yet, in every existence there is possibility for both tragedy and comedy. In the words of Frye, "If the characters were not qualified for tragedy, there would be no comedy."[8] Eric Bentley relates the close alliance of the two: "Comedy, like tragedy, is a way of trying to cope with despair, mental suffering, guilt, and anxiety."[9]

The Elements of Comedy

The essential elements of comedy are found in plot structure and character treatment. One example is the apparent distortion of a subject or a character type. A comic character usually seems to have a "bent" in some particular sense that makes him comical. Or the plot structure may be such that a character becomes helplessly intertwined in a set of circumstances that are distorted or out of balance. An example of a character distortion is Lady Bracknell in *The Importance of Being Earnest*. She is far more aristocratic and self-asserting than any woman we could imagine. Her sense of propriety is exaggerated. We see a distortion of plot when Ernest finds himself in a set of circumstances that result in his being engaged to two women at the same time. Seyler, in *The Craft of Comedy*, says, "Comedy is bound up with lack of proportion. It is technically dependent on accents of emphasis. It is not concerned with presenting a balanced whole: it consists in sharpening the angles of the complete character."[10]

A factor commonly found in the plot structure of comedy is the element of chance. The comic character who becomes tangled in a set of circumstances can do little to alter his or her fate, but must rely on chance. Consider the degree of chance involved in Jack Worthing discovering that he is a wealthy heir. Of course, one must not forget that it is the author's plot design and clever use of language that creates such "chance."

Another element of the comedy plot, also a direct result of the author's craftmanship, is what McCollom refers to as "amusing, discontinuous action." All of us remember the nonsensical and totally unrelated blunders in the classic Three Stooges movies. In the familiar comedy *You Can't Take It with You*, the grandfather collects snakes, the wife writes and loses plays, a young niece makes fudge and a young man delivers it, and the husband experiments with fireworks in the basement. Do these characters fit the divine average? No. And they are by chance involved in a series of disjointed and amusing actions. The comic character may be clever or foolish, wealthy or poor, old or young. Comedy depends on that character's clever or foolish handling of the situations in which he finds himself.

A comic character may be funny not because he stands apart as different but because he represents a large group that is participating in some folly. An example can be found in Aristophanes' comedy *Lysistrata*. Audiences in ancient Greece laughed heartily when all the women joined the hero Lysistrata in her militant stand, for at that time women were not citizens, and such an action was outrageous. McCollom reminds us that "where tragedy focuses attention on a single hero, comedy keeps its eye on the spectacle of human folly."[11]

Just as the role of a comic character is written differently from that of the tragic, so the portrayal of the two is different. Some aspect of the comic character must be heightened, exaggerated, or distorted. Certain aspects of the character's personality must be picked out and played up for their comic value. When playing the serious role, an actor attempts to become involved in the character, to feel as the character, and to experience events as the character would. This is true to a lesser extent in portraying the comic character, which requires that the actor take a more objective look at the role. Seyler, in her notes to an actor, warns that complete sincerity in a comic role would rob it of its humor. She advises the actor to "stand outside" the character to some extent.[12] In the case of Lady Bracknell and Cecily Cardew, we can see the validity of the advice. For it is in appearing to believe in the sincerity of a thing known to be false that humor is achieved.

Another important element of comedy that can be woven into both plot and character is tempo, or pace. The speed of the actors' speech and movements and of the development of the plot are directly related to the humorous result. *The Front Page*, a humorous look at newspaper work in the 1930s in America, is fast paced. News reporters run in and out of scenes as stories break and they race for the "scoop." It is the pace of this play that is crucial to its humorous effect. In *The Elements of Drama*, Styan begins a chapter with the following:

> When dramatic impressions follow one another in a related se-
> quence, a new quality arises because they must follow one an-
> other at a certain speed in time. . . . This "tempo" is a quality
> every dramatist is anxious to command, because it affects the
> rhythm of his play and enhances its effect. When he orchestrates
> his action, his sense of the rhythm of his scene may be the deep-
> est of his motives for adopting a particular structural arrange-
> ment.[13]

Tempo is especially important to the comic actor. Whereas
smooth movement, speech, and deportment may be needed for
the serious role, some deviation from this is desirable for the
comic role. Erratic movement and irregular speech can be vital elements of playing a comic role.

To understand comedy of all varieties, it is helpful to think of it in
terms of a continuum. You may recall the terms "high comedy"
and "low comedy" mentioned in chapter 3. What exactly do they
measure? Generally speaking, low comedy refers to comedy
achieved primarily from movement and physical pranks and pratfalls; high comedy refers to comedy achieved through the spoken
line. The former is essentially visual, while the latter is primarily
intellectual in appeal. Imagine a continuum labelled "high comedy" at one end and "low comedy" at the other. All of the comic
plays would fit in somewhere between the two along the line. At
the "low" end would be the Three Stooges type of pratfall humor.
Near the "high" end would be intricate, quick-witted conversa-
tional plays such as *The Importance of Being Earnest.* And in between
we would find the other comedies involving varying degrees of intellectual and physical humor. Toward the low comedy end we
would place the farce, *A Servant of Two Masters,* in which the actors
throw vegetables at each other, characters are disguised as other
characters, and amazing feats of gymnastics are performed. Near
the high comedy end, we would find plays with complicated plot
development and clever verbose characters such as Shaw's *Major
Barbara.* Henri Bergson makes this observation about the variety
within comedy: "It is only in its lower aspects, in light comedy and
farce, that comedy is in striking contrast to reality: the higher it
rises, the more it approximates to life; in fact, there are scenes in
real life so closely bordering on high-class comedy that the stage
might adopt them without changing a single word."[14] Whether we
appreciate comedy for its lightness or seriousness, whether we relate better to its visual or intellectual appeal, we all love to laugh—
we all enjoy the comedy.

The Value of Comedy

What is the worth of comedy to a society and to the individual? Why has it become so vital and so necessary a part of our lives? Have we come to need and to depend on it? In an article by Oliver Goldsmith, we find this observation. "For some years tragedy was the reigning entertainment; but of late it has entirely given way to comedy, and our best efforts are now exerted in these lighter kinds of composition."[15] How has this come to be and why?

A list of some of the many feelings associated with laughter might include: tension relief, incongruity, behavior modification (because of the derision of others), insight, contempt, pleasure, and condescension. Laughter has long been used to correct the behavior of others. We have all laughed to humiliate or to embarrass someone. We see this device for humor used again and again in comic plays. A character deviates in some way from the norm expected by the audience, and the audience laughs as a method of recognizing (and correcting) this behavior. Lysistrata is not a typical woman of the ancient Greek culture. Women were, for the most part, not independent or assertive during that era. So it was hilarious that a woman would be so daring as to propose to stop the war, and, furthermore, to succeed! The laughter elicited in this kind of circumstance is provoked from a comparison made by the viewer between current standards and the standards of the play's time period.

We chuckle when we recognize traits in ourselves revealed to us through characters on the stage. Comedy becomes instructive when it helps us gain this kind of personal insight. Tension relief through laughter is heard at the horror movie. And in the theatre, when tension has built to some kind of climax that shocks or surprises, the audience will often laugh. Incongruity elicits laughter, for example, when we recognize a character as "out of sync" in dress or behavior. A nurse in a striped sundress performing her duties would provoke laughter because we expect her to be dressed in white. Any number of factors may elicit our laughter, but in almost all those cases, we feel better as a result.

Comedy helps us to fulfill a need—the need to laugh. Eric Bentley once said, "When we get up tomorrow morning, we may well be able to do without our tragic awareness for an hour or two, but we shall desperately need our sense of the comic."[16] Simply watching the evening news can be cause for depression. In our helpless situation, laughter may be the only tonic we feel we have left. The theatre, through its comedies, offers us relief from the seriousness of everyday life by giving us an opportunity to laugh.

Victorian Comedy: *The Importance of Being Earnest*

Victorian England before the turn of the century, the era in which Oscar Wilde created his plays, was a period of transition and great change. Electricity had made its appearance and most theatres were equipped with incandescent bulbs, but gaslight was still a more controllable and better understood medium for lighting stages. Many of the playwrights approached their audiences as if they were Elizabethans or ancient Greeks. Productions of Shakespeare drew the public. The melodramatic actors of the era were important to the success of a play; their performances were often more notable than the substance of the drama.

In the last decade of the nineteenth century, English audiences were introduced to the realistic works of Norwegian playwright Henrick Ibsen, as well as two of their own—George Bernard Shaw and Oscar Wilde. Shaw ridiculed the frivolity of English drama, the ''well-made play,'' melodramatic acting, and the spectacular productions of the classics. A talented and prominent writer and playwright, Shaw broke with the past with his thought-provoking plays. Oscar Wilde's brilliant use of language and comedic approach made a similar break with the Victorian theatre. While other playwrights avoided facing issues and creating conflict, Wilde showed audiences and critics the shallowness of their society.

Wilde's play, *The Importance of Being Earnest*, is set in upper-class Victorian England, where ''proper'' behavior, manners, and decorum were essential, and the ''right'' family ties were a prerequisite to a ''good'' marriage. A major character is Jack Worthing, a handsome, likeable fellow, but one without the family ties that would insure his marriage into ''good'' society. When two young ladies believe that his name is Earnest, however, they fall head over heels in love. The name is so sincere, so brave and true, and so ''earnest,'' that they are sure the bearer of the name must be likewise.

When *The Importance of Being Earnest* was first produced in 1895, it was treated lightly by critics. Wilde was accused of writing a play without substance and worth. (Wilde's former plays had dealt with societal restraints and taught tolerance.) One writer said that it was ''a sort of sublime farce, meaningless and delightful.''[17] Other critics questioned why Wilde had bothered to write such a frivolous play. With time and distance, critics have come to see that the play is anything but frivolous. Although at first glance the dialogue may appear trivial, it is clear that Wilde was dealing with some serious subjects. He was posing some questions about the morality of the Victorian era as well as the social standards and behavior it espoused. The play, though superficially trivial, proposes ideas that are anything but trivial.

The Importance of Being Earnest
A Trivial Comedy for Serious People
Oscar Wilde

Characters

>JOHN WORTHING, J.P. of the Manor House, Woolton,
>   Hertfordshire
>ALGERNON MONCRIEFF, his friend
>REV. CANON CHASUBLE, D.D., Rector of Woolton
>MERRIMAN, butler to Mr. Worthing
>LANE, Mr. Moncrieff's man-servant
>LADY BRACKNELL
>HON. GWENDOLINE FAIRFAX, her daughter
>CECILY CARDEW, John Worthing's ward
>MISS PRISM

Scene

>ACT I. Algernon Moncrieff's Rooms in Half Moon Street, W.
>ACT II. The Garden at the Manor House, Woolton.
>ACT III. Morning-room at the Manor House, Woolton.

Act I

ALGY'S rooms in Half Moon Street

(Door up R.C. and door L.; fireplace C. The room is luxuriously furnished and artistically. Cigarettes, bread and butter, cucumber sandwiches on writing-table up L. Piano heard off L. The curtain then rises. LANE is arranging afternoon tea on table C. and after piano has ceased ALGY enters L.)

ALGY: (L.C.) Did you hear what I was playing, Lane?
LANE: (Coming down C.) I didn't think it polite to listen, sir. (L.C.)
ALGY: I'm sorry for that. Have you got the cucumber sandwiches cut for Lady Bracknell?

LANE: (*Goes up for sandwiches and brings them down*) Yes, sir. (*Hands them*)

ALGY: (L.C., *takes one or two off plate and goes* R., *and sits on sofa*) Oh, by the way, Lane, I see from your book that on Thursday night, when Lord Shoreham and Mr. Worthing were dining with me, eight bottles of champagne are entered as having been consumed.

LANE: (R.C., *up stage, arranging tea-table*) Yes, sir; eight bottles and a pint.

ALGY: Why is it that at a bachelor's establishment the servants   20 invariably drink the champagne? I ask merely for information.

LANE: I attribute it to the superior quality of the wine, sir. I have often observed that in *married* households, the champagne is *rarely* of a first-rate brand.

ALGY: Good Heavens! Is marriage so demoralizing as that?

LANE: (*Gravely*) I believe it is a very pleasant state, sir. (*Goes up for bread and butter*) I have had very little experience of it myself, up to the present. I have only been married *once*. That was in consequence of a misunderstanding between myself and the young person. (*Moves* R.C.)   30

ALGY: (*Crosses* L.C. *to table*) I don't know that I am much interested in your family life, Lane.

LANE: (L.) No, sir—(*Takes something from down* L. *and moves up* C. *to* R.)—it is not a very interesting subject. I never think of it myself.

ALGY: Very natural, I am sure. That will do, Lane, thank you.

LANE: Thank you, sir. (*Exit up* R.)

ALGY: (C.) Lane's views on marriage seem somewhat lax. Really, if the lower orders don't set us a good example, what on earth is the use of them? They seem, as a class, to have absolutely   40 no sense of their moral responsibility.

LANE: (*Enters* R. *Announcing*) Mr. Ernest Worthing. (*Enter* JACK R. *Exit* LANE R.)

ALGY: (C. *of table*) How do you do, my dear Ernest? What brings you up to town? (*Eating sandwiches*)

JACK: (R.C.) Oh, pleasure, pleasure! What else should bring one anywhere? (*Putting hat on table*) Eating as usual, I see, Algy!

ALGY: (L.C., *stiffly*) I believe it is customary in good society to take some slight refreshment at five o'clock. Where have you been since last Thursday? (*Goes away to* L. *of table*)   50

JACK: Oh, in the country.

ALGY: What on earth do you *do* there?

JACK: (*Pulling off his gloves*) When one is in town one amuses oneself. When one is in the country one amuses *other* people; it is excessively boring.

ALGY: (R.C.) And who are the people you amuse?

JACK: (*Airily*) Oh, neighbors, neighbors!

ALGY: Got nice neighbors in your part of Shropshire?

JACK: Perfectly horrid! Never speak to any of them.

ALGY: (*Crosses to back of table*) How immensely you must amuse   60
them. (*Goes over and takes sandwich*) By the way, Shropshire is
your county?

JACK: Eh? Shropshire? Yes, of course. (*Rising and crossing* C.)
Hallo! Why all these cups? Why cucumber sandwiches? Who
is coming to tea?

ALGY: Oh, merely Aunt Augusta and Gwendoline.

JACK: How perfectly delightful!

ALGY: Yes, that is all very well, but I am afraid Aunt Augusta
won't quite approve of your being here.

JACK: (C., *putting down gloves*) May I ask why?   70

ALGY: My dear fellow, the way you flirt with Gwendoline is
perfectly disgraceful. It is almost as bad as the way
Gwendoline flirts with you.

JACK: I am in love with Gwendoline. I have come up to town
expressly to propose to her.

ALGY: I thought you had come up for pleasure? I call that
business. (*Sitting* L. *of table*)

JACK: How utterly unromantic you are! (*Sitting* R.C. *table.*)

ALGY: I really don't see anything romantic in proposing. It is
very romantic to be in love. But there is nothing romantic   80
about a definite proposal. Why, one may be accepted. One
usually is, I believe. Then the excitement is all over. The very
esence of romance is uncertainty. (JACK *makes as if to take a
sandwich.* ALGY *takes up plate and puts it on his knee*) Please don't
touch the cucumber sandwiches. They are ordered specially
for Aunt Augusta. (*Takes one and eats it*)

JACK: Well, you have been eating them all the time.

ALGY: That is quite a different matter. She is my aunt. (*Rises;
takes plate from below*) Have some bread and butter. The bread
and butter is for Gwendoline. Gwendoline is devoted to bread   90
and butter.

JACK: (*Rises and takes bread and butter away*) And very good bread
and butter it is, too.

ALGY: Well, my dear fellow, you need not eat it as if you were
going to eat it all. You behave as if you were married to her
already. You are not married to her already, and I don't think
you ever will be.

JACK: Why on earth do you say that?

ALGY: Well, in the first place, girls never marry the men they flirt
with. Girls don't think it right.   100

JACK: Oh, that is nonsense.

ALGY: It isn't. It is a great truth. It accounts for the extraordinary

number of bachelors that one sees all over town. In the second
place, I don't give my consent.

JACK: Your consent!

ALGY: My dear fellow, Gwendoline is my first cousin; and before
I allow you to marry her you will have to clear up the whole
question of Cecily. (*Crosses in front to door* R.; *rings bell*)

JACK: Cecily! (*Moving*) What on earth do you mean? What do
you mean, Algy, by Cecily? I don't know anyone of the name   *110*
of Cecily.

ALGY: (*Walks down* R.) Lane, bring me that cigar case Mr.
Worthing left in the smoking-room the last time he dined
here.

LANE: Yes, sir. (*Exit* R. ALGY *returns* C.)

JACK: (C.) Do you mean to say you have had my cigar case all
this time? I wish to goodness you had let me know. I have
been writing frantic letters to Scotland Yard about it. I was
nearly offering a large reward.

ALGY: (*Crossing* R.) Well, I wish you *would* offer one. I happen to   *120*
be more than usually hardup.

(*Enter* LANE)

JACK: There is no good offering a large reward now that the
thing is found. (LANE *comes down* C. *with cigar case on salver.*
JACK *is about to take it.* ALGY *takes it and moves down* R.)

ALGY: I think it rather mean of you, Ernest, I must say. (*Opens
case and examines it*) However, it makes no matter, for now that
I look at the inscription inside, I find the thing isn't yours after
all. (*Turning away.*)   *130*

JACK: Of course it is mine. You have seen me with it a hundred
times, and you have no right whatsoever to read what is
written inside. It is a very ungentlemanly thing to read a
private cigar case.

ALGY: (*Turning to* JACK) Yes, but this is not your cigar case. This
cigar case is a present from someone of the name of Cecily,
and you said you didn't know anyone of that name.

JACK: Well, if you want to know, Cecily happens to be my aunt.

ALGY: Your aunt! (*Goes away and returns* C. *again.*)

JACK: Yes. Charming old lady she is, too. Lives at Tunbridge   *140*
Wells. (*Moves to him*) Just give it back to me, Algy! (*Tries to take
case.*)

ALGY: (*Retreating to back of sofa*) But why does she call herself
Little Cecily, if she is your aunt and lives at Tunbridge Wells?
(*Reading*) "From Little Cecily, with her fondest love."

JACK: (*Moving to sofa and kneeling upon it*) My dear fellow, what on
earth is there in that? Some aunts are tall, some aunts are not
tall. That is a matter that surely an aunt may be allowed to

decide for herself. You seem to think that every aunt should
be exactly like your aunt! (*Second grab for case*) That is absurd!   150
For Heaven's sake, give me back my cigar case. (*Bends across
sofa.*)

ALGY: Yes. But why does your aunt call you her uncle? "From
little Cecily, with her fondest love to her dear Uncle Jack."
(JACK *gradually moves round to* R. *of sofa.* ALGY *gradually moves
round to* R.C.) There is no objection, I admit, to an aunt being a
small aunt, but why an aunt, no matter what her size may be,
should call her own nephew her uncle, I can't quite make out.
(JACK *moves* L.) Besides, your name isn't Jack at all. It is Ernest.

JACK: It isn't Ernest, it's Jack! (*Moves* L.)   160

ALGY: (*Going round back of sofa to* R.C.) You always told me it was
Ernest. I have introduced you to everyone as Ernest. You
answer to the name of Ernest. You look as if your name was
Ernest. You are the most earnest looking person I ever saw in
my life. It is perfectly absurd your saying that your name isn't
Ernest. It's on your cards. Here is one of them. (*Taking it from
case*) Mr. Ernest Worthing, B_4, The Albany. I'll keep this as a
proof that your name is Ernest if ever you attempt to deny it to
me, or to Gwendoline, or to anyone else. (*Puts card in pocket.*)

JACK: Well, my name is Ernest in town and Jack in the country.   170
And the cigar case was given me in the country. (*Sits* C.)

ALGY: Yes, but that does not account for the fact that your small
Aunt Cecily who lives at Tunbridge Wells calls you her dear
uncle. (JACK *sits* R. *of table.* ALGY *puts case behind back*) Now, tell
me the whole thing. I may mention that I have always
suspected you of being a confirmed and secret Bunburyist,
and I am quite sure of it now.

JACK: Bunburyist! What on earth do you mean by a Bunburyist?

ALGY: I'll reveal to you the meaning of that incomparable
expression as soon as you are kind enough to inform me why   180
you are Ernest in town and Jack in the country. (*Moving to
him.*)

JACK: Well, produce my cigar case first. (*Sits* R.C. *on arm of settee.*)

ALGY: Here it is. (*Hands cigar case*) Now produce your
explanation.

JACK: (*Sits* C. ALGY *sits* R. *of sofa*) Well, old Mr. Thomas Cardew,
who adopted me when I was a little boy, made me, in his will,
guardian to his granddaughter, Miss Cecily Cardew. Cecily,
who addresses me as her uncle, from motives of respect that
you could not possibly appreciate, lives at my place in the   190
country, under the charge of her admirable governess, Miss
Prism.

ALGY: (*Rises; crosses* C.) Where is that place in the country, by the
way?

JACK: That is nothing to you, dear boy. You are not going to be
invited. I may tell you candidly that the place is not in
Shropshire.

ALGY: I suspected that, my dear fellow. I have Bunburyed all
over Shropshire on two separate occasions. Now go on. Why
are you Ernest in town and Jack in the country? (*Returns and*   200
sits on arm R.C.)

JACK: My dear Algy, when one is placed in the position of
guardian, one has to adopt a very high moral tone on all
subjects. It's one's duty to do so. And as a high moral tone
can hardly be said to conduce very much to either one's health
or happiness, in order to get up in town I have always
pretended to have a younger brother of the name of Ernest,
who lives at the Albany, and gets into the most dreadful
scrapes. There, my dear Algy, is the whole truth, pure and
simple.   210

ALGY: The truth is rarely pure and never simple. (*Rises; crosses to
him*) What you are is a Bunburyist. You are one of the most
advanced Bunburyists I know.

JACK: What on earth do you mean?

ALGY: You have invented a very useful younger brother called
Ernest, in order that you may be able to come up to town as
often as you like. I have invented an invaluable permanent
invalid called Bunbury, in order that I may go down into the
country whenever I choose. Bunbury is perfectly invaluable. If
it wasn't for Bunbury's extraordinary bad health, for instance, 220
I wouldn't be able to dine with you at the Carlton tonight, for I
have been really engaged to Aunt Augusta for more than a
week.

JACK: I haven't asked you to dine with me anywhere tonight.

ALGY: I know. You are absurdly careless about sending out
invitations. It is very foolish of you. Nothing annoys people so
much as not receiving invitations.

JACK: You had much better dine with your Aunt Augusta.

ALGY: (*Sits* R.C. *on sofa*) I haven't the smallest intention of doing
anything of the kind. To begin with, I dined there on Monday, 230
and once a week is quite enough to dine with one's own
relations. In the second place, whenever I do dine there I am
always treated as a member of the family, and sent down with
either no woman at all or two. In the third place, I know
perfectly well who she will place me next to tonight. She will
place me next to Mary Farquhar, who always flirts with her
own husband across the dinner-table. That is not very
pleasant. Indeed, it is not even decent—and that sort of thing
is enormously on the increase. The amount of women in
London who flirt with their own husbands is perfectly   240

scandalous. It looks so bad. It is simply washing one's clean
linen in public. Besides, now that I know you are a confirmed
Bunburyist, I naturally want to talk to you about Bunburying.
I want to tell you the rules.

JACK: I'm not a Bunburyist at all. If Gwendoline accepts me, I am
going to kill my brother; indeed, I think I'll kill him in any
case. Cecily is a little too much interested in him. It is rather a
bore. So I am going to get rid of Ernest. And I strongly advise
you to do the same with Mr.—with your invalid friend who
has the absurd name.   250

ALGY: Nothing will induce me to part with Bunbury, and if you
ever get married, which seems to be extremely problematic,
you will be very glad to know Bunbury. A man who marries
without knowing Bunbury has a very tedious time of it.

JACK: That is nonsense. If I marry a charming girl like
Gwendoline, and she is the only girl I ever saw in my life that
I would marry, I certainly don't want to know Bunbury.

ALGY: (*Rises*) Then your wife will. (*Rising and moving to him*) You
don't seem to realize, my dear fellow, that in married life *three*
is company, and two is none. (*Bell.* JACK *rises, goes* L., *and*   260
returns L.C.) Ah, that must be Aunt Augusta. (*Moving to* JACK)
Now, if I get her out of the way for ten minutes, so that you
can have an opportunity of proposing to Gwendoline, may I
dine with you tonight at the Carlton?

JACK: I suppose so, if you want to.

ALGY: Yes, but you must be serious about it. I hate people who
are not serious about meals; it is so shallow of them.

LANE: (*Enters* R.) Lady Bracknell and Miss Fairfax. (ALGY *moves* R.
to meet them. Enter LADY BRACKNELL *and* GWENDOLINE)

LADY BRACKNELL: Well, dear Algernon, I hope you are behaving   270
well. (*Shakes hands; moves* R.)

ALGY: I'm feeling well, Aunt Augusta.

LADY BRACKNELL: That's not quite the same thing; in fact, the
two rarely go together. Good afternoon, Mr. Worthing. How
d'ye do?

ALGY: (*To* GWENDOLINE) Dear me, you *are* smart! (*Moves away to*
L. *of table.*)

GWENDOLINE: (*Crosses* L.) I am always smart. (*Crossing to* JACK C.)
Aren't I, Mr. Worthing? (ALGY R.C.)

JACK: You are quite perfect, Miss Fairfax. (ALGY *gets* L. *of table.*)   280

LADY BRACKNELL: I'm sorry if we are a little late, Algernon, but I
was obliged to call on dear Lady Harbury. (*Enter* LANE R.C.,
carrying teapot, which he puts on table; he then moves up to desk) I
hadn't been there since her poor husband's death. I never saw
a woman so altered; she looks quite twenty years *younger*. I'll
have a cup of tea and one of those nice cucumber sandwiches

you promised me. (ALGY *table* L.C.) Won't you come and sit here, Gwendoline?

GWENDOLINE: Thanks, Mamma, I'm quite comfortable where I am.   290

ALGY: (*Picking up empty plate and moving* C.) Good heavens, Lane! (LANE *moves down to him* L. GWENDOLINE *and* JACK *move up* R.C.) Why, are there no cucumber sandwiches? I ordered them specially.

LANE: There were no cucumbers in the market this morning, sir. I went down twice. (*Takes plate*)

ALGY: No cucumbers?

LANE: No, sir—not even for ready money.

ALGY: That will do, Lane, thank you.

LANE: Thank you, sir. (*Exit* R.)   300

ALGY: I'm greatly distressed, Aunt Augusta, about there being no cucumbers—not even for ready money.

LADY BRACKNELL: It really makes no matter, Algernon. I had some crumpets with Lady Harbury, who seems to me to be living entirely for pleasure now.

ALGY: I hear that her hair has turned quite gold from grief. (*Moves to* R.C. *with two cups of tea*)

LADY BRACKNELL: It certainly has changed color. From what cause, I, of course, can't say. (ALGY *crosses and hands tea; he then gets round back of sofa and sits* R. *of her*) Thank you. I've   310 quite a treat for you tonight, Algernon. (JACK *gives* GWENDOLINE *tea at back of* L.C. *table.*) I am going to send you down with Mary Farquhar. She is such a nice young woman, and so attentive to her husband. It's delightful to watch them.

ALGY: (R.C.) I am afraid, Aunt Augusta, I shall have to give up the pleasure of dining with you tonight after all. (*Sits*)

LADY BRACKNELL: I hope not, Algernon. It would put my table completely out. Your uncle would have to dine upstairs. Fortunately he's accustomed to that. (JACK *and* GWENDOLINE *return back* C.)   320

ALGY: It is a great bore, but the fact is I have just had a telegram to say that my poor friend Bunbury is very ill again. (*Exchanges glances with* JACK) They seem to think I should be with him.

LADY BRACKNELL: It is very strange. This Mr. Bunbury seems to suffer from curiously bad health.

ALGY: Yes; poor Bunbury is a dreadful invalid.

LADY BRACKNELL: Well, I must say, Algernon, that I think it is high time that Mr. Bunbury made up his mind whether he was going to live or die. This shilly-shallying with the question is absurd. Nor do I in any way approve of this modern   330 sympathy with invalids. I consider it morbid. Illness of any kind is hardly a thing to be encouraged in others. Health is the primary duty of life. I am always telling that to your poor uncle, but he never seems to take any notice—as far as improvement in his many ailments goes. I would be much obliged if you would ask Mr. Bunbury, from me, to be kind enough not to have a relapse on Saturday, for I rely on you to arrange my music for me. It is my last reception—and one wants *something* that will encourage conversation—particularlv at the end of the season when everyone has practically said   340 whatever they have to say.

ALGY: I'll speak to Bunbury, Aunt Augusta—if he is still conscious—(*Rising, taking her cup and crossing* L.)—and I think I can promise you he'll be all right on Saturday. Of course the music is a great difficulty. (JACK *takes* GWENDOLINE'S *cup to table*) But I'll run over the program I've drawn out, if you will come into the next room for a moment. (*Crosses to table with two cups*)

LADY BRACKNELL: Thank you, Algernon. It is very thoughtful of you. (*Rising and following him*) I'm sure the program will be   350 delightful, after a few expurgations. Gwendoline, you will follow.

GWENDOLINE: Certainly, Mamma. (*Crossing over, moves front of sofa* R. *Exit* LADY BRACKNELL *with* ALGY L., *leaving door open*)

JACK: Charming day it has been, Miss Fairfax.

GWENDOLINE: Pray don't talk to me about the weather, Mr. Worthing. Whenever people talk to me about the weather, I feel quite certain that they mean something else; and that makes me so nervous.

JACK: I do mean something else.   360

GWENDOLINE: I thought so.

JACK: And I would like to be allowed to take advantage of Lady Bracknell's temporary absence—

GWENDOLINE: I would certainly advise you to do so. Mamma has a way of coming back suddenly into a room that I have had to speak to her about.

JACK: (*Crosses to door, shuts it, and returns to* GWENDOLINE) Miss Fairfax, ever since I met you I have admired you more than any girl I have ever met since I met you.

GWENDOLINE: Yes, I am quite aware of that fact. And I often   370 wish that in public, at any rate, you had been more demonstrative. For me, you have always had an irresistible fascination. Even before I met you I was far from indifferent to you. (JACK *looks at her in amazement*) We live, as I hope you know, Mr. Worthing, in an age of ideals. The fact is constantly mentioned in the more expensive monthly magazines. And my ideal has always been to love someone of the name of Ernest. (JACK *backs* R.C. *to* C. *and walks down*) There is

something in that name that inspires absolute confidence. The
moment Algernon first mentioned to me that he had a friend   *380*
called Ernest I *knew* I was destined to love you.

JACK: You really love me, Gwendoline?

GWENDOLINE: Passionately!

JACK: Darling! You don't know how happy you've made me.
(*Sitting* L. *of her*)

GWENDOLINE: My own *Ernest*! (*Embracing* JACK)

JACK: Of course. But you don't really mean to say that you
couldn't love me if my name wasn't Ernest?

GWENDOLINE: But your name *is* Ernest. (*Releases him*)

JACK: Yes, I know it is. But supposing it was something else? Do   *390*
you mean to say you couldn't love me then?

GWENDOLINE: Oh, that is clearly a metaphysical speculation, and
like all metaphysical speculations has very little reference to
the actual facts of life, as we know them.

JACK: Personally, darling, to speak quite candidly, I don't care
much about the name of Ernest—I don't think the name suits
me at all.

GWENDOLINE: It suits you perfectly. It is a divine name. It has a
music of its own. It produces vibration.

JACK: Well, really, Gwendoline, I must say that I think there are   *400*
lots of other much nicer names. I think Jack, for instance, a
charming name.

GWENDOLINE: Jack! No, there is very little music in the name
Jack, if any at all, indeed. It does not thrill. It produces
absolutely *no* vibrations. I have known several Jacks, and they
all without exception were more than usually plain. Besides,
Jack is a notorious domesticity for John! And I pity any
woman who is married to a man called John. She would
probably never be allowed to know the entracing pleasure of a
single moment's solitude. The only really *safe* name is Ernest.   *410*

JACK: Gwendoline, I must get christened at once—I mean we
must get married at once.

GWENDOLINE: (*Surprised*) Married, Mr. Worthing? (*They both rise*)

JACK: (*Astounded*) Well—surely. You know that I love you, and
you led me to believe, Miss Fairfax, that you were not
absolutely indifferent to me.

GWENDOLINE: I adore you. But you haven't proposed to me yet.
Nothing has been *said* at all about marriage. The subject has
not even been touched upon.

JACK: Well—may I propose to you now?   *420*

GWENDOLINE: I think it would be an admirable opportunity.
(*Sitting on sofa again*) To spare you any possible disappointment,
Mr. Worthing, I think it only fair to tell you quite frankly
beforehand that I am fully determined to accept you.

JACK: Then, Gwendoline, you will marry me? (*Goes on his knees*)

GWENDOLINE: Of course I will, darling. (*Putting arms round his neck*) How long you have been about it! I am afraid you have had very little experience in how to propose.

JACK: My own one, I have never loved anyone in the world but you.   430

GWENDOLINE: Yes, but men often propose for practice. Oh. Ernest, what wonderfully blue eyes you have. They are quite, quite blue. I hope you will always look at me just like that, especially when there are other people present.

LADY BRACKNELL: (*Enters L.*) Mr. Worthing! (JACK *tries to get up.* GWENDOLINE *restrains him*) Rise, sir, from this semi-recumbent posture. It is most indecorous.

GWENDOLINE: Mamma! (*He tries to rise; she restrains him*) I must beg you to *retire.* This is no place for you. (*Another movement from* JACK) Besides, Mr. Worthing has not quite finished yet.   440

LADY BRACKNELL: Finished what, may I ask?

GWENDOLINE: I am engaged to Mr. Worthing, Mamma. (*Rising and helping him up*)

LADY BRACKNELL: Pardon me, you are not engaged to anyone. (*Crosses C.*) When you do become engaged to anyone, I or your father, should his health permit him, will inform you of the fact. An engagement should always come on a young girl as a surprise, pleasant or unpleasant, as the case may be. It is hardly a matter that she should be allowed to arrange for herself. And now I have a few questions to put to you, Mr.   450
Worthing. And while I am making these inquiries, you, Gwendoline, will wait for me below in the carriage. (*Moves L. a little*)

GWENDOLINE: (*Reproachfully*) Mamma!

LADY BRACKNELL: (*Severely*) In the carriage, Gwendoline! (GWENDOLINE *and* JACK *move up R. and blow kisses to each other behind* LADY BRACKNELL'S *back.* LADY BRACKNELL *looks vaguely about as if she cannot understand what the noise is; finally turns*) Gwendoline, the carriage!

GWENDOLINE: Yes, Mamma. (*Exits R.*)   460

LADY BRACKNELL: (*Sitting down L.C.*) You can take a seat, Mr. Worthing. (*Looks in her pocket for notebook and pencil*)

JACK: Thank you, Lady Bracknell. I prefer standing. (*Comes down C.*)

LADY BRACKNELL: (*Pencil and notebook in hand*) I feel bound to tell you that you are not *down* on my list of eligible young men; although I have the same list as the dear Duchess of Bolton has. We work together, in fact. However, I am quite ready to enter your name, should your answers be what a really affectionate mother requires. Do you smoke?   470

JACK: Well, yes, I must admit I smoke.

LADY BRACKNELL: I am glad to hear it. A man should always have an occupation of some kind. There are far too many idle men in London as it is. How old are you?

JACK: Thirty-five.

LADY BRACKNELL: A very good age to be married at. I have always been of opinion that a man who desires to get married should either know everything or nothing. Which do you know?

JACK: I know nothing, Lady Bracknell. (*Moving* R.)   480

LADY BRACKNELL: I am pleased to hear it. I do not approve of anything that tampers with natural ignorance. Ignorance is like a delicate, exotic fruit; touch it and the bloom has gone. What is your income?

JACK: Between seven and eight thousand a year.

LADY BRACKNELL: (*Makes a note in her book*) In land or in investments?

JACK: In investments, chiefly. (*Sitting sofa* R.C.)

LADY BRACKNELL: That is satisfactory. What between the duties expected of one during one's lifetime and the duties exacted   490 from one after one's death, land has ceased to be either a profit or a pleasure. It gives one position and prevents one from keeping it up. That's all that can be said about land.

JACK: I have a country house, with some land, of course, attached to it; about fifteen hundred acres, I believe, but I don't depend on that for my real income. As far as I can see, the poachers are the only people who make anything out of it.

LADY BRACKNELL: A country house? How many bedrooms? Well, that point can be cleared up afterwards. (*Makes note*) You have a *town* house, I hope? A girl with a simple unspoiled nature   500 like Gwendoline could hardly be expected to reside in the country.

JACK: Well, I own a house in Belgrave Square, but it is let by the year to Lady Bloxham. Of course I can get it back whenever I like, at six months' notice.

LADY BRACKNELL: (*Severely*) Lady Bloxam? I don't know her.

JACK: Oh, she goes about very little. She's a lady considerably advanced in years.

LADY BRACKNELL: Ah, nowadays that is no guarantee of respectability of character. What number in Belgrave Square?   510

JACK: One hundred and forty-nine.

LADY BRACKNELL: (*Closing pocket-book*) The unfashionable side. I thought there was something! However, that could easily be altered. Now to minor matters. Are your parents living? (*Turning to* JACK)

JACK: I have lost both parents.

LADY BRACKNELL: Both? To lose one parent may be regarded as a misfortune—to lose both seems like carelessness. Who was your father? He seems to have been a man of wealth. Was he born in what the Radical papers call the purple of commerce, *520* or did he rise from the ranks of the aristocracy?

JACK: I am afraid I really don't know. The fact is, Lady Bracknell, I said I had lost my parents. It would be nearer the truth to say that my parents seem to have lost me—I don't actually know who I am, by birth. I was—well—I was found. (*Rises*)

LADY BRACKNELL: Found!

JACK: The late Mr. Thomas Cardew, an old gentleman of a very charitable and kindly disposition, found me, and gave me the name of Worthing, because he happened to have a first-class ticket for Worthing in his pocket at the time. *530*

LADY BRACKNELL: *Where* did the charitable gentleman who had a first-class ticket for Worthing find you?

JACK: (*Gravely*) In a handbag.

LADY BRACKNELL: A handbag!

JACK: (*Very seriously*) Yes, Lady Bracknell. I was in a handbag—a somewhat large leather handbag, with handles to it—an ordinary handbag, in fact.

LADY BRACKNELL: In what locality did this Mr. Thomas Cardew come across this ordinary handbag?

JACK: In the cloakroom at Victoria Station. It was given him in *540* mistake for his own.

LADY BRACKNELL: (*Rising*) Mr. Worthing, I confess I feel somewhat bewildered by what you have just told me. To be born, or at any rate, bred, in a handbag, whether it had handles or not, seems to me to display a contempt for the ordinary decencies of family life that remind one of the worst excesses of the French Revolution—and I presume you know what that unfortunate movement led to? As for the particular locality in which the handbag was found, a cloakroom at a railway station might serve to conceal a social *550* indiscretion—has probably, indeed, been used for that purpose before now—but it can hardly be regarded as an assured basis for a recognized position in good society.

JACK: May I ask you then what you would advise me to do? I need hardly say I would do anything in the world to insure Gwendoline's happiness.

LADY BRACKNELL: I would strongly advise you, Mr. Worthing, to try and acquire some relations as soon as possible, and to make a definite effort to produce, at any rate, one parent, of either sex, before the season is quite over. *560*

JACK: Well, I don't see how I can possibly manage to do that. I can produce the handbag at any moment. It is in my dressing-room at home. I really think *that* should satisfy you, Lady Bracknell.

LADY BRACKNELL: (*Crossing*) Me, sir? What has it to do with me? You can hardly imagine that I and Lord Bracknell would dream of allowing our only daughter—a girl brought up with the utmost care—to marry into a cloakroom, and form an alliance with a handbag. Good morning, Mr. Worthing. (*Exits R.*) 570

JACK: Good morning. (ALGERNON, *inside, strikes up the "Wedding March." JACK looks perfectly furious, then runs across and off L. into room.*) For goodness' sake, don't play that ghastly tune, Algy! (*Re-enters and goes C.*) How idiotic you are!

ALGY: (*Enters L. Cheerily*) Didn't it go off all right, old boy? You don't mean to say Gwendoline refused you? (*Moves up to desk and gets cigarettes, brings down box and offers JACK one*)

JACK: Oh, as far as Gwendoline is concerned, we are engaged. Her mother is perfectly unbearable. Never met such a gorgon. You don't think there is any chance of Gwendoline becoming 580 like her mother in about a hundred and fifty years, do you, Algy?

ALGY: (*Moving down R.C., drawlingly and sententiously*) All women become like their mothers. That is their tragedy. No man does. That's *his*. (*Puts box on C. table*)

JACK: Is that clever? (*Sits sofa R.*)

ALGY: It is perfectly phrased, and quite as true as any observation in civilized life need be.

JACK: I am sick to death of cleverness. Everybody is clever nowadays. You can't go anywhere without meeting clever 590 people. The thing has become an absolute public nuisance. I wish to goodness we had a few fools left.

ALGY: We have.

JACK: I should extremely like to meet them. What do they talk about?

ALGY: The fools? Oh, about the clever people, of course. (*Brings chair to C. and sits*) By the way, did you tell Gwendoline the truth about your being Ernest in town and Jack in the country?

JACK: (*In a very patronizing manner*) My dear fellow, the truth isn't quite the sort of thing one tells to a nice sweet, refined girl. 600 What extraordinary ideas you have about the way to behave to a woman.

ALGY: The only way to behave to a woman is to make love to her if she is pretty, and to someone else if she is plain.

JACK: Oh, that is nonsense.

ALGY: What about your brother? What about the *profligate* Ernest?

JACK: Oh, before the end of the week I shall have got rid of him;

I'll say he died in Paris of apoplexy. Lots of people die of
apoplexy quite suddenly, don't they?   *610*

ALGY: Yes, but it's hereditary, my dear fellow. It's a sort of thing
that runs in families. You had much better say a severe chill.

JACK: You are sure a severe chill isn't hereditary or anything of
that kind?

ALGY: Of course it isn't.

JACK: Very well, then. My poor brother Ernest is carried off
suddenly in Paris, by a severe chill. That gets rid of him.

ALGY: But I thought you said that—Miss Cardew was a little too
much interested in your poor brother Ernest?

JACK: Oh, that is all right. Cecily is not a silly, romantic girl at all. *620*
She has a capital appetite, and goes on long walks, and pays
no attention at all to her lessons.

ALGY: I should like to see Cecily.

JACK: I will take very good care you never do. She is excessively
pretty, and she is only just eighteen.

ALGY: Have you told Gwendoline that you have an excessively
pretty young ward who is only just eighteen?

JACK: Oh, one doesn't blurt these things out to people. Cecily
and Gwendoline are perfectly certain to be extremely great
friends. I bet you anything you like that half an hour after they *630*
have met they will be calling each other sister.

ALGY: (*Rising and putting chair back*) Women only do that when
they have called each other a lot of other things first. Now, my
dear boy, if we want to get a good table at the Carlton we
really must go and dress. I'm hungry.

JACK: (C.) I never knew you when you weren't. (*Crosses* L.C.)

ALGY: (R.C.) What shall we do after dinner? Go to a theatre?

JACK: Oh, no! I *loathe* listening.

ALGY: Well, let us go to the Club?

JACK: Oh, no! I *hate* talking.   *640*

ALGY: Well—(*Goes up* C.)—we might trot round to the Empire at
ten.

JACK: Oh, no! I can't bear *looking* at things.

ALGY: Well, what *shall* we do?

JACK: Oh, nothing.

LANE: (*Enters* R.) Miss Fairfax. (*Enter* GWENDOLINE R. *She goes
down* C. *Exit* LANE, *leaving door open*)

ALGY: Gwendoline, upon my word.

GWENDOLINE: (*Turning him round*) Algy, kindly turn your back. I
have something very particular to say to Mr. Worthing.   *650*

ALGY: Really, Gwendoline, I don't think I can allow this at all.

GWENDOLINE: Algy, pray oblige me by turning your back. (*Turns
him round again.* ALGY *turns away up* C. *to fireplace. Moving down*
R.C. *to* JACK) Ernest, we may never be married. From the

expression on mamma's face I fear we never shall. Few
parents nowadays pay any regard to what their children say to
them. The old-fashioned respect for the young is rapidly dying
out. (R.C.) Whatever influence I ever had over mamma I lost at
the age of three. But though she may prevent us from
becoming man and wife, and I may marry someone else, and   660
marry often, nothing that she can possibly do can alter my
eternal devotion to you.

JACK: (R.) Dear Gwendoline!

GWENDOLINE: (R.C.) The story of your romantic origin, as related
to me by mamma, with unpleasing comments, has naturally
stirred the deeper fibres of my nature. Your Christian name is
an irresistible fascination. (*Embracing him*) The simplicity of
your character makes you exquisitely incomprehensible to me
(*Getting away a little*) Your town address at the Albany I have.
What is your address—(*Taking out notebook*)—in the country?   670

JACK: The Manor House, Woolton, Hertfordshire. (ALGY *writes
the address on shirt cuff, then picks up railway guide*)

GWENDOLINE: How long do you remain in town? (*Goes a little* R.)

JACK: Till Monday.

GWENDOLINE: Good! Algy, you may turn around now.

ALGY: Thanks, I've turned round already.

GWENDOLINE: (*To* ALGY) You may also ring the bell.

JACK: You will let me see you to your carriage, my own darling.

GWENDOLINE: Certainly.

JACK: (*To* LANE, *who now appears in hall*) I will see Miss Fairfax   680
out.

LANE: Yes, sir.

(*Exit* JACK *and* GWENDOLINE R.C. LANE *enters room and presents two
letters on salver to* ALGY, *who is seated at desk up* C. *It is to be
surmised that they are bills, for* ALGY *tears them up*)

ALGY: A glass of sherry, Lane.

LANE: Yes, sir. (*Hands sherry*)

ALGY: To-morrow, Lane, I'm going Bunburying.   690

LANE: Yes, sir.

ALGY: I shall probably not be back till Monday. You can put up
my dress clothes, my smoking jacket, and all the Bunbury
suits.

LANE: Yes, sir. (*Handing sherry*)

ALGY: (*Rising and coming down* R.) I hope tomorrow will be a fine
day, Lane.

LANE: It never is, sir.

ALGY: Lane, you are a perfect pessimist.

LANE: I do my best to give satisfaction, sir.   700

(*Exit* L. ALGY *crosses* C. *to table and puts glass down*)

JACK: (*Enters* R.C.) There's a sensible, intellectual girl; the only girl I ever cared for in my life. (ALGY *is laughing immoderately*) What on earth are you so amused at?

ALGY: (C.) Oh, I'm a little anxious about poor Bunbury, that is all.

JACK: (R.C.) If you don't take care, your friend Bunbury will get you into a serious scrape some day.

ALGY: I love scrapes. They are the only things that are never   710
serious.

JACK: Oh, that's nonsense. Algy; you never talk anything but nonsense.

ALGY: Nobody ever does. Besides, I love nonsense!

(JACK *looks indignantly and leaves the room.* ALGERNON *lights a cigarette, reads shirt cuff, and smiles*)

The Manor House, Woolton, Hertfordshire.

Act II

Garden at the Manor House

(*Door leading into house* R. *The garden is an old-fashioned one, full of roses, yew hedges, etc. Time of year, July. Basket chairs, and table covered with books.* MISS PRISM *discovered seated* L. *of table.* CECILY *up* R., *watering flowers*)

MISS PRISM: (C. *on settee, calling*) Cecily! Cecily! Surely it is more Moulton's duty to water the flowers than yours. Your German grammar is on the table. Pray open it at page fifteen. We will repeat yesterday's lesson.

CECILY: But I don't like German. It isn't at all a becoming   10
language. I know perfectly well that I always look quite plain after my German lesson.

MISS PRISM: Child, you know how anxious your guardian is that you should improve yourself in every way. He laid particular stress on your German, as he was leaving for town yesterday.

CECILY: Dear Uncle Jack is so very serious—sometimes he is so serious that I think he cannot be quite well. (*Puts down can and moves to* R. *of stage*)

MISS PRISM: Your guardian enjoys the best of health—and his gravity of demeanor is specially to be commended in one so   20
comparatively young as he is. I know no one who has a higher sense of duty and responsibility.

CECILY: (*Moving* R. *of* C. *table*) I suppose that is why he so often looks a little bored when we three are together.

MISS PRISM: Cecily, I am surprised at you! Mr. Worthing has many troubles in his life. Idle merriment and triviality would be out of place in his conversation. You must remember his constant anxiety about that unfortunate young man, his brother.

CECILY: I wish Uncle Jack would allow him to come here   *30* sometimes. We might have a good influence over him, Miss Prism. I am sure you certainly would. (*Goes* C. *and sitting* R. *of table*) You know German and geology, and things of that kind, that influence a man so much. (*Begins to write in her diary*)

MISS PRISM: (*Shaking her head*) I do not think that even I would produce any effect on a character that, according to his own brother's admission, is irretrievably weak and vacillating. Indeed, I am not sure that I would desire to reclaim him. I am not in favor of this modern mania for turning bad people into good people at a moment's notice. You must put away your   *40* diary, Cecily. I really don't see why you should keep a diary at all.

CECILY: I keep a diary in order to enter the wonderful secrets of my life. If I didn't write them down I would probably forget all about them.

MISS PRISM: Memory, my dear Cecily, is the diary we all carry about with us.

CECILY: Yes, but it usually chronicles the things that have never happened and couldn't possibly have happened. I believe that memory is responsible for nearly all the novels that Mudie   *50* sends us. (*Puts diary on table*)

MISS PRISM: Do not speak slightingly of novels, Cecily. I wrote one myself in earlier days.

CECILY: *Was* your novel ever published?

MISS PRISM: Alas, no. The manuscript unfortunately was abandoned. (CECILY *looks at her, then rises and moves up* C.) I use the word in the sense of lost or mislaid. To your work, child; these speculations are profitless.

CECILY: (*Going* L., *back of table*) But I see dear Doctor Chasuble coming up through the garden.   *60*

MISS PRISM: (*Rising and advancing* L.) Doctor Chasuble! This is indeed a pleasure.

CANON CHASUBLE: (*Enters through the door* L. *in garden wall*) And how are we this morning? (*Crosses and shakes hands*) Miss Prism, you are, I trust, well?

CECILY: (*Behind table*) Miss Prism has just been complaining of a slight headache. I think it would do her so much good to have a short stroll with you in the park, Dr. Chasuble.

MISS PRISM: Cecily, I have not mentioned anything about a headache. (*Sits*)   *70*

CECILY: No, dear Miss Prism, I know that, but I felt instinctively that you had a headache. Indeed, I was thinking about it, and not about my German lesson, when the dear rector came in.

CHASUBLE: I hope, Cecily, you are not inattentive. (*Sits* C.)

CECILY: Oh, I am afraid I am.

CHASUBLE: That is strange. Were I fortunate enough to be Miss Prism's pupil I would hang upon her lips. (MISS PRISM *glares.* CECILY *moves up behind table*) I spoke metaphorically—the metaphor was drawn from bees. Ahem! Mr. Worthing, I suppose, has not returned from town yet. 80

MISS PRISM: We do not expect him till Monday afternoon.

CHASUBLE: Ah, yes, he usually likes to spend his Sunday in London. He is not one of those whose sole aim is enjoyment, as, by all accounts, that unfortunate young man, his brother, seems to be. (*Rising*) But I must not disturb Egeria and her pupil any longer. (*Moves over toward her*)

MISS PRISM: (*Rising*) Egeria? My name is Letitia, Doctor.

CHASUBLE: A classical allusion merely, drawn from the Pagan authors. I will see you both, no doubt, at evensong?

MISS PRISM: I think, dear Doctor, I will have a stroll with you. I 90 find I have a headache after all, and a walk might do it good.

CHASUBLE: With pleasure, Miss Prism, with pleasure. We might go as far as the schools and back.

MISS PRISM: (*Crossing to* CECILY, R.C.) That will be delightful. Cecily, you will read your "Political Economy" in my absence; the chapter on the "Fall of the Rupee" you may omit. (*Returns*) It is somewhat too exciting for a young girl. (*Exit* L. *with* CHASUBLE)

CECILY: (*Picks up books and throws them back on table*) Horrid Political Economy! Horrid Geography! (*Rises; stands* L. *of table*) 100 Horrid, horrid German!

MERRIMAN: (*Enters* R. *Presents card on salver*) Mr. Ernest Worthing has just driven over from the station. He has brought his luggage with him.

CECILY: "Mr. Ernest Worthing, B₄, The Albany, W." Uncle Jack's brother! Did you tell him that Mr. Worthing was in town? (*Moves to front of table*)

MERRIMAN: Yes, Miss. He seemed very much disappointed. I told him that you and Miss Prism were in the garden. He said he was anxious to speak to you privately for a moment. 110

CECILY: Ask Mr. Ernest Worthing to come out here. I suppose you had better speak to the housekeeper about a room for him.

MERRIMAN: Yes, Miss. (*Exits* R.)

CECILY: I have never met any really wicked person before. I feel rather frightened. (*Moves* L.C.) I am afraid he will look just like anyone else. (*Enter* ALGY, *very gay and debonnaire. He is shown in by* MERRIMAN) He does!

ALGY: (*Raising his hat*) You are my little cousin, Cecily; I'm sure.

CECILY: You are under some strange mistake. I am not little. In   120
fact, I believe I am more than usually tall for my age. (ALGY *is taken aback*) But I am Cousin Cecily. You, I see from your card, are Uncle Jack's brother—my Cousin Ernest. My wicked Cousin Ernest.

ALGY: I am not really wicked at all, Cousin Cecily. You mustn't think I am wicked.

CECILY: If you are not, then you have certainly been deceiving us all in a very inexcusable manner. I hope you have not been leading a double life, pretending to be wicked and being really good all the time. That would be hypocrisy.   130

ALGY: (*Looking at her in amazement*) Oh! Of course I have been rather reckless.

CECILY: I am glad to hear it. (*Sitting on settee*)

ALGY: In fact, now you mention the subject, I have been very bad in my own small way.

CECILY: I don't think you should be so proud of that, though I am sure it must have been very pleasant.

ALGY: It is much pleasanter being here with you. (*Sitting* R.C.)

CECILY: I can't understand how you are here at all. Uncle Jack won't be back till Monday afternoon.   140

ALGY: This is a great disappointment, as I am obliged to go up on Monday morning.

CECILY: I think you had better wait till Uncle Jack arrives. I know he wants to speak to you about your emigrating.

ALGY: About my what? (*Startled*)

CECILY: Your emigrating. He is sending you to Australia.

ALGY: Australia! (*Rising and moving* R.C.) I'd sooner die.

CECILY: Well, he said at dinner on Wednesday night you would have to choose between this world, the next world, and Australia.   150

ALGY: Oh, well. (*Returning and sitting* C.) The accounts I have received of Australia and the next world are not encouraging. This world is good enough for me, Cousin Cecily.

CECILY: Yes, but are you good enough for it?

ALGY: I'm afraid I'm not that. That is why I want you to reform me. You might make that your mission, if you don't mind, Cousin Cecily.

CECILY: I'm afraid I've no time this afternoon.

ALGY: Well, would you mind my reforming myself, this afternoon?   160

CECILY: It is rather quixotic of you—but I think you should try.

ALGY: I will. I feel better already.

CECILY: You are looking a little worse. (*Rising*)

ALGY: That is because I am hungry.

CECILY: (*Crossing* R. *to steps*) How thoughtless of me. (*Crosses* R.C. ALGY *rises and follows*) I should have remembered that when one is going to lead an entirely new life, one requires regular and wholesome meals. (*Moves to door* R.) Won't you come in?

ALGY: Thank you. (*Moving to her*) Won't you give me a rose?

CECILY: A Marechal Niel? (*Picks up scissors and looks up right back*) 170

ALGY: No, I'd sooner have a pink rose.

CECILY: Why? (*Cuts flower*)

ALGY: Because *you* are like a pink rose, Cousin Cecily.

CECILY: I don't think it can be right for you to talk to me like that. Miss Prism never says such things to me.

ALGY: Then Miss Prism is a very short-sighted old lady. (CECILY *offers him rose and puts it in his buttonhole*) You are the prettiest girl I ever saw.

CECILY: Miss Prism says that all good looks are a snare.

ALGY: They are a snare that every sensible man would like to be 180 caught in.

CECILY: Oh, I don't think I would care to catch a sensible man. I wouldn't know what to talk to him about. (*Exeunt into house* R.)

MISS PRISM: (*Enters with* CHASUBLE *from door* L., *crossing* C., *then sits* R. *of table*) Where is Cecily? You are too much alone, dear Doctor Chasuble. You should get married. A misanthrope I can understand—a womanthrope, never!

CHASUBLE: Believe me, I do not deserve so Neologistic a phrase. The precept, as well as the practice, of the Primitive Church was distinctly against matrimony.   190

MISS PRISM: That is obviously the reason why the Primitive Church has not lasted up to the present day. And you do not seem to realize, dear Doctor, that by persistently remaining single, a man converts himself into a permanent public temptation. Men should be more careful; this very celibacy leads weaker vessels astray.

CHASUBLE: (*On settee*) But is a man not equally attractive when married?

MISS PRISM: No married man is ever attractive except to his wife.

CHASUBLE: And often, I've been told, not even to her. (*Putting* 200 *his hand over hers on table*)

MISS PRISM: But where is Cecily? (*Rises and moves to steps*)

CHASUBLE: (*Rising and moving* L.) Perhaps she followed us to the schools.

(*Enter* JACK *from back of garden* R. *He comes* C. *is dressed entirely in black.* MISS PRISM *shakes his hand.* JACK *takes out his handkerchief and puts it to his eyes*)

MISS PRISM: Mr. Worthing!

CHASUBLE: Mr. Worthing.   *210*

MISS PRISM: This is indeed a surprise. We did not look for you till Monday afternoon.

JACK: (*Shakes* MISS PRISM'S *hand in a tragic manner*) I have returned sooner than I expected. Doctor Chasuble, I hope you are well.

CHASUBLE: Dear Mr. Worthing, I trust this garb of woe does not betoken some terrible calamity.

JACK: My brother!

MISS PRISM: More shameful debts and extravagancies?

CHASUBLE: Still leading his life of pleasure?   *220*

JACK: (*Shaking his head*) Dead! (*Putting handkerchief to his eyes*)

CHASUBLE: Your brother Ernest dead?

JACK: Quite dead.

MISS PRISM: What a lesson for him. I trust he will profit by it. (*Sits* R.)

CHASUBLE: Mr. Worthing, I offer you my sincere condolences. You have at least the consolation of knowing that you were always the most generous and forgiving of brothers.

JACK: (*Handkerchief business*) Poor Ernest. He had many faults, but it is a sad blow.   *230*

CHASUBLE: Very sad indeed. Were you with him at the end?

JACK: No, he died abroad in Paris. I had a telegram last night from the manager of the Grand Hotel.

CHASUBLE: Was the cause of his death mentioned?

JACK: A severe chill, it seems.

CHASUBLE: (*Raising his hand*) None of us are perfect. I myself am particularly susceptible to draughts. Will the—interment take place here?

JACK: No. He seems to have expressed the desire to be buried in Paris. (CHASUBLE *helps* JACK *to sit* C.)   *240*

CHASUBLE: In Paris. (*Shakes his head*) I fear that hardly points to any very serious state of mind at the last. You would no doubt wish me to make some slight allusion to this tragic domestic affliction next Sunday. (JACK *presses his hand convulsively*) My sermon on the meaning of the manna in the Wilderness can be adapted to almost any occasion, joyful or, as in the present case, distressing. (*Long pause*) I have preached it at harvest celebrations, christenings, confirmations, on days of humiliation and festal days. The last time I delivered it was in the Cathedral, as a charity sermon on behalf of the Society for   *250* the Prevention of Discontent Among the Upper Classes. The Bishop, who was present, was much *struck* by some of the analogies I drew.

JACK: (*Rising*) Ah, that reminds me, you mentioned christenings,

I think, Doctor Chasuble. I suppose you know how to christen, all right? (CHASUBLE *looks astounded*) I mean, of course, you are continually christening, aren't you?

MISS PRISM: It is, I regret to say, one of the Rector's most constant duties in this parish. I have often spoken to the poorer classes on the subject. But they don't seem to know what thrift is.   260

CHASUBLE: (*Moving* C. *to* JACK) But is there any particular infant in whom you are interested, Mr. Worthing? Your brother was, I believe, unmarried, was he not?

JACK: (*Mournfully*) Oh, yes. Quite unmarried.

MISS PRISM: (*Bitterly*) People who live entirely for pleasure usually are.

JACK: Oh, it is not for any child, dear Doctor. I am very fond of children. No, the fact is, I would like to be christened myself, this afternoon, if you have nothing better to do.   270

CHASUBLE: But surely, Mr. Worthing, you have been christened already.

JACK: I don't remember anything about it. Of course, I don't know if the thing would bother you in any way, or if you think I am a little too old now.

CHASUBLE: Not at all. The sprinkling and indeed immersion of adults is a perfectly canonical practice.

JACK: Immersion? (*With a shudder*)

CHASUBLE: Oh, no. You need have no apprehensions. Sprinkling is all that is necesssary, or indeed I think advisable. 280 Our weather is so changeable. What hour would you wish the ceremony to be performed?

JACK: (C.) Oh, I might trot round about five, if that would suit you.

CHASUBLE: (L.C.) Oh, perfectly! In fact I have two similar ceremonies to perform at that time. A case of twins that occurred recently in one of the outlying cottages on your own estate. Poor Jenkins, the carter, a most hard-working man.

JACK: Oh! I don't see much fun in being christened along with other babies. It would be childish. Would half-past five do?   290

CHASUBLE: Admirably, admirably! (*Takes out watch*) And now, dear Mr. Worthing, I will not intrude any longer into a house of sorrow. I would merely beg you not to be too much bowed down by grief. What seem to us bitter trials are often blessings in disguise. (*Moves* L.)

MISS PRISM: (*Moving up* R.C.) This seems to me a blessing of an *extremely obvious* kind. (*Rises and moves round back stage to* L.)

CECILY: (*Enters* R.) Uncle Jack! Oh, I *am* pleased to see you back. What horrid clothes you have got on. Do go and change them.

MISS PRISM: Cecily!   300

CECILY: (*Goes toward* JACK. *He kisses her brow in a melancholy manner*) What is the matter, Uncle Jack? (JACK *turns away, crying*) Do look happy! You look as if you had toothache, and I have got such a surprise. (MISS PRISM *has moved over to* L. *to* DR. CHASUBLE) Who do you think is in the dining-room? Your brother!

JACK: Who?

CECILY: Your brother Ernest. He arrived here half an hour ago.

JACK: What nonsense! I haven't got a brother.

CECILY: Oh, don't say that! However badly he may have   310
behaved to you in the past, he is still your brother. You couldn't be so heartless as to disown him. I'll tell him to come out. And you will shake hands with him, won't you, Uncle Jack? (*Exits* R.)

CHASUBLE: These are very joyful tidings.

MISS PRISM: After we had all been resigned to his loss, his sudden return seems to me *peculiarly* distressing.

JACK: My brother is in the dining-room? I don't know what it all means? I think it is perfectly absurd. (*Enter* ALGY *and* CECILY R.
ALGY *goes* R. CECILY *goes to* R.C.) Good heavens! (*Motions him*   320
away) Go away.

ALGY: Brother John, I have come down from town to tell you that I am very sorry for all the trouble I have given you, and I intend to lead a better life in the future.

JACK: (*Glares at him and does not take his hand*) Go away.

CECILY: (*Coming down and touching him on the shoulder*) Uncle Jack, you are not going to refuse your own brother's hand?

JACK: Nothing will induce me to take his hand. I think his coming down here is disgraceful. He knows perfectly well why.   330

CECILY: Uncle Jack, do be nice. There is some good in everyone. Ernest has been telling me about his poor invalid friend whom he goes to visit so often. (JACK *walks up and down* C.)

ALGY: Of course I admit that the faults were all on my side. But I must say that I think brother John's coldness to me is peculiarly painful. I expected a more enthusiastic welcome, especially considering it is the first time I have come here. (JACK *moves up* R.C.)

CECILY: (*Pulling* JACK *across to* ALGY, L.C.) Uncle Jack, if you don't shake hands with Ernest I will never forgive you. (*Joins* MISS   340
PRISM, *who is with* DR. CHASUBLE, L.)

JACK: I suppose I must, then.

CHASUBLE: It's pleasant, is it not, to see so perfect a reconciliation? I think we might leave the two brothers together.

MISS PRISM: Cecily, you will come with me.

CECILY: Certainly, Miss Prism. (ALGY *gets* C. *Exeunt* CECILY *and*
MISS PRISM, *arm in arm, and* DR. CHASUBLE)

JACK: (*Down* R.C.; *shakes hands*) You young scoundrel! Algy, you
must get out of this place as soon as possible. I don't allow   *350*
any Bunburying here.

MERRIMAN: (*Enters* R.) I have put Mr. Ernest's things in the room
next to yours, sir. I suppose that is all right?

JACK: What?

MERRIMAN: Mr. Ernest's luggage, sir. I have unpacked it and pu
it in the room next to your own.

ALGY: (*Takes off hat and puts it on table*) I am afraid I can't stay
more than a week this time. (*Looks after* CECILY)

JACK: Merriman, order the dog-cart at once. Mr. Ernest has been
suddenly called back to town.   *360*

MERRIMAN: Yes, sir. (*Exit* R.)

ALGY: (*Turning to* JACK) Jack, Cecily is a darling.

JACK: You are not to talk of Miss Cardew like that. I don't like it.

ALGY: Well, I don't like your clothes. You look perfectly
ridiculous in them. Why on earth don't you go up and
change? It is perfectly childish to be in deep mourning for a
man who happens to be staying for a week with you in your
own house as a guest. I call it grotesque.

JACK: You are certainly not staying with me for a week as a guest
or anything else. You have got to leave—by the four-five train. *370*

ALGY: I certainly won't leave you as long as you are in
mourning. It would be most unfriendly. If I were in mourning
you would stay with me, I suppose. I should think it very
unkind if you didn't.

JACK: Well, will you go if I change my clothes?

ALGY: Yes, if you are not too long. I never saw anybody take so
long to dress, and with such little result.

JACK: Well, at any rate, that is better than being always
overdressed, as you are. (*Exit* R.)

ALGY: I'm in love with Cecily. (*Enter* CECILY L.) I must see her   *380*
before I go. Ah, there she is!

CECILY: Oh, I merely came back to water the flowers. I thought
you were with Uncle Jack.

ALGY: He's gone to order the dog-cart for me.

CECILY: Oh, is he going to take you for a nice drive?

ALGY: He's going to send me away.

CECILY: Then we have got to part. (*Moves to seat* L.C. *and sits*)

ALGY: (*After a pause*) I'm afraid so. (*Sits beside her*)

MERRIMAN: (*Enters* R.) The dog-cart is at the door, sir.

CECILY: It can wait, Merriman—(*Rises*)—for—five minutes.   *390*
(*Crossing* R.C.)

MERRIMAN: Yes, Miss. (*Exit* R.)

ALGY: (*Pulls out his watch; rises*) I hope, Cecily, I shall not offend
you if I state quite frankly and openly that you seem to me to
be in every way the visible personification of absolute
perfection.

CECILY: I think your frankness does you great credit, Ernest. If
you will allow me I will copy your remarks into my diary.
(*Goes over to table and begins writing in diary*)

ALGY: Do you really keep a diary? (*Sitting* C.) I'd give anything to   *400*
look at it. May I?

CECILY: Oh, no! (*Puts hand over it*) You see, it is simply a very
young girl's record of her own thoughts and impressions, and
consequently not meant for publication. But pray, Ernest,
don't stop. I delight in taking down dictation. I have reached
"absolute perfection." (*Sits* R.C.) You can go on. I am quite
ready for more.

ALGY: (*Speaking very rapidly*) Cecily, ever since I first looked upon
your wonderful and incomparable beauty, I have dared to love
you wildly, passionately, devotedly, hopelessly.   *410*

CECILY: I don't think you should tell me that you love me wildly,
passionately, devotedly, hopelessly. Hopelessly doesn't seem
to make much sense, does it?

ALGY: Cecily! (*Rising; leaning over the table*)

MERRIMAN: (*Enters* R.) The dog-cart is waiting, sir.

ALGY: (*Rises, crossing* R. *back*) Tell it to come round next week at
the same hour.

MERRIMAN: (*Looking at* CECILY, *who makes no sign*) Yes, sir. (*Exit*
R.)

CECILY: (*Rising and moving* C.) Uncle Jack would be very much   *420*
annoyed if he knew you were staying on till next week, at the
same hour.

ALGY: Oh, I don't care about Jack. I don't care for anybody in
the whole world but you. I love you, Cecily. You will marry
me, won't you?

CECILY: You silly boy! Of course. Why, we have been engaged
for the last three months.

ALGY: For the last three months?

CECILY: Yes. It will be exactly three months on Thursday.

ALGY: (*Sits on table*) But how did we become engaged?   *430*

CECILY: Well—(*Sits on sofa* L.C.)—ever since dear Uncle Jack first
confessed to us that he had a younger brother who was very
wicked and bad, you, of course, have formed the chief topic of
conversation between myself and Miss Prism. And, of course,
a man who is much talked about is always very attractive. One
feels there must be something in him after all. I daresay it was
foolish of me, but I fell in love with you, Ernest.

ALGY: Darling! And when was the engagement actually settled?

(ALGY *embraces* CECILY)

CECILY: On the 14th of April last. Worn out by your entire   440
ignorance of my existence, I determined to end the matter one
way or the other, and after a long struggle with myself, I
accepted you here. The next day I bought this little ring in
your name, and this is the little bangle with the true lover's
knot I promised you always to wear.

ALGY: Did I give you this? It's very pretty, isn't it?

CECILY: (*Rising and crossing* R.) Yes, you've wonderfully good
taste, Ernest. It's the excuse I've always given for your leading
such a bad life. (*Then moving up to table*) And this is the box in
which I keep all your dear letters. (*Kneels at table, opens box and*   450
produces letters tied up with blue ribbon)

ALGY: My letters! (*Standing* C.) But my own sweet Cecily, I have
never written—you any letters.

CECILY: You need hardly remind me of that, Ernest. I remember
only too well that I was forced to write your letters for you. I
wrote always three times a week, and sometimes oftener.

ALGY: Oh, do let me read them, Cecily!

CECILY: (*Sits* R.C. *table*) Oh, I couldn't possibly. They would
make you far too conceited. (*Replaces box*)

ALGY: (*Crossing to her and kneeling*) What a perfect angel you are,   460
Cecily!

CECILY: You dear romantic boy! (*He kisses her. She puts her fingers*
through his hair) I hope your hair curls naturally. Does it?

ALGY: Yes, darling, with a little help from others.

CECILY: I am so glad!

ALGY: You'll never break off our engagement, Cecily?

CECILY: I don't think I could break it off, now that I have actually
met you. Besides, of course, there is the question of your
name.

ALGY: (*With head on her shoulder*) Yes, of course. (*Nervously*)   470

CECILY: You must not laugh at me, darling, but it had always
been a girlish dream of mine to love someone whose name
was Ernest. (*Both rise and move* R.C.) There is something in that
name that seems to inspire absolute confidence. I pity any
poor married woman whose husband is not called Ernest.

ALGY: But, my dear child, do you mean to say you could not
love me if I had some other name?

CECILY: But what name?

ALGY: Oh, any name you like—Algernon, for instance—

CECILY: But I don't like the name of Algernon. (*Crossing* C. ALGY   480
follows)

ALGY: Well, my own dear, sweet, loving little darling, I really
can't see why you should object to the name of Algernon. It is
not at all a bad name. In fact, it is rather an aristocratic name.

But seriously, Cecily, if my name was Algy, couldn't you love me?

CECILY: I might respect you, Ernest. I might admire your character, but I fear I would not be able to give you my undivided attention.

ALGY: Ahem! Cecily! (*Picking up hat*) Your rector here is, I   490
suppose, thoroughly experienced in the practice of all the rights and ceremonials of the church?

CECILY: Oh, yes. Doctor Chasuble is a most learned man. He has never written a single book, so you can imagine how much he knows.

ALGY: I must see him at once on a matter of important christening—I mean business. (*Crossing* L.) I'll be back in no time. (*Kisses her. Exit* L.)

CECILY: What an impetuous boy he is! (*Moves up to chair*) I like his hair so much. I must enter his proposal in my diary. (*Goes*   500
over and sits down R. *of* C. *table*)

MERRIMAN: (*Enters* R.) A Miss Fairfax has just called to see Mr. Worthing. On very important business, Miss Fairfax states.

CECILY: Isn't Mr. Worthing in his library?

MERRIMAN: Mr. Worthing went over in the direction of the Rectory some time ago.

CECILY: Pray ask the lady to come out here. Mr. Worthing is sure to be back soon. And you can bring tea.

MERRIMAN: Yes, Miss. (*Exit* R.)

CECILY: Miss Fairfax! I suppose one of the many elderly good   510
women who are associated with Uncle Jack in some of his philanthropic work in London. I don't quite like women who are interested in philanthropic work. I think it is so forward of them. (*Rising; moving* L.C.)

MERRIMAN: (*Enters* R.) Miss Fairfax. (*Enter* GWENDOLINE R. *Exit* MERRIMAN R.)

CECILY: (*Advancing to meet her,* C.) Pray let me introduce myself to you. My name is Cecily Cardew.

GWENDOLINE: (C.) Cecily Cardew! (*Moving to her and shaking hands*) What a very sweet name. Something tells me that we   520
are going to be *great friends*. I like you already more than I can say. My first impressions of people are never wrong.

CECILY: How nice of you to like me so much after we have known each other such a comparatively short time. (*Pause*) Pray sit down.

GWENDOLINE: (*Still standing up front of* C. *chair*) I may call you Cecily, may I not?

CECILY: With pleasure.

GWENDOLINE: And you will always call *me* Gwendoline, won't you?   530

CECILY: If you wish.

GWENDOLINE: Then that is all settled, is it not?

CECILY: I hope so. (*Pause. They both sit together,* CECILY L.C., GWENDOLINE C.)

GWENDOLINE: Perhaps this might be favorable for my mentioning who I am. My father is Lord Bracknell. You have never *heard* of papa, I suppose?

CECILY: I don't think so.

GWENDOLINE: *Outside* the family circle, papa, I am glad to say, is entirely unknown. I think that is quite as it should be. The home seems to me to be the proper sphere for the man. Cecily, mamma, whose views on education are remarkably strict, has brought me up to be extremely short-sighted. It's part of her system, so you do not mind my looking at you through my glasses? 540

CECILY: Oh, not at all, Gwendoline. I am very fond of being looked at.

GWENDOLINE: (*Long pause. After examining* CECILY *carefully through lorgnette*) You are here on a short visit, I suppose?

CECILY: Oh, no! I live here. 550

GWENDOLINE: (*Severely*) Really? Your *mother*, no doubt, or some female relative of advanced years, resides here also.

CECILY: Oh, no! I have no mother, nor, in fact, any relations.

GWENDOLINE: Indeed?

CECILY: My dear guardian, with the assistance of Miss Prism, has the arduous task of looking after me.

GWENDOLINE: Your guardian?

CECILY: Yes, I am Mr. Worthing's ward.

GWENDOLINE: Oh! It is strange he never mentioned to me that he had a ward. How secretive of him. He grows more interesting hourly. I am not sure, however, that the news inspires me with feelings of unmixed delight. (*Rises and walks* R.C.) I am very fond of you, Cecily. I have liked you ever since I met you. But I am bound to state that, now I know that you are Mr. Worthing's ward, I cannot help expressing the wish that you were—well, just a little older than you seem to be—and not quite so very alluring in appearance. In fact, if I may speak candidly—(*Returning* C.) 560

CECILY: Pray do! I think that whenever one has anything unpleasant to say, one should always be quite candid. 570

GWENDOLINE: Well, to speak with perfect candor, Cecily, I wish that you were fully thirty-five—(*Sits on sofa,* R. *of* CECILY)—and more than usually plain for your age. Ernest has a strong, upright nature. He is the very soul of truth and honor. But even men of the noblest possible moral character are extremely susceptible to the influence of the physical charms of others.

CECILY: I beg your pardon, Gwendoline. Did you say Ernest?

GWENDOLINE: Yes.

CECILY: Oh, but it is not Mr. Ernest Worthing who is my
guardian. It is his brother—his elder brother.   *580*

GWENDOLINE: Ernest never mentioned to me that he had a
brother.

CECILY: I am sorry to say they have not been on good terms for a
long time.

GWENDOLINE: Ah, that accounts for it. And now I think of it, I
have never heard any man mention his brother. The subject
seems distasteful to most men. Of course you are quite, quite
sure that it is not Mr. *Ernest* Worthing who is your guardian?

CECILY: Quite sure. (*Pause*) In fact, I am going to be *his*.

GWENDOLINE: (*Inquiringly*) I beg your pardon?   *590*

CECILY: (*Rather shy and confidingly*) Dearest Gwendoline, there is
no reason why I should make any secret of it to you. Our little
county newspaper is sure to chronicle the fact next week. Mr.
Ernest Worthing and I are engaged to be married.

GWENDOLINE: (*Quite politely, rising, crossing* R.C.) My darling
Cecily, I think there must be some *slight* error. Mr. Ernest
Worthing is engaged to *me*. The announcement will appear in
the *Morning Post* on Saturday at the latest.

CECILY: (*Very politely, rising, and moving* R.C.) I am *afraid* you must
be under some misconception. Ernest proposed to me exactly   *600*
ten minutes ago. (*Shows diary*)

GWENDOLINE: (*Examines diary through her lorgnette carefully*) It is
certainly very curious, for he asked *me* to be his *wife* yesterday
afternoon at five-thirty. If you would care to verify the
incident, pray do so. I never travel without my diary. (*Produces
her diary*) I am so sorry, dear Cecily, if it is any disappointment
to you, but I am afraid I have the prior claim.

CECILY: It would distress me more than I can tell you, dear
Gwendoline, if it caused you any mental or physical anguish,
but I feel bound to point out that since Ernest proposed to *you*   *610*
he has clearly changed his mind.

GWENDOLINE: (*Meditatively*) If the poor fellow has been
entrapped into any foolish promise, I shall consider it my duty
to rescue him at *once*, and with a *firm hand*. (*Moves a little* R.C.)

CECILY: (*Thoughtfully and sadly, moving slowly* L.) Whatever
unfortunate entanglement my dear boy may have got into, *I*
will never reproach him with it, *after* we are married. (*Moves
down* C.)

GWENDOLINE: (*Moving* C.) do you allude to me, Miss Cardew, as
an entanglement? You are presumptuous. On an occasion of   *620*
this kind, it becomes more than a moral duty to speak one's
mind—it becomes a pleasure.

CECILY: (*Moving up* C. *to* GWENDOLINE) Do you suggest, Miss Fairfax, that I entrapped Ernest into an engagement? How dare you? This is no time for wearing the shallow mask of manners. When I see a *spade* I call it a *spade*.

(*Enter* MERRIMAN. *He carries a salver, tablecloth and plate stand.* GWENDOLINE *is about to make a retort. The presence of a servant exercises a restraining influence under which both girls chafe*)   630

GWENDOLINE: (*Satirically*) I am glad to say that I have never seen a spade. It is obvious that our social spheres have been *widely* different.
MERRIMAN: Shall I lay tea here as usual, Miss?

(GWENDOLINE *moves up* R. *and returns, moving* L.C.)

CECILY: (*Sternly, in a clear voice*) Yes, as usual.
                                                                                                        640
(MERRIMAN *begins to clear table and lay cloth. Long pause.* CECILY *and* GWENDOLINE *glare at each other, then separate and move respectively* L. *and* R.)

GWENDOLINE: (*Looking round, moving back* R., *and coming down* C.) Quite a well-kept garden this is, Miss Cardew.
CECILY: So glad you like it, Miss Fairfax. (*Moving* L. *and then to* R.C.)
GWENDOLINE: I had no idea there were any flowers in the country.   650
CECILY: Oh, flowers are as common here, Miss Fairfax, as people are in London.

(SERVANT *enters from house, carrying tray set with tea things. He hands it to* MERRIMAN, *who places it on table and remains waiting.* SERVANT *exits into house and re-enters with wicker table, on which are plates and cover dishes containing uncut cake, muffins, and tea-cake.* SERVANT *puts table* R. *of* R.C. *chair, then exits into house*)

GWENDOLINE: Personally, I cannot understand how anybody   660
manages to exist in the country, if anybody who is anybody does. The country always bores me to death. (*Sits* R.)
CECILY: Ah! That is what the newspapers call agricultural depression, is it not? I believe the aristocracy are suffering very much from it just at present. It is almost an epidemic amongst them, I have been told. May I offer you some tea, Miss Fairfax? (*Sits* C. *and begins to pour out tea*)
GWENDOLINE: (*With elaborate politeness*) Thank you. (*Aside*) Detestable girl! But I require tea!
CECILY: (*Sweetly*) Sugar?   670
GWENDOLINE: (*Superciliously*) No, thank you. Sugar is *not* fashionable any more. (CECILY *looks angrily at her, takes up tongs*

again, and puts four lumps of sugar into the cup which she then places on salver that MERRIMAN *is holding*)

CECILY: (*Severely*) Cake, or bread and butter?

GWENDOLINE: (*In a bored manner*) Bread and butter, please. (CECILY *is about to put bread and butter on tray*) Cake is rarely seen at the best houses nowadays.

(CECILY *cuts a large slice of cake, and puts it on* MERRIMAN'S *tray.*   680
MERRIMAN *moves to back of tree, picks up plate-stand, goes down* L. *of* GWENDOLINE, *places plate-stand beside her, hands tea, and puts cake on stand. Exit* MERRIMAN *into house.* GWENDOLINE *drinks the tea and makes a grimace, puts down cup at once, reaches out her hand for bread and butter, looks at it and finds it is cake, rises in indignation and moves* C.)

GWENDOLINE: (*Rises, crossing to table*) You have filled my cup with lumps of *sugar*, and though I asked most distinctly for bread and butter, you have given me cake. (*Both put down their*   690 *cups*) I am known for the gentleness of my disposition, and the extraordinary sweetness of my nature, but I warn you, Miss Cardew, you may go too far.

CECILY: (*Rising*) To save my poor, innocent, trusting boy from the machinations of any other girl, there are *no* lengths to which I would not go.

GWENDOLINE: From the moment I saw you I distrusted you. I felt that you were false and deceitful. I am never deceived in such matters. My first impressions of people are invariably right. (*Stamping foot*)   700

CECILY: It seems to me, Miss Fairfax, that I am trespassing on your valuable time. No doubt you have many other calls of a similar character to make in the neighborhood. (GWENDOLINE *goes away* R. *Enter* JACK *from* R.)

GWENDOLINE: Ernest! My own Ernest!

JACK: (*Advancing to* R.C.) Gwendoline, darling! (*Offers to kiss her*)

GWENDOLINE: (*Drawing back*) A moment! May I ask if you are engaged to be married to this young lady? (*Points to* CECILY)

JACK: (*Laughing*) To dear little Cecily! Of course not! What could have put such an idea into your pretty little head?   710

GWENDOLINE: Thank you. You may! (*Offers her cheek*)

CECILY: (*Very sweetly*) I knew there must be some misunderstanding, Miss Fairfax. The gentleman whose arm is at present round your waist is my dear guardian, Mr. John Worthing.

GWENDOLINE: I beg your pardon. (*Moves back* R.C.)

CECILY: This is my Uncle Jack.

GWENDOLINE: (*Receding*) Jack! Oh! (*Enter* ALGY *from* L.)

CECILY: Here is Ernest!

ALGY: (*Goes straight over to* L. *of* CECILY *without noticing anyone* 720
else) My own love! (*Offers to kiss her*)

CECILY: (*Drawing back*) A moment! Ernest, may I ask if you are
engaged to be married to this young lady?

ALGY: (*Looking round*) To what young lady? Gwendoline!
(*Laughing*) Of course not! What could have put such an idea
into your pretty little head?

CECILY: Thank you! (*Presenting her cheek to be kissed*) You may.
(ALGY *kisses her*)

GWENDOLINE: (*Crosses* C.) I felt there was some slight error, Miss
Cardew. The gentleman who is now embracing you is my 730
cousin, Mr. Algernon Moncrieff.

CECILY: (*Breaking away from* ALGY) Algernon Moncrieff? Oh! (*To*
ALGY) Are you called Algernon?

ALGY: I cannot deny it!

CECILY: Oh! (*Crosses to* GWENDOLINE. *The* TWO GIRLS *move* C.
*toward each other and put their arms round each other's waists as if
for protection*)

GWENDOLINE: Is your name really John?

JACK: (*Standing rather proudly*) I could deny it if I liked—I could
deny anything if I liked. But my name certainly is John. It has 740
been John for years.

CECILY: (*to* GWENDOLINE) A gross deception has been practiced
on both of us.

GWENDOLINE: My poor wounded Cecily!

CECILY: My sweet wronged Gwendoline!

GWENDOLINE: (*Slowly and seriously*) You will call me sister, will
you not? (*They embrace.* JACK *and* ALGY *groan and walk up and
down* R. *and* L.)

CECILY: (*Rather brightly*) There is just one question I would like to
be allowed to ask my guardian. (ALGY *comes down* L. JACK *comes* 750
down R.)

GWENDOLINE: An admirable idea! Mr. Worthing, there is just
one question I would like to be permitted to put to you. Where
is your brother Ernest? We are both engaged to be married to
your brother Ernest, so it is a matter of some importance to us
to know where your brother Ernest is at present.

JACK: (*Slowly and hesitatingly*) Gwendoline—Cecily. (*Crossing* C.)
It is very painful for me to be forced to speak the truth. (ALGY
sinks on L.C. *sofa*) It is the first time in my life that I have ever
been reduced to such a painful position, and I am really quite 760
inexperienced in doing anything of the kind. However, I will
tell you quite frankly that I *have* no brother Ernest. I have no
brother at all. I never had a brother in my life. And I certainly
have not the smallest intention of ever having one in the
future. (ALGY, *who has been seated down* L., *turns in chair*)

CECILY: (*Surprised*) No brother at all?

JACK: (*Cheerily*) None!

GWENDOLINE: (*Severely approaching him*) Have you never had a brother of any kind?

JACK: (*Pleasantly*) Never. Not even of any kind. (*Crossing L. to ALGY and sitting R. of sofa R.C.*)   770

GWENDOLINE: I am afraid it is quite clear, Cecily, that neither of us is engaged to be married to anyone. (*Crossing to CECILY C.*)

CECILY: It is not a very pleasant position for a young girl to suddenly find herself in, is it?

GWENDOLINE: Let us go into the house. (*Taking CECILY away up R.*) They will hardly venture to come after us there.

CECILY: No, men are so cowardly, aren't they? (*Exeunt into house with scornful look R. ALGY kicks JACK, and JACK returns it spitefully*)   780

JACK: This ghastly state of things is what you call Bunburying, I suppose.

ALGY: Yes, and a perfectly wonderful Bunbury it is. The most wonderful Bunbury I have ever had in my life.

JACK: Well, you've no right whatsoever to Bunbury here.

ALGY: That is absurd. One has a right to Bunbury anywhere one chooses. Every serious Bunburyist knows that.

JACK: Serious Bunburyists! Good heavens! (*Rises, crosses to C. and moves up C.*)

ALGY: (*Rising*) Well, one must be serious about something, if one   790 wants to have any amusement in life. I happen to be serious about Bunburying. What on earth you are serious about I haven't got the remotest idea. About everything, I should fancy. You have such an absolutely trivial nature.

JACK: (*Coming C.*) Well, the only small satisfaction I have in the whole of this wretched business is that your friend Bunbury is quite exploded. You won't be able to run down to the country quite so often as you used to do, Algy. And a very good thing, too. (*JACK moves R.*)

ALGY: Your brother is a little off color, isn't he, dear Jack? You   800 won't be able to disappear to London quite so frequently as your wicked custom was. And not a bad thing either.

JACK: (*Coming C.*) As for your conduct toward Miss Cardew, I must say that your taking in a sweet, simple, innocent girl like that is quite inexcusable. To say nothing of the fact that she is *my* ward.

ALGY: I can see no possible defense at all for your deceiving a brilliant, clever, thoroughly experienced young lady like Miss Fairfax. To say nothing of the fact that she is *my cousin*. (*Sits R. end of settee*)   810

JACK: I wanted to be engaged to Gwendoline, that is all. I love her.

ALGY: Well, I simply wanted to be engaged to Cecily. I adore her.

JACK: There is certainly no chance of your marrying Miss Cardew. (*Sits* C.)

ALGY: I don't think there is much likelihood, Jack, of you and Miss Fairfax being united. (*Takes muffins and sits* L.C.)

JACK: How can you sit there, calmly eating muffins, when we are in this horrible trouble, I can't make out. You seem to me to be perfectly heartless.   820

ALGY: Well, I can't eat muffins in an agitated manner. The butter would probably get on one's cuffs. One should always eat muffins quite calmly. It is the only way to eat them.

JACK: I say it is perfectly heartless your eating muffins at all under the circumstances.

ALGY: (JACK *sits* C.*after pouring tea*) When I am in trouble, eating is the only thing that consoles me. Indeed, when I am really in great trouble, as anyone who knows me intimately will tell you, I refuse everything except food and drink. At the present moment I am eating muffins because I am unhappy. Besides, I   830 am particularly fond of muffins. (*Picks muffin dish up*)

JACK: (*Rising*) Well, that is no reason why you should eat them all in that greedy way. (*Takes muffin from* ALGY)

ALGY: (*Picks up tea-cake dish, offering tea-cake, rising*) I wish you would take tea-cake instead. I don't like tea-cake.

JACK: Good heavens! I suppose a man may eat his own muffins in his own garden.

ALGY: But you have just said it was perfectly heartless to eat muffins.

JACK: I said it was perfectly heartless of you under the   840 circumstances. That is a very different thing.

ALGY: That may be. But the muffins are the same. (*They change plates.* ALGY *goes to head of table*)

JACK: Algy, I wish to goodness you would go. (*Puts tea-cake on table*)

ALGY: I cannot. (*Sits on settee* L.C.) I have just made arrangements with Dr. Chasuble to be christened at a quarter to six, under the name of Ernest. (*Sits* L.C. *on sofa*)

JACK: (*Sits* R. *of table*) My dear fellow, the sooner you give up that nonsense the better. (*Pouring out tea*) I made arrangements this   850 morning with Doctor Chasuble to be christened myself at five-thirty, and I naturally will take the name of Ernest. Gwendoline would wish it. We can't both be christened Ernest. It would be absurd. Besides, I have a perfect right to be christened if I like. There is no evidence at all that I ever have been christened by anybody. I should think it extremely probable I never was so, and so does Doctor Chasuble. It is

entirely different in your case. You have been christened
already. (*Crossing* R.C.)

ALGY: Yes, but I have not been christened for years.   860

JACK: Yes, but you have been christened. That is the important
thing.

ALGY: Quite so. (*Rises and moves to him*) So I know my
constitution can stand it. If you are not quite sure about your
ever having been christened, I must say I think it rather
dangerous your venturing on it now. It might make you
unwell. (*Business simultaneously*) You can hardly have forgotten
that someone very closely connected with you was very nearly
carried off this week in Paris, by a severe chill. (JACK *eats
muffins again*) Jack, you are at the muffins again. I wish you   870
wouldn't. (*Takes them*) I told you I was particularly fond of
muffins.

JACK: Algy, I have already told you to go. I don't want you here.
Why don't you go?

ALGY: (*Sits* R.C.) I haven't quite finished my tea yet.

(*Ring curtain down.* ALGY *sits back of table and takes* JACK'S *cup of tea
and begins to drink it*)

JACK: You are drinking my tea.

ALGY: It's not your tea. You are eating my muffins—   880

JACK: They are not your muffins—

(*Curtain down by this.* JACK *groans and sinks on to settee*)

Act III

Morning-room at the Manor House

(*Double doors up* R.C., *window* L., *fireplace* R., *chair* R. *of table out
toward* C. GWENDOLINE *and* CECILY *discovered at window* L.)

GWENDOLINE: The fact that they did not at once follow us into
the house, as anyone else would have done, seems to me to
show that they have some sense of shame left.

CECILY: They have been eating muffins. That looks like
repentance.

GWENDOLINE: They're looking at us—what effrontery!

CECILY: They're approaching; that's very forward of them. (JACK   10
passes window, followed by ALGY)

GWENDOLINE: Let us preserve a dignified silence.

CECILY: Certainly. It's the only thing to do now.

(*Both move down* L. *Enter* JACK, R. *of* ALGY. *They whistle*)

GWENDOLINE: This dignified silence seems to produce an
unpleasant effect.

(ALGY *moves down* L. JACK *moves down* R.C.)

20

CECILY: Most distasteful!

GWENDOLINE: But we will not be the first to speak.

CECILY: Certainly not.

GWENDOLINE: (*Crossing* C.) Mr. Worthing, I have something very
particular to ask you. Much depends on your reply.

CECILY: (*Moving to* ALGY C.) Mr. Moncrieff, kindly answer me the
following question: Why did you pretend to be my guardian's
brother?

ALGY: In order that I might have an opportunity of meeting you.

CECILY: (*Crossing* C. *to* GWENDOLINE. ALGY *moves down* L.) That   30
certainly seems a satisfactory explanation, does it not? (JACK
R.)

GWENDOLINE: (*Crossing to* JACK, *who comes down* C.) Mr.
Worthing, what explanation can you offer to me for
pretending to have a brother? Was it in order that you might
have an opportunity of coming up to town to see me as often
as possible?

JACK: Certainly, Miss Fairfax.

(JACK *and* ALGY *both move together like Siamese twins in every*   40
movement until both say "Christened this afternoon." First to front of
sofa, then fold hands together, then raise eyes to ceiling, then sit on
sofa, unfold hands, lean back, tilting up legs with both feet off ground,
then twitch trousers above knee, à la dude, so as not to crease them;
then both feet on ground, fold hands together on knees and look
perfectly unconcerned)

GWENDOLINE: (*Moving to* CECILY) Their explanations appear to be
quite satisfactory.

GWENDOLINE: You think we should forgive them?   50

CECILY *and* GWENDOLINE: (*Together*) Yes. No, I mean, no.

GWENDOLINE: True! I had forgotten. There are principles at stake
that one cannot surrender. Which of us should tell them? The
task is not a pleasant one.

CECILY: Could we not both speak at the same time?

GWENDOLINE: An excellent idea! Will you take the time from me?

CECILY: Certainly. (*Business of beating time*)

GWENDOLINE *and* CECILY: (*Speaking together and facing their*
respective sweethearts) Your Christian names are still an
insuperable barrier. That is all.   60

JACK: (*To* ALGY) Will you take the time from me?

JACK *and* ALGY: (*Speaking together*) Our Christian names! Is that
all? But we are going to be christened this afternoon.

GWENDOLINE: (*Crosses to* JACK R.) For my sake you are prepared
to do this terrible thing?

JACK: I am!

CECILY: (*To* ALGY L.C.) To please me you are ready to face this fearful ordeal?

ALGY: I am!

GWENDOLINE: (R.C. *to* CECILY) How absurd to talk of the equality   70
of the sexes. Where questions of self-sacrifice are concerned, men are infinitely beyond us.

JACK: We are!

CECILY: (*To* GWENDOLINE) They have moments of physical courage of which we women know absolutely nothing.

GWENDOLINE: (*To* JACK) Darling! (*They embrace* R.C.)

ALGY: (*To* CECILY) Darling! (*The embrace* L.C.)

(*They fall into each other's arms. Enter* MERRIMAN R.C., *coughs loudly on entering, seeing the situation*)   80

MERRIMAN: Ahem! ahem! Lady Bracknell!

JACK: Good heavens!

(*Enter* LADY BRACKNELL. *The couples separate.* JACK *and* GWENDOLINE *move down* R. *Exit* MERRIMAN)

LADY BRACKNELL: Gwendoline! What does this mean?

GWENDOLINE: Merely that I am engaged to be married to Mr. Worthing, Mamma.   90

LADY BRACKNELL: Sit down! (*Points to her to sit on sofa* R.C.; *turns to* JACK) Apprised, sir, of my daughter's sudden flight by her trusty maid, whose confidence I purchased by means of a small coin, I followed her at once by a luggage train. Of course, Mr. Worthing, you will clearly understand that all communication between yourself and my daughter must cease immediately from this moment. On this point as, indeed, on all points, I am firm.

JACK: I am engaged to be married to Gwendoline, Lady Bracknell. (*Sits beside* GWENDOLINE)   100

LADY BRACKNELL: You are nothing of the kind, sir. (*Turns and sits. To* ALGY) And now as regards Algernon—Algernon!

ALGY: Yes, Aunt Augusta. (*Crosses* L.C. JACK *moves and sits* R.C.)

LADY BRACKNELL: May I ask if it is in this house that your invalid friend, Mr. Bunbury, resides?

ALGY: Oh, no! Bunbury doesn't live here. Bunbury is somewhere else at present. In fact Bunbury is dead!

LADY BRACKNELL: Dead? When did Mr. Bunbury die? His death must have been extremely sudden.

ALGY: Bunbury has exploded—I mean—Oh, I killed Bunbury this   110
afternoon. (*Look from* LADY BRACKNELL) I mean poor Bunbury died this afternoon. I should say the doctors found out that Bunbury could not live—so Bunbury died. (ALGY *holds*

CECILY'S *hand.* JACK *and* GWENDOLINE R.)

LADY BRACKNELL: Really, he seems to have had great confidence in the opinion of his physicians. I am glad, however, that he made up his mind at the last to some definite course of action, and acted under proper medical advice. And now that we have buried Mr. Bunbury at last, may I ask, Mr. Worthing, who is that young lady whose hand my nephew Algernon is now holding in what seems to me a peculiarly unnecessary manner?   120

JACK: (*Rising*) That, Lady Bracknell, is Miss Cecily Cardew, my ward. (LADY BRACKNELL *bows coldly to* CECILY)

ALGY: I am engaged to be married to Cecily, Aunt Augusta.

LADY BRACKNELL: I beg your pardon!

CECILY: Mr. Moncrieff and I are engaged to be married, Lady Bracknell.

LADY BRACKNELL: (*With a shiver*) I do not know whether there is anything peculiarly exciting in the air of this part of Hertfordshire, but the amount of engagements that go on seems to me considerably above the proper average that statistics have laid down for our guidance. I think some preliminary inquiry on my part would not be out of place. Mr. Worthing, who is Miss Cardew?   130

JACK: (*Looks perfectly furious but restrains himself. In a clear, cold voice*) Miss Cardew is the granddaughter of the late Mr. Thomas Cardew, of 149, Belgrave Square, S.W.; Gervase Park, Dorking, Surrey; and the Glen, Fifeshire, N. B.

LADY BRACKNELL: That sounds not unsatisfactory. Three addresses always inspire confidence, even in tradesmen. So far I am satisfied.   140

JACK: (C. *very irritably*) I have also in my possession, you will be pleased to hear, certificates of Miss Cardew's birth, registration, baptism, whooping cough, vaccination, confirmation, and the measles, both the German and the English variety.

LADY BRACKNELL: (*Calmly*) Ah! A life crowded with incident, I see. Though perhaps somewhat too exciting for a young girl. I am not myself in favor of premature experiences. (*Rises; looks at her watch*) Gwendoline, the time approaches for our departure. We have not a minute to lose. (*Rises and moves* R.C.) As a matter of form, Mr. Worthing, I had better ask you if Miss Cardew has any little fortune.   150

(GWENDOLINE *rises*)

JACK: Oh, about a hundred and thirty thousand pounds in the funds. That is all. (LADY BRACKNELL *sits* R.C.) Good-bye, Lady Bracknell. So pleased to have seen you.   160

LADY BRACKNELL: A moment, Mr. Worthing. A hundred and thirty thousand pounds! And in the funds! Miss Cardew seems to be a most attractive young lady, now that I look at her. (*To* CECILY) Come here, dear. (CECILY *goes across.* JACK *moves to back of sofa*) Sweet child, your dress is sadly simple, and your hair seems almost as nature might have left it. But we can soon alter all that. A thoroughly experienced French maid produces a marvellous result in a very brief space of time. I remember recommending one to young Lady Lancing, and after three months her own husband did not know her.   *170*

JACK: (R.C.) And after six months nobody knew her.

LADY BRACKNELL: Kindly turn round, sweet child. (CECILY *turns completely round*) Algernon!

ALGY: Yes, Aunt Augusta! (*Moving* R.C. *to* CECILY)

LADY BRACKNELL: There are distinct social possibilities in Miss Cardew. (JACK *moves over to back of sofa*)

ALGY: (*Kissing* CECILY) Cecily is the sweetest, dearest, prettiest girl in the whole world. And I don't care twopence about social possibilities.

LADY BRACKNELL: Never speak disrespectfully of society,   *180* Algernon. Only people who can't get into it do that. (*To* CECILY) Dear child, of course you know that Algernon has nothing but his debts to depend upon. But I do not approve of mercenary marriages. When I married Lord Bracknell I had no fortune of any kind. But I never dreamed for a moment of letting that stand in my way. Well, I suppose I must give my consent.

ALGY: Thank you, Aunt Augusta.

LADY BRACKNELL: Cecily, you may kiss me.

CECILY: (*Crosses to her; kisses her*) Thank you, Aunt Augusta.   *190*

LADY BRACKNELL: The marriage, I think, had better take place quite soon.

ALGY *and* CECILY: Thank you, Aunt Augusta. (*Moving* L.C.)

LADY BRACKNELL: To speak frankly, I am not in favor of long engagements; they give people the opportunity of finding out each other's characters before marriage, which I think is never advisable.

JACK: (*Moves from back of sofa* R. *to* R.C.) I beg your pardon for interrupting you, Lady Bracknell, but this engagement is quite out of the question. I am Miss Cardew's guardian. She cannot   *200* marry without my consent until she comes of age. That consent I absolutely decline to give.

LADY BRACKNELL: Upon what grounds, may I ask?

JACK: It pains me very much to have to speak frankly to you, Lady Bracknell, about your nephew, but I suspect him of being untruthful. (ALGY *and* CECILY *look at him in amazement*)

LADY BRACKNELL: Untruthful! My nephew Algernon! Impossible! He's an Oxonian.

JACK: (R.C.) I fear there can be no possible doubt about the matter. This afternoon, during my temporary absence in London, on an important question of romance, he obtained admission into my house by means of a false pretense of being my brother. Under an assumed name he succeeded in the course of the afternoon in alienating the affections of my only ward. He subsequently stayed to tea and devoured every single muffin. And what makes his conduct all the more heartless is that he was perfectly well aware from the first that I have no brother and that I never had a brother, not even of any kind. I distinctly told him so myself yesterday afternoon. 210

LADY BRACKNELL: Ahem! Mr. Worthing, after careful consideration, I have decided to entirely overlook my nephew's conduct to you. (To CECILY) Come here, sweet child (CECILY goes over) How old are you, dear? 220

CECILY: Well, I am really only eighteen, but I always admit to twenty when I go to evening parties.

LADY BRACKNELL: (In a meditative manner) Well, it will not be very long before you are of age and free from the restraints of tutelage. So I don't think your guardian's consent, after all, a matter of any importance.

JACK: (R.C., coming down C.) Pray excuse me, Lady Bracknell, for interrupting you again, but it is only fair to tell you that, according to the terms of her grandfather's will, Miss Cardew does not come legally of age till she is thirty-five. 230

LADY BRACKNELL: That does not seem to me to be a grave objection. Thirty-five is a very attractive age. London society is full of women of the very highest birth who have, of their own free choice, remained thirty-five for years.

CECILY: (Crossing L. to ALGY) Algy, could you wait for me till I was thirty-five?

ALGY: Of course I could, Cecily. You know I could. 240

CECILY: Yes, I felt it instinctively, but I couldn't wait all that time.

ALGY: Then what is to be done, Cecily?

CECILY: I don't know, Mr. Moncrieff. (CECILY moves up L. behind table. ALGY moves to JACK L.C.)

LADY BRACKNELL: My dear Mr. Worthing, as Miss Cardew states positively that she cannot wait till she is thirty-five—a remark which I am bound to say seems to me to show a somewhat impatient nature, I would beg of you to reconsider your decision. 250

JACK: (R.C.) But my dear Lady Bracknell, the matter is entirely in your own hands. The moment you consent to my marriage with Gwendoline, I will most gladly allow your nephew to form an alliance with my ward.

LADY BRACKNELL: (*Rising and drawing herself up*) Mr. Worthing, you must be quite aware that which you propose is out of the question.

(JACK *and* ALGY *walk up* C. *and down* C. *again*)

JACK: Then a passionate celibacy is all that any of us can look   260
forward to. (*Moves over to back of* L.C. *chair to* CECILY. ALGY *and* CECILY *move up* L.C.)

LADY BRACKNELL: That is not the destiny I propose for Gwendoline. Algernon, of course, can choose for himself. (*Pulls out her watch*) Come, dear. (GWENDOLINE *rises*) We must be going.

CHASUBLE: (*Enters* R.C.) Is everything quite ready for the christenings?

LADY BRACKNELL: (R.C.) Christenings, sir? Is not that somewhat premature?   270

CHASUBLE: (*Looking rather puzzled and pointing to* JACK *and* ALGY) Both these gentlemen have expressed a desire for immediate christening. (*Both bow*)

LADY BRACKNELL: At their age? The idea is grotesque and irreligious! (*To* ALGY) Algernon, I forbid you to be christened. I will not hear of such excesses. Lord Bracknell would be highly displeased if he learned that that was the way in which you wasted your time and money.

CHASUBLE: Am I to understand, then, that there are to be no christenings at all this afternoon?   280

JACK: I don't think that, as things now stand, it would be of any practical value to either of us, Doctor Chasuble.

CHASUBLE: I am grieved to hear such sentiments from you, Mr. Worthing. I must return to the church at once. Indeed, I have just been informed by the pew-opener that for the last hour and a half Miss Prism has been waiting for me in the vestry.

LADY BRACKNELL: (*Starting*) Miss Prism! Did I hear you mention a Miss Prism! (JACK *crosses* R. *to* GWENDOLINE. ALGY *crosses* L.C. *to* CECILY)

CHASUBLE: Yes, Lady Bracknell, I am on my way to join her.   290

LADY BRACKNELL: (*Anxiously*) Pray allow me to detain you for a moment. This matter may prove to be one of vital importance to Lord Bracknell and myself. Is this Miss Prism a female of repellant aspect, remotely connected with education?

CHASUBLE: (*Somewhat indignantly*) She is the most cultivated of ladies, and the very picture of respectability.

LADY BRACKNELL: (*Thoughtfully*) It is obviously the same person. May I ask what position she holds in your household?

CHASUBLE: (*Severely*) I am a celibate, madam! (*Moves up* L.)

JACK: (R., *interposing*) Miss Prism has been for the last three years 300 Miss Cardew's esteemed governess and valued companion.

LADY BRACKNELL: I must see this Miss Prism at once. Let her be sent for.

CHASUBLE: (*Looking off*) She approaches—she is nigh.

MISS PRISM: (*Enters* R.C. *hurriedly*) I was told you expected me in the vestry, dear Canon. I have been waiting for you there for an hour and three quarters. (*Catches sight of* LADY BRACKNELL, *who has fixed her with a stony stare.* MISS PRISM *grows pale and quails, looks anxiously round as if desirous to escape*)

LADY BRACKNELL: (*In a severe judicial voice*) Prism!   310

MISS PRISM: (*Bowing her head in shame*) Lady Bracknell!

LADY BRACKNELL: Come here, Miss Prism! (MISS PRISM *approaches* C. *in humble manner*) Prism! Where is that baby?

(*General consternation.* CHASUBLE *starts back in horror.* ALGY *and* JACK *pretend to be anxious to shield* CECILY *and* GWENDOLINE *from hearing a terrible scandal.* MISS PRISM *makes no answer*)

Thirty-four years ago, Prism, you left Lord Bracknell's house, number 104, Grosvenor Street, in charge of a perambulator   320 that contained a baby of the male sex. You never returned. A few weeks later, through the elaborate investigation of the Metropolitan Police, the perambulator was discovered at midnight, standing by itself in a remote corner of Hyde Park. It contained the manuscript of a three-volume novel of more than usually revolting sentimentality. (MISS PRISM *starts in involuntary indignation*) But the baby was not there. Prism! Where is that baby? (*Everyone looks at* MISS PRISM)

MISS PRISM: Lady Bracknell, I admit with shame that I do not know. I only wish I did. The plain facts of the case are these.   330 On the morning of the day you mention, a day that is forever branded on my memory, I prepared as usual to take the baby out in the perambulator. I had also with me a somewhat old but capacious handbag in which I intended to place the manuscript of a work of fiction that I had written during my few unoccupied hours. In a moment of mental abstraction, for which I can never forgive myself, I deposited the manuscript in the bassinette, and placed the baby in the handbag. (*Crossing* L.)

JACK: (*Has been listening attentively; comes* C.) But where did you   340 deposit the handbag?

MISS PRISM: Do not ask me, Mr. Worthing.

JACK: Miss Prism, this is a matter of no small importance to me. I insist on knowing where you deposited the handbag that contained the infant.

MISS PRISM: In the cloakroom at Victoria Station—the Brighton line. (*Quite crushed, sinks into chair* L.C.)

JACK: I must retire to my room for a moment. (*Exit* JACK R.C.)

CHASUBLE: (*Crossing* C. *behind table to sofa*) What do you think this means, Lady Bracknell? 350

LADY BRACKNELL: I dare not even suspect, Dr. Chasuble.

(*Noise heard overhead as if someone is throwing trunks about. Everyone looks up*)

CECILY: (*Looking up*) Uncle Jack seems strangely agitated.

CHASUBLE: Your guardian has a very emotional nature.

LADY BRACKNELL: This noise is extremely unpleasant. (*Noises heard overhead*)

CHASUBLE: (*Looking up*) It has stopped now. (*Goes up* L.) 360

LADY BRACKNELL: I wish he would arrive at some conclusion.

GWENDOLINE: This suspense is terrible. I hope it will last.

JACK: (*Enters* R.C. *with black leather handbag in his hand.* L.C., *rushing over to* MISS PRISM, *who is still seated* L.C.) Is this the handbag, Miss Prism? (*Hands it to her*) Examine it carefully before you speak. The happiness of more than one life depends on your answer.

MISS PRISM: It seems to be mine. (*Rises*) Yes, here is the injury it received through the upsetting of a Gower Street omnibus in younger and happier days. (*Opens bag. In a more confidential and* 370 *more joyful voice*) And here, on the lock, are my initials. The bag is undoubtedly mine. I am delighted to have it unexpectedly restored to me. It has been a *great* inconvenience being without it all these years.

JACK: (*In a pathetic voice*) Miss Prism, more is restored to you than the handbag. I was the baby you placed in it.

MISS PRISM: (*Amazed*) You?

JACK: (*Embracing her*) Yes—Mother!

MISS PRISM: (*Recoiling in indignant astonishment*) Mr. Worthing, I am unmarried! 380

JACK: Unmarried! I do not deny that this is a serious blow. But, after all, who has the right to cast a stone against one who has suffered? Cannot repentance wipe out an act of folly? Why should there be one law for men and another for women? Mother, I forgive you! (*Throws bag to* DR. CHASUBLE; *tries to embrace her again*)

MISS PRISM: (*After pause; still more indignant*) Mr. Worthing, there is some error. (*Pointing to* LADY BRACKNELL) There is the lady who can tell you who you really are. (*Retires* L. *and up to* DR. CHASUBLE *up* L.C., *and talks to* DR. CHASUBLE) 390

JACK: (*After a pause*) Lady Bracknell, I hate to seem inquisitive, but would you kindly inform me who I am?

LADY BRACKNELL: I am afraid that the news I have to give you will not altogether please you. (*Rising and going up* C.) You are the son of my poor sister, Mrs. Moncrieff, and consequently Algernon's elder brother.

JACK: Algy's elder brother! Then I have a brother after all! I knew I had a brother! I always said I had a brother. Cecily, how could you have ever doubted that I had a brother? (ALGY *crosses to him*) Dr. Chasuble, my unfortunate brother!   400 Gwendoline, my unfortunate brother!

GWENDOLINE: (*To* JACK) My own! But what own are you? What is your Christian name now that you have become someone else?

JACK: Good heavens! I had quite forgotten that point. Aunt Augusta, a moment. At the time when Miss Prism left me in the handbag, had I been christened already?

LADY BRACKNELL: (*Coming down* C., *quite calmly*) Every luxury that money could buy, including christening, had been lavished on you by your fond and doting parents.   410

JACK: Then I *was* christened! *That* is settled. Now, what name was I given? Let me know the worst.

LADY BRACKNELL: (*After a pause*) Being the eldest son, you were naturally christened after your father.

JACK: (*Irritably*) Yes, but what was our father's Christian name?

LADY BRACKNELL: I remember now that the General was called Ernest.

GWENDOLINE: Ernest! I felt from the first that you could have no other name.

JACK: Gwendoline, at last!   420

CHASUBLE: Letitia, at last!

MISS PRISM: Frederick, at last!   (*Together*)

ALGY: Cecily, at last!

GWENDOLINE: My own Ernest.

Tableau

Curtain

Understanding *The Importance of Being Earnest*

Triviality is Wilde's primary vehicle in this play for exposing the insincerity and pseudo-sophistication of British society of the time. Surely there is no more trivial a character than Algernon. Triviality is a game he plays. But Wilde gives us more than meets the eye in this character. We must not allow ourselves to be taken in by Algernon. He seems to be pleasant and sweet, but looking carefully into his behavior, we see lies and deception. And even "earnest" Jack has his shortcomings. He shies away from telling the truth when doing so would seem imprudent. When Algernon asks Jack if he will be truthful to Gwendoline, Jack replies, "Truth isn't quite the sort of thing one tells to a nice, sweet, refined girl." Elevating and keeping women on a pedestal was important during this period. Many deceptions were made in the name of "protecting women." Wilde is exposing here the silliness of such a practice.

Cecily and Gwendoline have been reared on triviality also. Gwendoline tells us she has been brought up to be shortsighted and therefore must use her glasses. Cecily and Gwendoline record everything in their diaries, and conveniently so, for they can "prove" their love for Earnest by reading dated passages. The height of this runaway triviality is reached at the end of the play when the unlikely Miss Prism becomes the key to Jack's identity. When her attention should be riveted on Jack, she is checking the initials on a handbag.

The plot and characters of this witty treatment of Victorian English society are handled with finesse by Wilde. The characters have a cold, unfeeling, almost mechanical way of handling issues we would consider serious. The Victorian era would not permit the display of feeling or affection, so these characters feel nothing. Life is a game played exactly by the rules. So it should not surprise us that Cecily and Gwendoline both fall in love with a name without having met the man. Both women clearly express that the sound and quality of the name are far more important than the moral quality of the man.

Lady Bracknell puts propriety and decorum first, even at the expense of an unhappy marriage. Marriage was generally arranged by guardians in drawing rooms, and the arrangement often favored finances over affection. Lady Bracknell is certainly not going to allow her niece to marry a man of unknown parentage. Even Jack has two identities for his own gratification, one for the city and another for the country. And he feels no shame at this deception.

In *The Importance of Being Earnest* we are offered a powerful statement on the rules of "proper" society. In this witty story of matchmaking and courtship ritual, we see the emptiness of Victorian values and moralism. The play reveals Victorian morality as a game devised for the amusement of the upper classes. The courtship game serves as a way to fill the idle hours for the likes of Lady Bracknell. Arbitrary matchmaking without regard for personal relationships is presented as common practice. It is truly ironic that the play ends with a near love match.

Using cliché characters, Wilde devises a well-made comic plot.

The hero of unknown birth, the long lost brother, and the protective guardian are caught up in a tale of romantic intrigue and a web of Victorian societal standards. These were times when a young man had to prove his love in order to gain a fair young lady, and both men offer to be rechristened in order to conform to the ideals of a lady who prefers a man named Earnest. All of this is laughable (especially when we learn that one of the gentlemen is already named Earnest!). In true comic tradition, the resolution comes when a relatively minor character, Miss Prism, reveals Jack's true identity.

Wilde adds a further humorous dimension to the play in the stylized movement of the actors. This can be fully appreciated only in viewing a performance. The movements detailed for these characters by Wilde are sophisticated, mechanical, and stylized. In the confrontation between Cecily and Gwendoline, the two women stand and sit in synchronization for comic effect. They turn, sit, and consult their diaries in stilted, almost mechanical, fashion. Later, they embrace as the men "pace and groan" and deliver lines in unison—as do the women. The choreography of this highly stylized scene underscores the way Wilde viewed society.

Wilde's characters have such straight-faced innocence when delivering the most absurd lines of dialogue that even reading the play becomes an enjoyable undertaking. When Jack says he has lost both parents, Lady Bracknell replies, "Both? . . . that seems like carelessness." When Algernon tells Cecily that he is not wicked, she retorts, "I hope you have not been leading a double life, pretending to be wicked and being really good all the time. That would be hypocrisy." At one point Jack comments that "divorces are made in Heaven." He admits to having a dual identity for convenience, but reprimands Algernon for producing a false impression of himself when he talks like a "dentist." A classic example of Wilde's brand of wit appears in these lines spoken by Jack: "All women become like their mothers; that is their tragedy. No man does. That's his."

The Importance of Being Earnest presents a view of civilization that is far from civilized. Some may regard the play as merely fun, but it is serious in its comments on the superficiality of Victorian society. This is not a play at which one can simply sit back, relax, and be entertained. Rather, it demands attentive intellectual involvement to keep pace with the lively repartee. The sociological and ethical implications of this fine comedy must not be overlooked. To do so would be to treat Wilde's work too lightly. As a subhead to the play's title, Wilde added "A Trivial Comedy for Serious People." In one of the few truths she speaks in the play, Lady Bracknell helps us realize our need of the play's truthful revelations when she admits, "We live, I regret to say, in an age of surfaces."

Arthur Ganz said, "*The Importance of Being Earnest* is a unique play. It stands alone among English comedies, not only because of the quality of its wit, but because it is an expression of Wilde's theories and attitudes, and no other writer has approached the theater with a comparable point of view."[18] Writer and critic Glenn Loney comments that the play is "an attack on Victorian solemnity, hypocrisy, priggishness and lack of true wit and manners."[19] These two comments taken together fairly assess this outstanding comedy by Oscar Wilde.

The Theatre of the Absurd: *The Leader*

Some writers have found the existing genres of comedy, drama, and tragedy to be inadequate to express ideas about the human condition in the twentieth century. Feeling the need to explore and express ideas about modern man and society in a new and innovative form, these writers have forged a theatre genre that bends or breaks many of the existing guidelines for playwriting. Some call this genre Avant-Garde or Experimental theatre, but Theatre of the Absurd is the most widely used name.

This recent trend in theatrical expression rejects the traditional methods of plot structure and character development, attempting instead, through new methods, to jolt us into a new awareness. Attempting to help clarify and define absurdism, one writer said:

> In my view, the Theatre of the Absurd, in its defeatist celebration of emptiness and despair, is very much a function of our era, though it derives many of its techniques and much of its nihilism from the theatre and philosophy of earlier periods. . . . Nonsense and violence are raw materials of the plays. They present a world turned topsy-turvy, where ordinary cause-effect relationships do not function. They offer a universe in which men cannot communicate with each other. Not infrequently, communication is impossible because there is nothing to understand. . . . Quite simply, what the major playwrights of the Absurd have to offer is a vision of despair.[20]

Making a more positive statement, another writer expressed the following:

> We may be shocked, sickened, or bewildered, . . . but we are also fumigated. We lose for a moment the make-believe we invent when we can no longer believe in ourselves.
>
> Ionesco tells us to "look at yourself with one eye and listen to yourself with the other." Linguistically, this highlights the absurdity of the theatre, but it is also wise advice.[21]

This new turn in playwriting began around the turn of the century, but its widespread exposure has been more recent. Absurdist writers that have gained prominence include Edward Albee, Harold Pinter, Eugene Ionesco, Jean Genet, and Samuel Beckett. Although they receive increasing attention for their absurdist writing, these authors might resent being categorized and defined.

The French philosopher Jean Paul Sartre commented once that absurdity is the fabric of man's existence. By looking at the totality of absurdist thought and theatrical expression, we may come to understand why the absurdists feel that they must "jolt" us into a new awareness. After reading and viewing some absurdists works, we may find that the Theatre of the Absurd is anything but absurd.

Theatre of the Absurd attempts to point out in highly unusual fashion some of the undesirable and shameful truths about human existence. It "pulls all the plugs" on sham and deception. It forces us to see ourselves as we are.

The tragi-comedy of absurdist drama reveals hopelessness and despair about the human condition. While comedy treats us to "happily ever after" endings, the Theatre of the Absurd sees no ending at all. Ionesco says, "The human drama is as absurd as it is painful. . . . There are no alternatives; if man is not tragic, he is ridiculous and painful, 'comic' in fact, and by revealing his absurdity one can achieve a sort of tragedy. In fact I think that man must either be unhappy . . . or stupid."[22] Another writer reports that Ionesco said, "Comic and tragic are merely two aspects of the same condition, and I have now reached the point where I find it hard to distinguish one from the other."[23]

The dialogue of absurdist drama points out the trivial, mundane, and often unspoken truths of our conversations. In Albee's *American Dream*, for example, the visitor is invited to "come in. Take off your dress and sit down." We are reminded of the times we have invited people into our home and instructed them to take off their coats. Why do we do this? When we are in a stiff, formal situation, we often think about when we can get out of those uncomfortable clothes, but ordinarily we don't verbalize such a thought. Why not? Absurdist plays break through such ordinary societal restraints. The absurdity of our behavior surfaces in the absurdist play.

We are often stunned by the language of the absurdist theatre. In Albee's *Who's Afraid of Virginia Woolf*, we are shocked by the harshness of the words. Surely, we think, people are not this cruel toward each other. Or are we perhaps reminded of a time when we were just as cruel? It is often the case in absurdist plays that we are not just laughing at the line, but at how close it hits to the truths and deeds of our own private lives. In *The Leader* by Ionesco, when the boy and girl meet and immediately fall in love, we may think that this is silly—unrealistic. But is it? What about the man and woman who meet over a martini and hours later whisper those same words, with the same absurd implications. The absurdist play attempts to break down some of the excuses and arguments we have constructed for our less-than-civilized behavior. It tries to shake us and force us to see ourselves as we really are, with all the veneer stripped away.

The absurdist play does not follow the traditional rules of structure. There is no attempt to draw realistic characters in lifelike situations. Language is used in nontraditional ways. The development of plot appears illogical, for it moves toward no specific climax or resolution. Establishing and maintaining contact between audience and actor, which is a primary goal in the traditional theatre, is altogether lacking in the comedy of the absurd. Wild exaggeration is used by the absurdist to mock rather than imitate. The traditional vehicles of comedy and tragedy are abandoned.

It has been said that one of the functions of absurdist theatre is to stretch possibility. We may find ourselves asking, How far should a playwright go? How much license does a playwright have? The absurdist would reply that there is no limit; there is no license! Using "banality, exaggeration, repetition, inconsequence, illogicality, dislocation, elevation, and nonverbal aspects . . . the idea is that theatre must have widest range, expanded horizons, delimited limits."[24]

The ideology behind the Theatre of the Absurd is existential. We exist. We are here. There is no hope, no deliverance. We need make no plans nor devise expectations. We await the end. Ionesco said, "I have tried to deal with themes that obsess me; with emptiness, with frustration, with this world, at once fleeting and crushing, with despair and death. The characters I have used are not fully conscious of their spiritual rootlessness, but they feel it instinctively and emotionally."[25] The absurdist seems to strike out at an unrecognizable foe, a dark shadow within the soul that defies form or shape but remains illusive and just out of reach.

Is Theatre of the Absurd a momentary diversion or is it a force to be reckoned with? Author William Saroyan wrote, "I suspect that the gimmicks, the vitality, the impudence, the disillusionment of the Theatre of the Absurd will find itself gradually absorbed into the mainstream of theatre tradition."[26] Eventually, we must come face to face with the ills and inadequacies within us and our society. We must admit empty relationships and sham alliances. Saroyan also said,

> Beckett and Ionesco are not mad. They have discovered the means by which to reveal, in acceptable and deeply moving terms, that the human race is mad, and that the world has been in an uncharted and unknown dimension of hopeless lunacy—if not criminality—for centuries, and is now away off in this dimension. . . . They lack size and rage. . . . All the same they are the scientists among playwrights so far.[27]

Perhaps through the jolting stimulation of the absurdist theatre, we will begin to search for the truth and for solutions to the problems.

Since World War II and the tragic possibilities of the nuclear bomb, the Theatre of the Absurd has gained in popularity and exposure. Of the postwar absurdist writers, one of the most stimulating is Ionesco. Donald Watson says Ionesco was "doing for the theatre what has already been done for other art forms by James Joyce, Picasso, and Stravinsky."[28] One of the qualities of Ionesco's plays is that they have meaning, although one may have to search for it in subtext. The Leader presents ideas concerning our choices for hero worship. Watson goes on to say that Ionesco "writes to provide audiences with a new kind of dramatic experience. The meaning is also in the means, and the key to the meaning is to be found in our knowledge of ourselves."[29] William Saroyan said of Ionesco's plays, "You can laugh out loud . . . as you read and . . . behold one of his plays, but your laughter isn't quite real, or at any rate, it isn't like any laughter you have ever known before."[30]

Reprinted courtesy of Grove Press, Inc.
196 West Houston Street, New York, NY 10014

The Leader
Eugene Ionesco

Characters

THE ANNOUNCER	THE GIRL-FRIEND	THE GIRL-ADMIRER
THE YOUNG LOVER	THE ADMIRER	THE LEADER

(*Standing with his back to the public, centre-stage, and with his eyes fixed on the up-stage exit, the* ANNOUNCER *waits for the arrival of the* LEADER. *To right and left, riveted to the walls, two of the* LEADER'S ADMIRERS, *a man and a girl, also wait for his arrival*)

ANNOUNCER: (*after a few tense moments in the same position*) There he is! There he is! At the end of the street! (*Shouts of 'Hurrah!' etc., are heard.*) There's the leader! He's coming, he's coming nearer! (*Cries of acclaim and applause are heard from the wings.*) It's better if he doesn't see us . . . (*The* TWO ADMIRERS *hug the* 10 *wall even closer.*) Watch out! (*The* ANNOUNCER *gives vent to a brief display of enthusiasm.*) Hurrah! Hurrah! The leader! The leader! Long live the leader! (*The* TWO ADMIRERS, *with their bodies rigid and flattened against the wall, thrust their necks and heads as far forward as they can to get a glimpse of the* LEADER.) The leader! The leader! (*The* TWO ADMIRERS *in unison:*) Hurrah! Hurrah! (*Other 'Hurrahs!' mingled with 'Hurrah! Bravo!' come from the wings and gradually die down.*) Hurrah! Bravo!

(*The* ANNOUNCER *takes a step up-stage, stops, continues up-stage,* 20 *followed by the* TWO ADMIRERS, *saying as he goes: 'Ah! Too bad! He's going away! He's going away! Follow me quickly! After him!' The* ANNOUNCER *and the* TWO ADMIRERS *leave crying: 'Leader! Leeeeader! Lee-ee-eader!' (This last 'Lee-ee-eader!' echoes in the wings like a bleating cry.*)

(*Silence. The stage is empty for a few brief moments. The* YOUNG LOVER *enters right, and his* GIRL-FRIEND *left; they meet centrestage.*)

YOUNG LOVER: Forgive me, Madame, or should I say   30
   Mademoiselle?
GIRL-FRIEND: I beg your pardon, I'm afraid I don't happen to
   know you!
YOUNG LOVER: And I'm afraid I don't know you either!
GIRL-FRIEND: Then neither of us knows each other.
YOUNG LOVER: Exactly. We have something in common. It
   means that between us there is a basis of understanding on
   which we can build the edifice of our future.
GIRL-FRIEND: That leaves me cold, I'm afraid.
(*She makes as if to go*)   40
YOUNG LOVER: Oh, my darling, I adore you.
GIRL-FRIEND: Darling, so do I!   (*They embrace*)

YOUNG LOVER: I'm taking you with me, darling. We'll get married straightaway.

(*They leave left. The stage is empty for a brief moment*)

ANNOUNCER: (*enters up-stage followed by the* TWO ADMIRERS) But the leader swore that he'd be passing here.

ADMIRER: Are you absolutely sure of that?

ANNOUNCER: Yes, yes, of course.

GIRL-ADMIRER: Was it really on his way?   50

ANNOUNCER: Yes, yes. He should have passed by here, it was marked on the Festival programme . . .

ADMIRER: Did you actually see it yourself and hear it with your own eyes and ears?

ANNOUNCER: He told someone. Someone else!

ADMIRER: But who? Who was this someone else?

GIRL-ADMIRER: Was it a reliable person? A friend of yours?

ANNOUNCER: A friend of mine who I know very well.

(*Suddenly in the background one hears renewed cries of 'Hurrah! and*   60
'Long live the leader!')

That's him now! There he is! Hip! Hip! Hurrah! There he is! Hide yourselves! Hide yourselves!

(*The* TWO ADMIRERS *flatten themselves as before against the wall, stretching their necks out towards the wings from where the shouts of acclamation come; the* ANNOUNCER *watches fixedly upstage his back to the public*)

ANNOUNCER: The leader's coming. He approaches. He's   70
bending. He's unbending. (*At each of the* ANNOUNCER'S *words, the* ADMIRERS *give a start and stretch their necks even farther; they shudder.*) He's jumping. He's crossed the river. They're shaking his hand. He sticks out his thumb. Can you hear? They're laughing. (*The* ANNOUNCER *and the* TWO ADMIRERS *also laugh.*) Ah . . . ! they're giving him a box of tools. What's he going to do with them? Ah . . . ! he's signing autographs. The leader is stroking a hedgehog, a superb hedgehog! The crowd applauds. He's dancing, with the hedgehog in his hand. He's embracing his dancer. Hurrah! Hurrah! (*Cries are heard in the*   80
wings.) He's being photographed, with his dancer on one hand and the hedgehog on the other . . . He greets the crowd . . . He spits a tremendous distance.

GIRL-ADMIRER: Is he coming past here? Is he coming in our direction?

ADMIRER: Are we really on his route?

ANNOUNCER: (*turns his head to the* TWO ADMIRERS) Quite, and don't move, you're spoiling everything . . .

GIRL-ADMIRER: But even so . . .

ANNOUNCER: Keep quiet, I tell you! Didn't I tell you he'd   *90*
promised, that he had fixed his itinerary himself. . . . (*He turns
back up-stage and cries.*) Hurrah! Hurrah! Long live the leader!
(*Silence*) Long live, long live, the leader! (*Silence*) Long live,
long live, long live the lead-er! (*The* TWO ADMIRERS, *unable to
contain themselves, also give a sudden cry of:*) Hurrah! Long live
the leader!

ANNOUNCER: (*to the* ADMIRERS) Quiet, you two! Calm down!
You're spoiling everything! (*Then, once more looking up-stage,
with the* ADMIRERS *silenced.*) Long live the leader! (*Wildly
enthusiastic.*) Hurrah! Hurrah! He's changing his shirt. He   *100*
disappears behind a red screen. He reappears! (*The applause
intensifies.*) Bravo! Bravo! (*The* ADMIRERS *also long to cry 'Bravo'
and applaud; they put their hands to their mouths to stop
themselves.*) He's putting his tie on! He's reading his
newspaper and drinking his morning coffee! He's still got his
hedgehog . . . He's leaning on the edge of the parapet. The
parapet breaks. He gets up . . . he gets up unaided! (*Applause,
shouts of 'Hurrah!'*) Bravo! Well done! He brushes his soiled
clothes.

TWO ADMIRERS: (*stamping their feet*) Oh! Ah! Oh! Oh! Ah! Ah!   *110*
ANNOUNCER: He's mounting the stool! He's climbing piggyback,
they're offering him a thin-ended wedge, he knows it's meant
as a joke, and he doesn't mind, he's laughing.

(*Applause and enormous acclaim*)

ADMIRER: (*to the* GIRL-ADMIRER) You hear that? You hear? Oh! If I
were king . . .
GIRL-ADMIRER: Ah . . . ! the leader! (*This is said in an exalted tone*)
ANNOUNCER: (*still with his back to the public*) He's mounting the   *120*
stool. No. He's getting down. A little girl offers him a bouquet
of flowers . . . What's he going to do? He takes the flowers . .
. He embraces the little girl . . . calls her 'my child' . . .
ADMIRER: He embraces the little girl . . . calls her 'my child' . . .
GIRL-ADMIRER: He embraces the little girl . . . calls her
'my child' . . .
ANNOUNCER: He gives her the hedgehog. The little girl's crying
. . . Long live the leader! Long live the leead-er!
ADMIRER: Is he coming past here?
GIRL-ADMIRER: Is he coming past here?   *130*
ANNOUNCER: (*with a sudden run, dashes out up-stage*) He's going
away! Hurry! Come on!

(*He disappears, followed by the* TWO ADMIRERS, *all crying 'Hurrah!
Hurrah!' The stage is empty for a few moments. The* TWO LOVERS
*enter, entwined in an embrace; they halt centre-stage and separate; she
carries a basket on her arm.*)

GIRL-FRIEND: Let's go to the market and get some eggs!

YOUNG LOVER: Oh! I love them as much as you do!   *140*

(*She takes his arm. From the right the* ANNOUNCER *arrives running, quickly regaining his place, back to the public, followed closely by the* TWO ADMIRERS, *arriving one from the left and the other from the right; the* TWO ADMIRERS *knock into the* TWO LOVERS *who were about to leave right.*)

ADMIRER: Sorry!

YOUNG LOVER: Oh! Sorry!

GIRL-ADMIRER: Sorry! Oh! Sorry!   *150*

GIRL-FRIEND: Oh! Sorry, sorry, sorry, so sorry!

ADMIRER: Sorry, sorry, sorry, oh! sorry, sorry, so sorry!

YOUNG LOVER: Oh, oh, oh, oh, oh, oh! So sorry, everyone!

GIRL-FRIEND: (*to her* LOVER) Come along, Adolphe! (*To the* TWO ADMIRERS:) No harm done!

(*She leaves, leading her* LOVER *by the hand.*)

ANNOUNCER: (*watching up-stage*) The leader is being pressed forward, and pressed back, and now they're pressing his   *160* trousers! (*The* TWO ADMIRERS *regain their places.*) The leader is smiling. Whilst they're pressing his trousers, he walks about. He tastes the flowers and the fruits growing in the stream. He's also tasting the roots of the trees. He suffers the little children to come unto him. He has confidence in everybody. He inaugurates the police force. He pays tribute to justice. He salutes the great victors and the great vanquished. Finally he recites a poem. The people are very moved.

TWO ADMIRERS: Bravo! Bravo! (*Then, sobbing:*) Boo! Boo! Boo!

ANNOUNCER: All the people are weeping. (*Loud cries are heard*   *170* *from the wings; the* ANNOUNCER *and the* ADMIRERS *also start to bellow.*) Silence! (*The* TWO ADMIRERS *fall silent; and there is silence from the wings.*) They've given the leader's trousers back. The leader puts them on. He looks happy! Hurrah! (*'Bravos', and acclaim from the wings. The* TWO ADMIRERS *also shout their acclaim, jump about, without being able to see anything of what is presumed to be happening in the wings.*) The leader's sucking his thumb! (*To the* TWO ADMIRERS:) Back, back to your places, you two, don't move, behave yourselves and shout: 'Long live the leader!'   *180*

TWO ADMIRERS: (*flattened against the wall, shouting*) Long live, long live the leader!

ANNOUNCER: Be quiet, I tell you, you'll spoil everything! Look out, the leader's coming!

ADMIRER: (*in the same position*) The leader's coming!

GIRL-ADMIRER: The leader's coming!

ANNOUNCER: Watch out! And keep quiet! Oh! The leader's going away! Follow him! Follow me!

(*The* ANNOUNCER *goes out up-stage, running; the* TWO ADMIRERS   190
leave right and left, whilst in the wings the acclaim mounts, then fades.
The stage is momentarily empty. The YOUNG LOVER, *followed by his*
GIRL-FRIEND, *appear left running across the stage right.*)

YOUNG LOVER: (*running*) You won't catch me! You won't catch
    me! (*Goes out*)
GIRL-FRIEND: (*running*) Wait a moment! Wait a moment!

(*She goes out. The stage is empty for a moment; then once more the*
TWO LOVERS *cross the stage at a run, and leave.*)   200

YOUNG LOVER: You won't catch me!
GIRL-FRIEND: Wait a moment!

(*They leave right. The stage is empty. The* ANNOUNCER *reappears*
up-stage, the ADMIRER *from the right, the* GIRL-ADMIRER *from the*
left. They meet centre.)

ADMIRER: We missed him!
GIRL-ADMIRER: Rotten luck!   210
ANNOUNCER: It was your fault!
ADMIRER: That's not true!
GIRL-ADMIRER: No, that's not true!
ANNOUNCER: Are you suggesting it was mine?
ADMIRER: No, we didn't mean that!
GIRL-ADMIRER: No, we didn't mean that!

(*Noise of acclaim and 'Hurrahs' from the wings.*)

ANNOUNCER: Hurrah!   220
GIRL-ADMIRER: It's from over there! (*She points up-stage.*)
ADMIRER: Yes, it's from over there! (*He points left.*)
ANNOUNCER: Very well. Follow me! Long live the leader!

(*He runs out right, followed by the* TWO ADMIRERS, *also shouting.*)

TWO ADMIRERS: Long live the leader! (*They leave. The stage is*
    empty for a moment. The YOUNG LOVER *and his* GIRL-FRIEND
    appear left; the YOUNG LOVER *exits up-stage; the* GIRL-FRIEND,
    after saying 'I'll get you!', runs out right. The ANNOUNCER *and the*   230
    TWO ADMIRERS *appear from up-stage. The* ANNOUNCER *says to the*
    ADMIRERS:) Long live the leader! (*This is repeated by the*
    ADMIRERS. *Then, still talking to the* ADMIRERS, *he says:*) Follow
    me! Follow the leader! (*He leaves up-stage, still running and*
    shouting:) Follow him!

(*The* ADMIRER *exits right, the* GIRL-ADMIRER *left into the wings.*

During the whole of this, the acclaim is heard louder or fainter
according to the rhythm of the stage action; the stage is empty for a
moment, then the LOVERS *appear from right and left, crying:)* 240

YOUNG LOVER: I'll get you!

GIRL-ADMIRER: You won't get me! (*They leave at a run, shouting:*)
  Long live the leader! (*The* ANNOUNCER *and the* TWO ADMIRERS
  emerge from up-stage, also shouting: 'Long live the leader', followed
  by the TWO LOVERS. *They all leave right, in single file, crying as*
  they run: 'The leader! Long live the leader! We'll get him! It's from
  over here! You won't get me!' They enter and leave, employing all
  the exits; finally, entering from left, from right, and from up-stage
  they all meet centre, whilst the acclaim and the applause from the 250
  wings becomes a fearful din. They embrace each other feverishly,
  crying at the tops of their voices:) Long live the leader! Long live
  the leader! Long live the leader!

(*Then, abruptly, silence falls*)

ANNOUNCER: The leader is arriving. Here's the leader. To your
  places! Attention!

(*The* ADMIRER *and the* GIRL-FRIEND *flatten themselves against the wall* 260
right; the GIRL-ADMIRER *and the* YOUNG LOVER *against the wall left;*
the two couples are in each other's arms, embracing.)

ADMIRER and GIRL-FRIEND: My dear, my darling!

GIRL-ADMIRER and YOUNG LOVER: My dear, my darling!

(*Meanwhile the* ANNOUNCER *has taken up his place, back to the*
audience, looking fixedly up-stage; a lull in the applause.)

ANNOUNCER: Silence. The leader has eaten his soup. He is 270
  coming. He is nigh.

(*The acclaim redoubles its intensity; the* TWO ADMIRERS *and the* TWO
LOVERS *shout:*)

ALL: Hurrah! Hurrah! Long live the leader! (*They throw confetti*
  before he arrives. Then the ANNOUNCER *hurls himself suddenly to*
  one side to allow the LEADER *to pass; the other four characters freeze*
  with outstretched arms holding confetti; but still say:) Hurrah!
  280

(*The* LEADER *enters from upstage, advances down-stage to centre; to*
the footlights, hesitates, makes a step to left, then makes a decision and
leaves with great, energetic strides by right, to the enthusiastic
'Hurrahs!' of the ANNOUNCER *and the feeble, somewhat astonished*
'Hurrahs!' of the other four; these, in fact, have some reason to be
surprised, as the LEADER *is headless, though wearing a hat. This is*
simple to effect: the actor playing the LEADER *needing only to wear an*
overcoat with the collar turned up round his forehead and topped with a
hat. The- man-in-an-overcoat-with-a-hat-without-a-head is a somewhat

surprising apparition and will doubtless produce a certain sensation.   290
After the LEADER's *disappearance, the* GIRL-ADMIRER *says:*)

GIRL-ADMIRER: But . . . but . . . the leader hasn't got a head!
ANNOUNCER: What's he need a head for when he's got genius!
YOUNG LOVER: That's true! (*to the* GIRL-FRIEND:) What's your
name? (*The* YOUNG LOVER *to the* GIRL-ADMIRER, *the* GIRL-ADMIRER
to the ANNOUNCER, *the* ANNOUNCER *to the* GIRL-FRIEND, *the*
GIRL-FRIEND *to the* YOUNG LOVER:) What's yours? What's yours?
What's yours? (*Then, all together, one to the other:*) What's your
name?   300

CURTAIN

Understanding *The Leader*

In this play, a group of unrelated characters with no names
yearn for a long awaited leader with no head. Tension and relaxation are achieved by periodic outbursts of enthusiasm from the
Announcer. This character reminds us of some sports an-
nouncers in his attempts to make "nothing" seem like something
that is terribly interesting and exciting. The Announcer "handles" the crowd, telling them when to cheer and where to look.
Like all good crowds, they obediently follow his directions.

We soon meet the young man and woman who meet, fall in
love, and discuss marriage, all in the space of nine lines. Then we
meet two admirers of the Leader, who mindlessly praise and ea-
gerly await him. On considering these characters and how they
follow the Announcer, we are reminded of the behavior often exhibited by groups. Awaiting the rock concert, the crowd chants,
applauds, and stamps, usually at the bidding of one instigator.
Audiences attending live television shows clap when the applause light goes on.

As the characters run in and out of the scene in jerky, discontinuous fashion, the Announcer supplies us with vital information
about the Leader: he petted a hedgehog; he "suffered the little
children" to come to him; he climbed a stool and got down again.
No one would be interested in such trivial detail, we may say. But
isn't it true that the public dotes on reports of what the president
had for breakfast or the size of the first lady's dress? A movie
star's hair style can become a national obsession, and a clothing
trademark, a requirement.

After such a build up, how do we react to the fact that the
Leader has no head? The absurdity of a headless leader is that he

is what the adoring crowds have made him. Publicity hype has often created a "star" out of someone who lacked talent.

At first reading, *The Leader* may make no sense at all; but on closer examination, we see that it has an important message. It challenges audiences to look closely at their political, social, and religious leaders. Are they "headless" leaders or do they have substance? Are they leaders who have proven their leadership or is it merely their publicity stunts that have proven effective?

In *Notes and Counter Notes,* Eugene Ionesco says of *The Leader* that it has "no real characters, just people without identity. . . . [It is] simply a sequence of events without sequence, a series of fortuitous incidents unlinked by cause and effect, inexplicable adventures, emotional states, an indescribable tangle, . . . steeped in contradiction. This may appear tragic or comic or both at the same time, for I am incapable of distinguishing one from the other. I only want to render my own strange and improbable universe."[31]

Suggested Reading

Corrigan, Robert W., ed. *Comedy: A Critical Anthology.* Boston, Mass.: Houghton Mifflin, 1971.

Hart-Davis, Rupert, ed. *The Letters of Oscar Wilde.* New York: Harcourt, Brace and World, 1962.

Lesnick, Henry, ed. *Guerilla Street Theatre.* New York: Avon Books, 1973.

McCollom, William. *The Divine Average: A View of Comedy.* Cleveland, Ohio: Case Western Reserve University Press, 1971.

Olson, Elder. *The Theory of Comedy.* Bloomington, Indiana: Indiana University Press, 1968.

Roose-Evans, James. *Experimental Theatre.* New York: Universe Books, 1970.

Seyler, Athene, and Stephen Haggard. *The Craft of Comedy.* New York: Theatre Arts, 1946.

Wilde, Larry. *The Great Comedians Talk about Comedy.* New York: Citadel Press, 1961.

9

Modern Drama

Drama, in contrast to tragedy and comedy which show us as better or worse than we are, attempts to show us as we are. Drama more nearly reflects the nature of private and public lives. Of course, no individual's daily life is as action packed as a two-hour drama, so the playwright seeks to capsulize the most vital details in a continuous action, omitting those of lesser importance. The dramatic writer concentrates on a few characters who embody the characteristics or ideals he or she wishes to pursue in the story.

A drama requires the reader or viewer to become intellectually involved. There are no exaggerated gestures or pratfalls as in a comedy, and no masterful soliloquies as in a tragedy. The masterful dramatic writer will develop and reveal the characters and plot so artistically that the audience understands not only what is said but also what is implied through subtext, suggestion, facial expression, and movement. The audience must be sensitive to language nuance, to subtle unspoken communication, and to the many levels of intellectual and emotional involvement between the characters.

The elements of drama are finely developed in a modern drama. The plot is a compressed piece of time in which characters in conflict attempt to have some control over the circumstances of their lives. Exposition is often brief but so brilliantly presented that every word is full of meaning. No line is to be ignored. The complications begin early, and we are quickly drawn into the circumstances in which the characters are embroiled. Often these complications have social significance, as in *Countess Julie*, where differences between social classes form the framework for the story.

The characters are all important in the modern drama, for example, Willy Loman in Arthur Miller's *Death of a Salesman* and Amanda and Laura Wingfield in Tennessee Williams's *The Glass Menagerie*. Through the troubled lives of these characters and the mistakes they make, we may come to a better understanding of ourselves and the problems we face. Unlike the characters of comedy, who represent distorted or stereotyped personages, or those of tragedy, whose goals and behaviors seem beyond our experience, the characters of a drama are people like us. They are psychologically complex, emotionally vulnerable, and instinctively motivated. We can recognize them as genuine, and we can believe in them and find kinship with them.

In the modern drama, the Method actor enjoys the challenge of playing characters that are psychological, social, emotional beings; they are complex characters, often no better and no worse than we are. The Method actor has the emotional resources for playing dramatic characters. Subtext plays an important role in the script and in the actor's portrayal. The author's intent—the Aristotelian "thought" element of drama—is a more modern one. Therefore, it is easier for us to understand and interpret.

Naturalism: *Countess Julie*

August Strindberg's play, *Countess Julie*, is considered by many to be a masterpiece of the naturalistic genre. Naturalism is concerned with man's struggle with and entrapment by basic urges or forces over which he has no control and which can be sordid and violent. The realist assumes that people can make choices; the naturalist does not assume this. *Countess Julie* takes place in the 1880s in Sweden. It explores the psychological and social ramifications of class consciousness, and it examines the personal struggles of two characters, Julie and Jean, who must deal with their personal attraction for each other as well as their desire to change places on the social ladder. Strindberg produced his outstanding works in the last quarter of the nineteenth century. He reveals much about his own family life, spiritual struggles, and psychological weaknesses in this play. *Countess Julie* depicts a sexual encounter that leads to a struggle for personal dominance and social change and is a good representative of the naturalistic tradition.

Naturalistic plays have realistic settings that seem to overwhelm the characters. Following the naturalistic mode, Strindberg sets this play in a manor house. But while plays of this era were usually set in a parlor or a drawing room, Strindberg chose the kitchen, complete with pots, pans, and table. The audience sees the room from one corner, a small, intimate acting area that contributes to the realism of the set. The manner and speech of the characters is relaxed and natural. There is no superfluous or stilted language impeding the smooth flow of dialogue. The dress of the characters reveals the relaxed relationships within the trio of characters. Kristin is attired as a cook; Julie is festively dressed for Midsummer's Eve. As we watch, Jean transforms himself from a valet to a gentleman.

Strindberg's use of the kitchen as the scene of the action acts as a visual force in this drama about the decay of the aristocracy. The kitchen is Kristin's domain; therefore, it becomes a relatively neutral ground for the meeting of Julie (upper class) and Jean (servant). The kitchen setting is a constant visual reminder that Miss Julie is out of her social place. It also reminds us that Jean feels comfortable here with Kristin. The kitchen has the ideal atmosphere for the events that unfold in this gripping one-act play.

Countess Julie

August Strindberg
translated by Edith and Warner Oland

Characters

COUNTESS JULIE, twenty-five years old
JEAN, a valet, thirty
KRISTIN, a cook thirty-five
FARM SERVANTS

Scene

The action takes place on Saint John's night, the mid-summer festival surviving from pagan times.

A large kitchen. The ceiling and walls are partially covered by draperies and greens. The back wall slants upward from left side

Reprinted courtesy of Branden Publishing Company,
17 Station Street Box 843, Brookline Village, MA 02147

of scene. On back wall, left, are two shelves filled with copper
kettles, iron casseroles and tin pans. The shelves are trimmed
with fancy scalloped paper. To right of middle a large arched
entrance with glass doors through which one sees a fountain
with a statue of Cupid, syringa bushes in bloom and tall poplars.
To left corner of scene a large stove with hood decorated with
birch branches. To right, servants' dining table of white pine and
a few chairs. On the end of table stands a Japanese jar filled with
syringa blossoms. The floor is strewn with juniper branches.

(*Near stove, an ice-box, sink and dish-table. A large old-fashioned bell
hangs over the door, to left of door a speaking tube.* KRISTIN *stands at
stove engaged in cooking something. She wears a light cotton dress and
kitchen apron.* JEAN *comes in wearing livery; he carries a large pair of
riding-boots with spurs, which he puts on floor.*)

JEAN: Tonight Miss Julie is crazy again, perfectly crazy.
KRISTIN: So—you're back at last.
JEAN: I went to the station with the Count and coming back I
    went in to the barn and danced and then I discovered Miss   *10*
    Julie there leading the dance with the gamekeeper. When she
    spied me, she rushed right toward me and asked me to waltz,
    and then she waltzed so—never in my life have I seen
    anything like it! Ah—she is crazy tonight.
KRISTIN: She has always been. But never so much as in the last
    fortnight, since her engagement was broken off.
JEAN: Yes, what about that gossip? He seemed like a fine fellow
    although he wasn't rich! Ach! they have so much nonsense
    about them. (*Seats himself at table*) It's queer about Miss Julie
    though—to prefer staying here at home among these people,   *20*
    eh, to going away with her father to visit her relatives, eh?
KRISTIN: She's probably shamefaced about breaking off with her
    intended.
JEAN: No doubt! but he was a likely sort just the same. Do you
    know, Kristin, how it happened? I saw it, although I didn't let
    on.
KRISTIN: No—did you see it?
JEAN: Yes, indeed, I did. They were out in the stable yard one
    evening and she was "training" him as she called it. Do you
    know what happened? She made him leap over her riding   *30*
    whip, the way you teach a dog to jump. He jumped it twice
    and got a lash each time; but the third time he snatched the
    whip from her hand and broke it into pieces. And then he
    vanished!
KRISTIN: Was that the way it happened? No, you don't say so!
JEAN: Yes, that's the way the thing happened. But what have
    you got to give me that's good, Kristin?

KRISTIN: (*She takes things from the pans on stove and serves them to him*) Oh, it's only a bit of kidney that I cut out of the veal steak for you.   40

JEAN: (*Smelling the food*) Splendid! My favorite delicacy. (*Feeling of plate*) But you might have warmed the plate.

KRISTIN: You're fussier than the Count, when you get started. (*Tweaks his hair*)

JEAN: Don't pull my hair! You know how sensitive I am.

KRISTIN: Oh—There, there! you know I was only loving you.

(JEAN *eats, and* KRISTIN *opens bottle of beer*)

JEAN: Beer on midsummer night—thank you, no! I have something better than that myself. (*Takes bottle of wine from drawer of table*) Yellow seal, how's that? Now give me a   50
glass—a wine glass you understand, of course, when one drinks the genuine.

KRISTIN: (*Fetches a glass. Then goes to stove and puts on casserole*) Heaven help the woman who gets you for a husband. Such a fuss budget!

JEAN: Oh, talk! You ought to be glad to get such a fine fellow as I am. And I don't think it's done you any harm because I'm considered your intended. (*Tastes wine*) Excellent, very excellent! Just a little too cold. (*Warms glass with hands*) We   60
bought this at Dijon. It stood at four francs a litre in the bulk; then of course there was the duty besides. What are you cooking now that smells so infernally?

KRISTIN: Oh, it's some devil's mess that Miss Julie must have for Diana.

JEAN: Take care of your words, Kristin. But why should you stand there cooking for that damned dog on a holiday evening? Is it sick, eh?

KRISTIN: Yes, it's sick. Diana sneaked out with the gatekeeper's mongrels and now something is wrong. Miss Julie can't stand   70
that.

JEAN: Miss Julie has a great deal of pride about some things—but not enough about others! Just like her mother in her lifetime; she thrived best in the kitchen or the stable, but she must always drive tandem—never one horse! She would go about with soiled cuffs but she had to have the Count's crest on her cuff buttons. And as for Miss Julie, she doesn't take much care of her appearance either. I should say she isn't refined. Why just now out there she pulled the forester from Anna's side and asked him to dance with her. We wouldn't do things that   80
way. But when the highborn wish to unbend they become vulgar. Splendid she is though! Magnificent! Ah, such shoulders and—

KRISTIN: Oh, don't exaggerate. I've heard what Clara says—who dresses her sometimes, I have.

JEAN: Ha! Clara—you women are always jealous of each other. I who've been out riding with her—!!! And such a dancer!

KRISTIN: Come now, Jean, don't you want to dance with me when I'm through?

JEAN: Of course I want to.   90

KRISTIN: That is a promise?

JEAN: Promise! When I say I will do a thing I do it! Thanks for the supper—it was excellent.

(*Pushes cork in the bottle with a bang.* MISS JULIE *appears in doorway, speaking to someone outside*)

JULIE: I'll be back soon, but don't let things wait for me.

(JEAN *quickly puts bottle in table drawer and rises very respectfully*   100
Enter MISS JULIE *who goes to* KRISTIN)

JULIE: Is it done? (KRISTIN *indicating* JEAN'S *presence*)

JEAN: (*Gallantly*) Have you secrets between you?

JULIE: (*Flipping handkerchief in his face*) Curious, are you?

JEAN: How sweet that violet perfume is!

JULIE: (*Coquettishly*) Impudence! Do you appreciate perfumes too? Dance—that you can do splendidly. (JEAN *looks towards the cooking stove*) Don't look. Away with you.

JEAN: (*Inquisitive but polite*) Is it some troll's dish that you are   110
both concocting for midsummer night? Something to pierce the future with and evoke the face of your intended?

JULIE: (*Sharply*) To see him one must have sharp eyes. (*To* KRISTIN) Put it into a bottle and cork it tight. Come now, Jean and dance a schottische with me.

JEAN: (*Hesitates*) I don't wish to be impolite to anyone but—this dance I promised to Kristin.

JULIE: Oh, she can have another—isn't that so, Kristin? Won't you lend Jean to me.

KRISTIN: It's not for me to say, if Miss Julie is so gracious it's not   120
for me to say no. (*To* JEAN) Go you and be grateful for the honor.

JEAN: Well said—but not wishing any offense I wonder if it is prudent for Miss Julie to dance twice in succession with her servant, especially as people are never slow to find meaning in—

JULIE: (*Breaking out*) In what? What sort of meaning? What were you going to say?

JEAN: (*Taken aback*) Since Miss Julie does not understand I must speak plainly. It may look strange to prefer one of   130
your—underlings—to others who covet the same honor—

JULIE: To prefer—what a thought! I, the lady of the house! I
   honor the people with my presence and now that I feel like
   dancing I want to have a partner who knows how to lead to
   avoid being ridiculous.
JEAN: As Miss Julie commands. I'm here to serve.
JULIE: (*Mildly*) You mustn't look upon that as a command.
   Tonight we are all in holiday spirits—full of gladness and rank
   is flung aside. So, give me your arm! Don't be alarmed
   Kristin, I shall not take your sweetheart away from you. (JEAN   140
   offers arm. They exit)
PANTOMIME: *Played as though the actress were really alone. Turns her
   back to the audience when necessary. Does not look out into the
   auditorium. Does not hurry as though fearing the audience might
   grow restless. Soft violin music from the distance, schottische time.*
   KRISTIN *hums with the music. She cleans the table; washes plate,
   wipes it and puts it in the china closet. Takes off her apron and then
   opens drawer of table and takes a small hand glass and stands it
   against a flower pot on table. Lights a candle and heats a hair pin
   with which she crimps her hair around her forehead. After that she*   150
   *goes to door at back and listens. Then she returns to table and sees the
   Countess' handkerchief, picks it up, smells of it, then smooths it out
   and folds it. Enter* JEAN)
JEAN: She is crazy I tell you! To dance like that! And the people
   stand grinning at her behind the doors. What do you say to
   that, Kristin?
KRISTIN: Oh, didn't I say she's been acting queer lately? But isn't
   it my turn to dance now?
JEAN: You are not angry because I let myself be led by the
   forelock?   160
KRISTIN: No, not for such a little thing. That you know well
   enough. And I know my place too—
JEAN: (*Puts arm around her waist*) You're a pretty smart girl,
   Kristin, and you ought to make a good wife.

(*Enter* MISS JULIE)

JULIE: (*Disagreeably surprised, but with forced gaiety*) You're a
   charming cavalier to run away from your partner.
JEAN: On the contrary, Miss Julie, I have hastened to my   170
   neglected one as you see.
JULIE: (*Changing subject*) Do you know, you dance wonderfully
   well! But why are you in livery on a holiday night? Take it off
   immediately.
JEAN: Will you excuse me—my coat hangs there. (*Goes* R. *and
   takes coat*)
JULIE: Does it embarrass you to change your coat in my

presence? Go to your room then—or else stay and I'll turn my
back.   180

JEAN: With your permission, Miss Julie. (*Exit* R. *One sees his arm
as he changes coat*)

JULIE: (*To* KRISTIN) Is Jean your sweetheart, that he is so devoted?

KRISTIN: Sweetheart? Yes, may it please you. Sweetheart—that's
what they call it.

JULIE: Call it?

KRISTIN: Oh Miss Julie has herself had a sweetheart and—

JULIE: Yes, we were engaged—

KRISTIN: But it came to nothing.
                                                                           190
(*Enter* JEAN *in black frock coat*)

JULIE. Très gentil, Monsieur Jean, très gentil.

JEAN: Vous voulez plaisanter, Mademoiselle.

JULIE: Et vous voulez parler français? Where did you learn that?

JEAN: In Switzerland where I was butler in the largest hotel at
Lucerne.

JULIE: Why, you look like a gentleman in your frock coat.
Charmant! (*Seats herself by table*)

JEAN: You flatter me!

JULIE: Flatter! (*Picking him up on the word*)   200

JEAN: My natural modesty forbids me to believe that you could
mean these pleasant things that you say to a—such as I
am—and therefore I allowed myself to fancy that you overrate
or, as it is called, flatter.

JULIE: Where did you learn to use words like that? Have you
frequented the theatres much?

JEAN: I have frequented many places, I have!

JULIE: But you were born here in this neighborhood?

JEAN: My father was a cottager on the district attorney's
property, and I saw Miss Julie as a child—although she didn't 210
see me!

JULIE: No, really?

JEAN: Yes, I remember one time in particular. But I mustn't talk
about that.

JULIE: Oh yes, do, when was it?

JEAN: No really—not now, another time perhaps.

JULIE: "Another time" is a good for nothing. Is it so dreadful
then?

JEAN: Not dreadful—but it goes against the grain. (*Turns and
points to* KRISTIN *who has fallen asleep in a chair near stove*) Look 220
at her.

JULIE: She'll make a charming wife! Does she snore too?

JEAN: No, but she talks in her sleep.

JULIE: (*Cynically*) How do you know that she talks in her sleep?

JEAN: (*Boldly*) I have heard her. (*Pause and they look at each other*)

JULIE: Why don't you sit down?

JEAN: I can't allow myself to do so in your presence.

JULIE: But if I command you?

JEAN: Then I obey.

JULIE: Sit down then. But wait—can't you get me something to drink first?   230

JEAN: I don't know what there is in the icebox. Nothing but beer probably.

JULIE: Is beer nothing? My taste is so simple that I prefer it to wine.

(JEAN *takes out beer and serves it on plate*)

JEAN: Allow me.

JULIE: Won't you drink too?

JEAN: I am no friend to beer—but if Miss Julie commands.   240

JULIE: (*Gaily*) Commands! I should think as a polite cavalier you might join your lady.

JEAN: Looking at it in that way you are quite right. (*Opens another bottle of beer and fills glass*)

JULIE: Give me a toast!

(JEAN *hesitates*)

JULIE: (*Mockingly*) Old as he is, I believe the man is bashful!

JEAN: (*On his knee with mock gallantry, raises glass*) A health to my lady of the house!   250

JULIE: Bravo! Now you must kiss my slipper. Then the thing is perfect.

(JEAN *hesitates and then seizes her foot and kisses it lightly*)

JULIE: Splendid! You should have been an actor.

JEAN: (*Rising*) But this mustn't go any further, Miss Julie. What if someone should come in and see us?

JULIE: What harm would that do?

JEAN: Simply that it would give them a chance to gossip. And if Miss Julie only knew how their tongues wagged just now—then—   260

JULIE: What did they say? Tell me. And sit down now.

JEAN: (*Sitting*) I don't wish to hurt you, but they used an expression—threw hints of a certain kind—but you are not a child, you can understand. When one sees a lady drinking alone with a man—let alone a servant—at night—then—

JULIE: Then what? And for that matter, we are not alone. Kristin is here.

JEAN: Sleeping! Yes.

JULIE: Then I shall wake her. (*Rises*) Kristin, are you asleep?   270

KRISTIN: (*In her sleep*) Bla—bla—bla—bla.

JULIE: Kristin! She certainly can sleep. (*Goes to* KRISTIN)

KRISTIN: (*In her sleep*) The Count's boots are polished—put on the coffee—soon—soon—soon. Oh—h-h-h—puh! (*Breathes heavily.* JULIE *takes her by the nose.*)

JULIE: Won't you wake up?

JEAN: (*Sternly*) Don't disturb the sleeping.

JULIE: (*Sharply*) What?

JEAN: Anyone who has stood over the hot stove all day long is tired when night comes. One should respect the weary.   280

JULIE: That's a kind thought—and I honor it. (*Offers her hand*) Thanks for the suggestion. Come out with me now and pick some syringas.

(KRISTIN has awakened and goes to her room, right, in a sort of sleepy, stupefied way)

JEAN: With Miss Julie?

JULIE: With me.

JEAN: But that wouldn't do—decidedly not.   290

JULIE: I don't understand you. Is it possible that you fancy that I—

JEAN: No—not I, but people.

JULIE: What? That I'm in love with my coachman?

JEAN: I am not presumptuous, but we have seen instances—and with the people nothing is sacred.

JULIE: I believe he is an aristocrat!

JEAN: Yes, I am.

JULIE: But I step down—

JEAN: Don't step down, Miss Julie. Listen to me—no one would   300 believe that you stepped down of your own accord; people always say that one falls down.

JULIE: I think better of the people than you do. Come—and try them—come! (*Dares him with a look*)

JEAN: Do you know that you are wonderful?

JULIE: Perhaps. But you are too. Everything is wonderful for that matter. Life, people—everything. Everything is wreckage, that drifts over the water until it sinks, sinks. I have the same dream every now and then and at this moment I am reminded of it. I find myself seated at the top of a high pillar and I see no 310 possible way to get down. I grow dizzy when I look down, but down I must. But I'm not brave enough to throw myself; I cannot hold fast and I long to fall—but I don't fall. And yet I can find no rest or peace until I shall come down to earth; and if I came down to earth I would wish myself down in the ground. Have you ever felt like that?

JEAN: No, I dream that I'm lying in a dark wood under a tall tree
and I would up—up to the top, where I can look far over the
fair landscape, where the sun is shining. I climb—climb, to
plunder the birds' nests up there where the golden eggs lie,   320
but the tree trunk is so thick, so smooth, and the first limb is
so high! But I know if I reached the first limb I should climb as
though on a ladder, to the top. I haven't reached it yet, but I
shall reach it, if only in the dream.

JULIE: Here I stand talking about dreams with you. Come now,
just out in the park. (*She offers her arm and they start*)

JEAN: We should sleep on nine midsummer flowers tonight and
then our dreams would come true.

(JULIE *turns,* JEAN *quickly holds a hand over his eye*)   330

JULIE: What is it, something in your eye?

JEAN: Oh, it is nothing—just a speck. It will be all right in a
moment.

JULIE: It was some dust from my sleeve that brushed against
you. Now sit down and let me look at it. (*Pulls him into a chair,
looks into his eye*) Now sit still, perfectly still. (*Uses corner of her
handkerchief in his eye. Strikes his hand*) So—will you mind? I
believe you are trembling, strong man that you are. (*Touching
his arm*) And such arms!   340

JEAN: (*Warningly*) Miss Julie!

JULIE: Yes, Monsieur Jean!

JEAN: Attention. Je ne suis qu' un homme!

JULIE: Will you sit still! So, now it is gone! Kiss my hand and
thank me!

(JEAN *rises*)

JEAN: Miss Julie, listen to me. Kristin has gone to bed now—will
you listen to me—   350

JULIE: Kiss my hand first.

JEAN: Listen to me—

JULIE: Kiss my hand first.

JEAN: Yes, but blame yourself.

JULIE: For what?

JEAN: For what? Are you a child at twenty-five? Don't you know
that it is dangerous to play with fire?

JULIE: Not for me. I am insured!

JEAN: No, you are not. But even if you are, there is inflammable
material in the neighborhood.   360

JULIE: Might that be you?

JEAN: Yes, not because it is I, but because I'm a young man—

JULIE: (*Scornfully*) With a grand opportunity—what inconceivable presumption! A Don Juan perhaps! Or a Joseph! On my soul, I believe he is a Joseph!

JEAN: You do?

JULIE: Almost.

(JEAN *rushes towards her and tries to take her in his arms to kiss her*) 370

JULIE: (*Gives him a box on the ear*) Shame on you.

JEAN: Are you in earnest, or fooling?

JULIE: In earnest.

JEAN: Then you were in earnest a moment ago, too. You play too seriously with what is dangerous. Now I'm tired of playing and beg to be excused that I may go on with my work. The Count must have his boots in time, and it is long past midnight. (*Picks up boots*)

JULIE: Put those boots away.   380

JEAN: No, that is my work which it is my duty to do, but I was not hired to be your plaything and that I shall never be. I think too well of myself for that.

JULIE: You are proud.

JEAN: In some things—not in others.

JULIE: Were you ever in love?

JEAN: We do not use that word, but I have liked many girls. One time I was sick because I couldn't have the one I wanted—sick, you understand, like the princesses in the Arabian Nights who could not eat nor drink for love sickness.   390

JULIE: Who was she? (JEAN *is silent*) Who was she?

JEAN: That you could not make me tell.

JULIE: Not if I ask you as an equal, as a—friend? Who was she?

JEAN: It was you!

(JULIE *seats herself*)

JULIE: How extravagant!

JEAN: Yes, if you will, it was ridiculous. That was the story I hesitated to tell, but now I'm going to tell it. Do you know   400 how people in high life look from the under world? No, of course you don't. They look like hawks and eagles whose backs one seldom sees, for they soar up above. I lived in a hovel provided by the state, with seven brothers and sisters and a pig; out on a barren stretch where nothing grew, not even a tree, but from the window I could see the Count's park walls with apple trees rising above them. That was the garden of paradise; and there stood many angry angels with flaming swords protecting it; but for all that I and other boys found the way to the tree of life—now you despise me.   410

JULIE: Oh, all boys steal apples.

JEAN: You say that, but you despise me all the same. No matter! One time I entered the garden of paradise—it was to weed the onion beds with my mother! Near the orchard stood a Turkish pavilion, shaded and overgrown with jessamine and honeysuckle. I didn't know what it was used for and I had never seen anything so beautiful. People passed in and out and one day—the door was left open. I sneaked in and beheld walls covered with pictures of kings and emperors and there were red-fringed curtains at the windows—now you understand what I mean—I—(*Breaks off a spray of syringa and puts it to her nostrils*) I had never been in the castle and how my thoughts leaped—and there they returned ever after. Little by little the longing came over me to experience for once the pleasure of—enfin, I sneaked in and was bewildered. But then I heard someone coming—there was only one exit for the great folk, but for me there was another, and I had to choose that.   *420*

(JULIE *who has taken the syringa lets it fall on table*)

Once out I started to run, scrambled through a raspberry hedge, rushed over a strawberry bed and came to a stop on the rose terrace. For there I saw a figure in a pink dress and white slippers and stockings—it was you! I hid under a heap of weeds, under, you understand, where the thistles pricked me, and lay on the damp, rank earth. I gazed at you walking among the roses. And I thought if it is true that the thief on the cross could enter heaven and dwell among the angels it was strange that a pauper child on God's earth could not go into the castle park and play with the Count's daughter.   *430*

JULIE: (*Pensively*) Do you believe that all poor children would have such thoughts under those conditions?   *440*

JEAN: (*Hesitates, then in a positive voice*) That all poor children—yes, of course, of course!

JULIE: It must be a terrible misfortune to be poor.

JEAN: (*With deep pain and great chagrin*) Oh, Miss Julie, a dog may lie on the couch of a Countess, a horse may be caressed by a lady's hand, but a servant—yes, yes, sometimes there is stuff enough in a man, whatever he be, to swing himself up in the world, but how often does that happen! But to return to the story, do you know what I did? I ran down to the mill dam and threw myself in with my clothes on—and was pulled out and got a thrashing. But the following Sunday when all the family went to visit my grandmother I contrived to stay at home; I scrubbed myself well, put on my best clothes, such as they were, and went to church so that I might see you. I saw you. Then I went home with my mind made up to put an end to myself. But I wanted to do it beautifully and without pain.   *450*

Then I happened to remember that elderberry blossoms are
poisonous. I knew where there was a big elderberry bush in
full bloom and I stripped it of its riches and made a bed of it in 460
the oat-bin. Have you ever noticed how smooth and glossy
oats are? As soft as a woman's arm.—Well, I got in and let
down the cover, fell asleep, and when I awoke I was very ill,
but didn't die—as you see. What I wanted—I don't know. You
were unattainable, but through the vision of you I was made
to realize how hopeless it was to rise above the conditions of
my birth.

JULIE: You tell it well! Were you ever at school?

JEAN: A little, but I have read a good deal and gone to the
theatres. And besides, I have always heard the talk of fine 470
folks and from them I have learned most.

JULIE: Do you listen then to what we are saying?

JEAN: Yes, indeed, I do. And I have heard much when I've been
on the coachbox. One time I heard Miss Julie and a lady—

JULIE: Oh, what was it you heard?

JEAN: Hm! that's not so easy to tell. But I was astonished and
could not understand where you had heard such things. Well,
perhaps at bottom there's not so much difference between
people and—people.

JULIE: Oh, shame! We don't behave as you do when we are 480
engaged.

JEAN: (*Eyeing her*) Are you sure of that? It isn't worth while to
play the innocent with me.

JULIE: I gave my love to a rascal.

JEAN: That's what they always say afterward.

JULIE: Always?

JEAN: Always, I believe, as I have heard the expression many
times before under the same circumstances.

JULIE: What circumstances?

JEAN: Those we've been talking about. The last time I— 490

JULIE: Silence. I don't wish to hear any more.

JEAN: Well, then I beg to be excused so I may go to bed.

JULIE: Go to bed! On midsummer night?

JEAN: Yes, for dancing out there with that pack has not amused
me.

JULIE: Then get the key for the boat and row me out over the
lake. I want to see the sun rise.

JEAN: Is that prudent?

JULIE: One would think that you were afraid of your reputation.

JEAN: Why not? I don't want to be made ridiculous. I am not 500
willing to be driven out without references, now that I am
going to settle down. And I feel I owe something to Kristin.

JULIE: Oh, so it's Kristin now—

JEAN: Yes, but you too. Take my advice, go up and go to bed.

JULIE: Shall I obey you?

JEAN: For once—for your own sake. I beg of you. Night is crawling along, sleepiness makes one irresponsible and the brain grows hot. Go to your room. In fact—if I hear rightly some of the people are coming for me. If they find us here—then you are lost.   510

(*Chorus is heard approaching, singing*)

> There came two ladies out of the woods
> Tridiridi-ralla tridiridi-ra.
> One of them had wet her foot,
> Tridiridi-ralla-la.
>
> They talked of a hundred dollars,
> Tridiridi-ralla tridiridi-ra.   520
> But neither had hardly a dollar,
> Tridiridi-ralla-la.
>
> The mitten I'm going to send you,
> Tridiridi-ralla tridiridi-ra.
> For another I'm going to jilt you,
> Tridiridi-ralla tridiridi-ra.

JULIE: I know the people and I love them and they respect me. Let them come, you shall see.   530

JEAN: No, Miss Julie, they don't love you. They take your food and spit upon your kindness, believe me. Listen to them, listen to what they're singing! No! Don't listen!

JULIE: (*Listening*) What are they singing?

JEAN: It's something suggestive, about you and me.

JULIE: Infamous! Oh horrible! And how cowardly!

JEAN: The pack is always cowardly. And in such a battle one can only run away.

JULIE: Run away? Where? We can't get out and we can't go to Kristin.   540

JEAN: Into my room then. Necessity knows no law. You can depend on me for I am your real, genuine, respectful friend.

JULIE: But think if they found you there.

JEAN: I will turn the key and if they try to break in I'll shoot. Come—come!

JULIE: (*Meaningly*) You promise me—?

JEAN: I swear . . . (*She exits* R. JEAN *follows her*)

BALLET: *The farm folk enter in holiday dress with flowers in their hats, a fiddler in the lead. They carry a keg of home-brewed beer and a smaller keg of gin, both decorated with greens which are placed on the* 550 *table. They help themselves to glasses and drink. Then they sing and dance a country dance to the melody of ''There came two ladies out of the woods.'' When that is over they go out, singing.*

(*Enter* JULIE *alone, sees the havoc the visitors have made, clasps her hands, takes out powder box and powders her face. Enter* JEAN *exuberant*)

JEAN: There, you see, and you heard them. Do you think it's possible for us to remain here any longer?   560

JULIE: No, I don't. But what's to be done?

JEAN: Fly! Travel—far from here!

JULIE: Travel—yes—but where?

JEAN: To Switzerland—to the Italian lakes. You have never been there?

JULIE: No—is it beautiful there?

JEAN: Oh, an eternal summer! Orange trees, laurels—oh!

JULIE: But what shall we do there?

JEAN: I'll open a first-class hotel for first-class patrons.

JULIE: Hotel?   570

JEAN: That is life—you shall see! New faces constantly, different languages. Not a moment for boredom. Always something to do night and day—the bell ringing, the trains whistling, the omnibus coming and going and all the time the gold pieces rolling into the till—that is life!

JULIE: Yes, that is life. And I—?

JEAN: The mistress of the establishment—the ornament of the house. With your looks—and your manners—oh, it's a sure success! Colossal! You could sit like a queen in the office and set the slaves in action by touching an electric button. The   580 guests line up before your throne and shyly lay their riches on your desk. You can't believe how people tremble when they get their bills—I can salt the bills and you can sweeten them with your most bewitching smile—ha, let us get away from here—(*Takes a timetable from his pocket*) immediately—by the next train. We can be at Malmö at 6:30, Hamburg at 8:40 tomorrow morning, Frankfort the day after and at Como by the St. Gothard route in about—let me see, three days. Three days!

JULIE: All that is well enough, but Jean—you must give me   590 courage. Take me in your arms and tell me that you love me.

JEAN: (*Hesitatingly*) I will—but I daren't—not again in this house. I love you of course—do you doubt that, Miss Julie?

JULIE: (*Shyly and with womanliness*) Miss Julie! Call me Julie! Between us there can be no more formality.

JEAN: I can't—There must be formality between us—as long as we are in this house. There is the memory of the past—and there is the Count, your father. I have never known anyone

else for whom I have such respect. I need only to see his
gloves lying in a chair to feel my own insignificance. I have   *600*
only to hear his bell to start like a nervous horse—and now as I
see his boots standing there so stiff and proper I feel like
bowing and scraping. (*Gives boots a kick*) Superstitions and
prejudices taught in childhood can't be uprooted in a moment.
Let us go to a country that is a republic where they'll stand on
their heads for my coachman's livery—on their heads shall
they stand—but I shall not. I am not born to bow and scrape,
for there's stuff in me—character. If I only get hold of the first
limb, you shall see me climb. I'm a coachman today, but next
year I shall be a proprietor, in two years a gentleman of   *610*
income; then for Roumania where I'll let them decorate me
and can, mark you, *can* end a count!

JULIE: Beautiful, beautiful!

JEAN: Oh, in Roumania, one can buy a title cheap—and so you
can be a countess just the same—my countess!

JULIE: What do I care for all that—which I now cast behind me.
Say that you love me—else, what am I, without it?

JEAN: I'll say it a thousand times afterwards, but not here. Above
all, let us have no sentimentality now or everything will fall
through. We must look at this matter coldly like sensible   *620*
people. (*Takes out a cigar and lights it*) Now sit down there and
I'll sit here and we'll talk it over as if nothing had happened.

JULIE: (*Staggered*) Oh, my God, have you no feeling?

JEAN: I? No one living has more feeling than I, but I can restrain
myself.

JULIE: A moment ago you could kiss my slipper and now—

JEAN: (Harshly) That was—then. Now we have other things to
think about.

JULIE: Don't speak harshly to me.

JEAN: Not harshly, but wisely. One folly has been   *630*
committed—commit no more. The Count may be here at any
moment, and before he comes, our fate must be settled. How
do my plans for the future strike you? Do you approve of
them?

JULIE: They seem acceptable enough. But one question. For such
a great undertaking a large capital is necessary, have you that?

JEAN: (*Chewing his cigar*) I? To be sure. I have my regular
occupation, my unusual experience, my knowledge of
different languages—that is capital that counts, I should say.

JULIE: But with all that you could not buy a railway ticket.   *640*

JEAN: That's true, and for that reason I'm looking for a backer
who can furnish the funds.

JULIE: How can that be done at a moment's notice?

JEAN: That is for you to say, if you wish to be my companion.

JULIE: I can't—as I have nothing myself.

(*A pause*)

JEAN: Then the whole matter drops—

650

JULIE: And—

JEAN: Things remain as they are.

JULIE: Do you think I could remain under this roof after—do you think I will allow the people to point at me in scorn, or that I can ever look my father in the face again? Never! Take me away from this humiliation and dishonor. Oh, what have I done! Oh, my God, what have I done! (*Weeping*)

JEAN: So, you are beginning in that tune now. What have you done? The same as many before you.

JULIE: And now you despise me. I am falling! I am falling!

JEAN: Fall down to my level, I'll lift you up afterwards.

660

JULIE: What strange power drew me to you—the weak to the strong—the falling to the rising, or is this love! This—love! Do you know what love is?

JEAN: I? Yes! Do you think it's the first time?

JULIE: What language, what thoughts.

JEAN: I am what life has made me. Don't be nervous and play the high and mighty, for now we are on the same level. Look here, my little girl, let me offer you a glass of something extra fine. (*Opens drawer of table and takes out wine bottle, then fills two glasses that have been already used*)

670

JULIE: Where did you get that wine?

JEAN: From the cellar.

JULIE: My father's Burgundy.

JEAN: What's the matter, isn't that good enough for the son-in-law?

JULIE: And I drink beer—I!

JEAN: That only goes to prove that your taste is poorer than mine.

JULIE: Thief!

JEAN: Do you intend to tattle?

680

JULIE: Oh ho! Accomplice to a house thief. Was I intoxicated—have I been walking in my sleep this night—midsummer night, the night for innocent play—

JEAN: Innocent, eh!

JULIE: (*Pacing back and forth*) Is there a being on earth so miserable as I.

JEAN: Why are you, after such a conquest? Think of Kristin in there, don't you think she has feelings too?

JULIE: I thought so a little while ago, but I don't any more. A servant is a servant.

690

JEAN: And a whore is a whore.

JULIE: (*Falls on her knees with clasped hands*) Oh, God in heaven,
  end my wretched life, save me from this mire into which I'm
  sinking—Oh save me, save me.

JEAN: I can't deny that it hurts me to see you like this.

JULIE: And you who wanted to die for me.

JEAN: In the oat-bin? Oh, that was only talk.

JULIE: That is to say—a lie!

JEAN: (*Beginning to show sleepiness*) Er—er almost. I believe I read
  something of the sort in a newspaper about a chimney-sweep   700
  who made a death bed for himself of syringa blossoms in a
  wood-bin—(*laughs*) because they were going to arrest him for
  non-support of his children.

JULIE: So you are such a—

JEAN: What better could I have hit on! One must always be
  romantic to capture a woman.

JULIE: Wretch! Now you have seen the eagle's back, and I
  suppose I am to be the first limb—

JEAN: And the limb is rotten—

JULIE: (*Without seeming to hear*) And I am to be the hotel's   710
  signboard—

JEAN: And I the hotel—

JULIE: And sit behind the desk and allure guests and overcharge
  them—

JEAN: Oh, that'll be my business.

JULIE: That a soul can be so degraded!

JEAN: Look to your own soul.

JULIE: Lackey! Servant! Stand up when I speak.

JEAN: Don't you dare to moralize to me. Lackey, eh! Do you
  think you have shown yourself finer than any maid-servant   720
  tonight?

JULIE: (*Crushed*) That is right, strike me, trample on me, I deserve
  nothing better. I have done wrong, but help me now. Help me
  out of this if there is any possible way.

JEAN: (*Softens somewhat*) I don't care to shirk my share of the
  blame, but do you think any one of my position would ever
  have dared to raise his eyes to you if you yourself had not
  invited it? Even now I am astonished—

JULIE: And proud.

JEAN: Why not? Although I must confess that the conquest was   730
  too easy to be exciting.

JULIE: Go on, strike me again—

JEAN: (*Rising*) No, forgive me, rather, for what I said. I do not
  strike the unarmed, least of all, a woman. But I can't deny that
  from a certain point of view it gives me satisfaction to know
  that it is the glitter of brass, not gold, that dazzles us from
  below, and that the eagle's back is grey like the rest of him.

On the other hand, I'm sorry to have to realize that all that I
have looked up to is not worth while, and it pains me to see
you fallen lower than your cook as it pains me to see autumn   740
blossoms whipped to pieces by the cold rain and transformed
into—dirt!

JULIE: You speak as though you were already my superior.

JEAN: And so I am! For I can make you a countess and you could
never make me a count.

JULIE: But I am born of a count, that you can never be.

JEAN: That is true, but I can be the father of counts—if—

JULIE: But you are a thief—that I am not.

JEAN: There are worse things than that, and for that matter when
I serve in a house I regard myself as a member of the family, a   750
child of the house as it were. And one doesn't consider it theft
if children snoop a berry from full bushes. (*With renewed
passion*) Miss Julie, you are a glorious woman—too good for
such as I. You have been the victim of an infatuation and you
want to disguise this fault by fancying that you love me. But
you do not—unless perhaps my outer self attracts you. And
then your love is no better than mine. But I cannot be satisfied
with that, and your real love I can never awaken.

JULIE: Are you sure of that?

JEAN: You mean that we could get along with such an   760
arrangement? There's no doubt about my loving you—you are
beautiful, you are elegant—(*Goes to her and takes her hand*)
accomplished, lovable when you wish to be, and the flame
that you awaken in man does not die easily. (*Puts arm around
her*) You are like hot wine with strong spices, and your
lips—(*Tries to kiss her. Julie pulls herself away slowly*)

JULIE: Leave me—I'm not to be won this way.

JEAN: How then? Not with caresses and beautiful words? Not by
thoughts for the future, to save humiliation? How then?

JULIE: How? I don't know. I don't know! I shrink from you as I   770
would from a rat. But I cannot escape from you.

JEAN: Escape with me.

JULIE: Escape? Yes, we must escape.—But I'm so tired. Give me a
glass of wine.

(JEAN *fills a glass with wine,* JULIE *looks at her watch*)

We must talk it over first for we have still a little time left.
(*She empties the glass and puts it out for more*)

JEAN: Don't drink too much. It will go to your head.   780

JULIE: What harm will that do?

JEAN: What harm? It's foolish to get intoxicated. But what did
you want to say?

JULIE: We must go away, but we must talk first. That is, I must speak, for until now you have done all the talking. You have told me about your life—now I will tell you about mine, then we will know each other through and through before we start on our wandering together.

JEAN: One moment, pardon. Think well whether you won't regret having told your life's secrets.   790

JULIE: Aren't you my friend?

JEAN: Yes. Sometimes. But don't depend on me.

JULIE: You only say that. And for that matter I have no secrets. You see, my mother was not of noble birth. She was brought up with ideas of equality, woman's freedom and all that. She had very decided opinions against matrimony, and when my father courted her she declared that she would never be his wife—but she did so for all that. I came into the world against my mother's wishes, I discovered, and was brought up like a child of nature by my mother, and taught everything that a   800 boy must know as well; I was to be an example of a woman being as good as a man—I was made to go about in boy's clothes and take care of the horses and harness and saddle and hunt, and all such things; in fact, all over the estate women servants were taught to do men's work, with the result that the property came near being ruined—and so we became the laughing stock of the countryside. At last my father must have awakened from his bewitched condition, for he revolted and ran things according to his ideas. My mother became ill—what it was I don't know, but she often had   810 cramps and acted queerly—sometimes hiding in the attic or the orchard, and would even be gone all night at times. Then came the big fire which of course you have heard about. The house, the stables—everything was burned, under circumstances that pointed strongly to an incendiary, for the misfortune happened the day after the quarterly insurance was due and the premiums sent in by father were strangely delayed by his messenger so that they arrived too late. (*She fills a wine glass and drinks*)

JEAN: Don't drink any more.   820

JULIE: Oh, what does it matter? My father was utterly at a loss to know where to get money to rebuild with. Then my mother suggested that he try to borrow from a man who had been her friend in her youth—a brick manufacturer here in the neighborhood. My father made the loan, but wasn't allowed to pay any interest, which surprised him. Then the house was rebuilt. (*Drinks again*) Do you know who burned the house?

JEAN: Her ladyship, your mother?

JULIE: Do you know who the brick manufacturer was?

JEAN: Your mother's lover?   *830*

JULIE: Do you know whose money it was?

JEAN: Just a moment, that I don't know.

JULIE: It was my mother's.

JEAN: The Count's—that is to say, unless there was a contract.

JULIE: There was no contract. My mother had some money
which she had not wished to have in my father's keeping and
therefore, she had entrusted it to her friend's care.

JEAN: Who kept it.

JULIE: Quite right—he held on to it. All this came to my father's
knowledge. He couldn't proceed against him, wasn't allowed *840*
to pay his wife's friend, and couldn't prove that it was his
wife's money. That was my mother's revenge for his taking
the reins of the establishment into his own hands. At that time
he was ready to shoot himself. Gossip had it that he had tried
and failed. Well, he lived it down—and my mother paid full
penalty for her misdeed. Those were five terrible years for me,
as you can fancy. I sympathized with my father, but I took my
mother's part, for I didn't know the true circumstances.
Through her I learned to distrust and hate men, and I swore to
her never to be a man's slave.   *850*

JEAN: But you became engaged to the District Attorney.

JULIE: Just to make him my slave.

JEAN: But that he didn't care to be.

JULIE: He wanted to be, fast enough, but I grew tired of him.

JEAN: Yes—I noticed that—in the stable-yard!

JULIE: What do you mean?

JEAN: I saw how he broke—the engagement.

JULIE: That's a lie. It was I who broke it. Did he say he broke
it—the wretch!

JEAN: I don't believe that he was a wretch. You hate men, Miss   *860*
Julie.

JULIE: Most of them. Sometimes one is weak—

JEAN: You hate me?

JULIE: Excessively. I could see you shot—

JEAN: Like a mad dog?

JULIE: Exactly!

JEAN: But there is nothing here to shoot with. What shall we do
then?

JULIE: (*Rousing herself*) We must get away from here—travel.

JEAN: And torture each other to death?   *870*

JULIE: No—to enjoy, a few days, a week—as long as we can. And
then to die.

JEAN: Die! How silly. I think it's better to start the hotel.

JULIE: (*Not heeding him*) By the Lake of Como where the sun is always shining, where the laurel is green at Christmas and the oranges glow.

JEAN: The Lake of Como is a rain hole, I never saw any oranges there except on fruit stands. But it's a good resort, and there are many villas to rent to loving couples. That's a very paying industry. You know why? They take leases for half a year at least, but they usually leave in three weeks. 880

JULIE: (*Naïvely*) Why after three weeks?

JEAN: Why? They quarrel of course, but the rent must be paid all the same. Then you re-let, and so one after another they come and go, for there is plenty of love, although it doesn't last long.

JULIE: Then you don't want to die with me?

JEAN: I don't want to die at all, both because I enjoy living and because I regard suicide as a crime to Him who has given us life. 890

JULIE: Then you believe in God?

JEAN: Yes. Of course I do, and I go to church every other Sunday—But I'm tired of all this and I'm going to bed.

JULIE: Do you think I would allow myself to be satisfied with such an ending? Do you know what a man owes to a woman he has——

JEAN: (*Takes out a silver coin and throws it on the table*) Allow me, I don't want to owe anything to anyone.

JULIE: (*Pretending not to notice the insult*) Do you know what the law demands? 900

JEAN: I know that the law demands nothing of a woman who seduces a man.

JULIE: (*Again not heeding him*) Do you see any way out of it but to travel?—wed—and separate?

JEAN: And if I protest against this misalliance?

JULIE: Misalliance!

JEAN: Yes, for me. For you see I have a finer ancestry than you, for I have no fire-bug in my family.

JULIE: How do you know?

JEAN: You can't prove the contrary. We have no family record 910 except that which the police keep. But your pedigree I have read in a book on the drawing room table. Do you know who the founder of your family was? It was a miller whose wife found favor with the king during the Danish War. Such ancestry I have not.

JULIE: This is my reward for opening my heart to anyone so unworthy, with whom I have talked about my family honor.

JEAN: Dishonor—yes, I said it. I told you not to drink because then one talks too freely and one should never talk.

JULIE: Oh, how I repent all this. If at least you loved me! *920*

JEAN: For the last time—what do you mean? Shall I weep, shall I
jump over your riding whip, shall I kiss you, lure you to Lake
Como for three weeks, and then—what do you want anyway?
This is getting tiresome. But that's the way it always is when
you get mixed up in women's affairs. Miss Julie, I see that you
are unhappy, I know that you suffer, but I can't understand
you. Among my kind there is no nonsense of this sort; we
love as we play—when work gives us time. We haven't the
whole day and night for it like you.

JULIE: You must be good to me and speak to me as though I were *930*
a human being.

JEAN: Be one yourself. You spit on me and expect me to stand it.

JULIE: Help me, help me. Only tell me what to do—show me a
way out of this!

JEAN: In heaven's name, if I only knew myself.

JULIE: I have been raving, I have been mad, but is there no
means of deliverance?

JEAN: Stay here at home and say nothing. No one knows.

JULIE: Impossible. These people know it, and Kristin.

JEAN: They don't know it and could never suspect such a thing. *940*

JULIE: (*Hesitating*) But—it might happen again.

JEAN: That is true.

JULIE: And the consequences?

JEAN: (*Frightened*) Consequences—where were my wits not to
have thought of that! There is only one thing to do. Get away
from here immediately. I can't go with you or they will
suspect. You must go alone—away from here—anywhere.

JULIE: Alone? Where? I cannot.

JEAN: You must—and before the Count returns. If you stay, we
know how it will be. If one has taken a false step it's likely to *950*
happen again as the harm has already been done, and one
grows more and more daring until at last all is discovered.
Write the Count afterward and confess all—except that it was
I. That he could never guess, and I don't think he'll be so
anxious to know who it was, anyway.

JULIE: I will go if you'll go with me.

JEAN: Are you raving again? Miss Julie running away with her
coachman? All the papers would be full of it and that the
Count could never live through.

JULIE: I can't go—I can't stay. Help me, I'm so tired—so weary. *960*
Command me, set me in motion—I can't think any
more,—can't act—

JEAN: See now, what creatures you aristocrats are! Why do you
bristle up and stick up your noses as though you were the
lords of creation. Very well—I will command you! Go up and

dress yourself and see to it that you have travelling money and then come down. (*She hesitates*) Go immediately.

(*She still hesitates. He takes her hand and leads her to door*)

JULIE: Speak gently to me, Jean.   970
JEAN: A command always sounds harsh. Feel it yourself now.

(*Exit* JULIE. JEAN *draws a sigh of relief, seats himself by the table, takes out a notebook and pencil and counts aloud now and then until* KRISTIN *comes in, dressed for church*)

KRISTIN: My heavens, how it looks here. What's been going on?
JEAN: Oh, Miss Julie dragged in the people. Have you been sleeping so soundly that you didn't hear anything?
KRISTIN: I've slept like a log.   980
JEAN: And already dressed for church!
KRISTIN: Ye-es, (*Sleepily*) didn't you promise to go to early service with me?
JEAN: Yes, quite so, and there you have my stock and front. All right. (*He seats himself.* KRISTIN *puts on his stock*)
JEAN: (*Sleepily*) What is the text today?
KRISTIN: St. John's Day! It is of course about the beheading of John the Baptist.
JEAN: I'm afraid it will be terribly long drawn out—that. Hey, you're choking me. I'm so sleepy, so sleepy.   990
KRISTIN: What have you been doing up all night? You are actually green in the face.
JEAN: I have been sitting here talking to Miss Julie.
KRISTIN: Oh, you don't know your place.

(*Pause*)

JEAN: Listen, Kristin.
KRISTIN: Well?
JEAN: It's queer about her when you think it over.   1000
KRISTIN: What is queer?
JEAN: The whole thing.

(*Pause.* KRISTIN *looks at half empty glasses on table*)

KRISTIN: Have you been drinking together, too?
JEAN: Yes!
KRISTIN: For shame. Look me in the eye.
JEAN: Yes.
KRISTIN: Is it possible? Is it possible?   1010
JEAN: (*After reflecting*) Yes, it is.
KRISTIN: Ugh! That I would never have believed. For shame, for shame!
JEAN: You are not jealous of her?

KRISTIN: No, not of her. But if it had been Clara or Sophie—then I would have scratched your eyes out. So that is what has happened—how I can't understand! No, that wasn't very nice!

JEAN: Are you mad at her?

KRISTIN: No, but with you. That was bad of you, very bad. Poor *1020* girl. Do you know what—I don't want to be here in this house any longer where one cannot respect one's betters.

JEAN: Why should one respect them?

KRISTIN: Yes, you can say that, you are so smart. But I don't want to serve people who behave so. It reflects on oneself, I think.

JEAN: Yes, but it's a comfort that they're not a bit better than we.

KRISTIN: No, I don't think so, for if they are not better there's no use in our trying to better ourselves in this world. And to think of the Count! Think of him who has had so much sorrow *1030* all his days? No, I don't want to stay in this house any longer! And to think of it being with such as you! If it had been the Lieutenant—if it had been a better man—

JEAN: What's that?

KRISTIN: Yes! You are good enough, to be sure, but there's a difference between people just the same. No, this I can never forget. Miss Julie who was always so proud and indifferent to men! One never would believe that she would give herself—and to one like you! She who was ready to have Diana shot because she would run after the gatekeeper's *1040* mongrels. Yes, I say it—and here I won't stay any longer and on the twenty-fourth of October I go my way.

JEAN: And then?

KRISTIN: Well, as we've come to talk about it, it's high time you looked around for something else, since we're going to get married.

JEAN: Well, what'll I look for? A married man couldn't get a place like this.

KRISTIN: No, of course not. But you could take a gatekeeper's job or look for a watchman's place in some factory. The *1050* government's plums are few, but they are sure. And then the wife and children get a pension—

JEAN: (*With a grimace*) That's all very fine—all that, but it's not exactly in my line to think about dying for my wife and children just now. I must confess that I have slightly different aspirations.

KRISTIN: Aspirations? Aspirations—anyway you have obligations. Think of those, you.

JEAN: Don't irritate me with talk about my obligations. I know my own business. (*He listens*) We'll have plenty of time for all *1060* this some other day. Go and get ready and we'll be off to church.

KRISTIN: (*Listening*) Who's that walking upstairs?

JEAN: I don't know—unless it's Clara.

KRISTIN: (*Starting to go*) It could never be the Count who has come home without anyone hearing him?

JEAN: (*Frightened*) The Count! I can't believe that. He would have rung the bell.

KRISTIN: God help us! Never have I been mixed up in anything like this! (*Exit* KRISTIN)   1070

(*The sun has risen and lights up the scene. Presently the sunshine comes in through windows at an angle.* JEAN *goes to door and motions. Enter* JULIE, *dressed for travelling, carrying a small bird cage covered with a cloth, which she places on a chair*)

JULIE: I am ready!

JEAN: Hush, Kristin is stirring!

(JULIE *frightened and nervous throughout following scene*)   1080

JULIE: Does she suspect anything?

JEAN: She knows nothing. But, good heavens, how you look!

JULIE: Why?

JEAN: You are pale as a ghost.

JULIE: (*Sighs*) Am I? Oh, the sun is rising, the sun!

JEAN: And now the troll's spell is broken.

JULIE: The trolls have indeed been at work this night. But, Jean, listen—come with me, I have money enough.

JEAN: Plenty?   1090

JULIE: Enough to start with. Go with me for I can't go alone—today, midsummer day. Think of the stuffy train, packed in with the crowds of people staring at one; the long stops at the stations when one would be speeding away. No, I cannot, I cannot! And then the memories, childhood's memories of midsummer day—the church decorated with birch branches and syringa blossoms; the festive dinner table with relations and friends, afternoon in the park, music, dancing, flowers and games—oh, one may fly, fly, but anguish and remorse follow in the pack wagon.   1100

JEAN: I'll go with you—if we leave instantly—before it's too late.

JULIE: Go and dress then. (*She takes up bird cage*)

JEAN: But no baggage! That would betray us.

JULIE: Nothing but what we can take in the coupé.

(JEAN *has picked up his hat*)

JEAN: What have you there?

JULIE: It's only my canary. I cannot, will not, leave it behind.

JEAN: So we are to lug a bird cage with us. Are you crazy? Let go   1110
of it.

JULIE: It is all I take from home. The only living creature that
cares for me. Don't be hard—let me take it with me.

JEAN: Let go the cage and don't talk so loud. Kristin will hear us.

JULIE: No, I will not leave it to strange hands. I would rather see
it dead.

JEAN: Give me the creature. I'll fix it.

JULIE: Yes, but don't hurt it. Don't—no, I cannot.

JEAN: Let go. I can.

JULIE: (*Takes the canary from cage*) Oh, my little siren. Must your   1120
mistress part with you?

JEAN: Be so good as not to make a scene. Your welfare, your life,
is at stake. So—quickly. (*Snatches bird from her and goes to
chopping block and takes up meat chopper*) You should have
learned how to chop off a chicken's head instead of shooting
with a revolver. (*He chops off the bird's head*) Then you wouldn't
swoon at a drop of blood.

JULIE: (*Shrieks*) Kill me, too. Kill me! You who can butcher an
innocent bird without a tremble. Oh, how I shrink from you. I
curse the moment I first saw you. I curse the moment I was   1130
conceived in my mother's womb.

JEAN: Come now! What good is your cursing, let's be off.

JULIE: (*Looks toward chopping block as though obsessed by thought of
the slain bird*) No, I cannot. I must see—hush, a carriage is
passing. Don't you think I can stand the sight of blood? You
think I am weak. Oh, I should like to see your blood
flowing—to see your brain on the chopping block, all your sex
swimming in a sea of blood. I believe I could drink out of your
skull, bathe my feet in your breast and eat your heart cooked
whole. You think I am weak; you believe that I love you   1140
because my life has mingled with yours; you think that I
would carry your offspring under my heart, and nourish it
with my blood—give birth to your child and take your name!
Hear, you, what are you called, what is your family name? But
I'm sure you have none. I should be ''Mrs. Gate-Keeper,''
perhaps, or ''Madame Dumpheap.'' You dog with my collar
on, you lackey with my father's hallmark on your buttons. I
play rival to my cook—oh—oh—oh! You believe that I am
cowardly and want to run away. No, now I shall stay. The
thunder may roll. My father will return—and find his desk   1150
broken into—his money gone! Then he will ring—that bell. A
scuffle with his servant—then sends for the police—and then I
tell all—everything! Oh, it will be beautiful to have it all over
with—if only that were the end! And my father—he'll have a
shock and die, and then that will be the end. Then they will

place his swords across the coffin—and the Count's line is
extinct. The serf's line will continue in an orphanage, win
honors in the gutter and end in prison.

JEAN: Now it is the king's blood talking. Splendid, Miss Julie!
Only keep the miller in his sack.   1160

(*Enter* KRISTIN *with prayer-book in hand.*)

JULIE: (*Hastening to* KRISTIN *and falls in her arms as though seeking
protection*) Help me, Kristin, help me against his man.

KRISTIN: (*Cold and unmoved*) What kind of performance is this for
a holy day morning? What does this mean—this noise and
fuss?

JULIE: Kristin, you are a woman,—and my friend. Beware of this
wretch.   1170

JEAN: (*A little embarrassed and surprised*) While the ladies are
arguing I'll go and shave myself. (JEAN *does*, R.)

JULIE: You must understand me—you must listen to me.

KRISTIN: No—I can't understand all this bosh. Where may you be
going in your traveling dress?—and he had his hat on! Hey?

JULIE: Listen to me, Kristin, listen to me and I'll tell you
everything.

KRISTIN: I don't want to know anything—

JULIE: You must listen to me—

KRISTIN: What about? Is it that foolishness with Jean? That   1180
doesn't concern me at all. That I won't be mixed up with, but
if you're trying to lure him to run away with you then we
must put a stop to it.

JULIE: (*Nervously*) Try to be calm now Kristin, and listen to me. I
can't stay here and Jean can't stay here. That being true, we
must leave—Kristin.

KRISTIN: Hm, hm!

JULIE: (*Brightening up*) But I have an idea—what if we three
should go—away—to foreign parts. To Switzerland and set up
a hotel together—I have money you see—and Jean and I would 1190
back the whole thing, you could run the kitchen. Won't that
be fine? Say yes, now—and come with us—then everything
would be arranged—say yes! (*Throws her arms around Kristin
and coaxes her*).

KRISTIN: (*Cold and reflecting*) Hm—hm!

JULIE: (*Presto tempo*) You have never been out and traveled,
Kristin. You shall look about you in the world. You can't
believe how pleasant traveling on a train is—new faces
continually, new countries—and we'll go to Hamburg—and
passing through we'll see the zoological gardens—that you   1200
will like—then we'll go to the theatre—and hear the
opera—and when we reach Munich there will be the

museum—there are Rubens and Raphaels and all the big painters that you know—you have heard of Munich—where King Ludwig lived—the King, you know, who went mad. Then we'll see his palace—a palace like those in the Sagas—and from there it isn't far to Switzerland—and the Alps, the Alps mind you with snow in midsummer. And there oranges grow and laurel—green all the year round if—

(JEAN *is seen in the doorway* R. *stropping his razor on the strop which* 1210 *he holds between his teeth and left hand. He listens and nods his head favorably now and then.* JULIE *continues, tempo prestissimo*)

And there we'll take a hotel and I'll sit taking the cash while Jean greets the guests—goes out and markets—writes letters—that will be life, you may believe—then the train whistles—then the omnibus comes—then a bell rings upstairs, then in the restaurant—and then I make out the bills—and I can salt them—you can't think how people tremble when they   1220 receive their bill—and you—you can sit like a lady—of course you won't have to stand over the stove—you can dress finely and neatly when you show yourself to the people—and you with your appearance—Oh, I'm not flattering, you can catch a husband some fine day—a rich Englishman perhaps—they are so easy to—(*Slowing up*) to catch—Then we'll be rich—and then we'll build a villa by Lake Como—to be sure it rains sometimes—but (*becoming languid*) the sun must shine too sometimes—although it seems dark—and if not—we can at least travel homeward—and come back—here—or some other place. 1230
KRISTIN: Listen now. Does Miss Julie believe in all this?

(JULIE *going to pieces*)

JULIE: Do I believe in it?
KRISTIN: Yes.
JULIE: (*Tired*) I don't know. I don't believe in anything any more. (*Sinks down on bench, and takes head in her hand on table*) In nothing—nothing!
KRISTIN: (*Turns to* R. *and looks toward* JEAN) So—you intended to run away?   1240
JEAN: (*Rather shamefaced comes forward and puts razor on table*) Run away? That's putting it rather strong. You heard Miss Julie's project, I think it might be carried out.
KRISTIN: Now listen to that! Was it meant that I should be cook—to that—
JEAN: (*Sharply*) Be so good as to use proper language when you speak of your mistress.
KRISTIN: Mistress?
JEAN: Yes.

KRISTIN: No—hear! Listen to him!   *1250*

JEAN: Yes, you listen—you need to, and talk less. Miss Julie is your mistress and for the same reason that you do not respect her now you should not respect yourself.

KRISTIN: I have always had so much respect for myself—

JEAN: That you never had any left for others!

KRISTIN: I have never lowered my position. Let any one say, if they can, that the Count's cook has had anything to do with the riding master or the swineherd. Let them come and say it!

JEAN: Yes, you happened to get a fine fellow. That was your good luck.   *1260*

KRISTIN: Yes, a fine fellow—who sells the Count's oats from his stable.

JEAN: Is it for you to say anything—you who get a commission on all the groceries and a bribe from the butcher?

KRISTIN: What's that?

JEAN: And you can't have respect for your master and mistress any longer—you, you!

KRISTIN: (*Glad to change the subject*) Are you coming to church with me? You need a good sermon for your actions.

JEAN: No, I'm not going to church today. You can go alone—and   *1270* confess your doings.

KRISTIN: Yes, that I shall do, and I shall return with so much forgiveness that there will be enough for you too. The Savior suffered and died on the cross for all our sins, and when we go to Him in faith and a repentant spirit He takes our sins on Himself.

JULIE: Do you believe that, Kristin?

KRISTIN: That is my life's belief, as true as I stand here. And that was my childhood's belief that I have kept since my youth, Miss Julie. And where sin overflows, there mercy overflows   *1280* also.

JULIE: Oh, if I only had your faith. Oh, if—

KRISTIN: Yes, but you see that is not given without God's particular grace, and that is not allotted to all, that!

JULIE: Who are the chosen?

KRISTIN: That is the great secret of the Kingdom of Grace, and the Lord has no respect for persons. But there the last shall be first.

JULIE: But then has he respect for the last—the lowliest person?

KRISTIN: (*Continuing*) It is easier for a camel to pass through the   *1290* eye of a needle than for a rich man to enter the Kingdom of Heaven. That's the way it is, Miss Julie. However—now I am going—alone. And on my way I shall stop in and tell the stable boy not to let any horses go out in case anyone wants to get away before the Count comes home. Good bye.

(*Exit* KRISTIN)

JEAN: Such a devil. And all this on account of your confounded
    canary!
JULIE: (*Tired*) Oh, don't speak of the canary—do you see any way
    out—any end to this?   *1300*
JEAN: (*Thinking*) No.
JULIE: What would you do in my place?
JEAN: In your place—wait. As a noble lady, as a
    woman—fallen—I don't know. Yes, now I know.
JULIE: (*She takes up razor from table and makes gestures saying*) This?
JEAN: Yes. But I should not do it, mark you, for there is a
    difference between us.
JULIE: Because you are a man and I am a woman? What other
    difference is there?
JEAN: That very difference—of man and woman.
JULIE: (*Razor in hand*) I want to do it—but I can't. My father   *1310*
    couldn't either that time when he should have done it.
JEAN: No, he was right, not to do it—he had to avenge himself
    first.
JULIE: And now my mother revenges herself again through me.
JEAN: Haven't you loved your father, Miss Julie?
JULIE: Yes, deeply. But I have probably hated him too, I must
    have—without being aware of it. And it is due to my father's
    training that I have learned to scorn my own sex. Between
    them both they have made me half man, half woman. Whose
    is the fault for what has happened—my father's? My   *1320*
    mother's? My own? I haven't anything of my own. I haven't a
    thought which was not my father's—not a passion that wasn't
    my mother's. And last of all from my betrothed the idea that
    all people are equal. For that I now call him a wretch. How can
    it be my own fault then? Throw the burden on Jesus as Kristin
    did? No, I am too proud, too intelligent, thanks to my father's
    teaching.—And that a rich man cannot enter the Kingdom of
    Heaven—that is a lie, and Kristin, who has money in the
    savings bank—she surely cannot enter there. Whose is the
    fault? What does it concern us whose fault it is? It is I who   *1330*
    must bear the burden and the consequences.
JEAN: Yes, but—

(*Two sharp rings on bell are heard.* JULIE *starts to her feet.* JEAN
changes his coat)

JEAN: The Count—has returned. Think if Kristin has—(*Goes up to
    speaking tube and listens*)
JULIE: Now he has seen the desk!

JEAN: (*Speaking in the tube*) It is Jean, Excellency. (*Listens*) Yes,   1340
  Excellency. (*Listens*) Yes, Excellency,—right
  away—immediately, Excellency. Yes—in half an hour.
JULIE: (*In great agitation*) What did he say? In Heaven's name,
  what did he say?
JEAN: He wants his boots and coffee in a half hour.
JULIE: In half an hour then. Oh, I'm so tired—I'm incapable of
  feeling, not able to be sorry, not able to go, not able to stay,
  not able to live—not able to die. Help me now. Command
  me—I will obey like a dog. Do me this last service—save my
  honor. Save his name. You know what I have the will to   1350
  do—but cannot do. You will it and command me to execute
  your will.
JEAN: I don't know why—but now I can't either.—I don't
  understand myself. It is absolutely as though this coat does
  it—but I can't command you now. And since the Count spoke
  to me—I can't account for it—but oh, it is that damned servant
  in my back—I believe if the Count came in here now and told
  me to cut my throat I would do it on the spot.
JULIE: Make believe you are he—and I you. You could act so well
  a little while ago when you knelt at my feet. Then you were a   1360
  nobleman—or haven't you ever been at the theatre and seen
  the hypnotist—(JEAN *nods*) He says to his subject "Take the
  broom," and he takes it; he says, "Sweep," and he sweeps.
JEAN: Then the subject must be asleep!
JULIE: (*Ecstatically*) I sleep already. The whole room is like smoke
  before me—and you are like a tall black stove, like a man clad
  in black clothes with a high hat; and your eyes gleam like the
  hot coals when the fire is dying; and your face a white spot
  like fallen ashes. (*The sunshine is coming in through the windows
  and falls on* JEAN. JULIE *rubs her hands as though warming them*   1370
  before a fire) It is so warm and good—and so bright and quiet!
JEAN: (*Takes razor and puts it in her hand*) There is the broom, go
  now while it's bright—out to the hay loft—and(*He whispers in
  her ear*)
JULIE: (*Rousing herself*) Thanks. And now I go to rest. But tell me
  this—the foremost may receive the gift of Grace? Say it, even if
  you don't believe it.
JEAN: The foremost? No, I can't say that. But wait, Miss
  Julie—you are no longer among the foremost since you are of
  the lowliest.   1380
JULIE: That's true, I am the lowliest—the lowliest of the lowly.
  Oh, now I can't go. Tell me once more that I must go.
JEAN: No, now I cannot either—I cannot.
JULIE: And the first shall be last—
JEAN: Don't think. You take my strength from me, too, so that

I become cowardly.—What—I thought I heard the bell!—No!
To be afraid of the sound of a bell! But it's not the bell—it's
someone behind the bell, the hand that sets the bell in
motion—and something else that sets the hand in motion. But
stop your ears, stop your ears. Then he will only ring louder   1390
and keep on ringing until it's answered—and then it is too
late! Then come the police—and then—(*Two loud rings on bell
are heard.* JEAN *falls in a heap for a moment, but straightens up
immediately*) It is horrible! But there is no other way. Go.

(JULIE *goes out resolutely*)

Curtain.

Understanding *Countess Julie*

Strindberg created two psychologically complex individuals
that are aspiring to be something other than what they are. We
come to understand each as a complex personality that represents a certain social status, heredity, and environment, and we
see the effects that other strong personalities have had on them.
That the play takes place on a warm Midsummer's Eve adds to
the excitement and tension that surrounds the two characters. (In
Sweden, Midsummer's Eve is celebrated with dancing and merrymaking.) Advancing to its conclusion without intermission,
this play propels its characters with a momentum that does not
allow them or the audience a moment to pause and take stock of
what has happened.

Julie is determined to change her fate, perhaps tragically so. We
witness her casual flirtation with danger and Jean's calculated,
cautious reactions. The characters are so honest in their feelings
and expressions that we clearly understand their yearnings and
needs. Strindberg says of them, "My souls (or characters) are ag-
glomerations of past and present cultures, scraps from books and
newspapers, fragments of humanity, torn shreds of once fine
clothing that has become rags, in just the way that a human soul
is patched together."[1]

The character of Julie probably was drawn from different
women Strindberg had known and from his own personality.
Just as Julie blames some of her problems on the fact that she was
reared by her father because her mother was not present after her
early years, Strindberg believed that his personal problems were
related to his relationship with his parents. He was the child of a

tailor's daughter and a shipping agent who claimed nobility.[2] He felt that his father and mother represented the highest and lowest classes in society. This dualism is realized in the characters of Julie and Jean. Julie's wish to "fall" from her pedestal and Jean's to "rise" from his position of servitude reflect Strindberg's feelings about his parents and his own place in society.

Julie's feelings about her parents affect her relations with others. Her father's weakness has caused her to dislike men, and her mother's early dominance taught Julie to be willful. (Jean is aware that Julie used a riding crop on her fiancé to get him to jump like an animal.) Yet we also see in her a desire to be seductive and to give in to a man—indeed to be "beneath" him. Julie feels she can dominate any man, so she puts aside her aristocratic station in life as she plays seductive games with Jean. She willfully touches him, stroking his masculine ego with comments about his physical attractiveness. He warns her of what may happen, but she ignores the warnings. Later, in an effort to explain away her behavior, she imagines herself to be in love with Jean.

Jean, the valet, wants to climb out of servitude into a position of influence. Perhaps Jean sees Julie as a way of doing this. In this conflict between the sexes, Jean is allowed to win. Unlike Julie's fiancé, there is nothing weak about Jean. He is refined, almost arrogant. He prefers the count's wine while Julie drinks beer. As Strindberg describes Jean, "He has now educated himself to the point where he is a potential gentleman. He has proved a quick student, possesses finely developed senses . . . and an eye for beauty. . . . He has learned the secrets of good society, is polished but coarse underneath, he knows how to wear a tail-coat, but can offer us no guarantee that his body is clean underneath it."[3]

We come to see some unattractive facets of Jean's nature when we witness the plight of the bird on the chopping block and become aware of the fate intended for Julie. Jean is not faint of heart—he is a match for Julie. He respects her; he warns her of what can happen. But he stands in fear and awe of Kristin, who knows him too well and disapproves of his behavior. Her approval would represent a kind of religious sanction that Jean knows he will never attain. Yet his strength and initiative will probably find for him a lucrative and respected position in his own social class. He is inferior only in social station. He holds his position with the count in reverence and cowers when he hears the valet's bell. He has the soul of a servant.

Kristin is a balance point for these two characters who represent opposite ends of a social continuum. She is a servant but is content with her station. She is happy with the conventional morality of her life. She is an ordinary character against whom we can measure the deviations of the characters of Julie and Jean.

The male-female battle inherent in this play is rooted in the nature of these two characters. Julie is both a seductress and a naive child. She wants Jean to dominate her, but she also wants to control him. This duality was probably inspired by Strindberg's own troubled marriages. Julie displays at times a strong aggressive streak in her character; yet, at other times, she is a kitten awaiting a stroking hand. She needs tenderness but tries to appear invulnerable. Robert Brustein suggests that "the heroine lacks honor and decency, pursuing her ends by subtle, insidious, and generally unconscious means."[4] Jean aspires to own a hotel. While he appears docile, he harbors violent, aggressive feelings. He courts Julie with tales of his childhood, only to admit later that they were lies. He wants a higher place in society and will use Julie to get it. At the end of the play neither character appears to be the clear winner. Although he may someday own a hotel, Jean is still a cowering servant; and Julie has lost her honor and faces death. The servant lives, still a servant, but Julie cannot live without her honor.

The religious-moral theme in this play reveals the author's developing and changing mores. Throughout his life, Strindberg vascillated between belief in and denial of God and religion. In the characters of Julie and Jean, this ambivalence can be seen, and in Kristin, a third, more conventional perspective is given. In his characterization of Kristin, we can sense Strindberg's contempt for conventional Christianity. He feels that in some ways it is as weak and ineffectual as a woman. Yet he allows Kristin to be solidly happy and satisfied with her life and station. She alone is undaunted by the tumultuous events involving Julie and Jean.

We see the elements of the drama expertly utilized in this play. The foreshadowing offered by Strindberg in the killing of the canary, for example, is a masterpiece of preparation for the probable suicide of Julie. Strindberg gradually reveals the true nature of these characters. We learn of Jean's high aspirations as he requests a warm plate for his dinner, prefers wines to beer, speaks fluent French, and scolds Julie for awakening Kristin. We discover Julie through her treatment of her fiancé and the pregnant dog. We come to see her frustrated and inaccurate perception of herself in her social class. Slowly and deliberately, the way we replace a first impression with a more informed estimate of a person, we discover the real nature, motivation, and desires of these two sensual, but cold and calculating persons.

The plot moves steadily forward toward its climax. We are not allowed a moment of lost concentration from the first flirtatious glances between Julie and Jean until Julie exits bearing the razor blade at the end of the play. We cannot help but feel that this play will have a tragic outcome.

Through this power struggle between a male and a female, Strindberg makes a powerful statement about changes in social position. A class system does not come crashing down overnight. One cannot move up or down the social scale simply by wanting to do so. Such changes can only take place gradually, and persons attempting to make such a change on their own are sure to meet disaster. Although Julie and Jean spend some intimate moments together, Julie cannot change the fact that she is the daughter of a count and that her deeds will bring embarrassment to her family. And Jean, with all his social aspirations and intimate moments with Julie, cannot deny that the tinkling of the servant's bell still frightens that soul of servitude within him. Changes of great magnitude cannot take place overnight. Realizing this and fearing discovery by the count, Jean knows he will again answer the bell and black the count's boots. Julie, no longer feeling able to claim her social position with dignity, sees death as her only alternative.

Suggested Reading

Hansberry, Lorraine. *A Raisin in the Sun*. New York: Random House, 1968.

Hatlen, Theodore. *Drama: Principles and Plays*, 2d ed. Englewood Cliffs, N.J.: Prentice-Hall, 1967.

Miller, Arthur. *Death of a Salesman*. New York: Viking Press, 1949.

Thompson, Alan. *The Anatomy of Drama*, 2d ed. New York: Books for Libraries Press, 1942.

10

Dramatic Criticism

The theatre critic has responsibilities to both the performance company and the public. He or she is bound to give a fair and accurate appraisal of the performance, commenting on the strengths and weaknesses of the production, explaining the nature of the play, and pointing out areas done well along with those found to be weak.

The obligations of a critic begin with advance preparations. The critic should know something about the play before seeing it. Reading and studying the script and researching the circumstances of its writing will give insight into the motivations and purposes of the author. While considering the production as an aesthetic whole, the conscientious critic must not lose sight of the contributions of the actors, costumes, lighting, sets, and so on. In a written evaluation, the critic should comment generally on the production. The first paragraphs may touch on the playwright, the social and political significance of the play, the aptness of the dialogue or beauty of the words, and the overall success of the author in creating a particular kind of effect or feeling. This introductory section should be followed by an analysis of the parts that make up the whole. For example, a critic may point out actors who have done exceptional work and certain technical aspects, especially those making an outstanding contribution and those that are weak or ineffective.

Three basic questions for play evaluation handed down to us by the German poet Johann Goethe (1749–1832) are still widely used. These questions help us discover the reasons why a production is or is not successful. Goethe believed that the critic must first ask, *What is the artist trying to do?* The word *artist* refers to those in each production area: author, director, actors, set designer, technicians. In script analysis, for example, the critic needs to understand what the author is attempting and to determine the play's genre, the period, and use of stylization or realism. Then he or she will be able to comment on how effectively the author's purpose was achieved. To assess an actor's portrayal, the critic tries to determine how well the actor understood the role. Comments on an actor's believability, style, and effectiveness can be made. Discussion of the technical elements points out if and how the intents of the author and director were achieved and reinforced by costumes, lighting, props, and so on.

The second question a critic must ask is, *How well has the artist done what he or she set out to do?* To answer this question, the critic may consider whether the production did or did not fulfill the requirements of its particular genre or style. Did the costumes serve to interpret the mood and tone of the play as well as the individual characters? Was the music appropriate? Did the actors interpret through gesture and voice the intentions of the author? In answer to these questions, the critic will point out strengths and weaknesses in the individual areas. Actors' individual performances may receive particular attention.

The third question a critic must ask is, *Was it worth doing?* Here again, the critic reacts from a personal vantage point. Personal preferences surface as he or she offers judgment on the quality and worth of the performance, on the author's accomplishment in writing this particular play, on the actors' willingness to ''give'' themselves to this kind of venture, and on the money spent and time involved.

A critic's reaction to a play production is, after all, the opinion of only one person. In the professional theatre, a handful of critics wield a great deal of power in their ability to determine the success or failure of a production. But whether in the professional theatre or in educational theatre, a critic's review is still one person's opinion.

There are a few pitfalls for the student critic. First and foremost, the negative connotation of the word *critical* must be dispelled. A critical evaluation is an assessment of a play and an effort to comment on all of its important elements. A critical eye is turned on the play production not to find mistakes or problems but rather to define the strengths and weaknesses of each element of the production and the production as a whole. It is sometimes the tendency of an inexperienced critic to be overly harsh and severe. He may not understand that a critique points out strong, positive characteristics as well as weak, ineffective ones.

No two critical play evaluations will be the same. If a group of individuals views a performance and each member then writes an evaluation of that performance, no two critiques will be the same, nor should they strive to be. A critic need not be concerned with whether or not his or her responses are typical of those of others. Each member of the audience views the play from a unique vantage point that varies with geographic location, nationality, personal preferences, education, age, maturity, state of physical, emotional, and mental health, and so on. These help form one's reactions. Some aspects one evaluator deems brilliant or beautiful may be assessed as shameful or pitiful by another.

The audience as a whole may alter or prejudice an individual's perception of what takes place. On some evenings, an audience may be uninhibited and freely express laughter or scorn. On other evenings of the same production, the audience may be quiet and reserved. Whether one goes alone or with a companion may also color one's perception of the play. Trivial details can color judgment. One must be consciously aware that these diversions and prejudices exist and try not to be swayed by them in a critique of a play.

The critic must explain "Why." Judgments, opinions, and comments should be supported and explained with specific examples and reasons. A critic should resist the temptation to be cute or clever and strive to be professional and objective. If the critic believes a production is weak or ineffectual, that opinion should be supported by specific examples.

The following is a list of questions the student critic will want to remember when preparing an evaluation:

1. Did the play fulfill the requirements of its genre? Did it satisfactorily develop plot, characters, and events? Did it have a fresh, interesting style and expressive language?
2. Was the production a smoothly integrated union of parts? Were blocking and movement appropriate?
3. Did the production adhere to the intent of the author? Did it have one clearly defined purpose or goal?
4. Did the actors provide spontaneous, believable behavior? Did they move, speak and gesture in accordance with the characters as set forth by the author? Did they employ emotional con-

trol according to the demands of the characters? Did they display teamwork and proper relationships with other characters? Did they remain involved and committed to their characterizations at all times?

5. Was the set appropriate to the play type and the author's intent? Did the lighting create the appropriate mood, time of day, and so on? Did costumes reveal period, style, and character? Were props authentic, believable, and properly handled?

The critic's job should never be taken lightly. A critic has a serious responsibility to assess each facet of the production. Onstage and backstage people will study every word the critic writes. Some may attempt to alter their methods or techniques based on negative criticism received in a review. The critic's responsibility to the entire production company is to provide a just and fair appraisal of what was attempted and what was accomplished.

Suggested Reading

Beckerman, Bernard. *Dynamics of Drama: Theory of Analysis.* New York: Knopf, 1970.

Coleman, Arthur, and Gary R. Tyler. *Drama Criticism.* Denver, Colo.: A. Swallow, 1966.

Shaw, George Bernard. *Dramatic Criticism.* New York: Hill and Wang, 1959.

Wright, Edward A., and Lenthiel H. Downs. *A Primer for Playgoers.* Englewood Cliffs, N.J.: Prentice-Hall, 1969.

Notes

1. Definitions: Theatre Terminology

1. Fran A. Tanner, *Creative Communication* (Pocatello, Idaho: Clark Pub. Co., 1973), p. 9.
2. Ibid., p. iii.
3. Constantin Stanislavski, *My Life in Art* (New York: Theatre Arts Books, 1924), p. 298.
4. Raymond Rizzo, *The Total Actor* (Indianapolis, Ind.: Odyssey Press, 1975), p. 94.
5. Sonia Moore, *The Stanislavski System* (New York: Viking Press, 1974), p. 14.
6. Charlotte Lee, *Oral Interpretation* (Boston, Mass.: Houghton Mifflin, 1965), p. v.

2. Theatre Conventions

1. George Kernodle and Portia Kernodle, *Invitation to the Theatre* (New York: Harcourt Brace Jovanovich, 1978), p. 4.
2. Ibid., p. 129.

3. Origins and Development of the Theatre

1. Vera M. Roberts, *On Stage: A History of Theatre* (New York: Harper and Row, 1962), p. 17.
2. George Freedley and John A. Reeves, *A History of the Theatre* (New York: Crown, 1941), p. 3.
3. Ibid.
4. Oscar G. Brockett, *History of the Theater,* 2d ed. (Boston, Mass.: Allyn and Bacon, 1974), p. 21.
5. Roberts, *On Stage,* pp. 25–26.

6. Brockettt, *History*, p. 26.

7. Ibid., p. 36.

8. Lois Spatz, *Aeschylus*, (Boston, Mass.: Twayne, 1982), p. 125.

9. Roberts, *On Stage*, p. 27.

10. Brockett, *History*, pp. 50–55.

11. Ibid., pp. 60–62.

12. Kenneth MacGowan and William Melnitz, *The Living Stage: A History of the World Theatre* (Englewood Cliffs, N.J.: Prentice-Hall, 1955), p. 88.

13. Brockett, *History*, p. 87.

14. MacGowan, and Melnitz, *Living Stage*, p. 88.

15. Ibid., p. 237.

16. Brockett, *History*, p. 419.

4. The Actor

1. Jerome Rockwood, *The Craftsmen of Dionysus* (Glenview, Ill.: Scott, Foresman, 1966), pp. 3–4.

2. Aaron Q. Sartain et al., *Psychology: Understanding Human Behavior* (New York: McGraw-Hill, 1967), p. 76.

3. Floyd L. Ruch, *Psychology and Life* (Glenview, Ill.: Scott, Foresman, 1968), p. 426.

4. William James, *Principles of Psychology*, vol. 2, 1890, reprint edition (New York: Dover Publications), pp. 449–50.

5. Ross Stagner and Charles M. Solley, *Basic Psychology: A Perceptual-Homeostatic Approach* (New York: McGraw Hill, 1970), p. 143.

6. Ibid., p. 134.

7. Ibid., p. 135.

8. Toby Cole and Helen Krich Chinoy, eds., *Actors on Acting* (New York: Crown, 1970), p. 629.

9. Ibid., p. 640.

10. Joshua Logan, "Foreword," in Sonia Moore, *The Stanislavski System* (New York: Viking, 1974) p. xiii.

11. John Gielgud, "Preface," in Moore, *Stanislavski System*, p. xi.

12. Cole and Chinoy, *Actors on Acting*, p. 478.

13. Rockwood, *Craftsmen*, p. 11.

14. Constantin Stanislavski, *An Actor's Handbook* (New York: Theatre Arts Books, 1963), p. 158.

15. Constantin Stanislavski, *My Life in Art* (New York: Theatre Arts Books, 1952), p. 465.

16. Rockwood, *Craftsmen*, p. 17.

17. Stanislavski, *Actor's Handbook*, p. 104.

18. Rockwood, *Craftsmen*, p. 61.

19. Stanislavski, *Actor's Handbook*, p. 94.

20. Ibid., p. 65.
21. Constantin Stanislavski, *Creating a Role* (New York: Theatre Arts Books, 1961), p. 11.
22. Fran A. Tanner, *Basic Drama Projects* (Pocatello, Id.: Clark Pub. Co., 1977), pp. 105–6.
23. Ibid.
24. Stanislavski, *Actor's Handbook*, p. 91.
25. Sarah Bernhardt, *The Art of the Theatre* (London: Geoffrey Bles, 1924), pp. 103–4.
26. Rockwood, *Craftsmen*, p. 11.
27. Stanislavski, *My Life in Art*, pp. 465–66.
28. Stanislavski, *Actor's Handbook*, p. 23.
29. Stanislavski, *Creating a Role*, p. 4.
30. Ibid.
31. Stanislavski, *Building a Character* (New York: Theatre Arts Books, 1949), p. 244.
32. Sonia Moore, *The Stanislavski System* (New York: Viking, 1974), p. 5.
33. Stanislavski, *Actor's Handbook*, p. 118.
34. Rockwood, *Craftsmen*, p. 33.
35. Stanislavski, *Building a Character*, p. 70.
36. Rockwood, *Craftsmen*, p. 15.
37. Stanislavski, *Building a Character*, p. 69.
38. Stanislavski, *Actor's Handbook*, p. 27.
39. Stanislavski, *My Life in Art*, p. 572.

7. Tragedy

1. Richard P. McKeon, *Aristoteles: The Basic Works of Aristotle* (New York: Random House, 1941), p. 631.
2. Whitney J. Oates and Eugene O'Neill, Jr. eds., *The Complete Greek Drama* (New York: Random House, 1938), p. xxviii.
3. James Kaufman, "Tragedy and Its Validating Conditions," *Comparative Drama*, 1, no. 1 (Spring 1967), p. 3.
4. Ibid., pp. 9–10.
5. Theodore Hatlen, *Drama: Principles and Plays* (Englewood Cliffs, N.J.: Prentice-Hall, 1967), p. 31.
6. McKeon, *Aristoteles*, p. 635.
7. Ibid., p. 640.
8. Ibid., p. 641.
9. Arthur Miller, "Tragedy and the Common Man," *Theatre Arts*, 35, no. 3 (March 1951), p. 48.
10. Philip W. Harsh, *A Handbook of Classical Drama* (Stanford, Calif.: Stanford University Press, 1944), p. 111.

11. Paul Roche, *The Oedipus Plays of Sophocles* (New York: New American Library, 1958), p. x.

12. George Freedley, *A History of the Theatre* (New York: Crown, 1941), p. 107.

13. A. C. Bradley, *Shakespearean Tragedy* (New York: Macmillan, 1960), p. 11.

14. Tucker Brooke, *Shakespeare's Principal Plays* (New York: Appleton Century Crofts, 1935), p. 576.

15. Terry Otten, "Woyzeck and Othello: The Dimensions of Melodrama," *Comparative Drama*, 12, no. 2 (1978), p. 126.

16. Larry S. Champion, *Shakespeare's Tragic Perspective* (Athens: University of Georgia Press, 1976), p. 153.

17. Bradley, *Shakespearean Tragedy*, p. 211.

18. Ibid., p. 226.

19. Ibid., p. 232.

20. Alfred Harbage, *Shakespeare: The Tragedies* (Englewood Cliffs, N.J.: Prentice-Hall, 1964), p. 76.

8. Comedy

1. Larry Wilde, *The Great Comedians Talk about Comedy* (New York: Citadel Press, 1961), flyleaf.

2. George Meredith, "An Essay on Comedy," in *Comedy: A Critical Anthology*, ed. Robert W. Corrigan (Boston, Mass.: Houghton Mifflin, 1971), p. 744.

3. Athene Seyler and Stephen Haggard, *The Craft of Comedy* (New York: Theatre Arts, 1946), p. 11.

4. Christopher Frye, "Comedy," in *Comedy: A Critical Anthology*, ed. Robert W. Corrigan (Boston, Mass.: Houghton Mifflin, 1971), p. 755.

5. William McCollom, *The Divine Average: A View of Comedy* (Cleveland, Ohio: Case Western Reserve University Press, 1971), p. 7.

6. Robert W. Corrigan, *Comedy: A Critical Anthology* (Boston, Mass.: Houghton Mifflin, 1971), p. xi.

7. Meredith, "An Essay on Comedy," p. 743.

8. Frye, "Comedy," p. 756.

9. Eric Bentley, "The Life of the Drama," in *Comedy: A Critical Anthology*, ed. Robert W. Corrigan (Boston, Mass.: Houghton Mifflin, 1971), p. 764.

10. Seyler and Haggard, *Craft of Comedy*, p. 12.

11. McCollom, *Divine Average*, p. 82.

12. Seyler and Haggard, *Craft of Comedy*, p. 13.

13. J. L. Styan, *The Elements of Drama* (Cambridge: University Press, 1967), p. 141.

14. Henri Bergson, "Laughter," in *Comedy: A Critical Anthology,* ed. Robert W. Corrigan (Boston, Mass.: Houghton Mifflin, 1971), p. 750.

15. John Gassner and Ralph Allen, *Theatre and Drama in the Making* (Boston, Mass.: Houghton Mifflin, 1964), p. 453.

16. Bentley, "Life of the Drama," p. 764.

17. Arthur Ganz, "The Meaning of 'The Importance of Being Earnest,' " *Modern Drama* (May 1963), p. 42.

18. Ibid.

19. Robert W. Corrigan, *Comedy: A Critical Anthology,* (Boston, Mass.: Houghton Mifflin, 1971), p. 333.

20. Glenn M. Loney, "Theatre of the Absurd: It Is Only a Fad," *Theatre Arts* (November 1962), pp. 20–22.

21. Faubion Bowers, "Theatre of the Absurd: It Is Here to Stay," *Theatre Arts* (November 1962), p. 65.

22. Eugene Ionesco, "The World of Eugene Ionesco," *The Tulane Drama Review* (October 1958), pp. 46–47.

23. Donald Watson, "The Plays of Ionesco," *The Tulane Drama Review* (October 1958), p. 48.

24. Bowers, "Theatre of the Absurd," p. 24.

25. Theodore Hatlen, *Drama: Principles and Plays* (Englewood Cliffs, N.J.: Prentice-Hall, 1967), p. 545.

26. William Saroyan, "Ionesco," *Theatre Arts* (July 1958), p. 25.

27. Ibid.

28. Donald Watson, "The Plays of Ionesco," *Tulane Drama Review* (October 1958), p. 49.

29. Ibid.

30. William Saroyan, "Ionesco," *Theatre Arts* (July 1958), p. 25.

31. Theodore Hatlen, *Drama: Principles and Plays.* (Englewood Cliffs, N.J.: Prentice-Hall, 1967), p. 554.

9. Modern Drama

1. Michael Meyer, *The Plays of Strindberg,* Vol. 1(New York: Modern Library, 1966), p. 103.

2. Robert Brustein, *Strindberg: Selected Plays and Prose* (New York: Holt, Rinehart, and Winston, 1964), p. xix.

3. Meyer, *Plays of Strindberg,* p. 105.

4. Brustein, *Strindberg,* p. xxix.

Bibliography

Altenbernd, Lynn, and Leslie L. Lewis. *A Handbook for the Study of Drama.* New York: Macmillan, 1966.

Arnold, Walter. "William James: Idea Man." *Saturday Review* 2 (Nov. 22, 1969): 75–76.

Arnott, Peter. *The Theatre in Its Time.* Boston, Mass.: Little, Brown, 1981.

" 'Arsenic and Old Lace' Done in Sign Language for the Deaf." *Newsweek*, May 18, 1942, p.56.

Bates, Barclay W. "The Lost Past in 'Death of a Salesman.' " *Modern Drama* 2, 2 (Sept. 1968): 164–72.

Beckerman, Bernard. *Dynamics of Drama: Theory of Analysis.* New York: Knopf, 1970.

Benedetti, Robert L. *The Actor at Work.* 3d ed. Englewood Cliffs, N.J.: Prentice-Hall, 1981.

Benston, Alice N. "From Naturalism to the Dream Play: A Study of the Evolution of Strindberg's Unique Theatrical Form." *Modern Drama* 7, 4 (Feb. 1965): 382–89.

Berthold, Margot. *A History of World Theatre.* New York: Frederick Ungar, 1972.

Bettina, Sister M., SSND. "Willy Loman's Brother Ben: Tragic Insight in 'Death of a Salesman.' " *Modern Drama* 4, 4 (Feb. 1962): 409–12.

Black, Walter J., ed. *The Works of William Shakespeare.* New York: Black's Readers Service, 1937.

Bliquez, Guerin. "Linda's Role in 'Death of a Salesman.' " *Modern Drama* 10, 4 (Feb. 1968): 383–86.

Boothe, John E. "Albee and Schneider Observe Something's Stirring." *Theatre Arts* 46, 3 (March 1961): 22–24, 78–79.

Bose, Tirthankar. "Oscar Wilde's Game of Being Earnest." *Modern Drama* 21, 1 (March 1978): 81–86.

Bowers, Faubion. "Theatre of the Absurd: It Is Here to Stay." *Theatre Arts* 46, 11 (Nov. 1962): 21, 23–24, 66–68.

Bowman, Walter P. and Robert H. Ball. *Theatre Language.* New York: Theatre Arts Books, 1961.

Boxandall, Lee. "The Theatre of Edward Albee. *Tulane Drama Review* 9, 4 (Summer 1965): 19–40.

Bradley, A. C. *Shakespearean Tragedy.* New York: Macmillan, 1960.

Brockett, Oscar G. *The Essential Theatre.* 2d ed. New York: Holt, Rinehart and Winston, 1980.

Brockett, Oscar G. *History of the Theatre.* 2d ed. Boston, Mass.: Allyn and Bacon, 1974.

Brooke, Tucker. *Shakespeare's Principal Plays.* New York: Appleton-Century-Crofts, 1935.

Brustein, Robert, ed. *Strindberg: Selected Plays and Prose.* New York: Holt, Rinehart and Winston, 1964.

Champion, Larry S. *Shakespeare's Tragic Perspective.* Athens: University of Georgia Press, 1976.

Coger, Leslie I., and Melvin R. White. *Readers Theatre Handbook.* Glenview, Ill.: Scott, Foresman, 1967.

Cohen, Robert. *Theatre.* Palo Alto, Calif.: Mayfield Pub. Co., 1981.

Corrigan, Robert W., ed. *Comedy: A Critical Anthology.* Boston, Mass.: Houghton Mifflin, 1971.

Corrigan, Robert W. *The World of the Theatre.* Glenview, Ill.: Scott, Foresman, 1979.

Corrigan, Robert W. *The Making of Theatre.* Glenview, Ill.: Scott, Foresman, 1981.

Cowhig, Ruth. "Actors, Black and Tawny, in the Role of Othello, and Their Critics." *Tulane Drama Review* 4, 2 (Feb. 1979): 133–46.

Curry, Ryder H., and Michael Porte. "The Surprising Unconscious of Edward Albee." *Drama Review* 7, 1 (Winter 1968–1969): 59.

Dannett, Sylvia G. L. *Profiles of Negro Womanhood,* vol. 2. New York: American Book–Stratford Press, 1966.

DeBosschere, Jean, illustrator. *Aristophanes: The Eleven Comedies.* New York: Horace Liveright, 1928.

DeCamp, L. Sprague. "Science Milestone: William James, Leader of American Psychology." *Science Digest* 43 (Jan. 1958): 86–91.

Driver, Tom F. "Strength and Weakness in Arthur Miller." *Tulane Drama Review* 4, 4(May 1960): 45–52.

Ellman, Richard, ed. *The Artist as Critic: Critical Writings of Oscar Wilde.* New York: Random House, 1969.

Fitts, Dudley, and Robert Fitzgerald. *Sophocles: The Oedipus Cycle.* New York: Harcourt, Brace and World, 1949.

Freedley, George, and John A. Reeves. *A History of the Theatre.* New York: Crown, 1941.

Frye, Northrop. *Fools of Time: Studies in Shakespearean Tragedy.* Toronto: University of Toronto Press, 1967.

Ganz, Arthur. "The Meaning of 'The Importance of Being Earnest.' " *Modern Drama* 6, 1 (May 1963): 42–52.

Gassner, John. "Strindberg in America." *Theater Arts* 33, 4 (May 1949): 49–52.

Gassner, John, and Ralph G. Allen. *Theatre and Drama in the Making.* Boston, Mass.: Houghton Mifflin, 1964.

Gilder, Rosamund. "On Broadway." *Theater Arts* 25, 3 (March 1941): 186.

Gross, Barry E. "Peddler and Pioneer in 'Death of a Salesman.' " *Modern Drama* 7, 4 (Feb. 1965): 405–10.

Hagopian, John V. "Arthur Miller: The Salesman's Two Cases." *Modern Drama* 6, 2 (Sept. 1963): 117–25.

Hansberry, Lorraine. *A Raisin in the Sun.* New York: Random House, 1968.

Hansberry, Lorraine. *To Be Young, Gifted and Black.* Englewood Cliffs, N.J.: Prentice-Hall, 1969.

Harbage, Alfred. *Shakespeare: The Tragedies.* Englewood Cliffs, N.J.: Prentice-Hall, 1964.

Harsh, Philip W. *A Handbook of Classical Drama.* Stanford, Calif.: Stanford University Press, 1944.

Hart-Davis, Rupert, ed. *The Letters of Oscar Wilde.* New York: Harcourt, Brace and World, 1962.

Hatlen, Theodore W. *Drama: Principles and Plays.* 2d ed. Englewood Cliffs, N.J.: Prentice-Hall, 1967.

Hatlen, Theodore W. *Orientation to the Theatre.* 3d ed. Englewood Cliffs, N.J.: Prentice-Hall, 1981.

Hawkes, Terence. *Shakespeare and the Reason.* London: Routeledge and Kegan Paul, 1964.

Heining, Ruth B. and Lyda Stillwell. *Creative Dramatics for the Classroom Teacher.* Englewood Cliffs, N.J.: Prentice-Hall, 1974.

Hosley, Richard. "The Origins of the So-Called Elizabethan Multiple Stage." *Drama Review* 12, 2 (Winter 1968): 28–50.

Idyll, Flatbush. "The Theatre." *New Yorker* 16 (Jan. 18, 1941): 34.

Ionesco, Eugene. "The World of Eugene Ionesco." *Tulane Drama Review* 3, 1 (Oct. 1958): 46–47.

Ionesco, Eugene. "My Thanks to the Critics," translated by Leo Kerz. *Theatre Arts* 44, 10 (Oct. 1960): 18–19.

James, William. *Principles of Psychology,* vol. 2. New York: Dover. (Originally published 1890.)

Joseph, Stephen. *Theatre in the Round.* New York: Taplinger, 1968.

Kaufmann, R. J. "Tragedy and Its Validating Conditions." *Comparative Drama* 1, 1 (Spring 1967): 3–18.

Kernodle, George, and Portia Kernodle. *Invitation to the Theatre.* New York: Harcourt, Brace, Jovanovich, 1978.

King, Nancy R. *A Movement Approach to Acting.* Englewood Cliffs, N.J.: Prentice-Hall, 1981.

Kott, Jan. *The Eating of the Gods.* New York: Random House, 1970.

Kurman, George. "Entropy and the 'Death' of Tragedy: Notes for a Theory of Drama." *Comparative Drama* 9, 4 (Winter 1975–76): 283–301.

Lamm, Martin. "Strindberg and the Theatre." *Tulane Drama Review* 6, 2 (Nov. 1961): 132–39.

Larrabee, Harold A. "William Jones' Impact upon American Education." *School and Society* 89 (Feb. 25, 1961): 84–86.

Lee, Charlotte I. *Oral Interpretation.* 3d ed. Boston, Mass.: Houghton Mifflin, 1955.

Lesky, Albin. *A History of Greek Literature.* New York: Crowell, 1963.

Lesnick, Henry, ed. *Guerilla Street Theatre.* New York: Avon Books, 1973.

Loney, Glenn M. "Theatre of the Absurd: It Is Only a Fad." *Theatre Arts* 46, 11 (Nov. 1962): 20,22,24,64–65.

Macgowan, Kenneth, and William Melnitz. *The Living Stage: A History of the World Theatre.* Englewood Cliffs, N.J.: Prentice-Hall, 1955.

McCollom, William. *The Divine Average: A View of Comedy.* Cleveland, Ohio: Case Western Reserve University Press, 1971.

McKeon, Richard. *Aristoteles: The Basic Works of Aristotle.* New York: Random House, 1941.

McKeon, Richard. *The Basic Works of Aristotle.* New York: Random House, 1941.

McKeon, Richard. *Introduction to Aristotle.* New York: Random House, 1947.

Meyer, Michael. *The Plays of Strindberg,* vol. 1. New York: Modern Library, 1966.

Mikhail, E. H. "The Four Act Version of 'The Importance of Being Earnest' " *Modern Drama* 11, 3 (Winter 1969): 263–66.

Miller, Arthur. *Death of a Salesman.* New York: Viking Press, 1949.

Miller, Arthur. "Tragedy and the Common Man." *Theatre Arts* 35, 3 (March 1951): 48–50.

Miller, Arthur. "Death of a Salesman." *Tulane Drama Review* 2, 3 (May 1958): 63–69.

Miller, Jordan Y. "Myth and the American Dream." *Modern Drama* 7, 2 (Sept. 1964): 190–98.

Misiak, Henry, and Virginia Sexton. *History of Psychology: An Overview.* New York: Grune and Stratton, 1966.

Moore, Sonia. *The Stanislavski System.* New York: Viking Press, 1974.

Moritz, Charles, ed. *Current Biography.* New York: H. W. Wilson Co., 1959.

Moss, Leonard. "Arthur Miller and the Common Man's Language." *Modern Drama* 7, 1 (May 1964): 52–59.

Nicoll, Allardyce. *The Development of the Theatre.* New York: Harcourt Brace Jovanovich, 1966.

Oates, Whitney J., and Eugene O'Neill, Jr. *The Complete Greek Drama,* vol. 2. New York: Random House, 1938.

O'Hara, John. "Brewster Bodies." *Newsweek* 17, 3 (Jan. 20, 1941): 63.

Olson, Elder. *Aristotle's "Poetics" and English Literature.* Chicago, Ill.: University of Chicago Press, 1965.

Olson, Elder. *The Theory of Comedy.* Bloomington: Indiana University Press, 1968.

"Othello." *Theatre Arts* 39, 4 (Nov. 1955): 67.

Otten, Terry. " 'Woyzeck' and 'Othello': The Dimensions of Melodrama." *Comparative Drama* 12, 2 (Summer 1978): 123–35.

Parker, Douglas, trans. *Aristophanes' Lysistrata.* New York: New American Library, 1964.

Paulson, Arvid, trans. *Seven Plays by August Strindberg.* New York: Bantam, 1968.

Poague, L. A. " 'The Importance of Being Earnest': The Texture of Wilde's Irony." *Modern Drama* 16, 3 and 4 (Dec. 1973): 251–57.

"A Raisin in the Sun." *Theatre Arts* 43, 5 (May 1959): 22–23.

Rizzo, Raymond. *The Total Actor.* Indianapolis, Ind.: Bobbs-Merrill, 1975.

Roberts, Vera M. *On Stage: A History of Theatre.* New York: Harper and Row, 1962.

Roche, Paul. *The Oedipus Plays of Sophocles.* New York: New American Library, 1958.

Rockwood, Jerome. *The Craftsmen of Dionysus.* Glenview, Ill.: Scott, Foresman, 1966.

Roose-Evans, James. *Experimental Theatre.* New York: Universe Books, 1970.

Rosenberg, Marvin. "Othello to the Life." *Theatre Arts* 42, 6 (June 1958): 58–61.

Ruch, Floyd L. *Psychology and Life.* Glenview, Ill.:Scott, Foresman, 1968.

Ryan, Paul R. "Olympic Theatre." *The Drama Review* 6, 4 (Dec. 1972): 63–85.

Saroyan, William. "Ionesco." *Theatre Arts* 42, 7 (July 1958): 25.

Sartain, Aaron Q., et al. *Psychology: Understanding Human Behavior.* New York: McGraw-Hill, 1967.

Schlveter, June. " 'Goats and Monkeys' and the 'Idiocy of Language': Handke's *Kaspar* and Shakespeare's *Othello*." *Modern Drama* 23, 1 (March 1980): 25–32.

Seyler, Athene, and Stephen Haggard. *The Craft of Comedy*. New York: Theatre Arts Books, 1946.

Southern, Richard. *Proscenium and Sight-Lines*. New York: Theatre Arts Books, 1964.

Spatz, Lois. *Aristophanes*. Boston, Mass.: Twayne Pub., 1978.

Sprinchorn, Evert. "Strindberg and the Greater Naturalism." *The Drama Review* 13, 2 (Winter 1968): 119–29.

Stagner, Ross and Charles M. Solley. *Basic Psychology: A Perceptual Homeostatic Approach*. New York: McGraw-Hill, 1970.

Stanislavski, Constantin. *An Actor Prepares*. New York: Theatre Arts Books, 1948.

Stanislavski, Constantin. *My Life in Art*. New York: Theatre Arts Books, 1948.

Stanislavski, Constantin. *Building a Character*. New York: Theatre Arts Books, 1949.

Stanislavski, Constantin. *Creating a Role*. New York: Theatre Arts Books, 1961.

Styan, J. L. *The Elements of Drama*. Cambridge: University Press, 1967.

Tanner, Fran A. *Basic Drama Projects*. Pocatello, Idaho: Clark Pub. Co., 1977.

Tanner, Fran A. *Creative Communication*. Pocatello, Idaho: Clark Pub. Co., 1977.

Thompson, Alan R. *The Anatomy of Drama*, 2d ed. New York: Books for Libraries Press, 1942.

Vinacke, W. Edgar. *Foundation of Psychology*. New York: American Book Co., 1968.

Watson, Donald. "The Plays of Ionesco." *The Tulane Drama Review* 3, 1 (Oct. 1958), 48–53.

Watt, Homer, et al. *Outlines of Shakespeare's Plays*. New York: Barnes and Noble, 1962.

Weales. "Arthur Miller: Man and His Image." *Tulane Drama Review* 7, 1 (Fall 1962): 165–80.

Webster, T. B. L. *Greek Theatre Production*. London: Methuen and Co., 1970.

Wild, John. *The Radical Empiricism of William James*. New York: Doubleday, 1969.

Wilde, Larry. *The Great Comedians Talk about Comedy*. New York: Citadel Press, 1961.

Wilde, Oscar. *The Importance of Being Earnest*, edited by Vincent Hopper and Gerald Lahey. New York: Barron's Educational Series, 1959.

Wilde, Oscar. *The Plays of Oscar Wilde*. New York: Random House, N.D.

"William James and the Psychology of the Present." *American Journal of Psychology* 55 (1942): 310.

Wilshire, Bruce. *William James and Phenomenology: A Study of "The Principles of Psychology."* Bloomington: Indiana University Press, 1968.

Wilson, Edwin. *The Theatre Experience.* New York: McGraw-Hill, 1980.

Woodbridge, Elizabeth. *The Drama: Its Law and Its Technique.* Boston, Mass.: Allyn and Bacon, 1898.

Wright, Edward A., and Lenthiel H. Downs. *A Primer for Playgoers.* Englewood Cliffs, N.J.: Prentice-Hall, 1969.

Wyatt, Euphemia V. R. ''The Drama.'' *Catholic World* 152 (Fall 1941): 599.

Index